ABOUT THE AUTHOR

Zara Slattery is a comic artist, illustrator and tutor, whose work was shortlisted for the Arts Foundation Futures Award 2020. She has created and collaborated on short story comics, including *Two Birds* and *Don't Call Me A Tomboy*. An extract from *Coma* was shortlisted for the Myriad First Graphic Novel Competition 2018.

ZARA SLATTERY

COMA

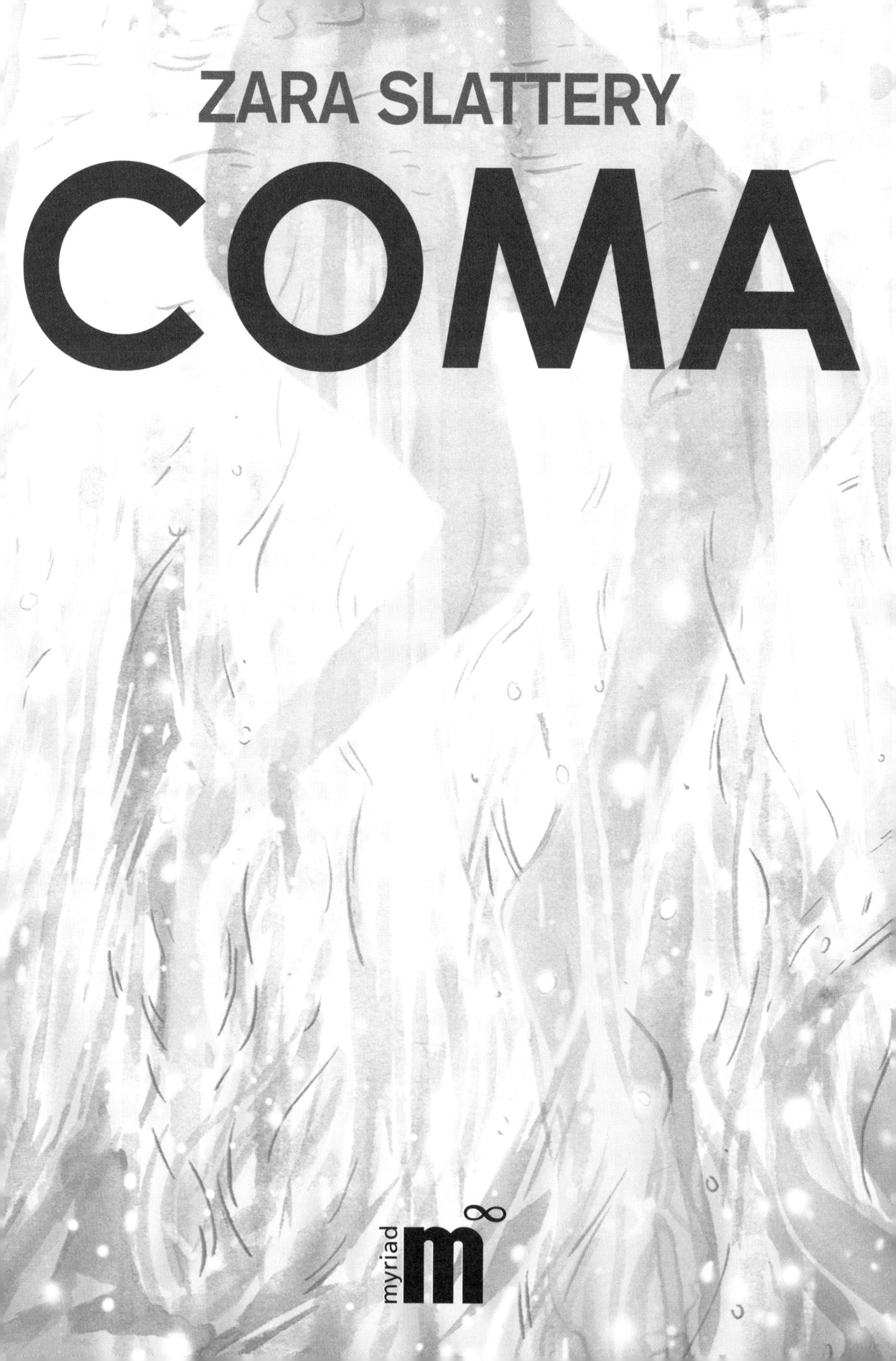

myriad

First published in 2021 by
Myriad Editions
www.myriadeditions.com

Myriad Editions
An imprint of New Internationalist Publications
The Old Music Hall, 106–108 Cowley Rd,
Oxford OX4 1JE

Reprinted 2021
3 5 7 9 10 8 6 4 2

A CIP catalogue record for this book
is available from the British Library

ISBN (paperback): 978-1-912408-66-5
ISBN (ebook): 978-1-912408-78-8

Printed in Poland
www.lfbookservices.co.uk

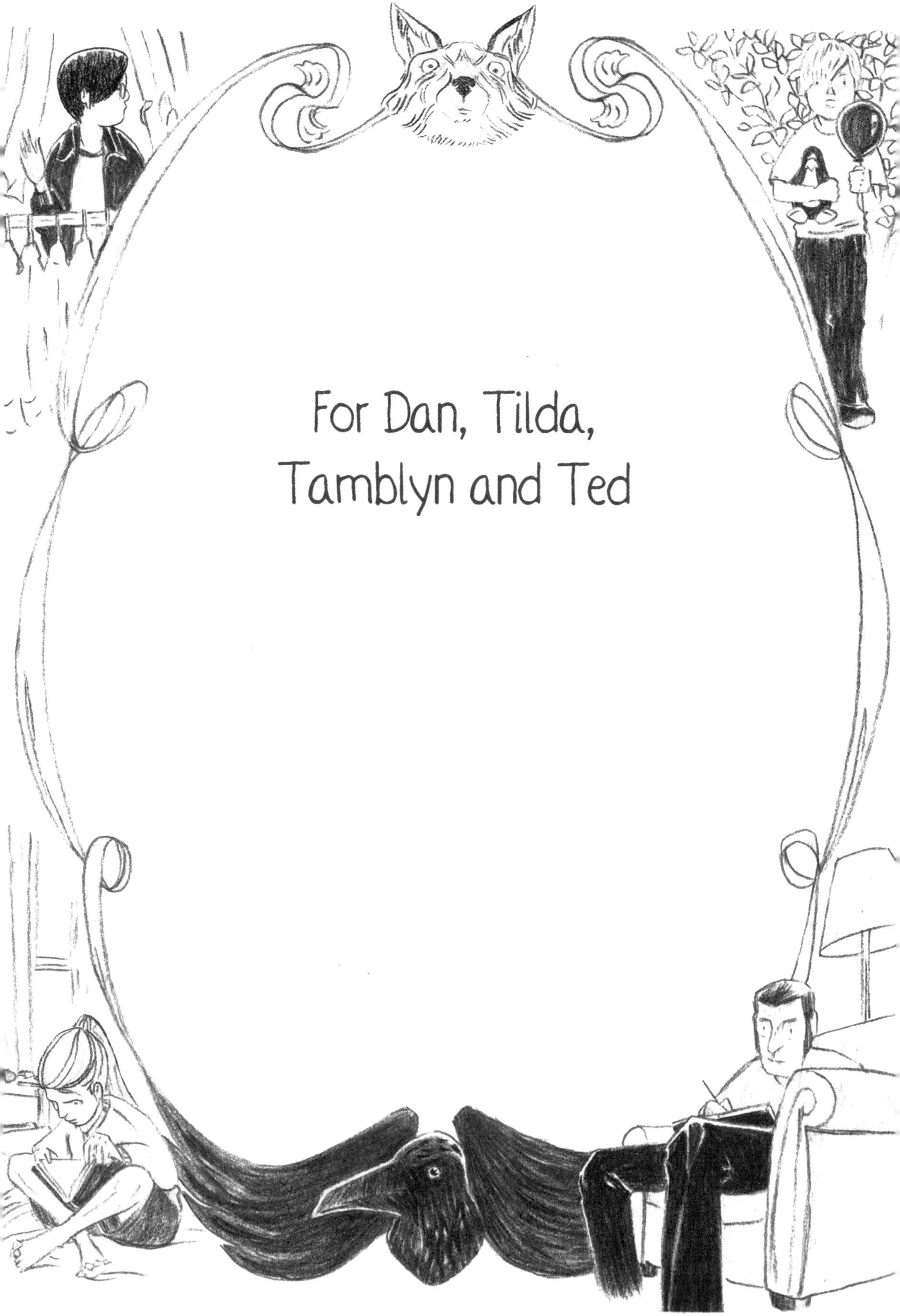

For Dan, Tilda,
Tamblyn and Ted

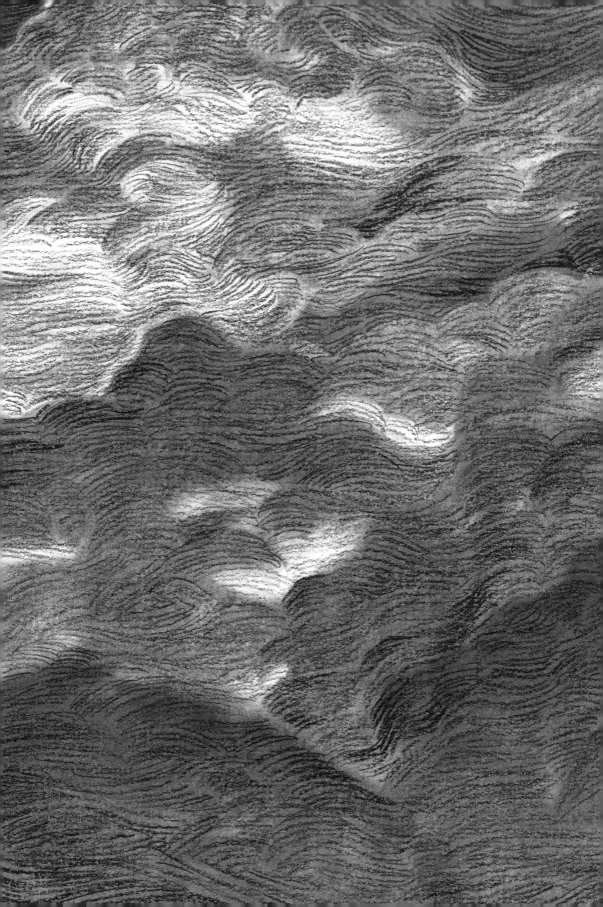

MAY 2013

The pain in my neck has become a pain in the arse, I tweeted as I lay in bed on the morning of 22nd May 2013. With a hot water bottle pressed to my neck, amused by my tweet, I watched a large flock of seagulls circle the rooftops opposite. I pondered their significance as their cries cut through the air and filled the sky outside my window.

Five weeks earlier my mother had died of pneumonia. As I sat at her hospital bedside, I developed a sore throat and later a temperature. In the days following her death, I lost my voice and was prescribed antibiotics. I was arranging her funeral, supporting my dad, who was himself unwell, and travelling between him and my family two hundred miles south. While the initial illness lifted, the sore throat lingered and, increasingly I found it hard to separate my physical and emotional states.

As the weeks went by, I dismissed my persistent sore throat, cared for my children, worked, partied and made plans to care for my dad. Life was full, and carried on in the same way until the day I stepped back into the corner of a table. I didn't give it a second thought until later that evening when I developed flu-like symptoms: headache, fatigue. The following day my thigh throbbed, and the day after that I lay in bed, tweeting as I watched seagulls circling the rooftops opposite.

The pain increased rapidly. After calling 111, I called my doctor and, in the intervening hours between then and my appointment, I called my husband, Dan. By the time we got to the GP surgery, Dan was holding me up and I was steadying myself on every surface I passed, be it car roofs or walls. Barely able to get up after sitting down, I was sent home with strong painkillers and told to come back if it got worse. I couldn't make it to the car without taking them first and a nurse invited me to wait it out in her room. But, the painkillers didn't kick in and I left the surgery dragging my body, grey and crying. When we got home, Dan helped me to bed. The white heat of pain was intense beyond words and I begged him to call an ambulance.

Despite the pain, I didn't imagine myself to be so ill. Soon after arriving at the hospital I drifted into black, only to 'wake' within the darkness. Initially I knew myself, and had enough awareness to question my surroundings, before being lost to an altered reality, one of fear and confusion. The experience would take me to the core of my being.

On waking, I believed there to be no blueprint — nothing had prepared me for the experience of the past fifteen days. Over time, I reflected on the emotions I'd felt and the visions I'd conjured, and while new to my story, they were not new to the human story. The blueprint was there all along connecting us through universal themes; embedded in our words, the language we speak, the stories we tell and the myths we're told.

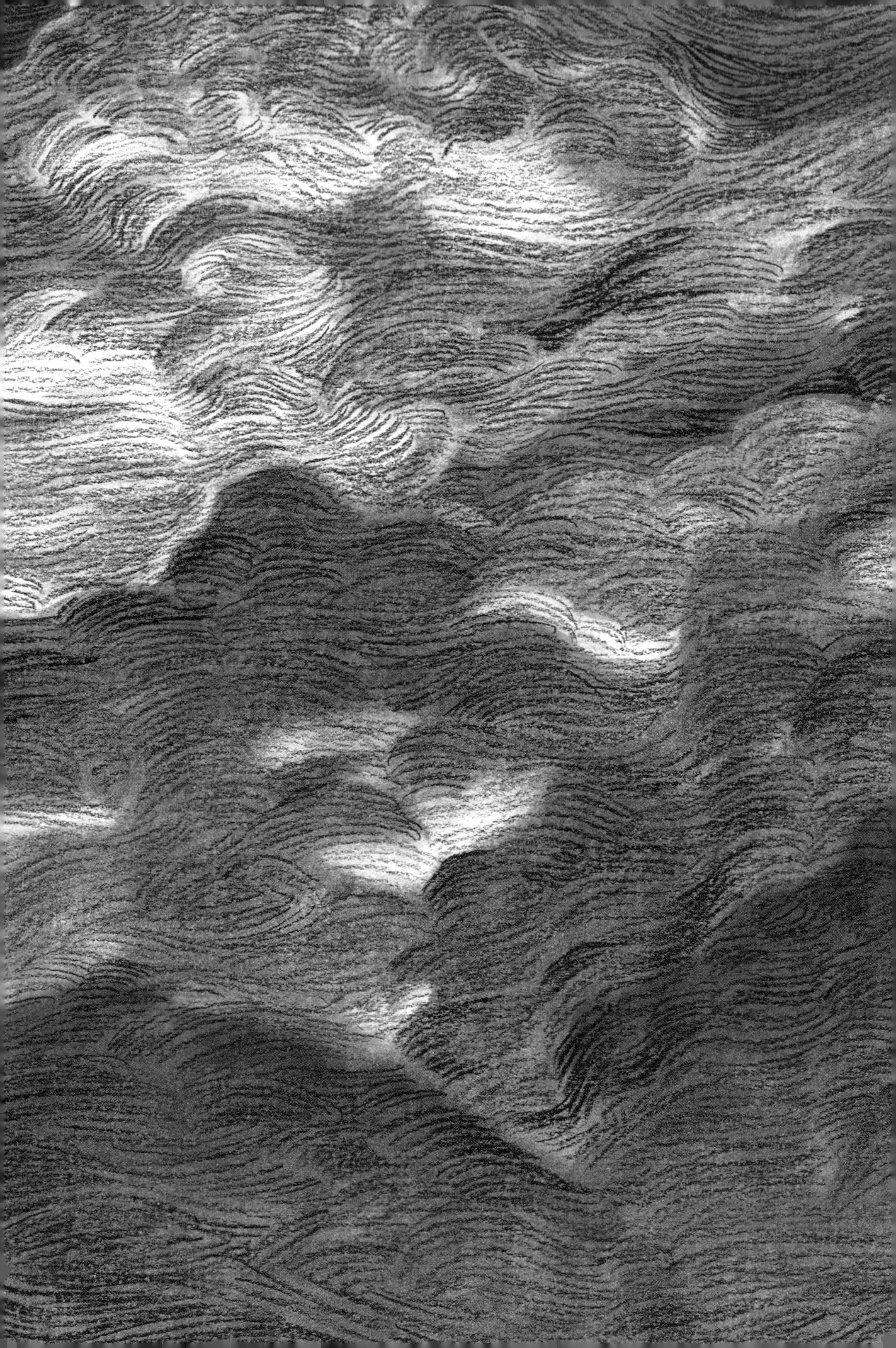

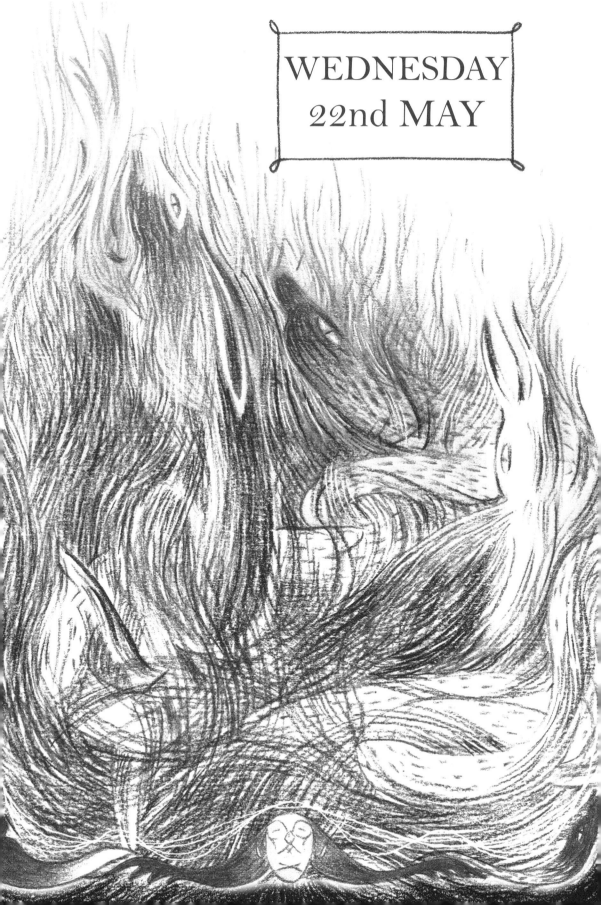

WEDNESDAY
22nd MAY

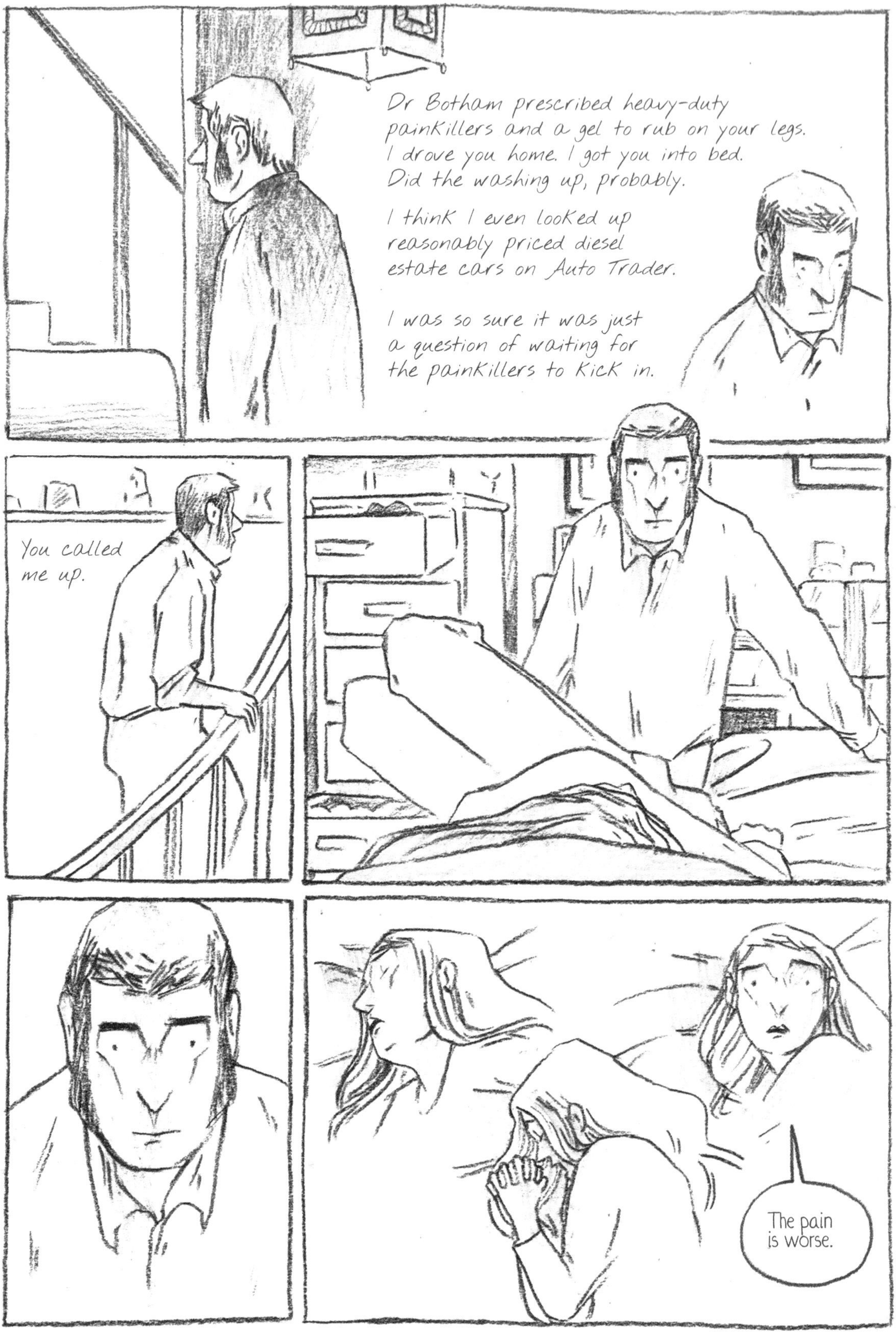
Dr Botham prescribed heavy-duty painkillers and a gel to rub on your legs. I drove you home. I got you into bed. Did the washing up, probably.
I think I even looked up reasonably priced diesel estate cars on Auto Trader.
I was so sure it was just a question of waiting for the painkillers to kick in.
You called me up.
The pain is worse.

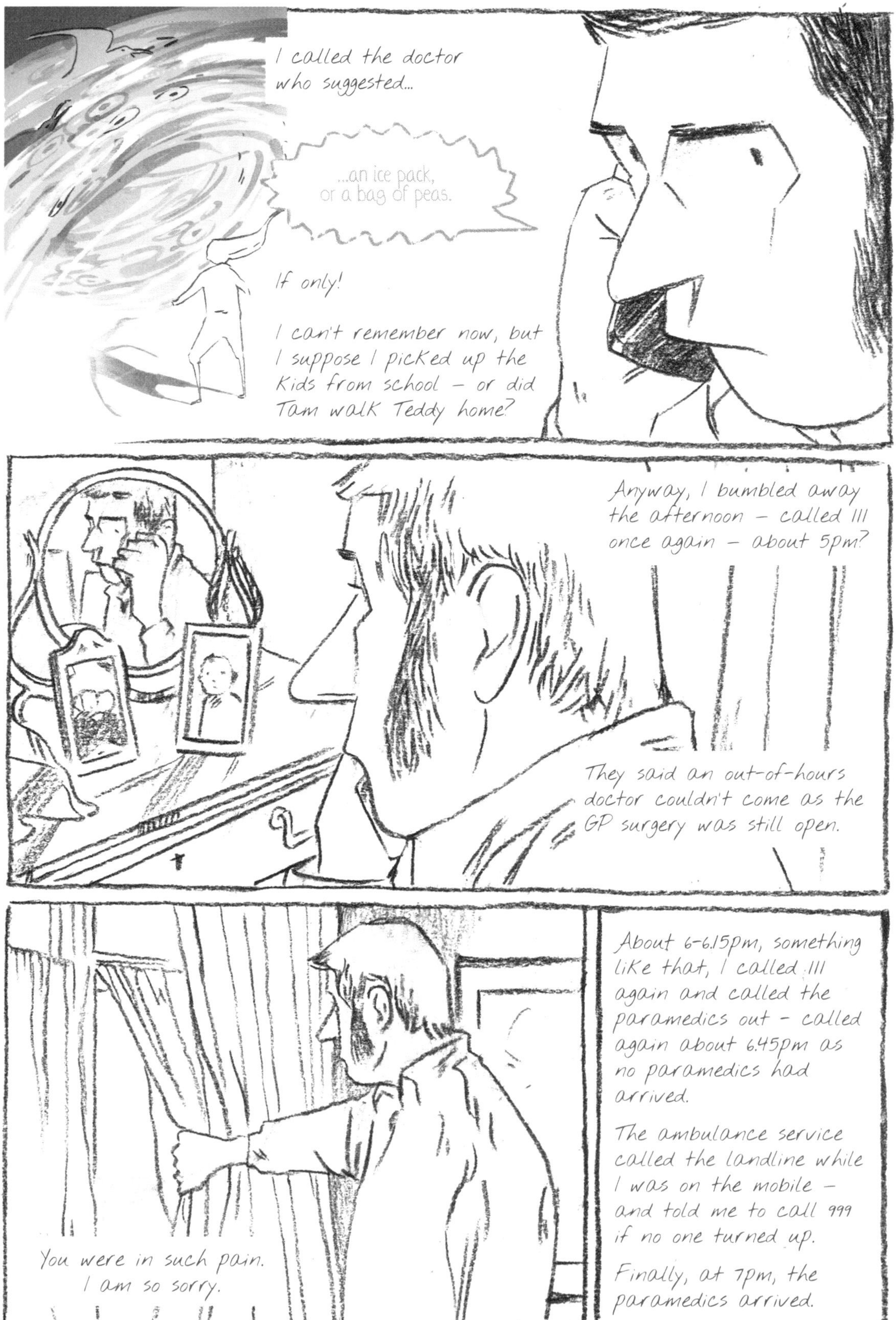
I called the doctor who suggested...
...an ice pack, or a bag of peas.
If only!
I can't remember now, but I suppose I picked up the kids from school – or did Tam walk Teddy home?
Anyway, I bumbled away the afternoon – called 111 once again – about 5pm?
They said an out-of-hours doctor couldn't come as the GP surgery was still open.
You were in such pain. I am so sorry.
About 6-6.15pm, something like that, I called 111 again and called the paramedics out – called again about 6.45pm as no paramedics had arrived.
The ambulance service called the landline while I was on the mobile – and told me to call 999 if no one turned up.
Finally, at 7pm, the paramedics arrived.

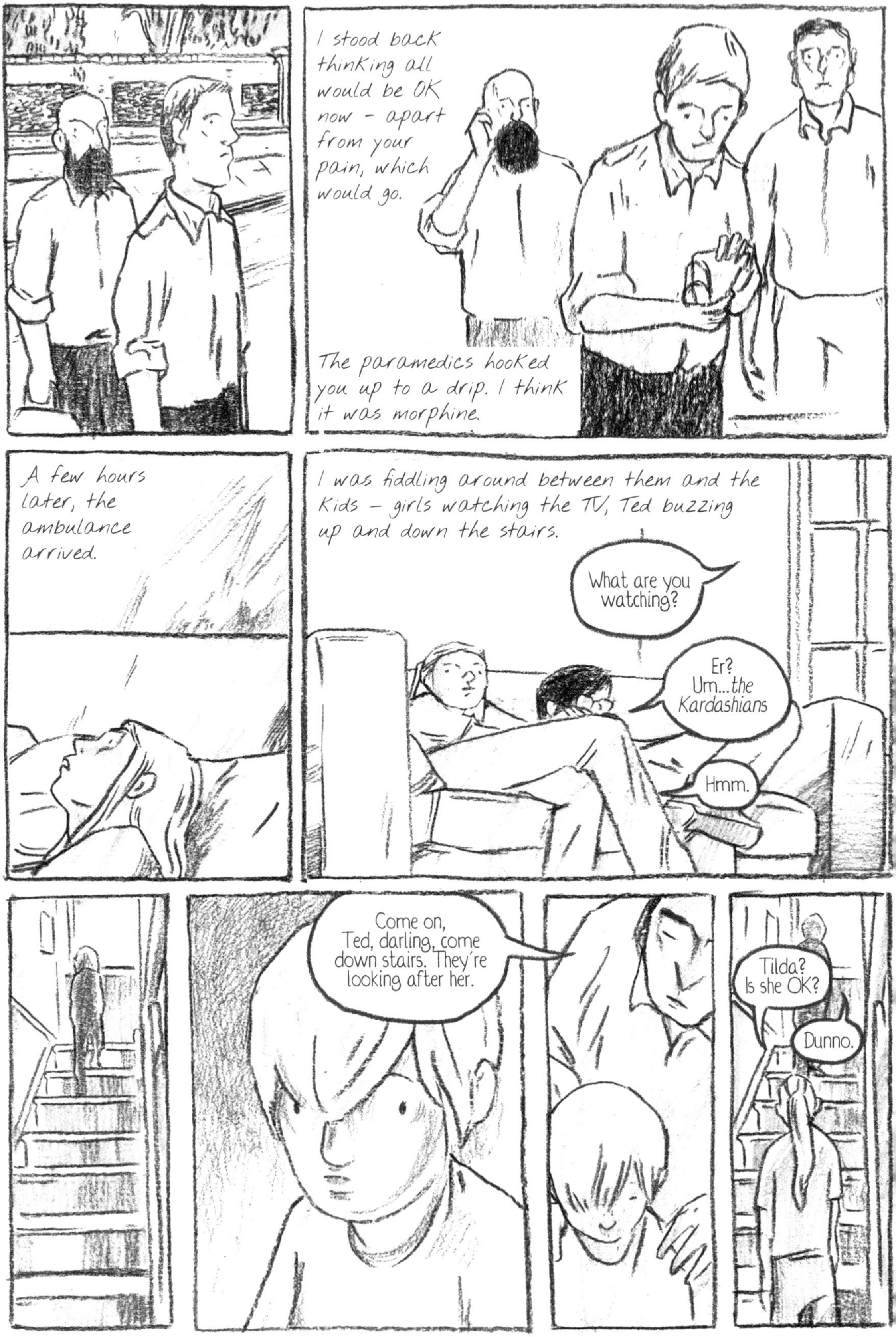

I stood back thinking all would be OK now - apart from your pain, which would go.
The paramedics hooked you up to a drip. I think it was morphine.
A few hours later, the ambulance arrived.
I was fiddling around between them and the kids - girls watching the TV, Ted buzzing up and down the stairs.
What are you watching?
Er? Um...the Kardashians
Hmm.
Come on, Ted, darling, come down stairs. They're looking after her.
Tilda? Is she OK?
Dunno.

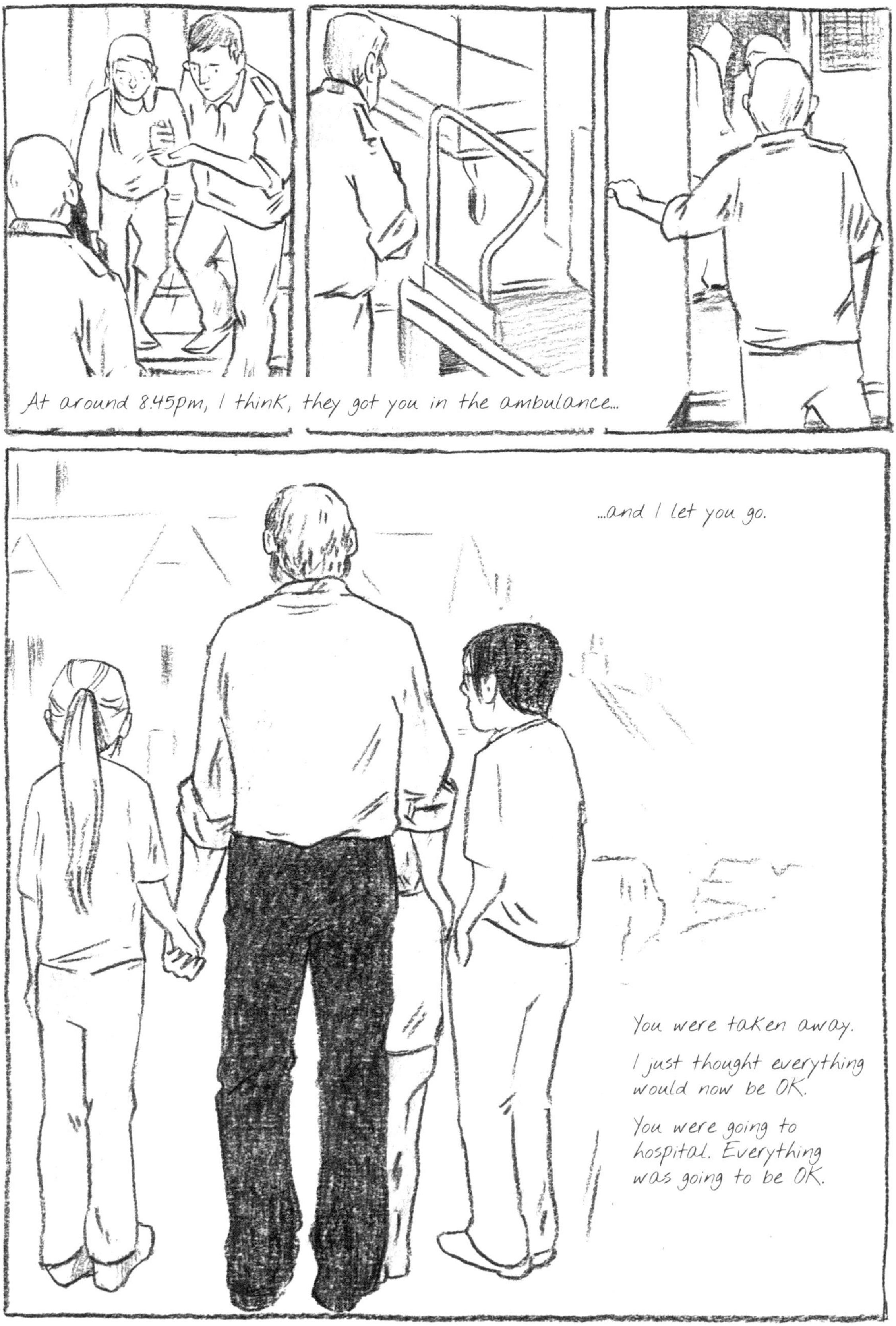
At around 8.45pm, I think, they got you in the ambulance...
...and I let you go.
You were taken away.
I just thought everything would now be OK.
You were going to hospital. Everything was going to be OK.

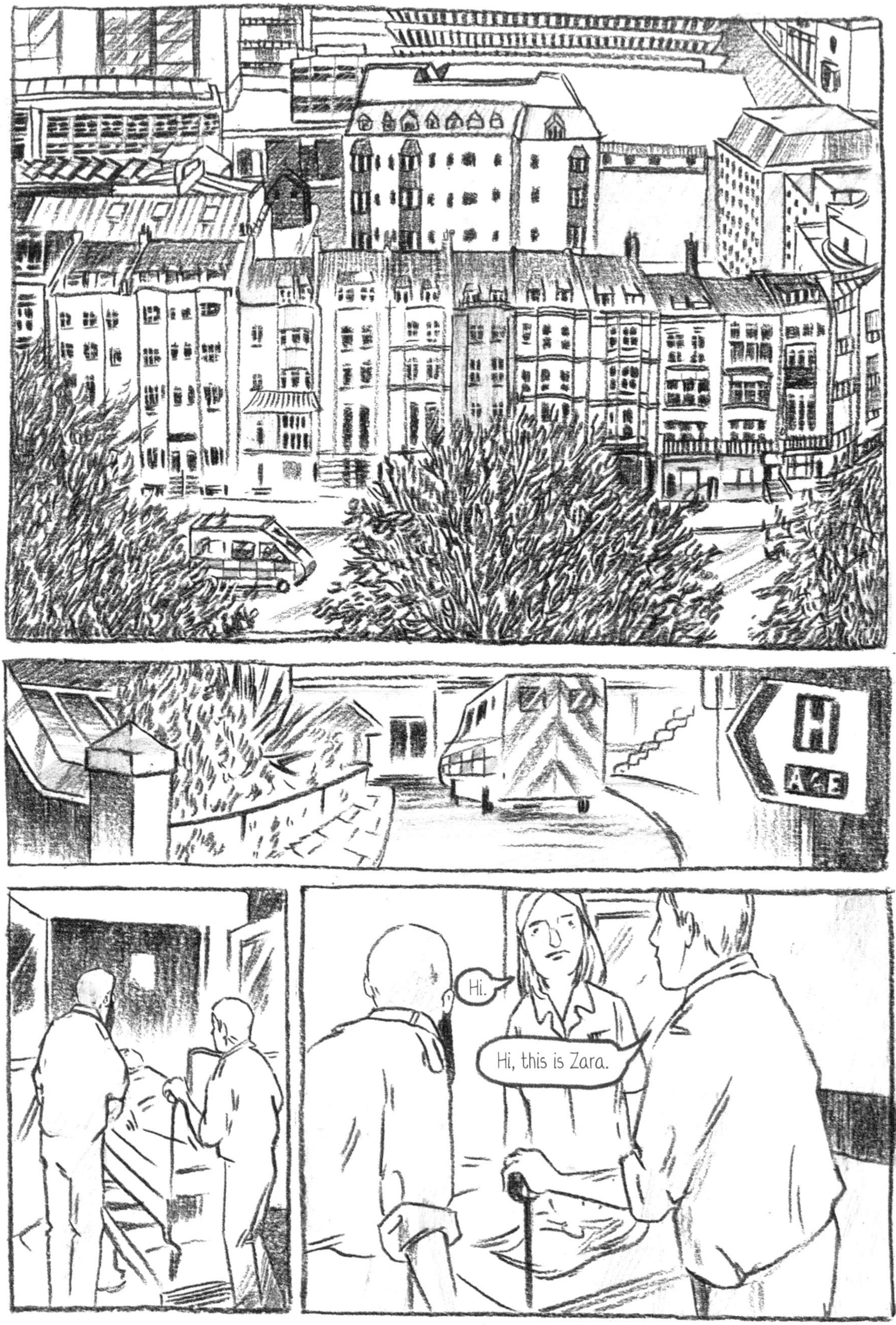
H
A&E
Hi.
Hi, this is Zara.

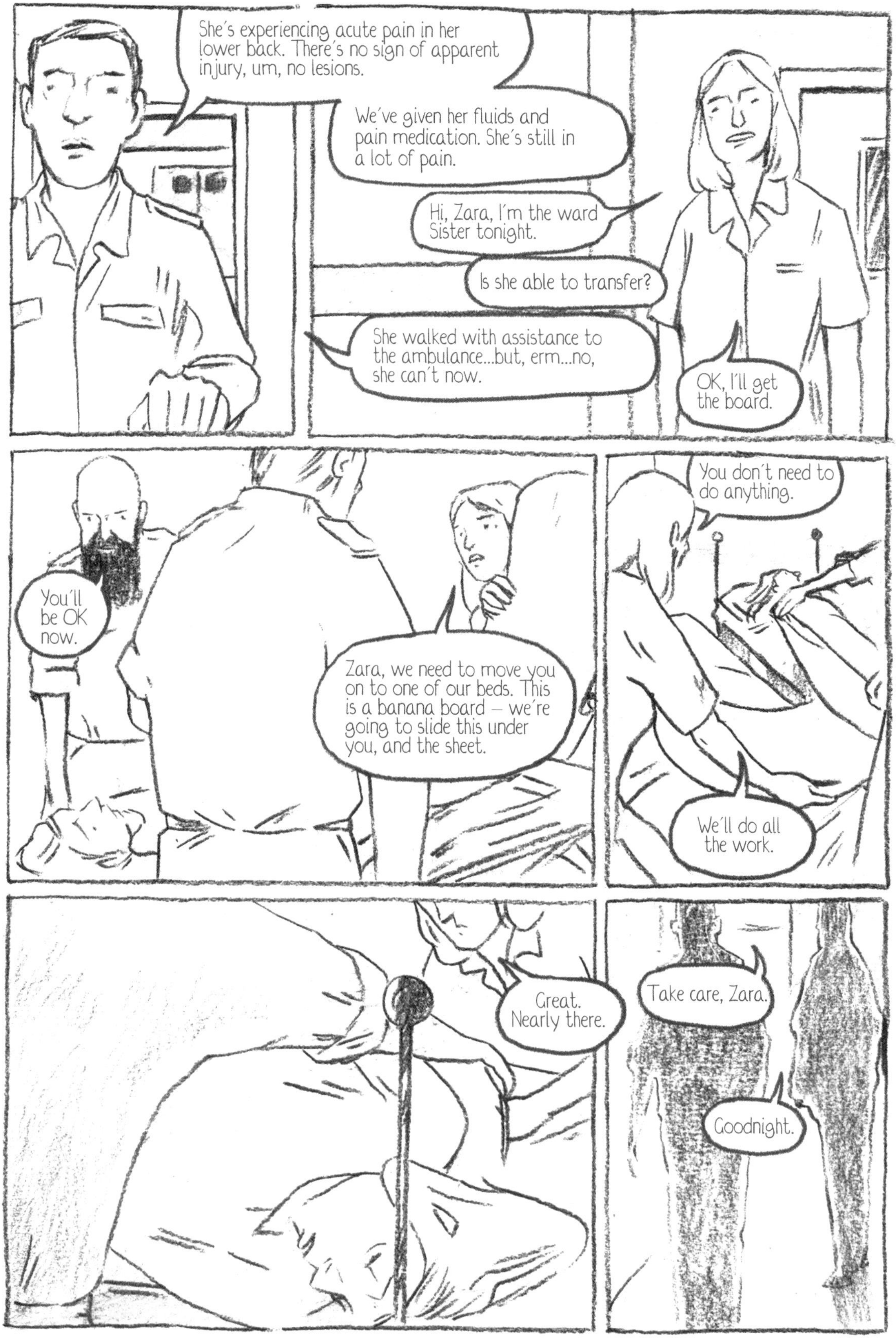
She's experiencing acute pain in her lower back. There's no sign of apparent injury, um, no lesions.
We've given her fluids and pain medication. She's still in a lot of pain.
Hi, Zara, I'm the ward Sister tonight.
Is she able to transfer?
She walked with assistance to the ambulance...but, erm...no, she can't now.
OK, I'll get the board.
You'll be OK now.
Zara, we need to move you on to one of our beds. This is a banana board – we're going to slide this under you, and the sheet.
You don't need to do anything.
We'll do all the work.
Great. Nearly there.
Take care, Zara.
Goodnight.

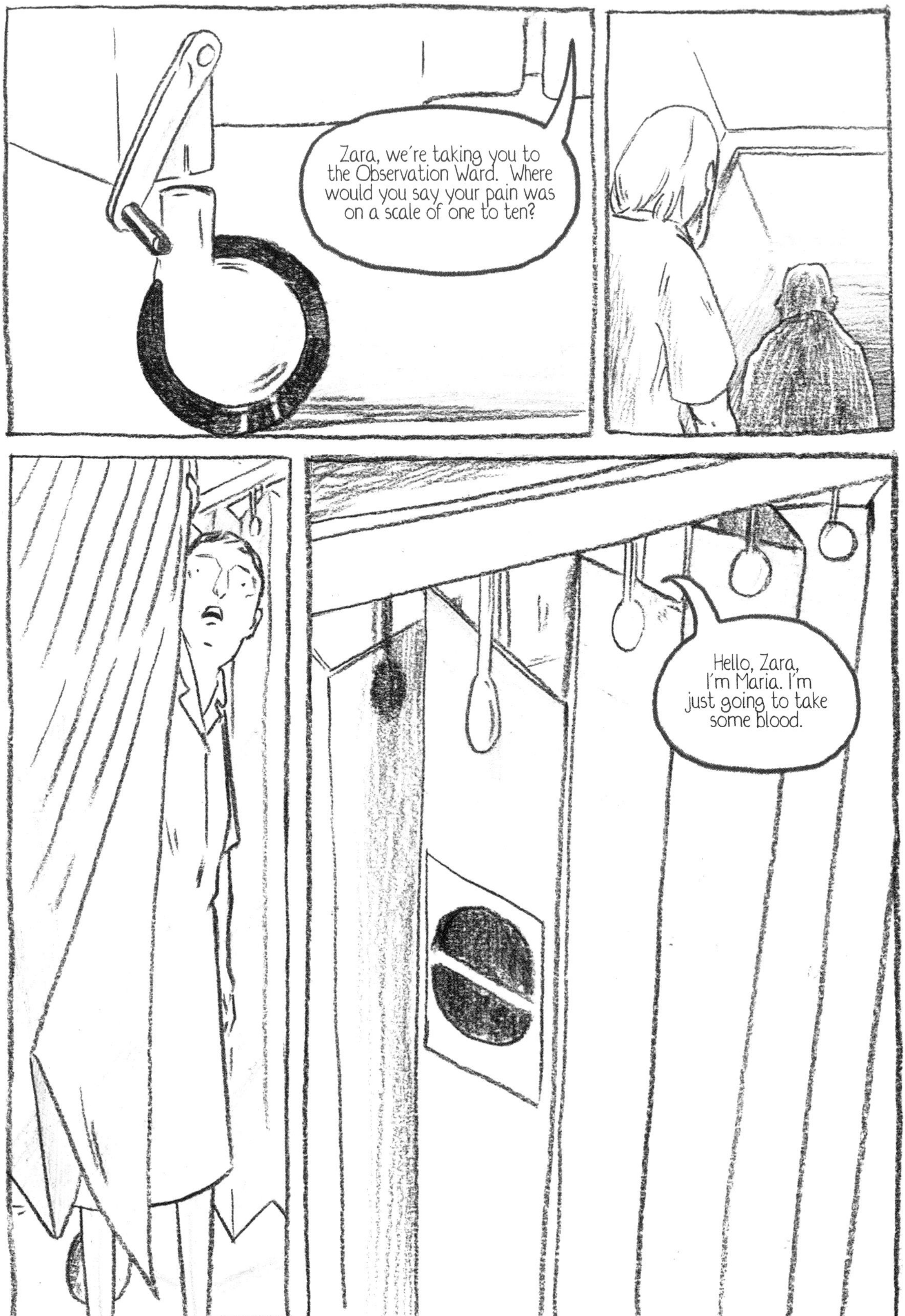
Zara, we're taking you to the Observation Ward. Where would you say your pain was on a scale of one to ten?
Hello, Zara, I'm Maria. I'm just going to take some blood.

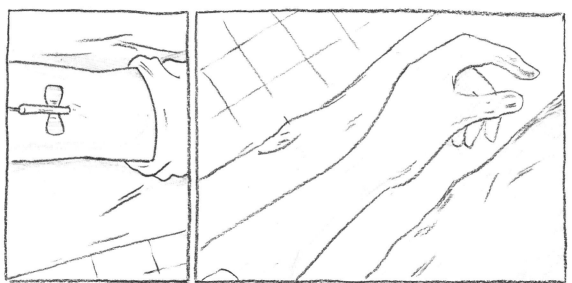

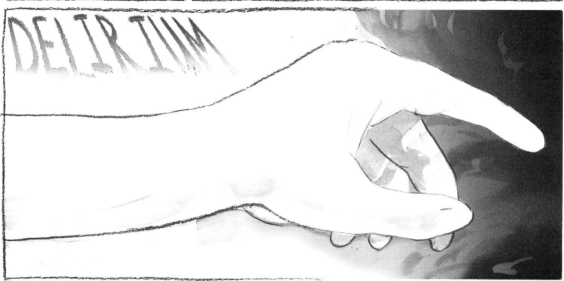

DELIRIUM

Meanwhile, within, the Ouroboros is awake...

...and its noxious clouds are gathering.

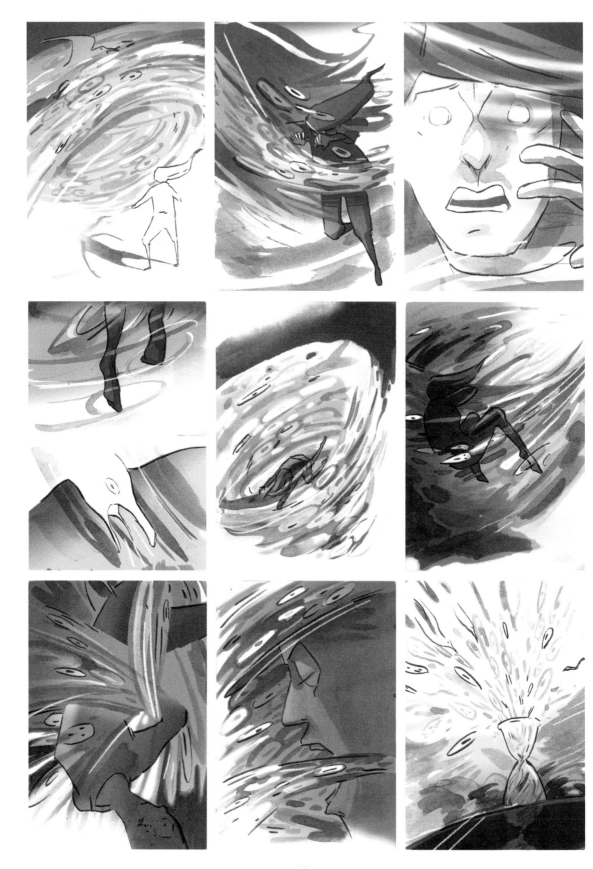

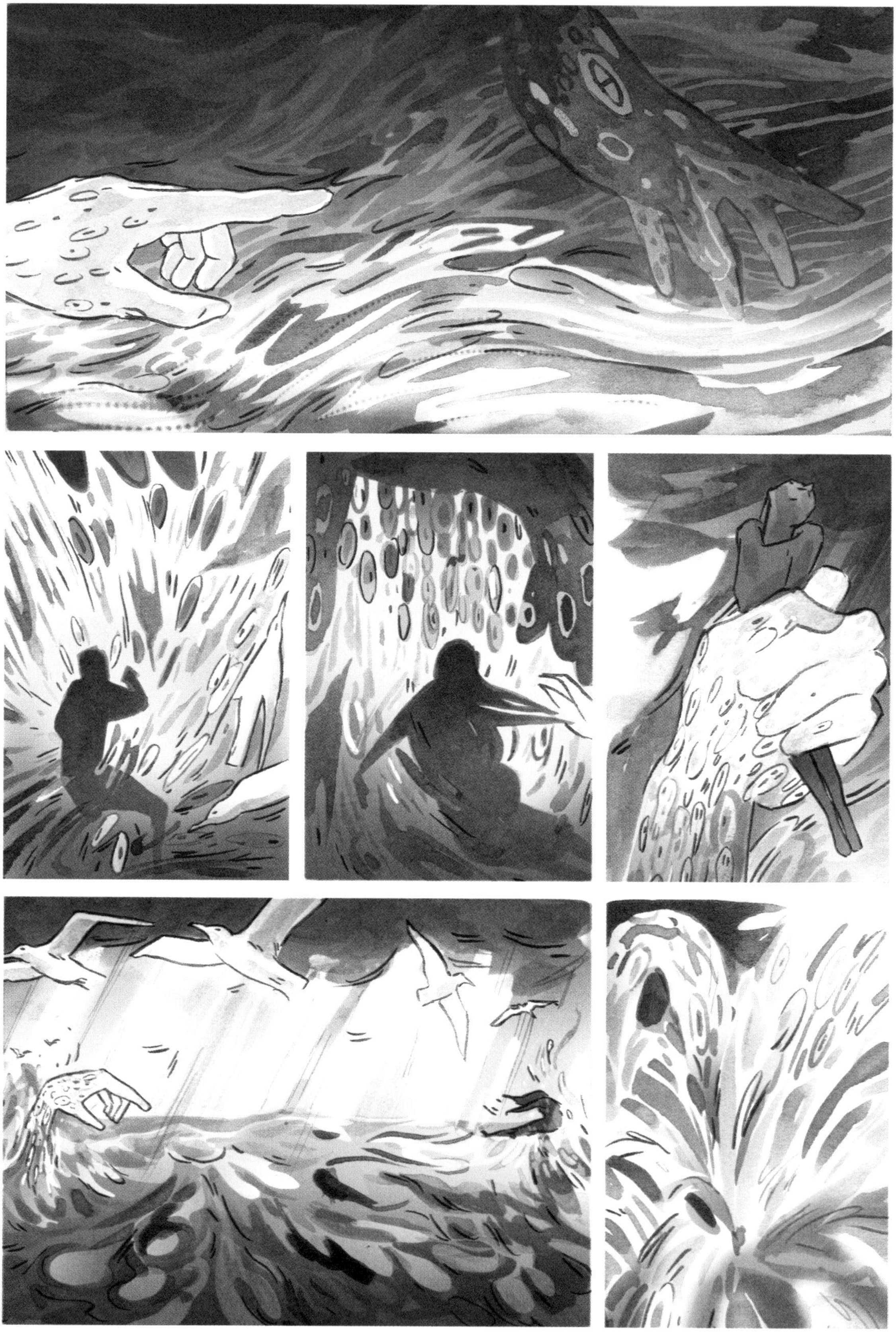

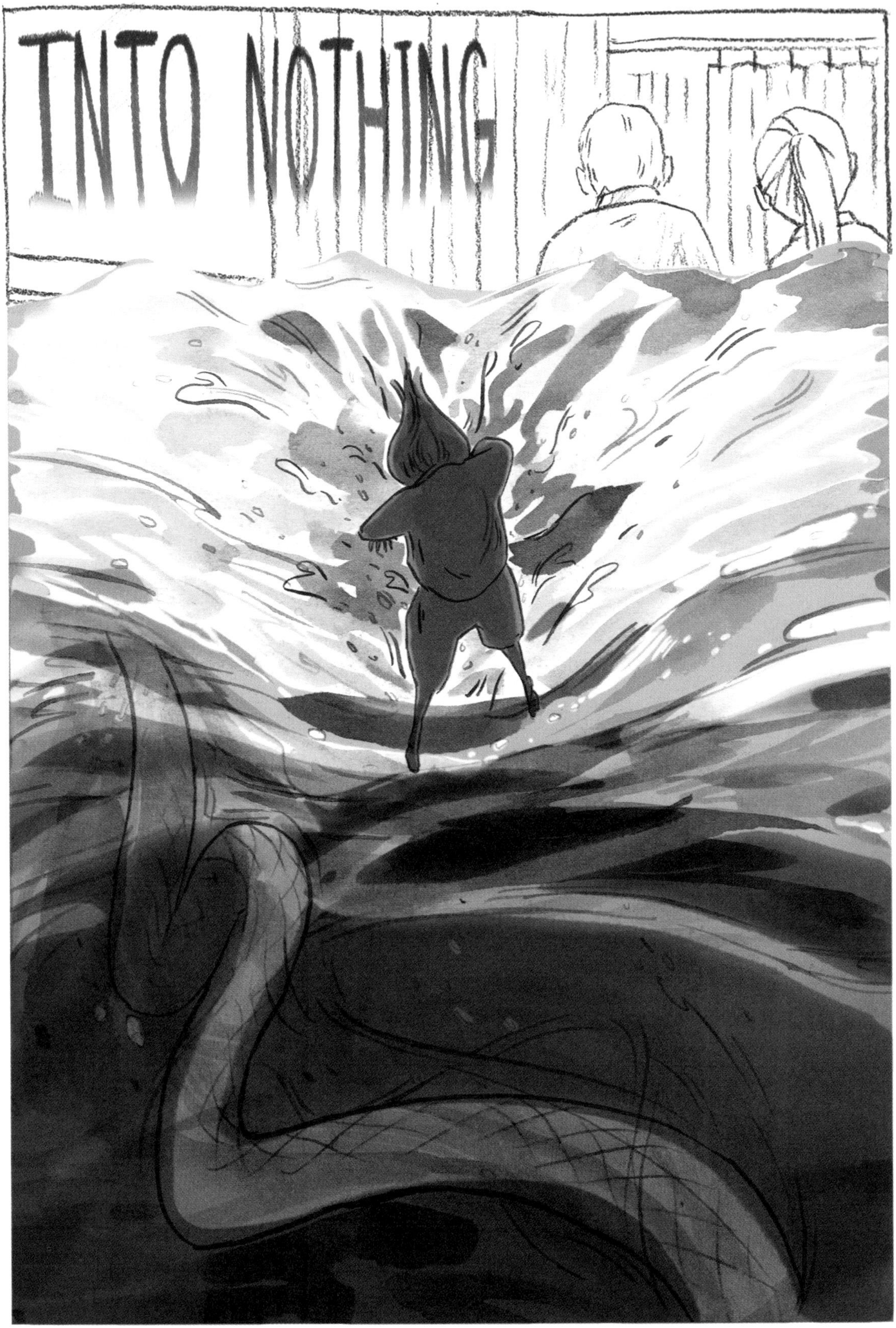
INTO NOTHING

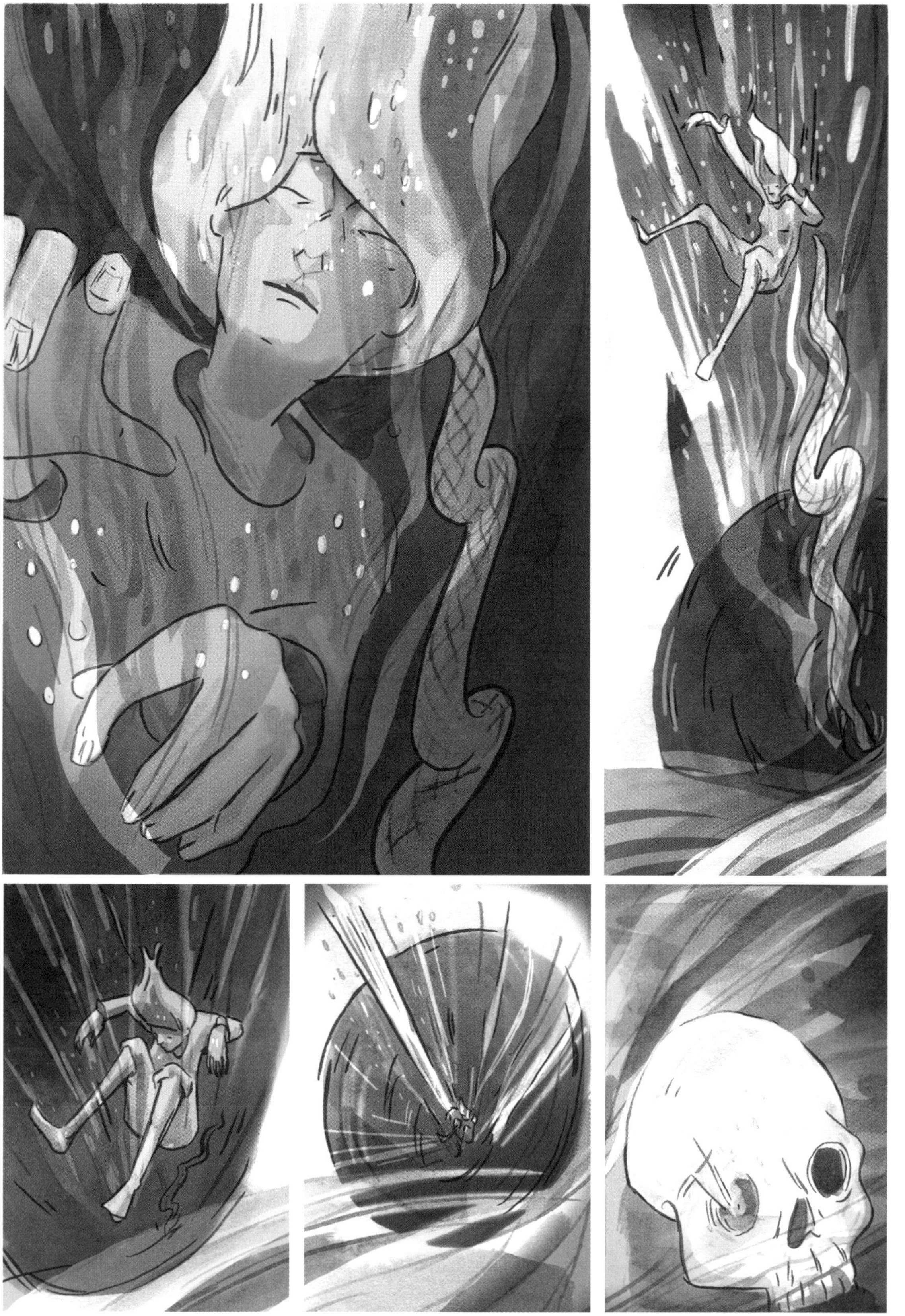

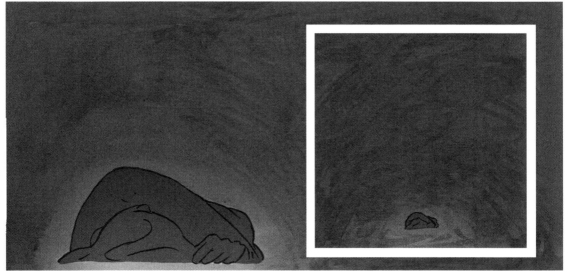

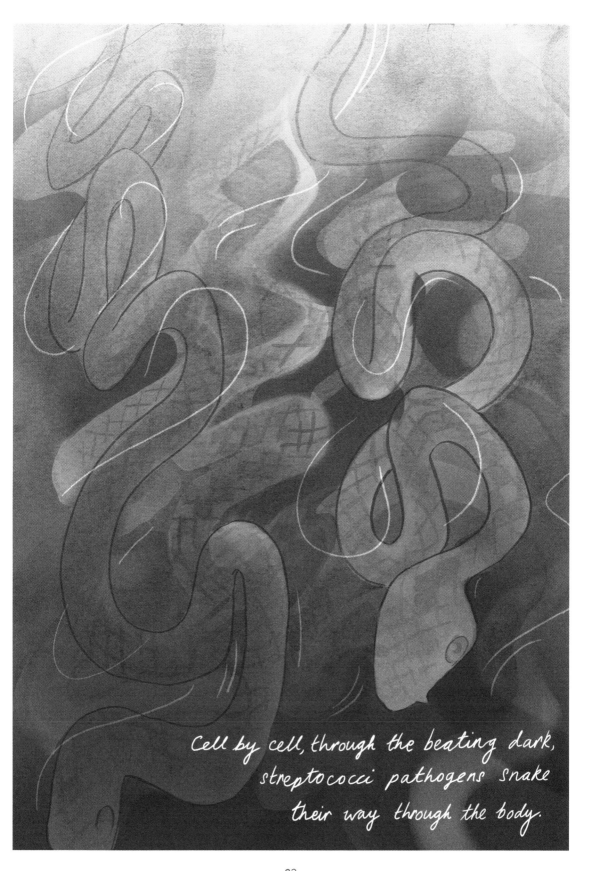

Cell by cell, through the beating dark, streptococci pathogens snake their way through the body.

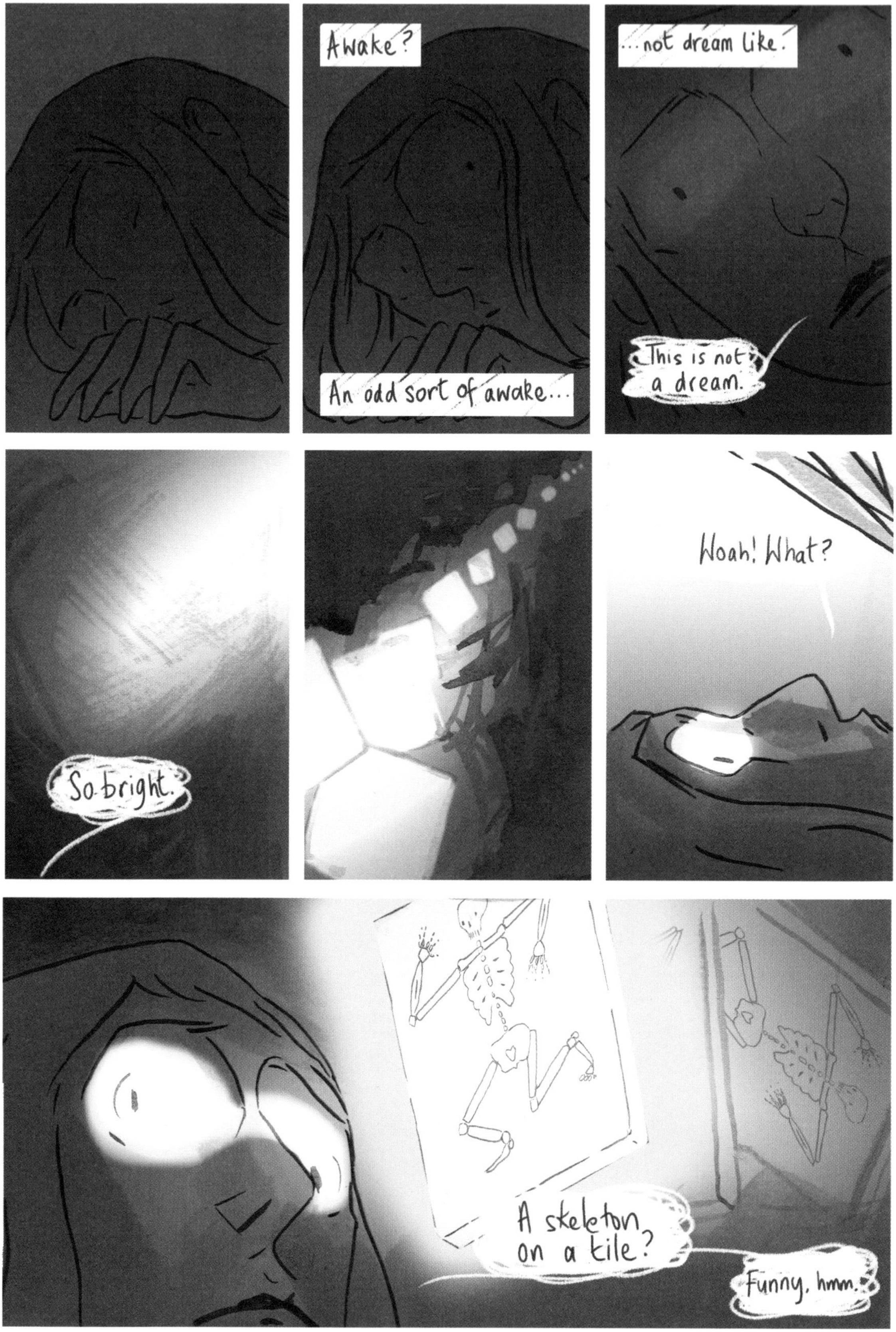

Awake?
An odd sort of awake...
...not dream like.
This is not a dream.
So bright.
Woah! What?
A skeleton on a tile?
Funny, hmm.

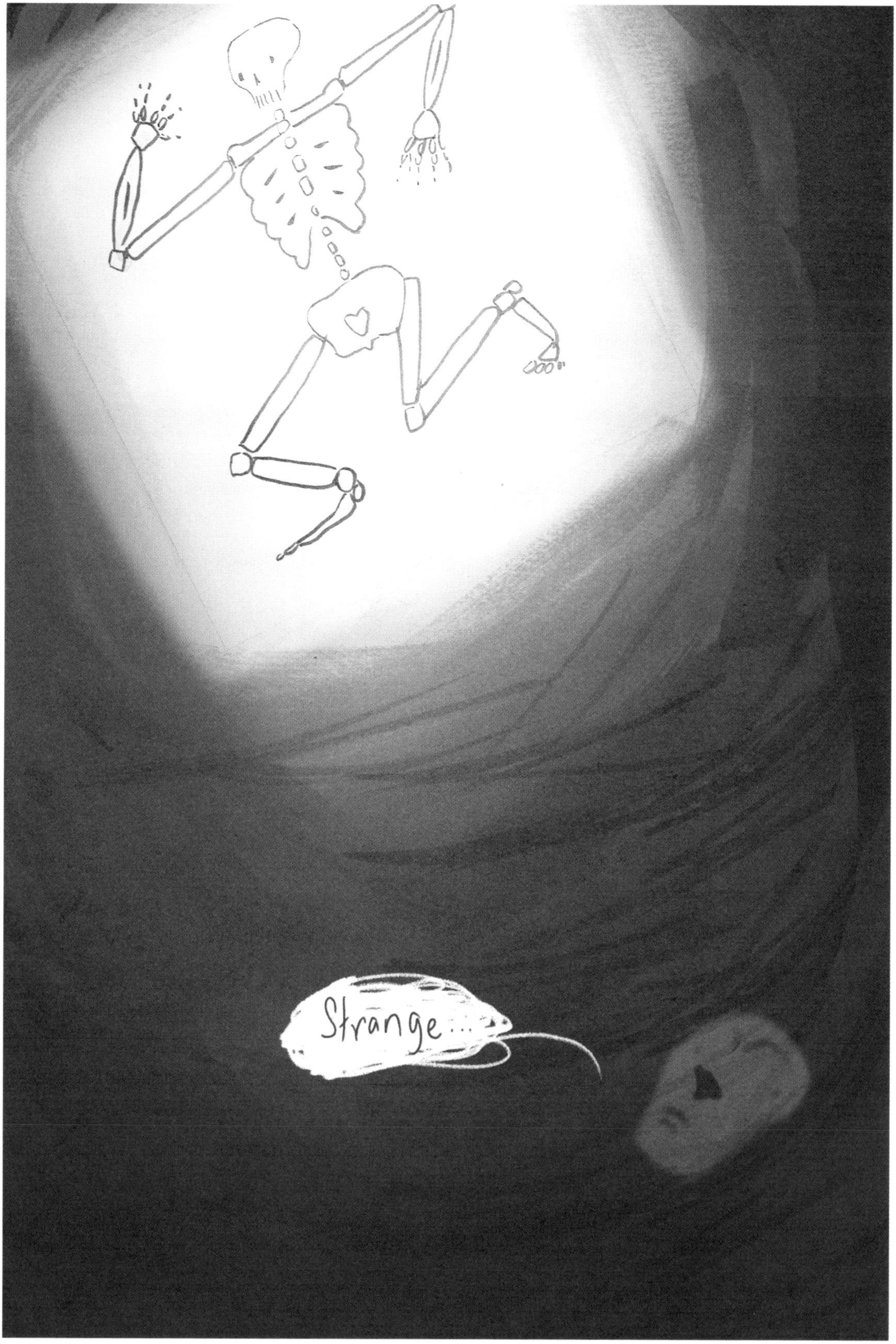
Strange...

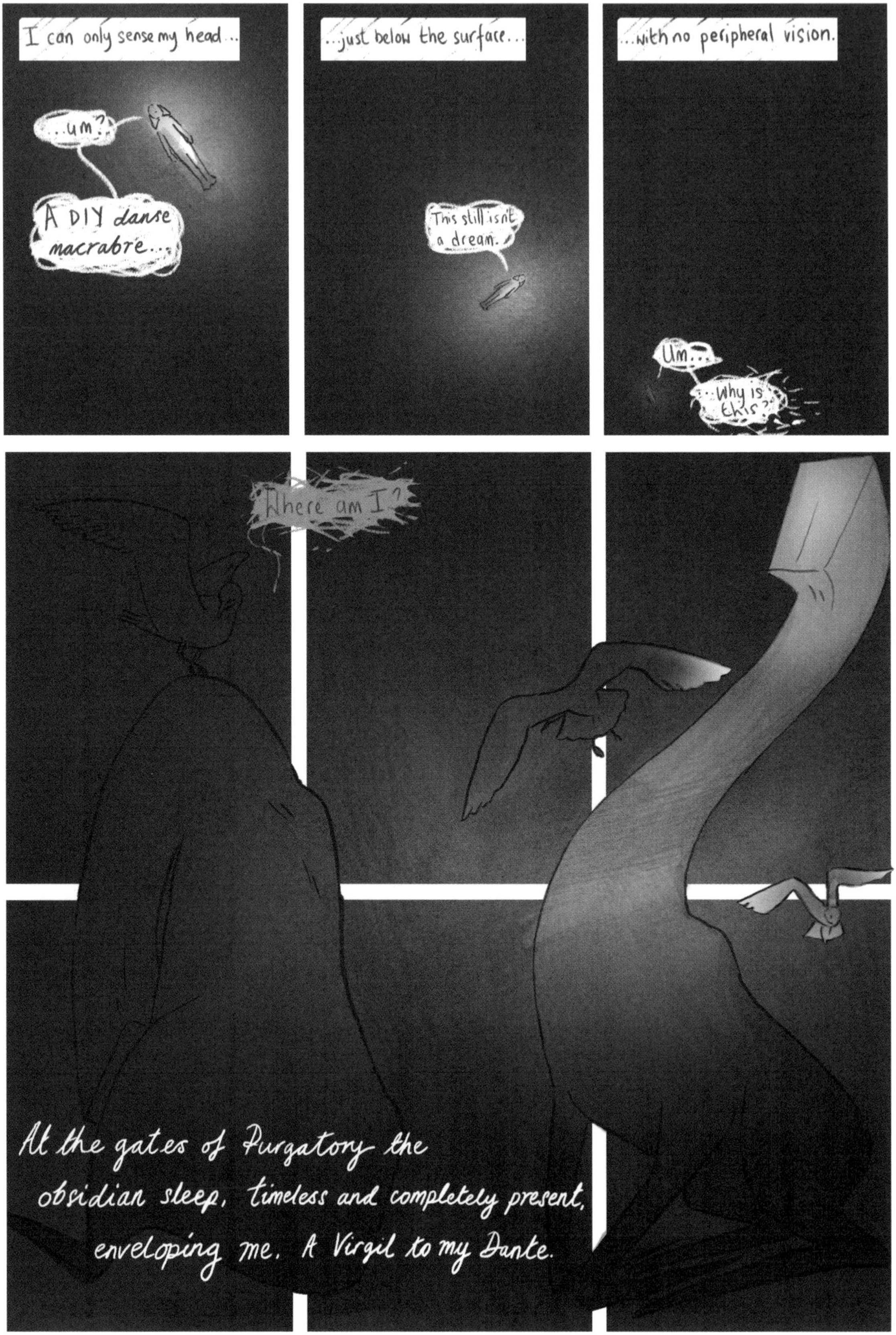
I can only sense my head...
...um?
A DIY danse macrabre...
...just below the surface...
This still isn't a dream.
...with no peripheral vision.
Um...
...why is this?
Where am I?
At the gates of Purgatory the obsidian sleep, timeless and completely present, enveloping me. A Virgil to my Dante.

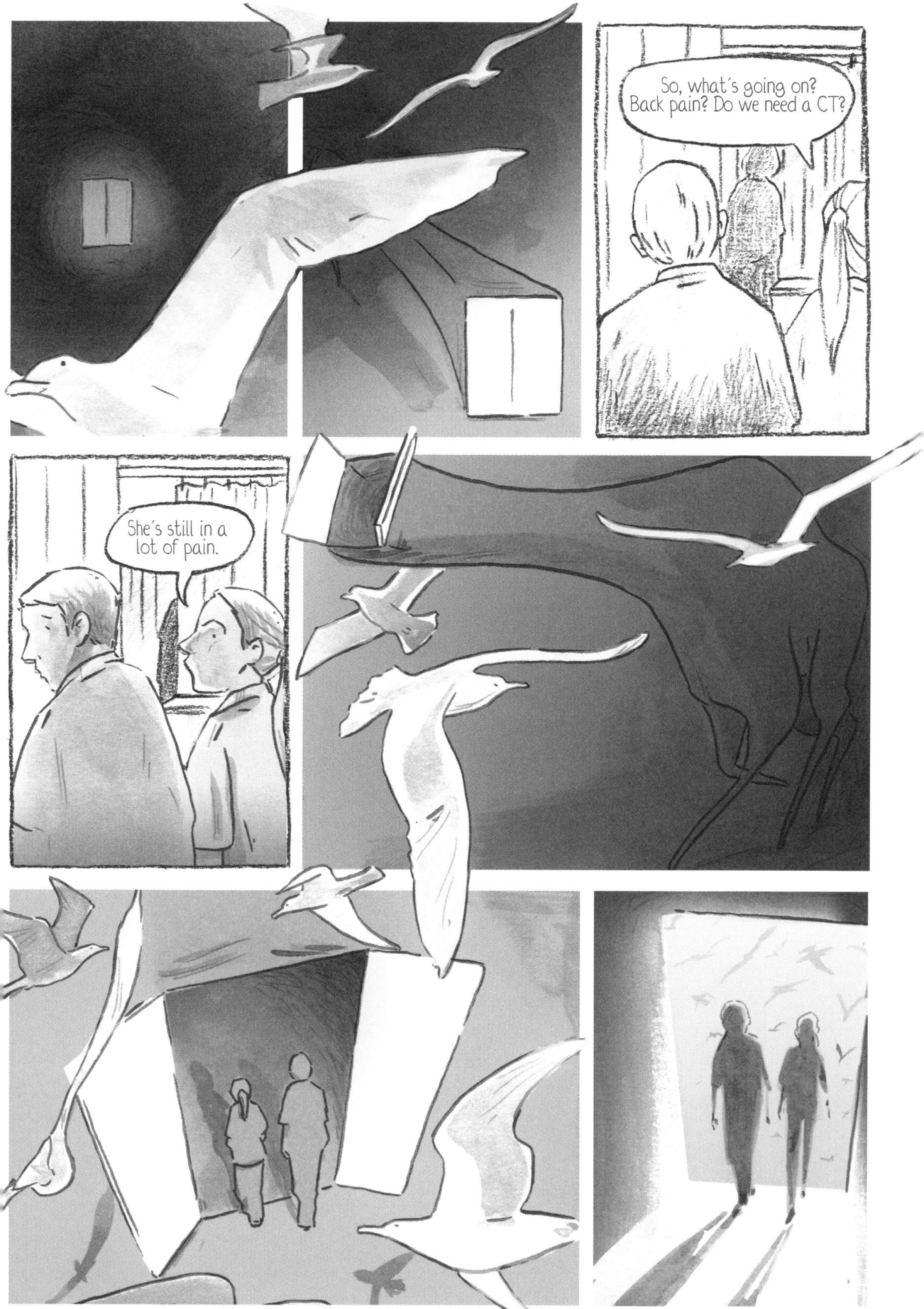
So, what's going on? Back pain? Do we need a CT?
She's still in a lot of pain.

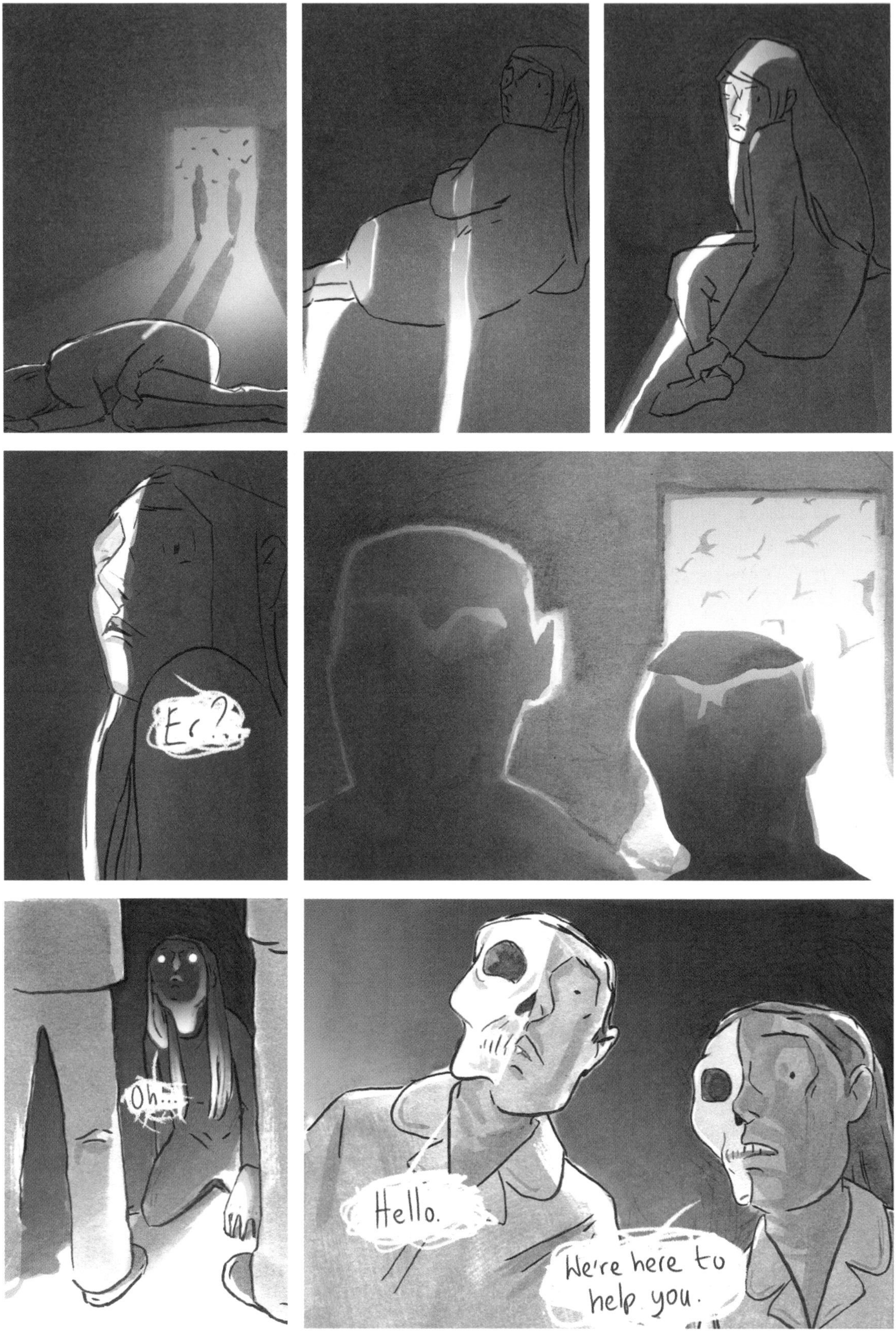
Er?..
Oh...
Hello.
We're here to help you.

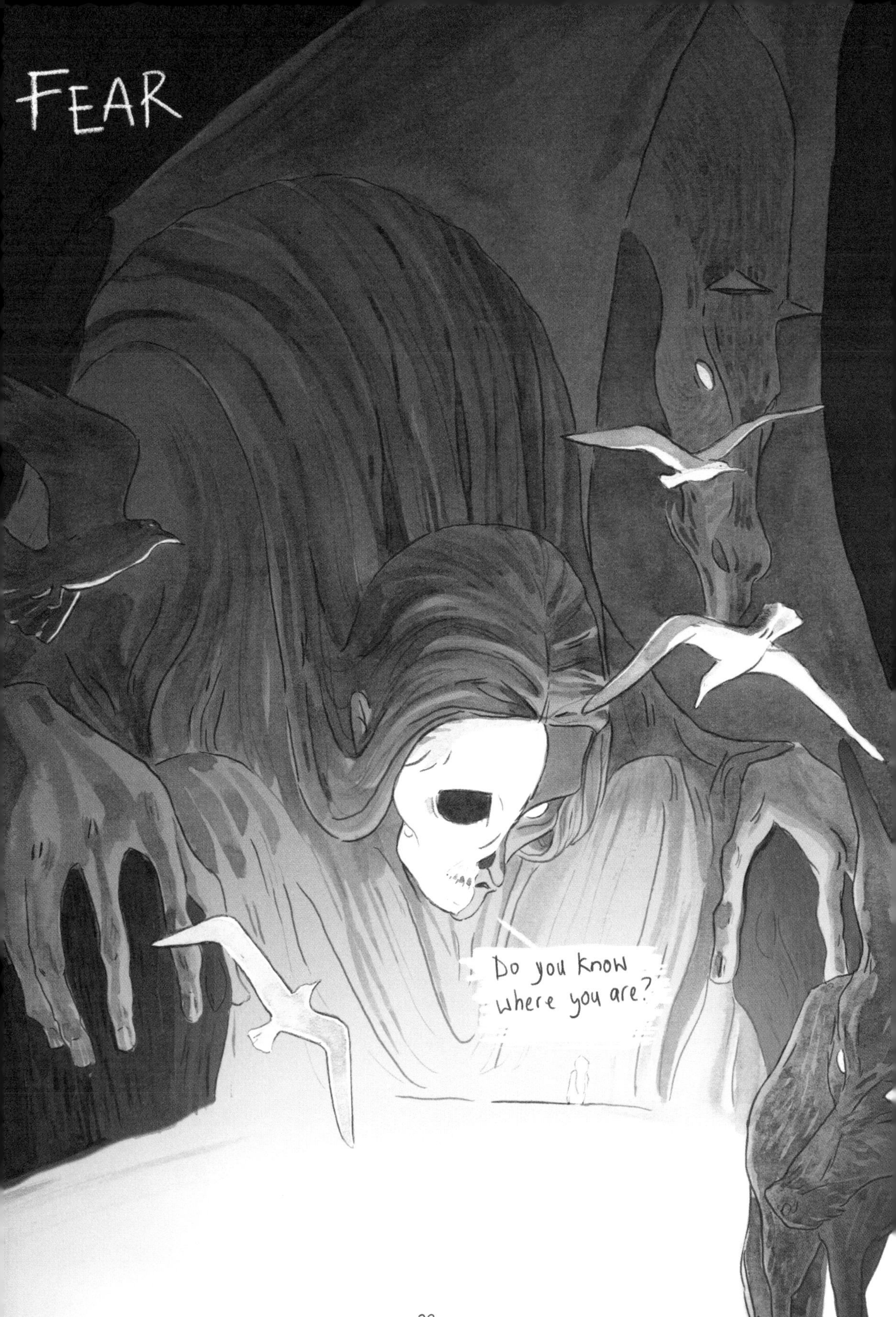
FEAR
Do you know where you are?

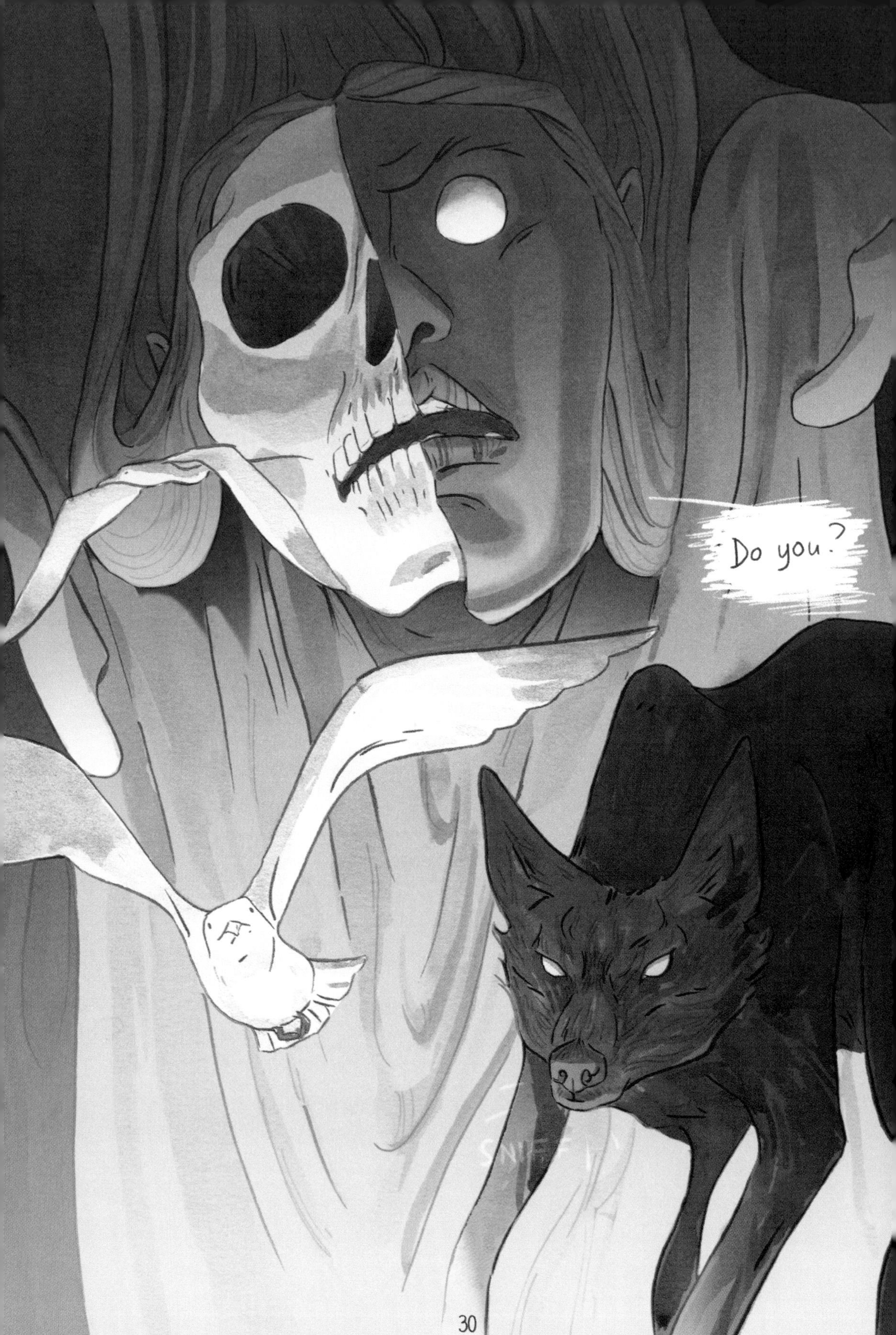
Do you?
SNIFF

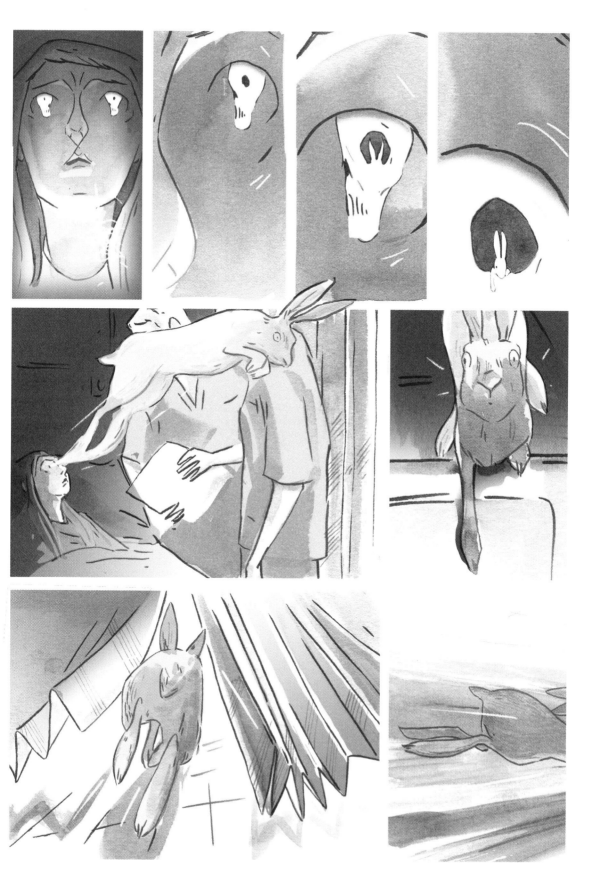

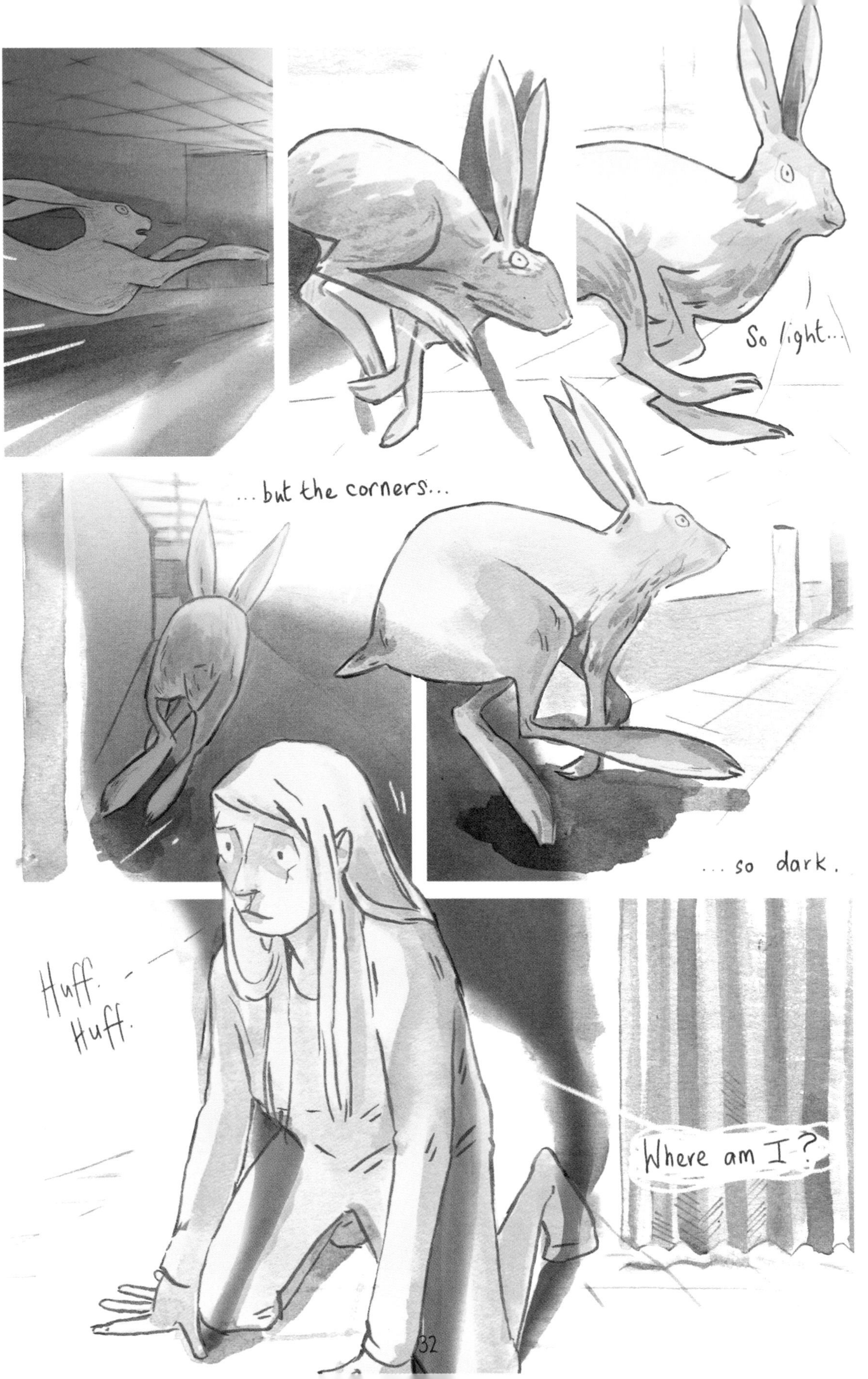
So light...
...but the corners...
...so dark.
Huff.
Huff.
Where am I?

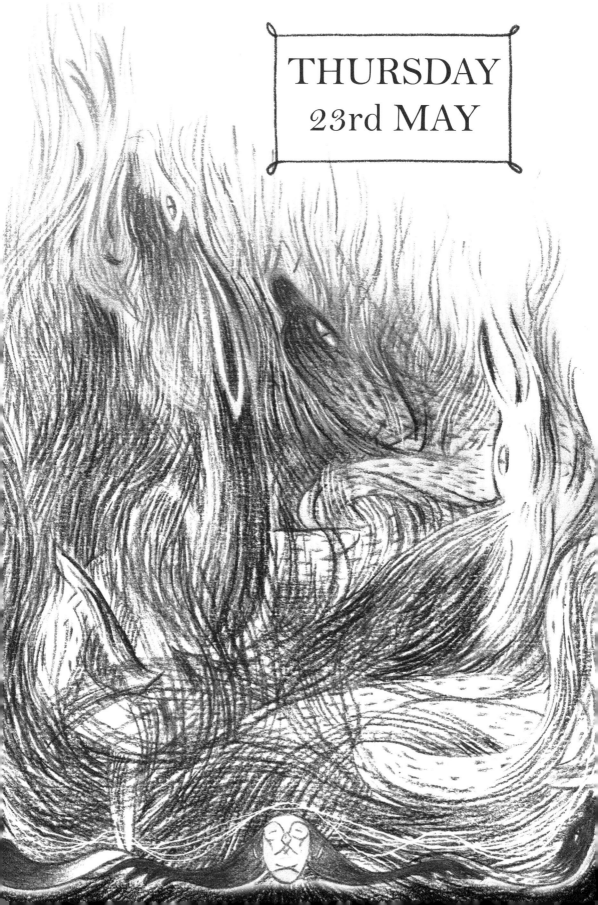

THURSDAY
23rd MAY

I woke up at 7am. Ted was up, I let Tam sleep in, got Tilda off to school.

It was past 9am, maybe 9.30am, when I called the hospital. I suddenly realised I didn't know what hospital you were in. I figured it was probably the Sussex.

You were in the A &E Observation Ward. You were having scans, they said it would take an hour or two.

I really wasn't worried.

My days are getting so mixed up. This was only Thursday.

Ted and Tam had to go to school, so of course I hadn't let Tam sleep in, that was the next day.

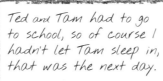

I must have called about 9.30am after getting back from school and having a coffee.

My only worry was that I might have to postpone visiting Dad again if you were infectious.

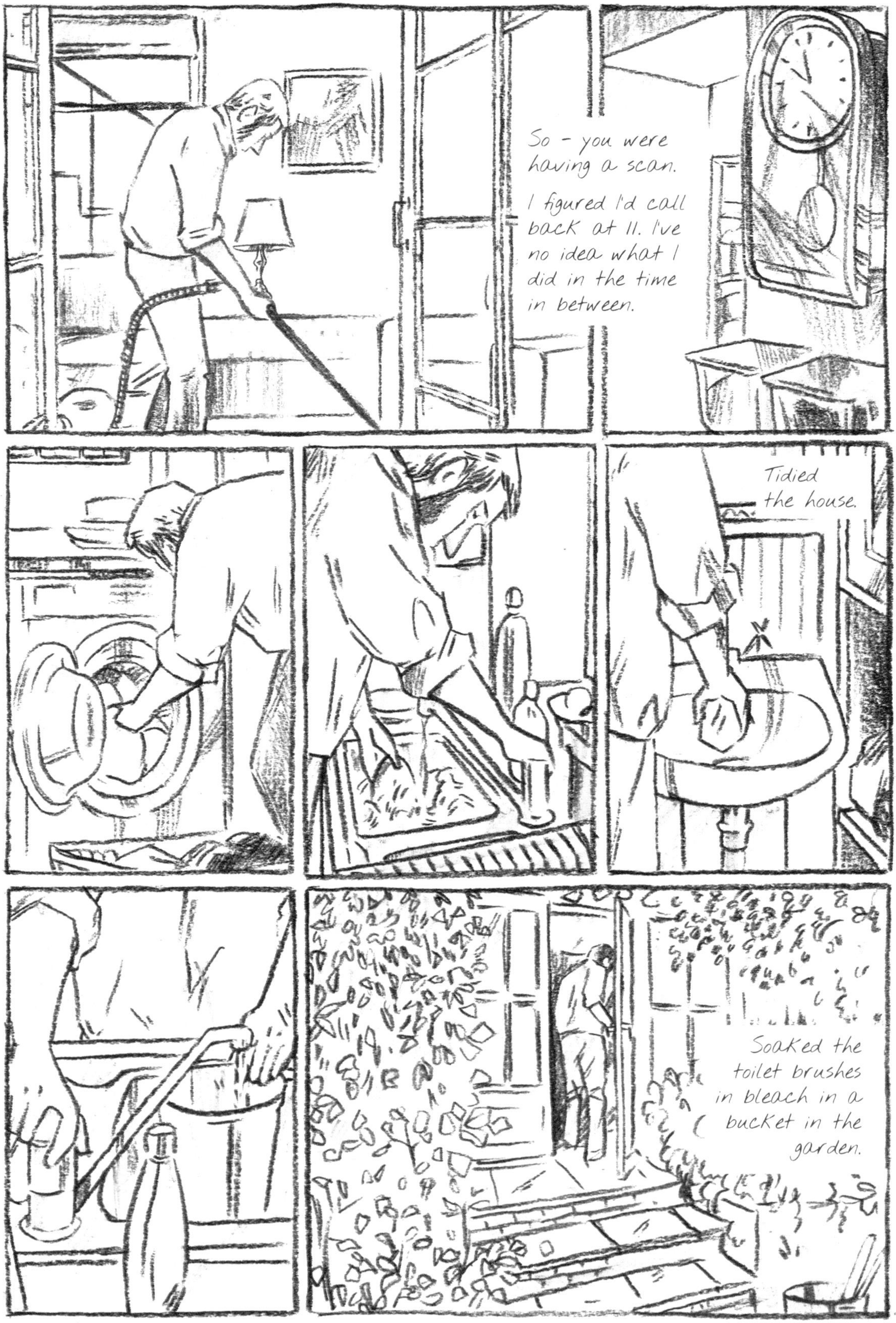
So – you were having a scan.
I figured I'd call back at 11. I've no idea what I did in the time in between.
Tidied the house.
Soaked the toilet brushes in bleach in a bucket in the garden.

I called again, midday?
I forgot, for some
reason, I can't
remember.
I didn't head down
until nearly 1pm.

Parked up in Sudeley
Street and came
to find you.

It was a
shock to
see you.

You looked so much worse.

Hi,
how are
you?

But the blood tests,
I thought, had been OK.
It still seemed nothing
too bad was wrong...

...apart from the pain.

About an hour in, someone
said one of the bloods
was inconclusive and they
needed to take another.

I kept peeping at the time
as I had to get Ted and
take him off to swimming.

Another half
hour or so and
you complained
about bruising on
your thigh.

Look!
Awwa...my leg...
Oww!

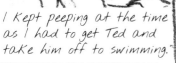

36

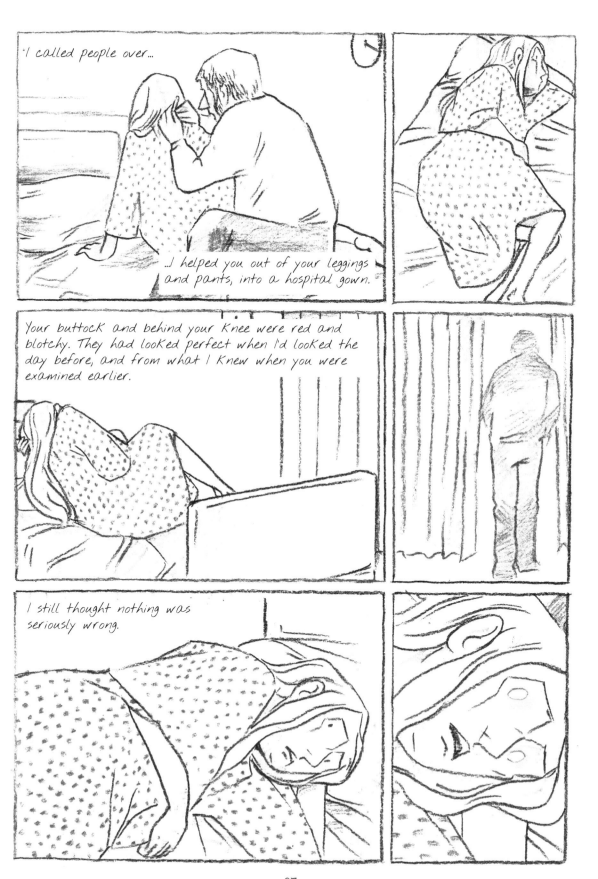

"I called people over...

...I helped you out of your leggings and pants, into a hospital gown.

Your buttock and behind your knee were red and blotchy. They had looked perfect when I'd looked the day before, and from what I knew when you were examined earlier.

I still thought nothing was seriously wrong.

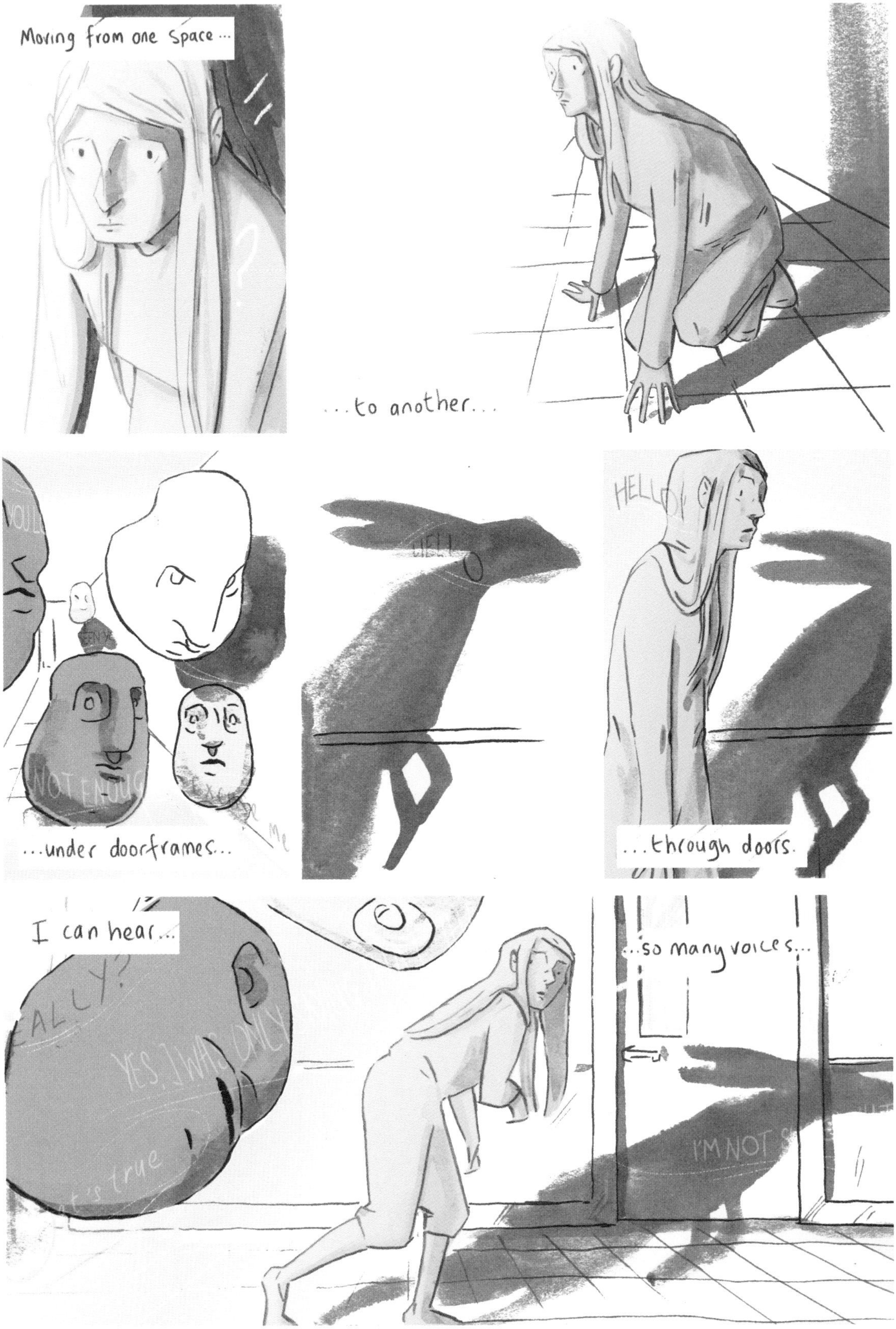
Moving from one space...
...to another...
...under doorframes...
...through doors.
I can hear...
...so many voices...

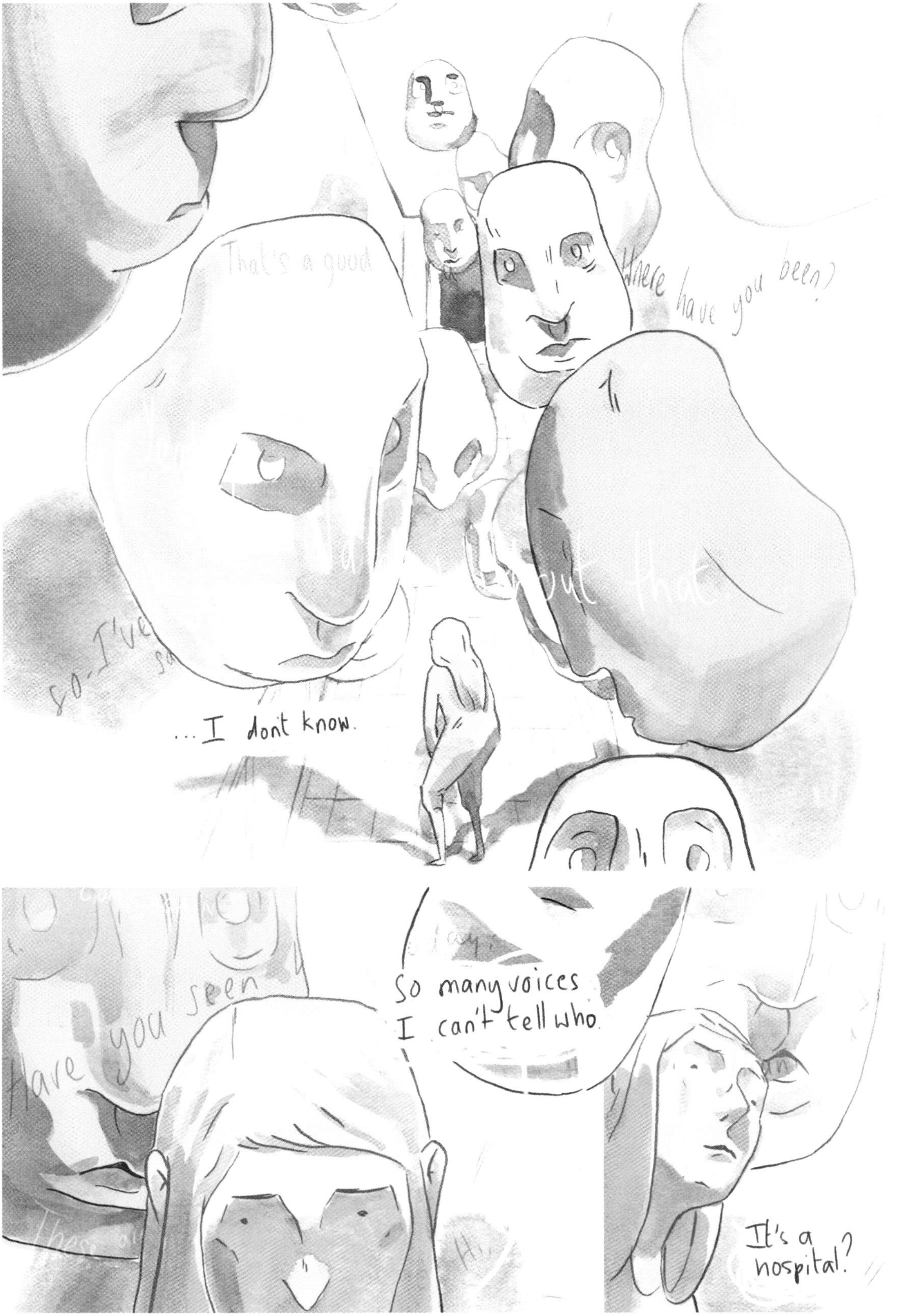
That's a good
Where have you been?
...I don't know.
Have you seen
So many voices
I can't tell who.
It's a hospital?

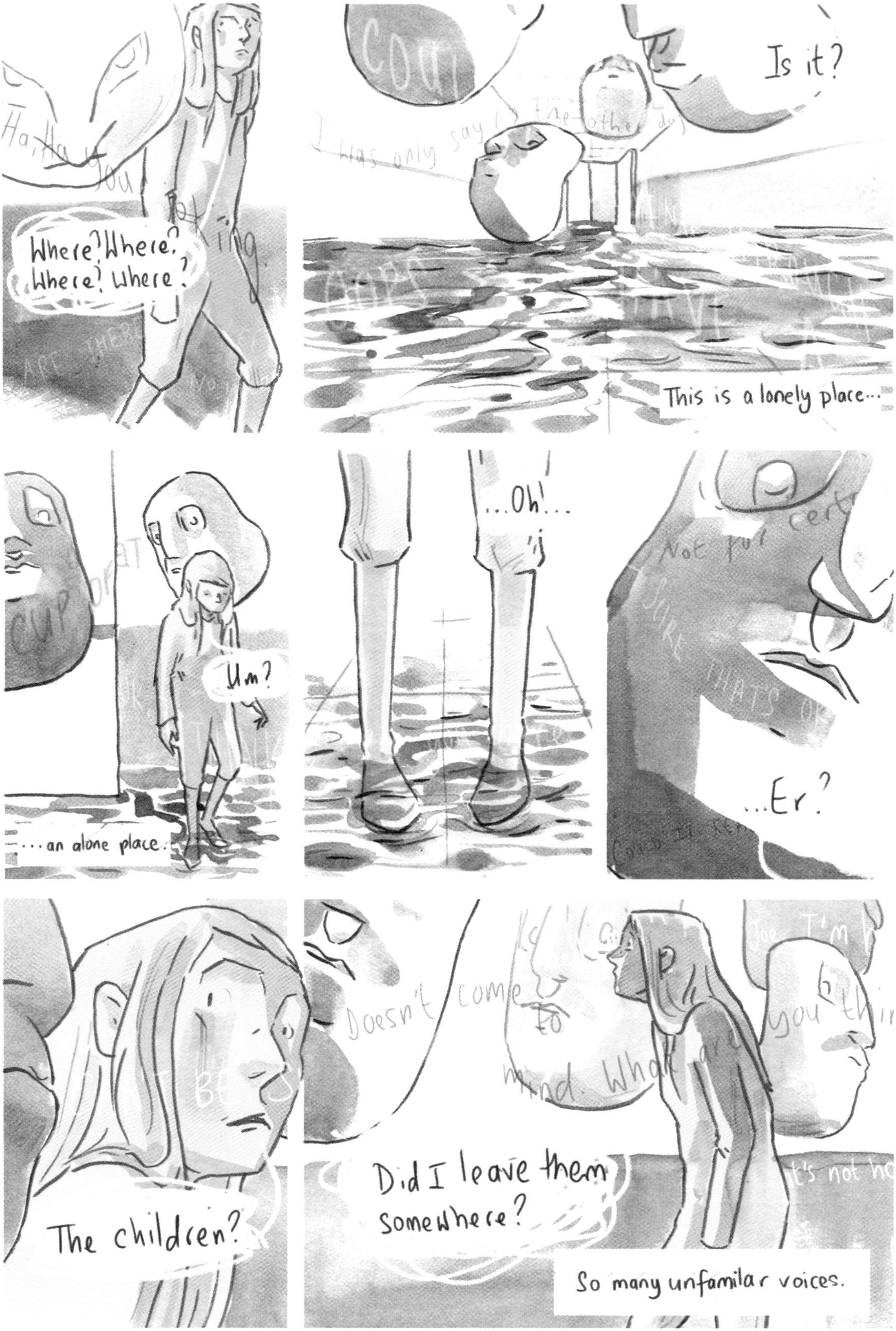
Where? Where? Where? Where?
Is it?
This is a lonely place...
Um?
...an alone place.
...Oh!...
...Er?
The children?
Did I leave them somewhere?
So many unfamilar voices.

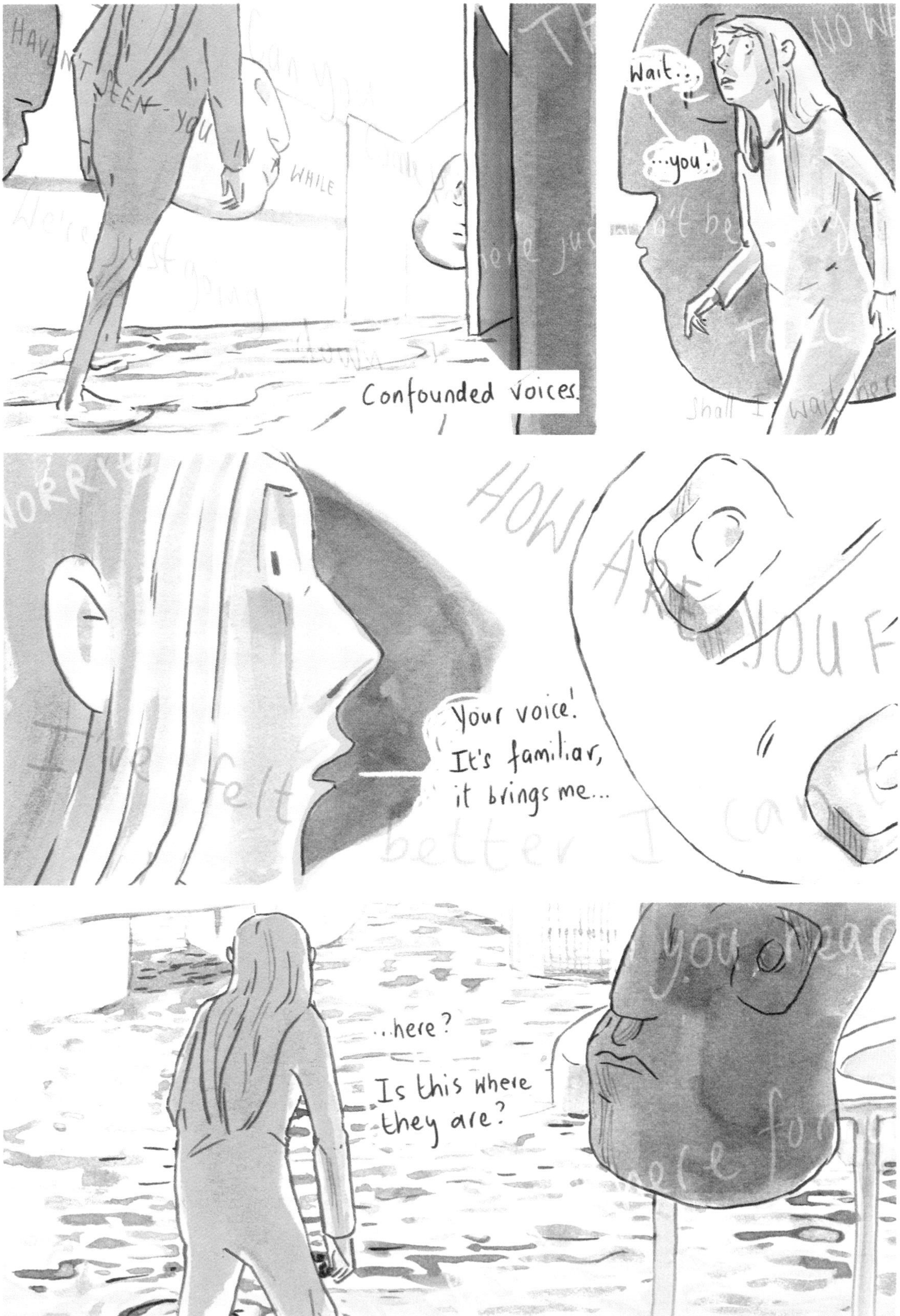
Confounded voices.
Wait...
...you!
Your voice! It's familiar, it brings me...
..here?
Is this where they are?

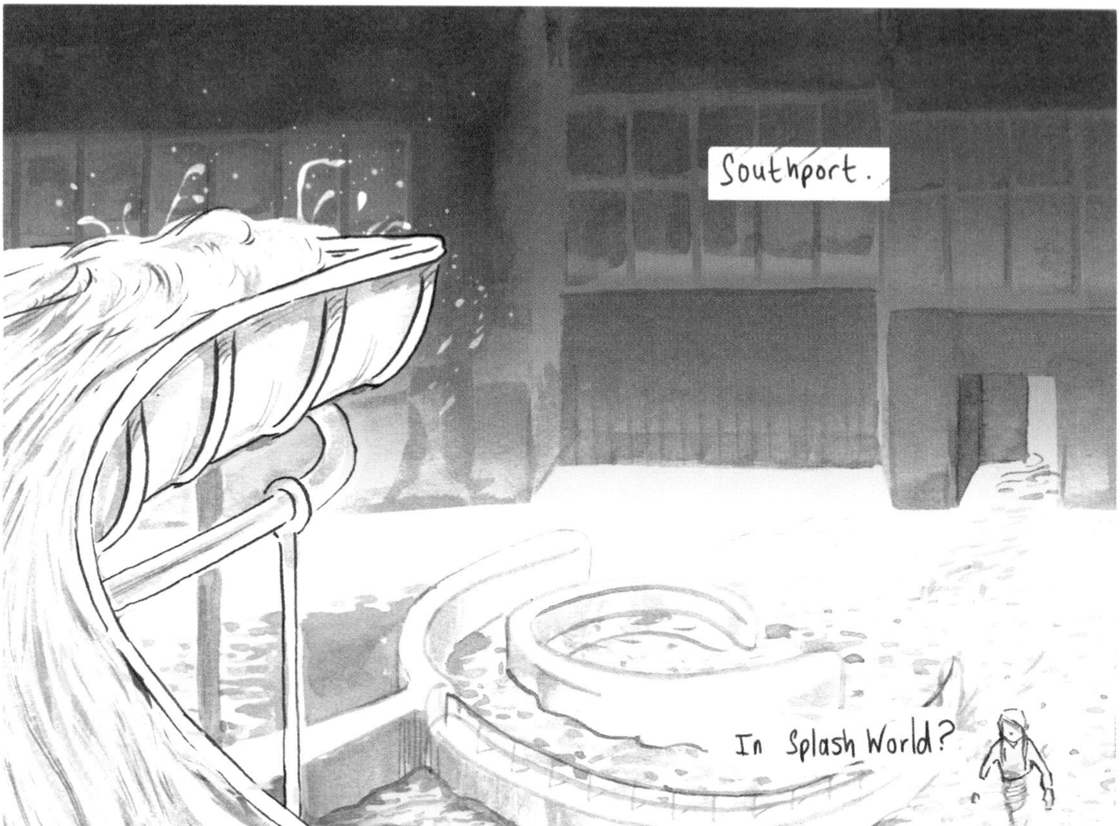
Southport.
In Splash World?

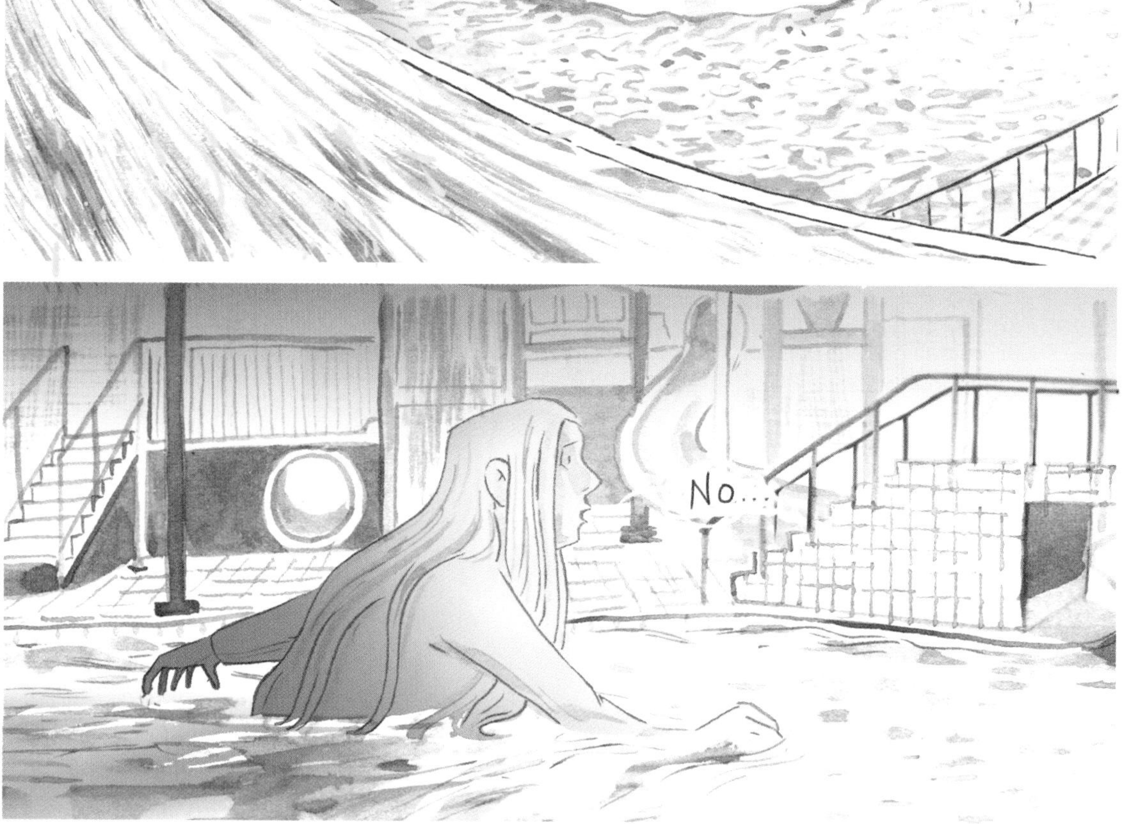
No...

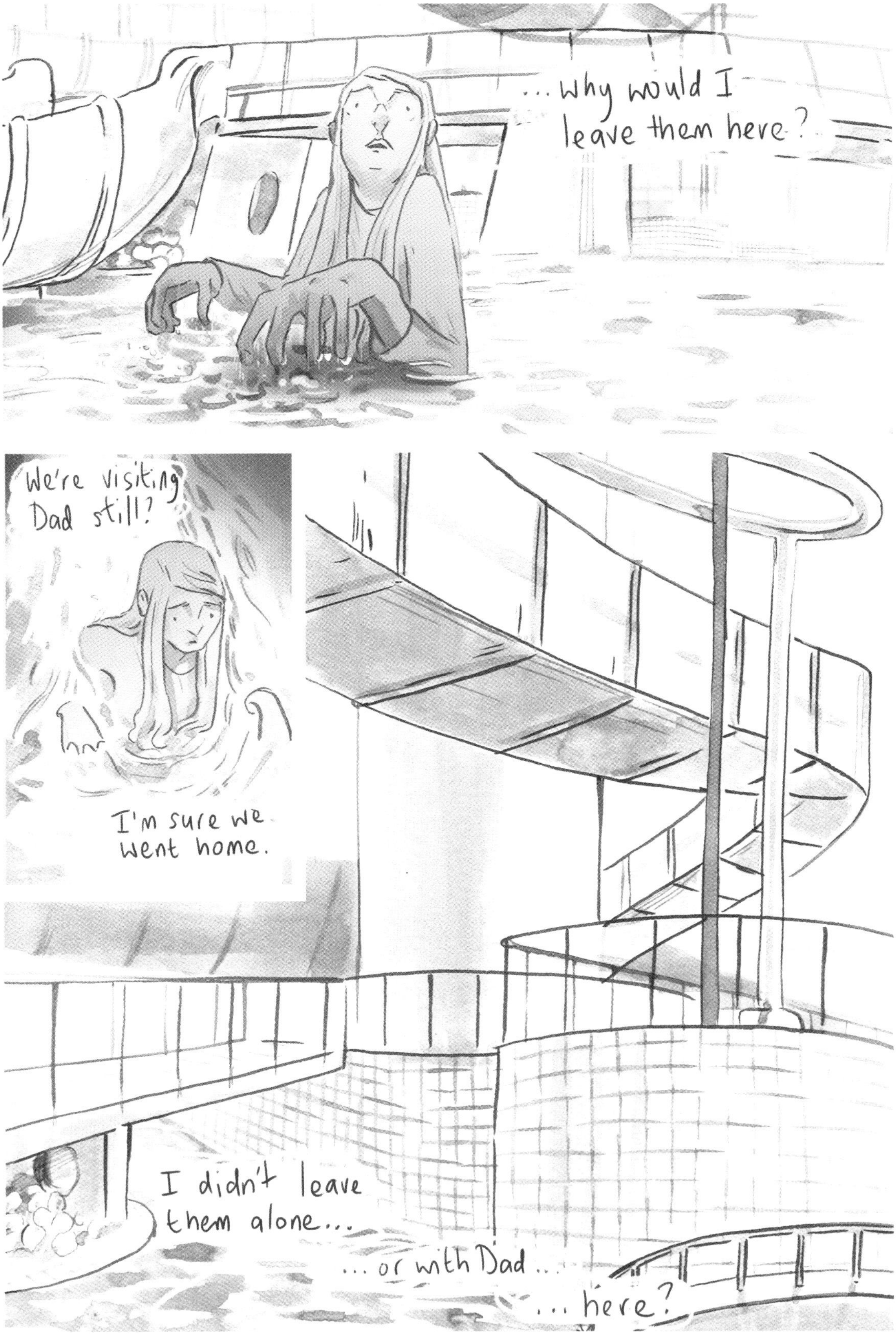
...why would I leave them here?
We're visiting Dad still?
I'm sure we went home.
I didn't leave them alone...
...or with Dad...
...here?

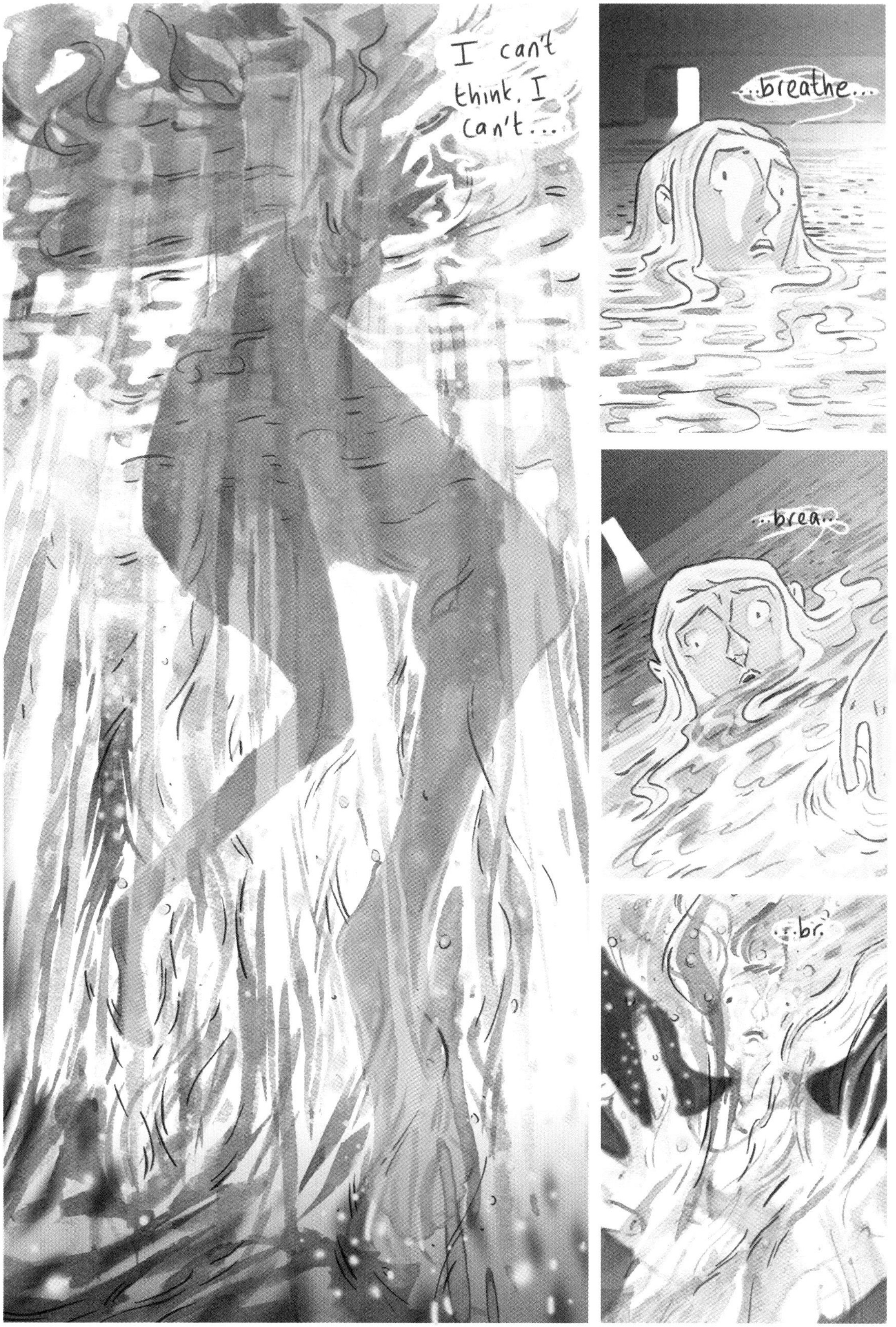
I can't think. I can't...
...breathe...
..brea..
..br.

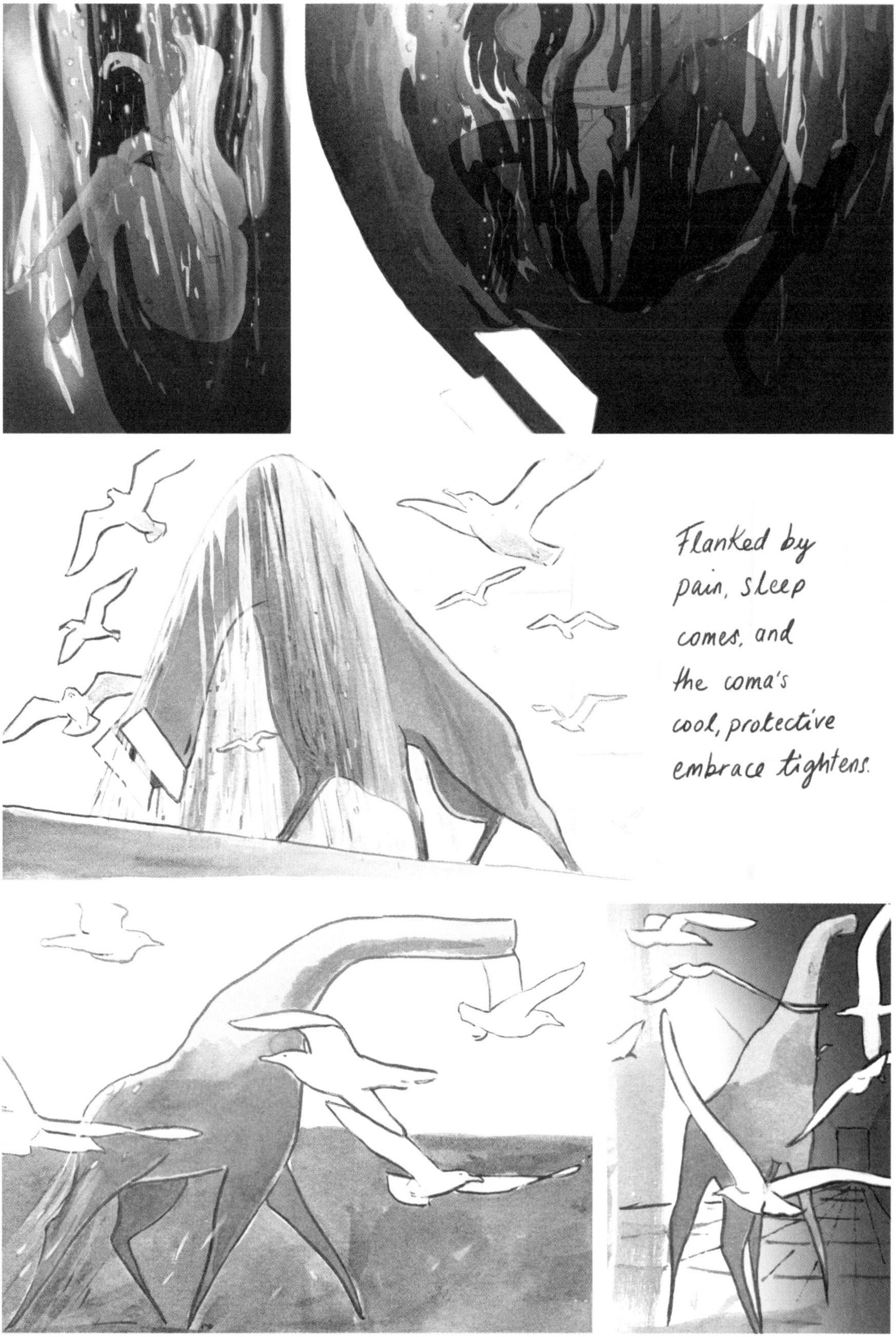
Flanked by pain, sleep comes, and the coma's cool, protective embrace tightens.

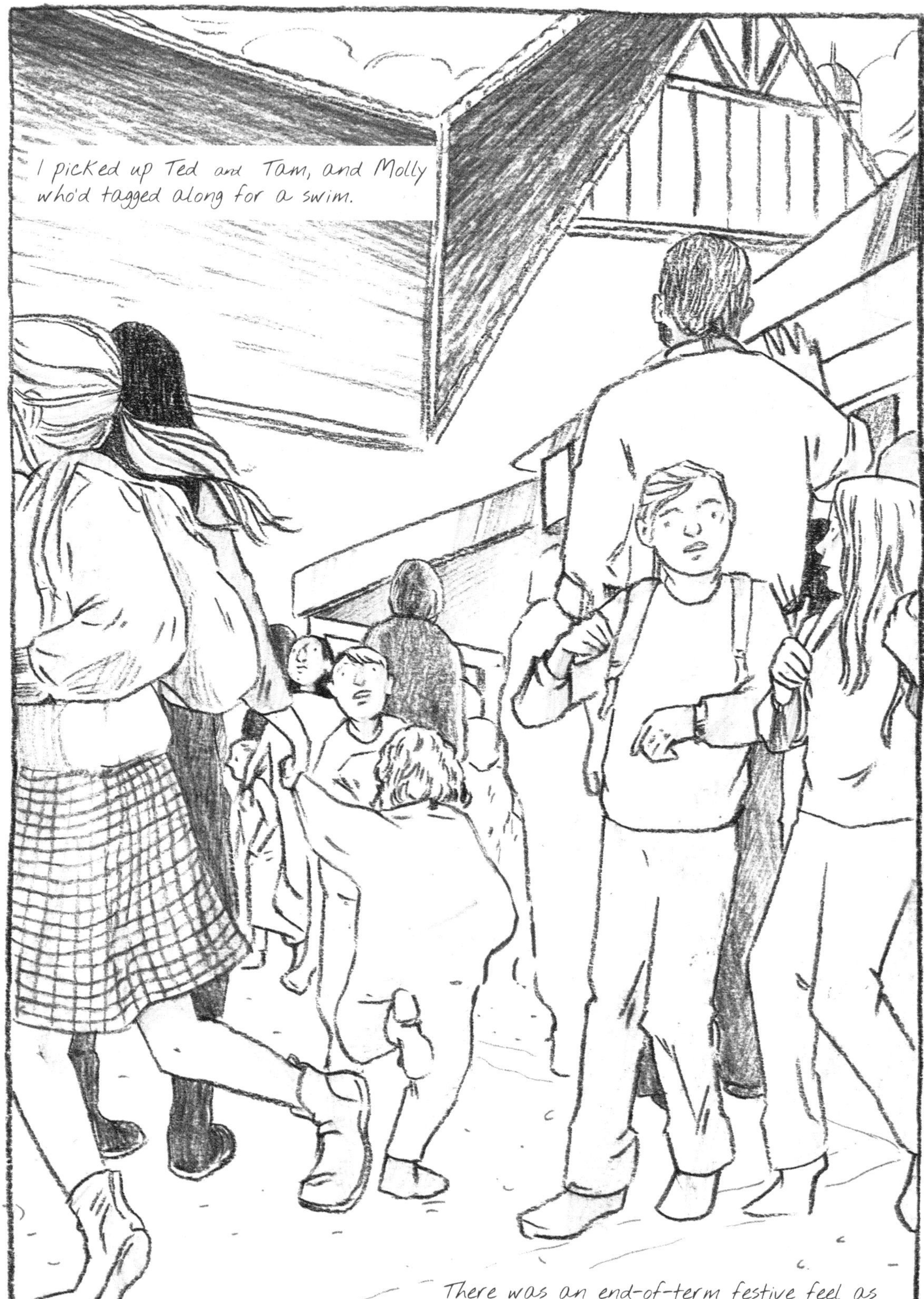
I picked up Ted and Tam, and Molly who'd tagged along for a swim.
There was an end-of-term festive feel as Friday was an inset day – then half term.

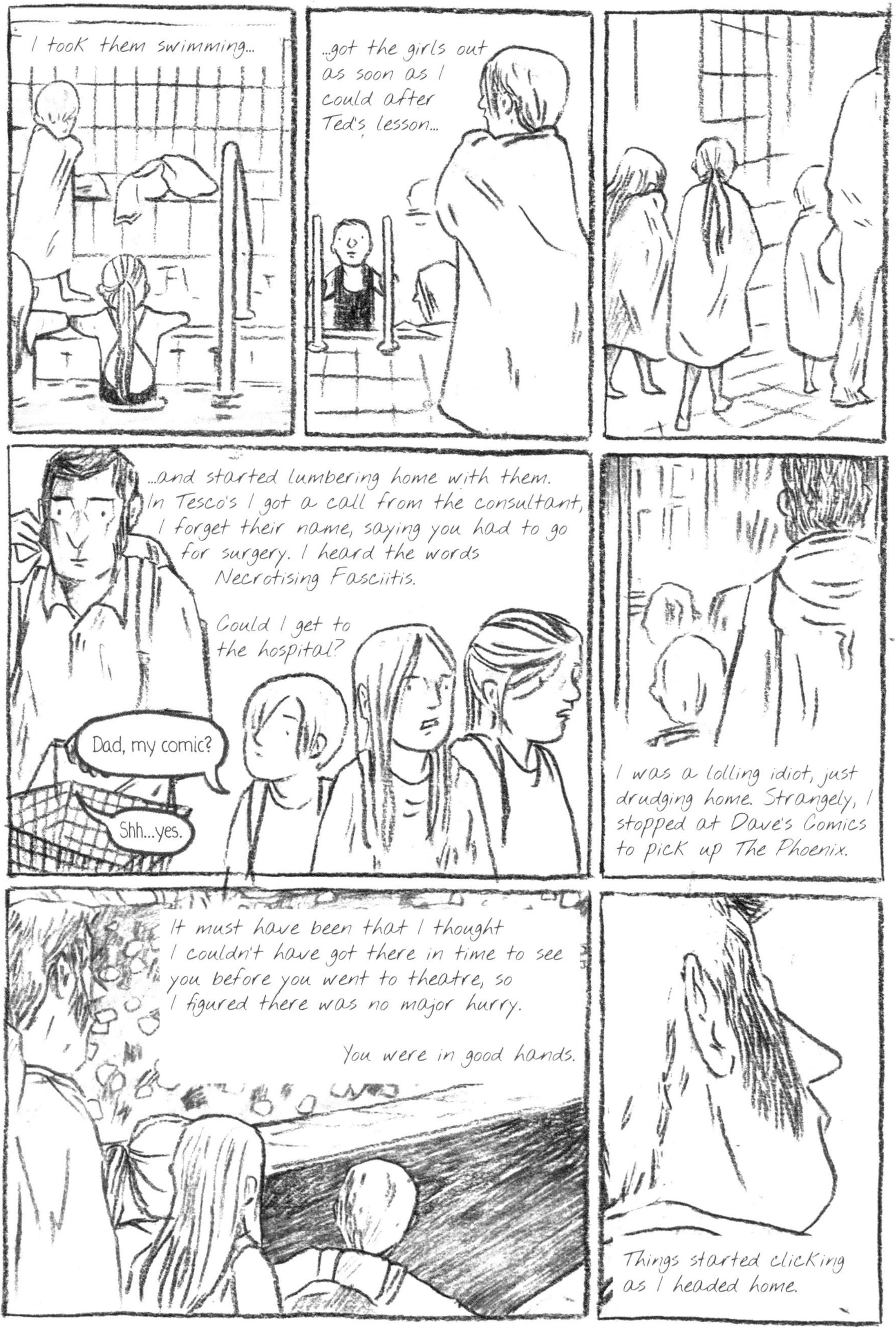
I took them swimming...
...got the girls out as soon as I could after Ted's lesson...
...and started lumbering home with them. In Tesco's I got a call from the consultant, I forget their name, saying you had to go for surgery. I heard the words Necrotising Fasciitis.
Could I get to the hospital?
Dad, my comic?
Shh...yes.
I was a lolling idiot, just drudging home. Strangely, I stopped at Dave's Comics to pick up The Phoenix.
It must have been that I thought I couldn't have got there in time to see you before you went to theatre, so I figured there was no major hurry.
You were in good hands.
Things started clicking as I headed home.

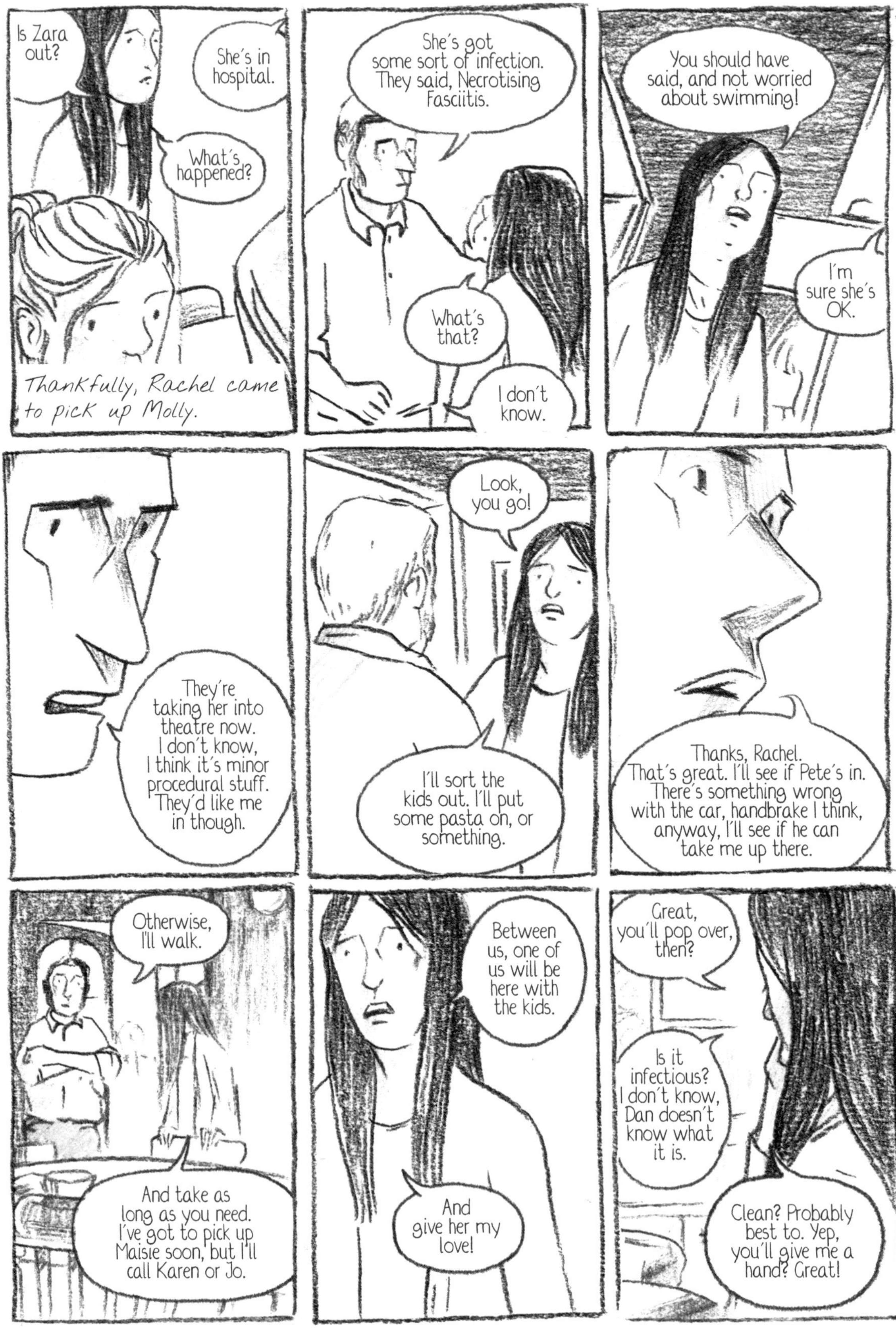
Is Zara out?
She's in hospital.
What's happened?
Thankfully, Rachel came to pick up Molly.
She's got some sort of infection. They said, Necrotising Fasciitis.
What's that?
I don't know.
You should have said, and not worried about swimming!
I'm sure she's OK.
They're taking her into theatre now. I don't know, I think it's minor procedural stuff. They'd like me in though.
Look, you go!
I'll sort the kids out. I'll put some pasta on, or something.
Thanks, Rachel. That's great. I'll see if Pete's in. There's something wrong with the car, handbrake I think, anyway, I'll see if he can take me up there.
Otherwise, I'll walk.
And take as long as you need. I've got to pick up Maisie soon, but I'll call Karen or Jo.
Between us, one of us will be here with the kids.
And give her my love!
Great, you'll pop over, then?
Is it infectious? I don't know, Dan doesn't know what it is.
Clean? Probably best to. Yep, you'll give me a hand? Great!

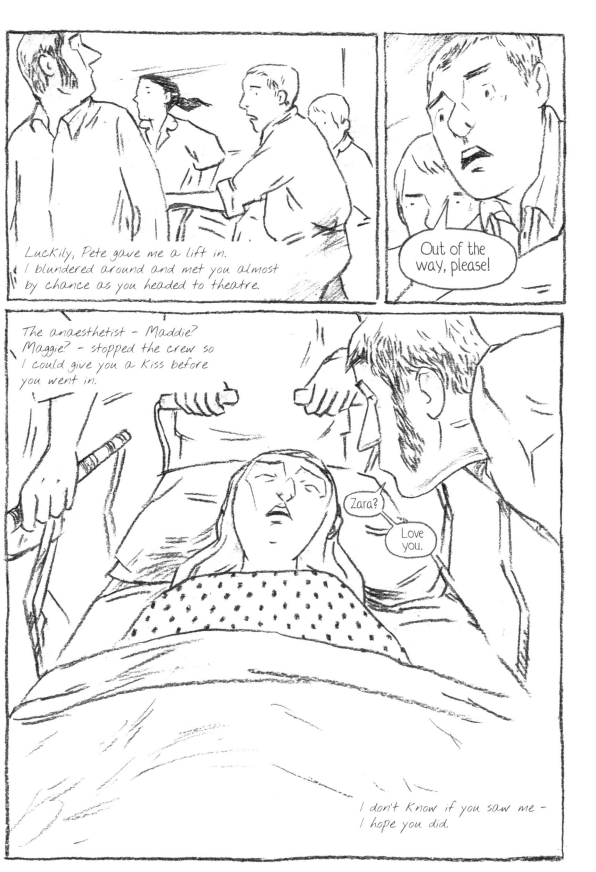

Luckily, Pete gave me a lift in.
I blundered around and met you almost
by chance as you headed to theatre.

Out of the way, please!

The anaesthetist — Maddie?
Maggie? — stopped the crew so
I could give you a kiss before
you went in.

Zara?

Love you.

I don't know if you saw me —
I hope you did.

49

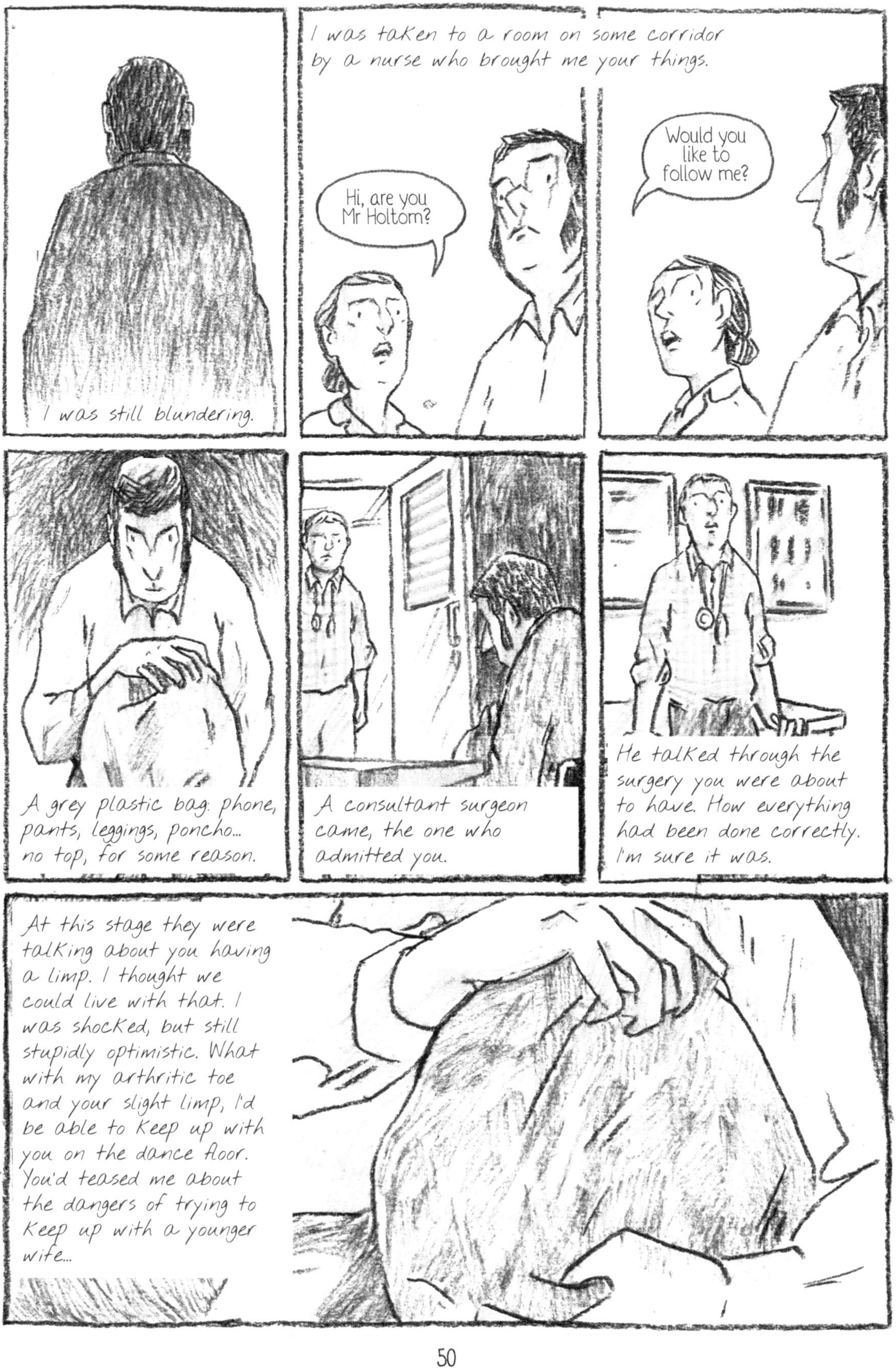
I was still blundering.
I was taken to a room on some corridor by a nurse who brought me your things.
Hi, are you Mr Holtom?
Would you like to follow me?
A grey plastic bag: phone, pants, leggings, poncho... no top, for some reason.
A consultant surgeon came, the one who admitted you.
He talked through the surgery you were about to have. How everything had been done correctly. I'm sure it was.
At this stage they were talking about you having a limp. I thought we could live with that. I was shocked, but still stupidly optimistic. What with my arthritic toe and your slight limp, I'd be able to keep up with you on the dance floor. You'd teased me about the dangers of trying to keep up with a younger wife...

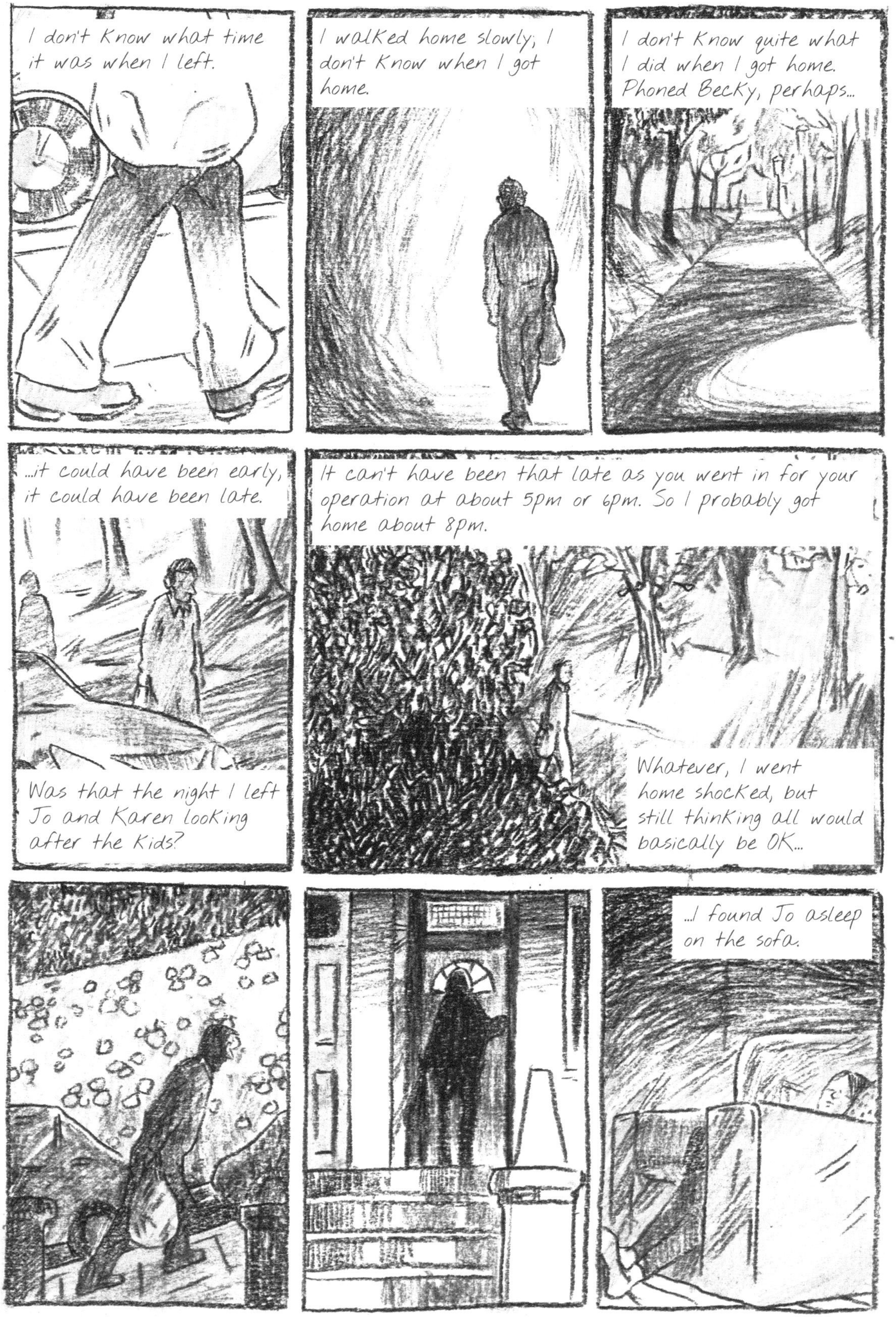
I don't Know what time it was when I left.
I walked home slowly; I don't Know when I got home.
I don't Know quite what I did when I got home. Phoned Becky, perhaps...
...it could have been early, it could have been late.
Was that the night I left Jo and Karen looking after the Kids?
It can't have been that late as you went in for your operation at about 5pm or 6pm. So I probably got home about 8pm.
Whatever, I went home shocked, but still thinking all would basically be OK...
...I found Jo asleep on the sofa.

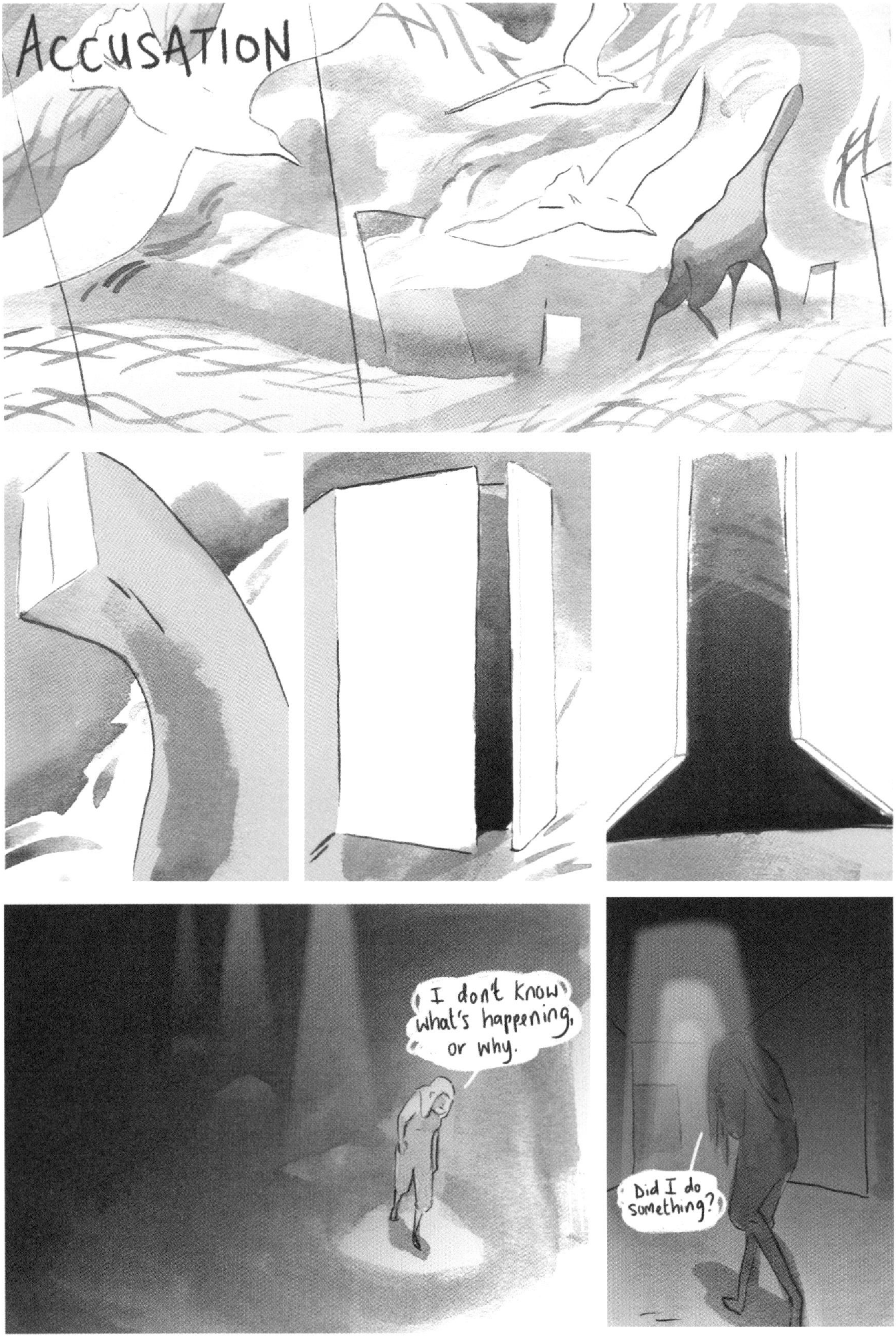
ACCUSATION
I don't know what's happening, or why.
Did I do something?

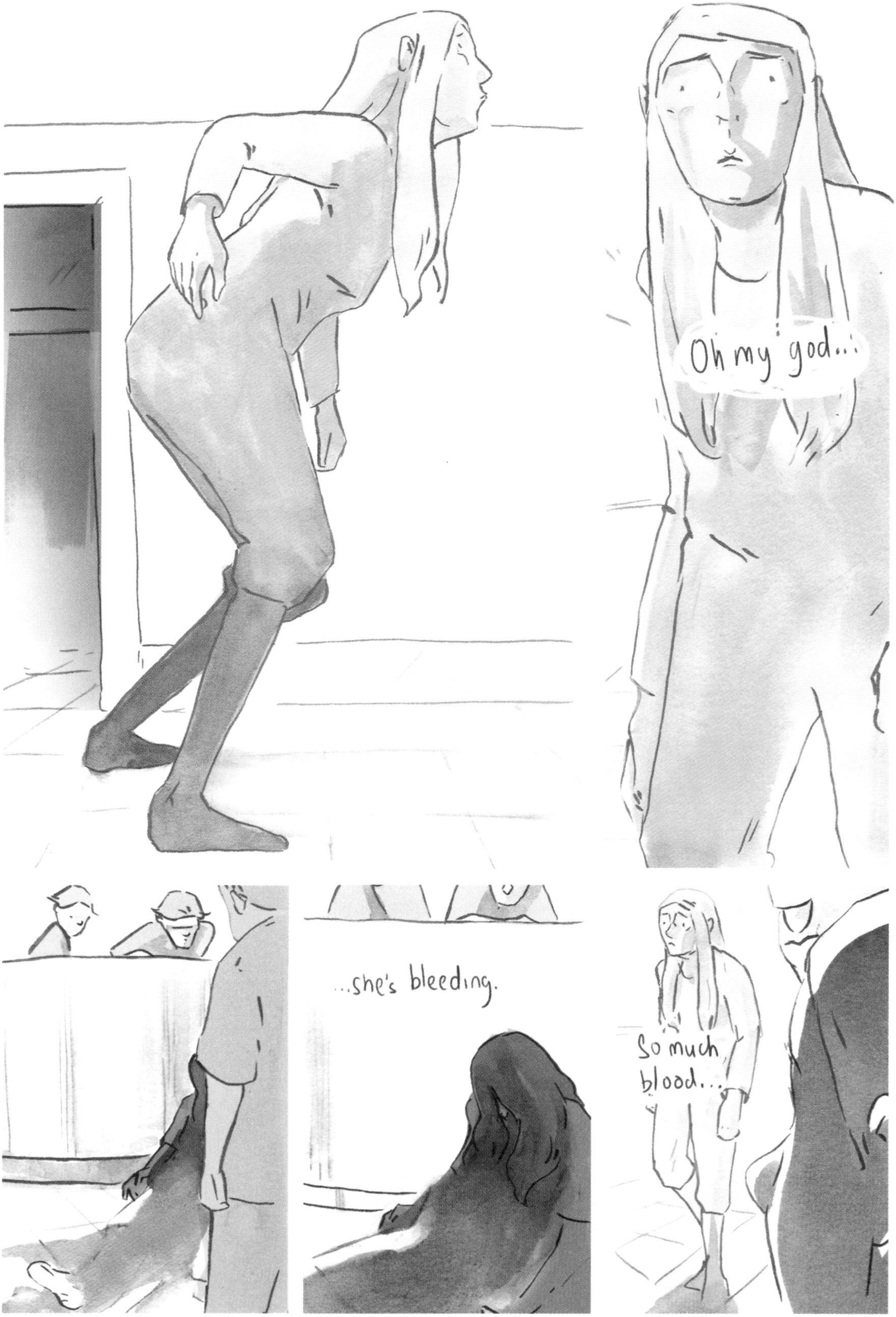

Oh my god...
...she's bleeding.
So much blood...

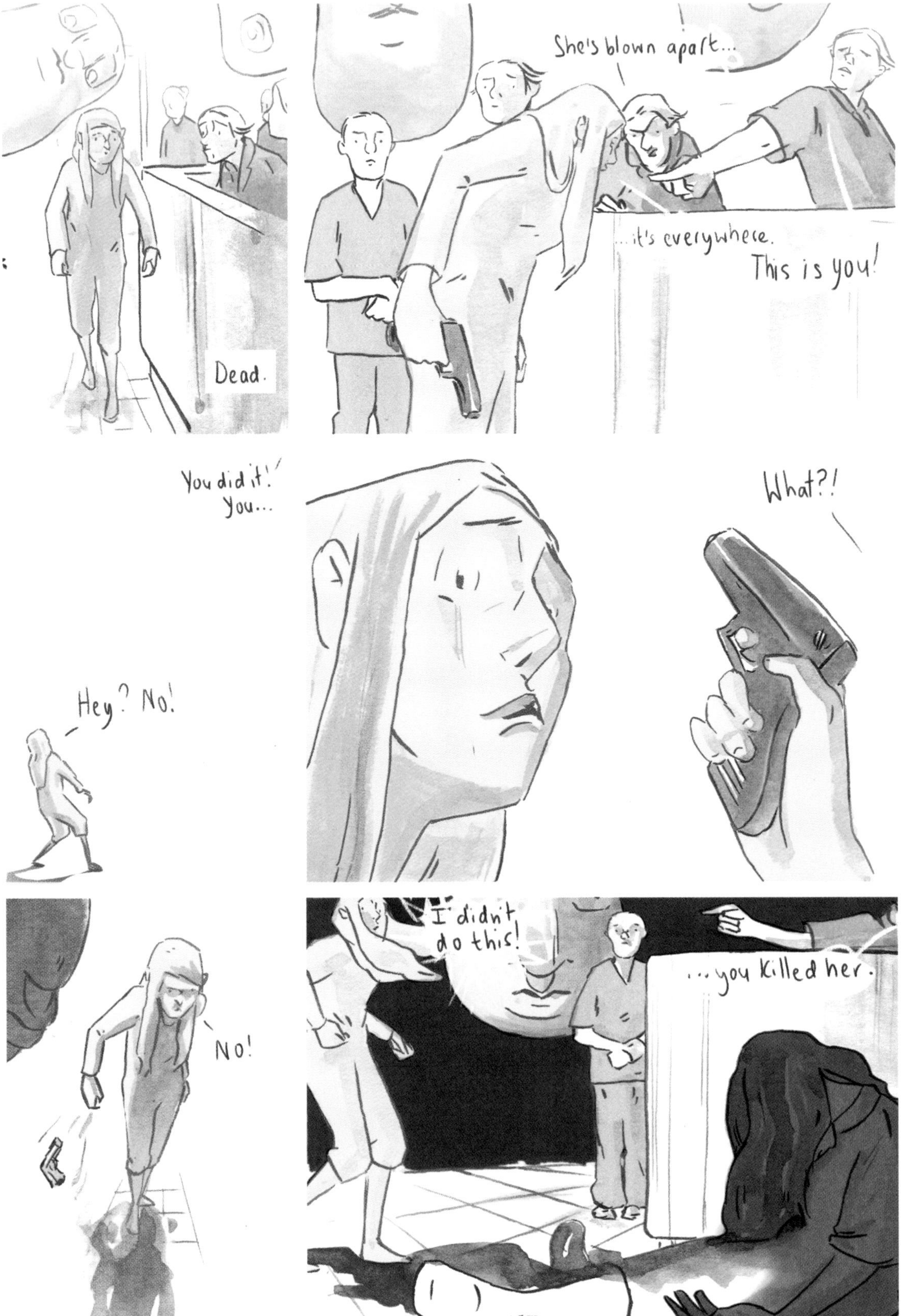
Dead.
She's blown apart...
...it's everywhere.
This is you!
You did it! You...
What?!
Hey? No!
No!
I didn't do this!
...you killed her.

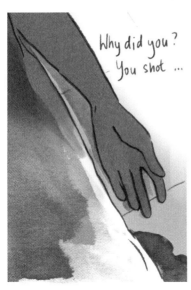

Why did you?
You shot ...

... my daughter...

...dead.

Is she pregnant?

She was.

Both are dead!

No!

Nooo...

What are you saying?
No, I...

She was one of us!
Trying to help you!

...I wouldn't I...no!

Who did this?

You did this!

It's not me!

55

Please...
...I couldn't.
I...
...see your...
...guilt.
We...
...See...
...you.

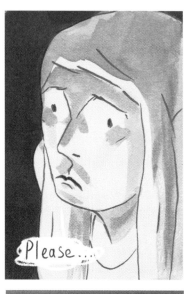

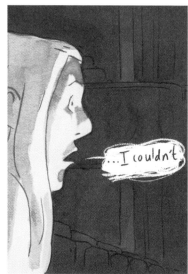

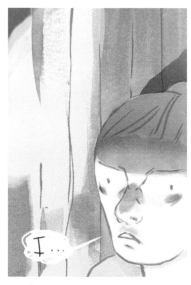

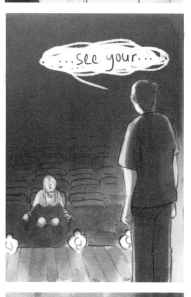

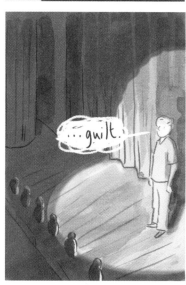

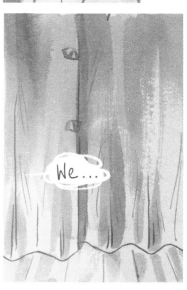

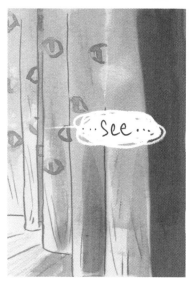

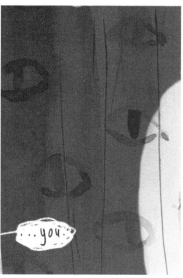

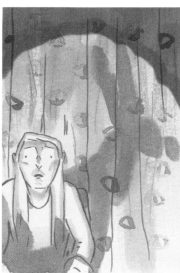

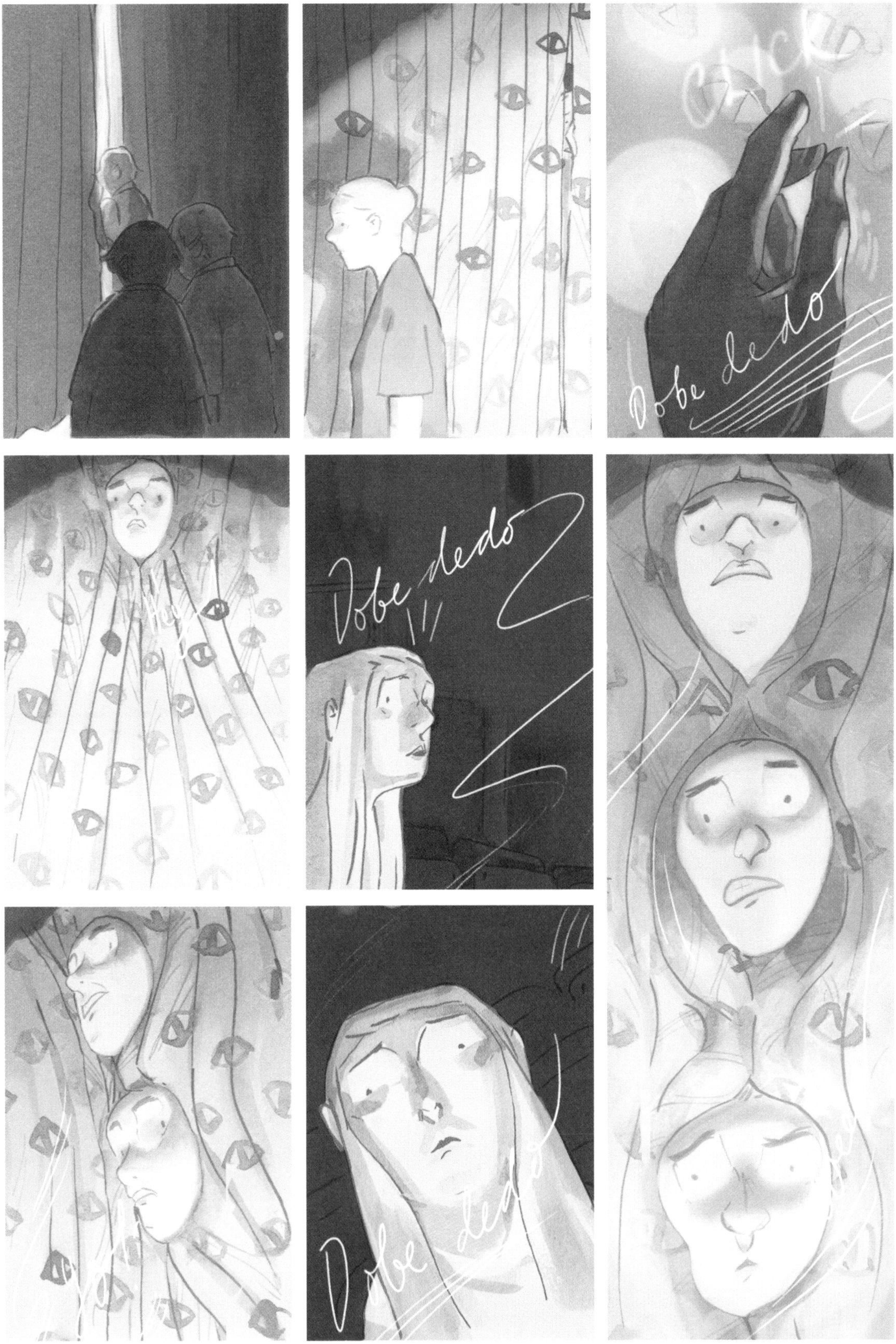
Click
Dobe dedo
Dobe dedo
Dobe dedo

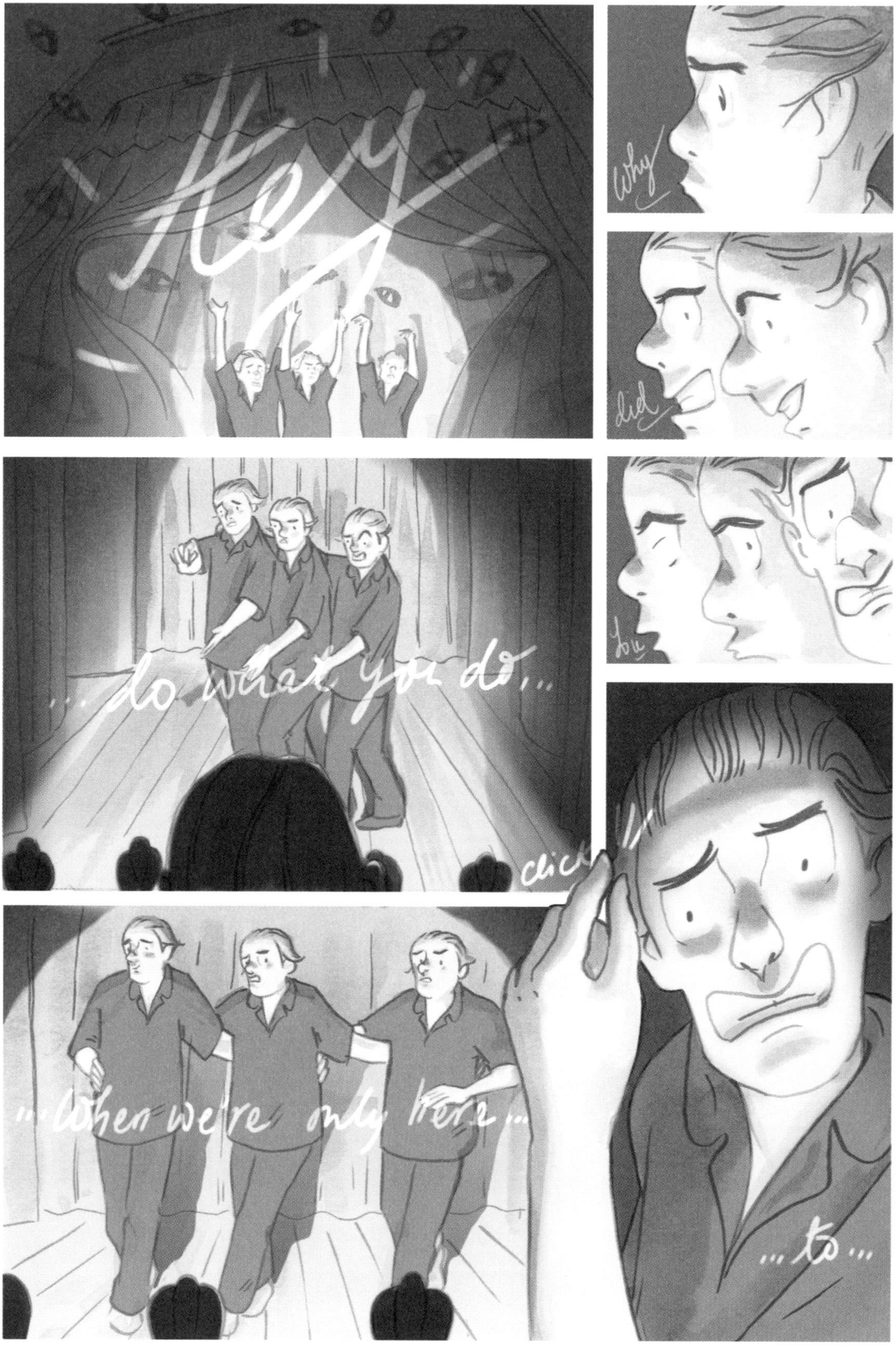
Hey
Why
did
You
...do what you do...
click
...When we're only here...
...to...

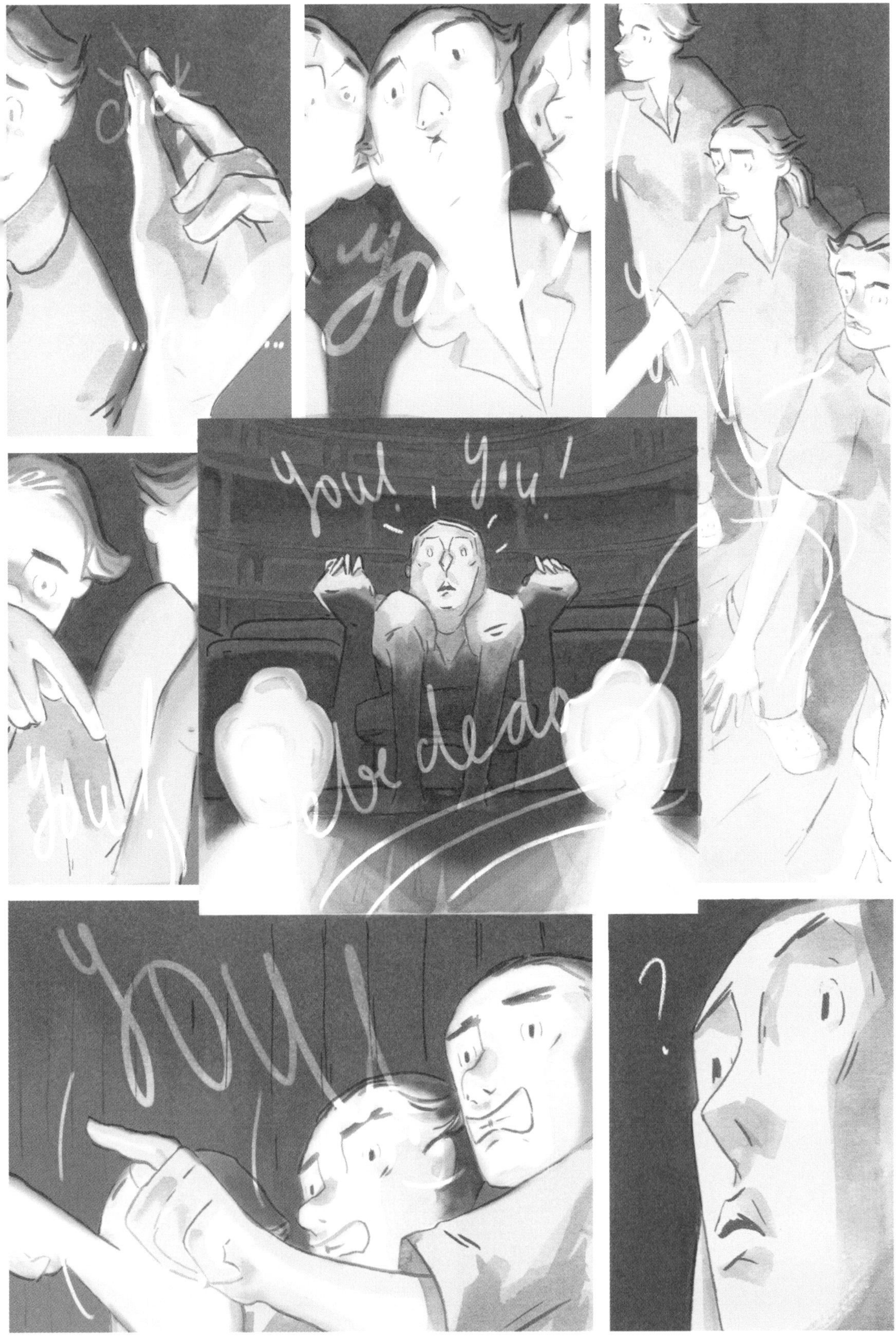
You! You!
YOU!
?

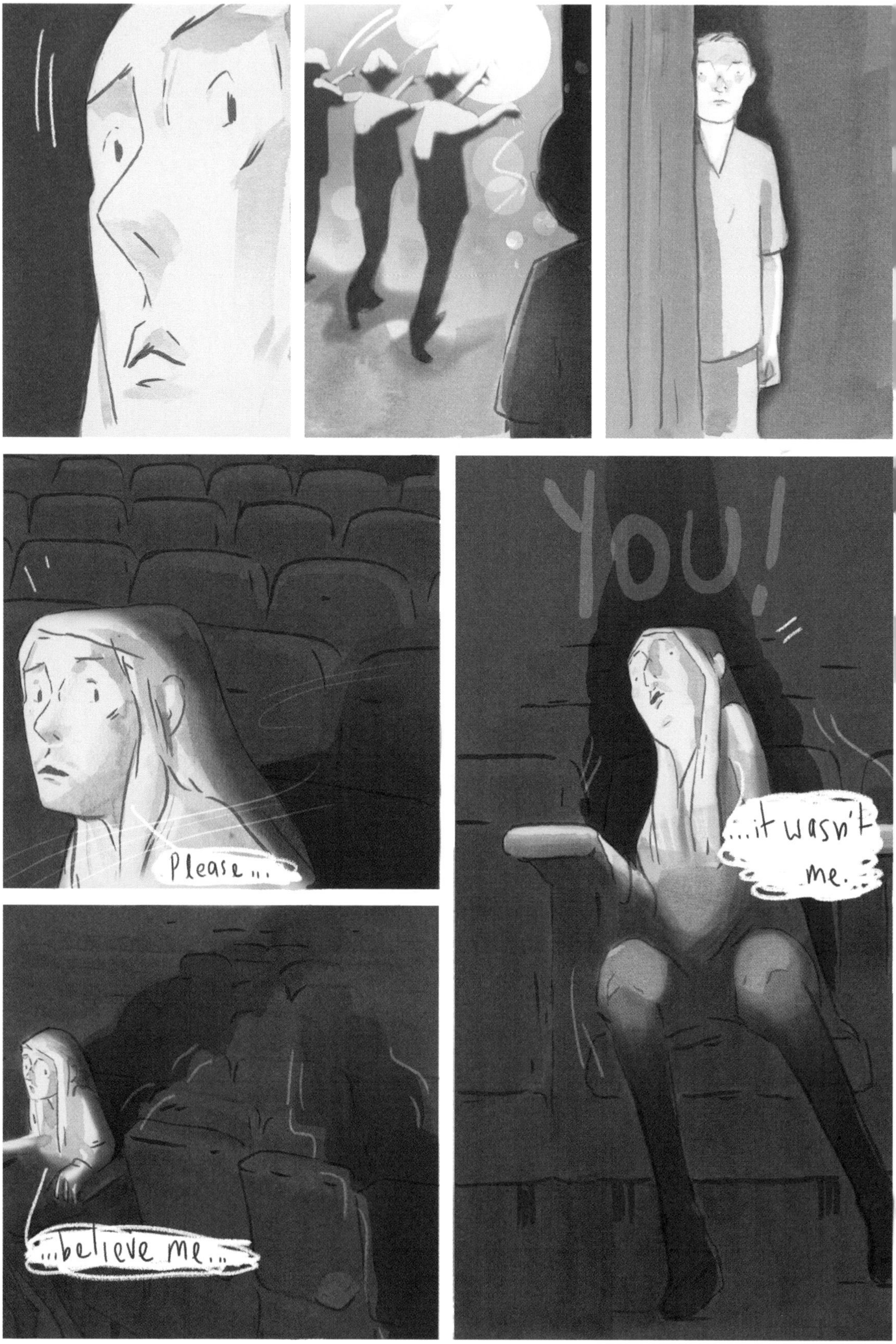
Please...
YOU!
...it wasn't me...
...believe me...

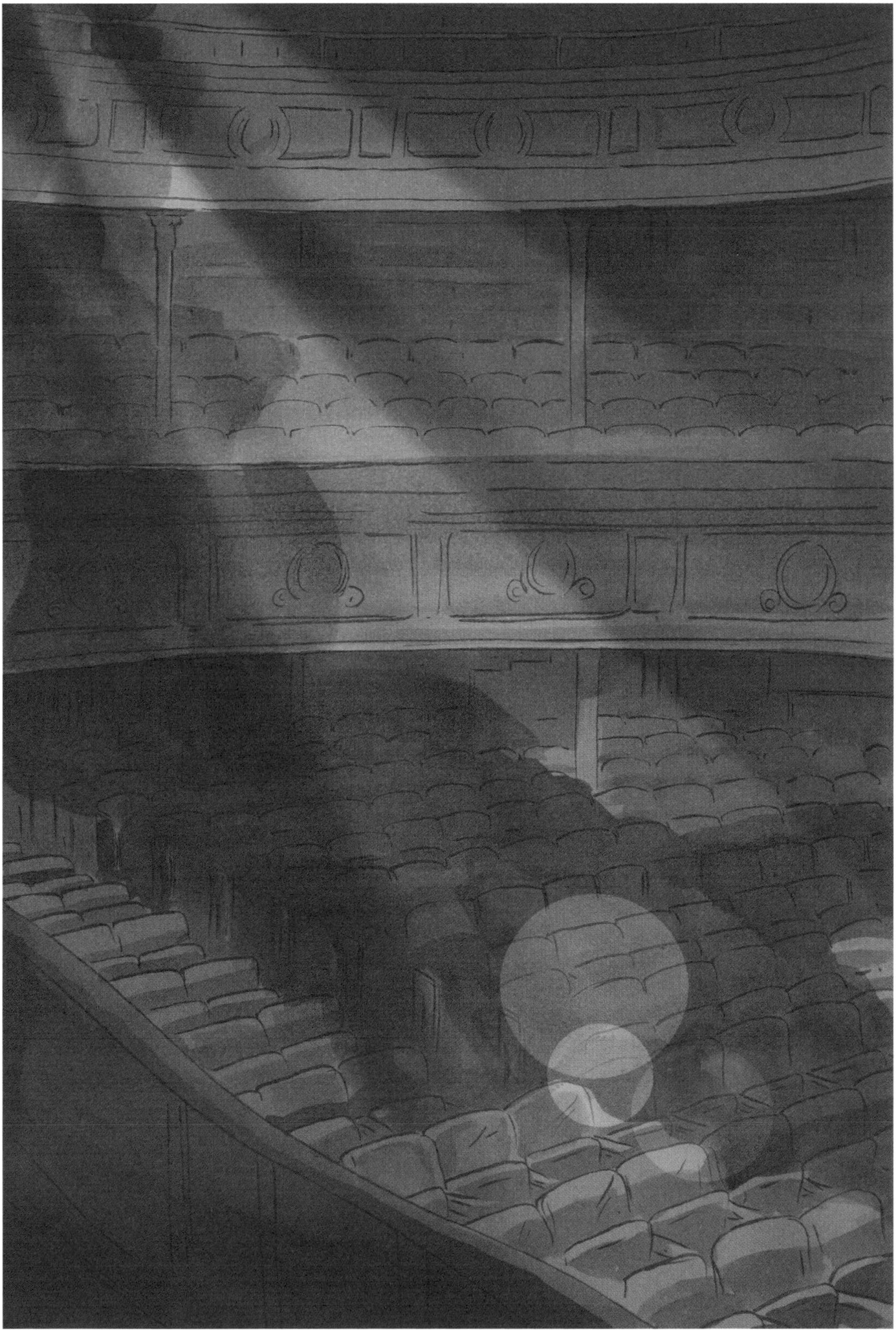

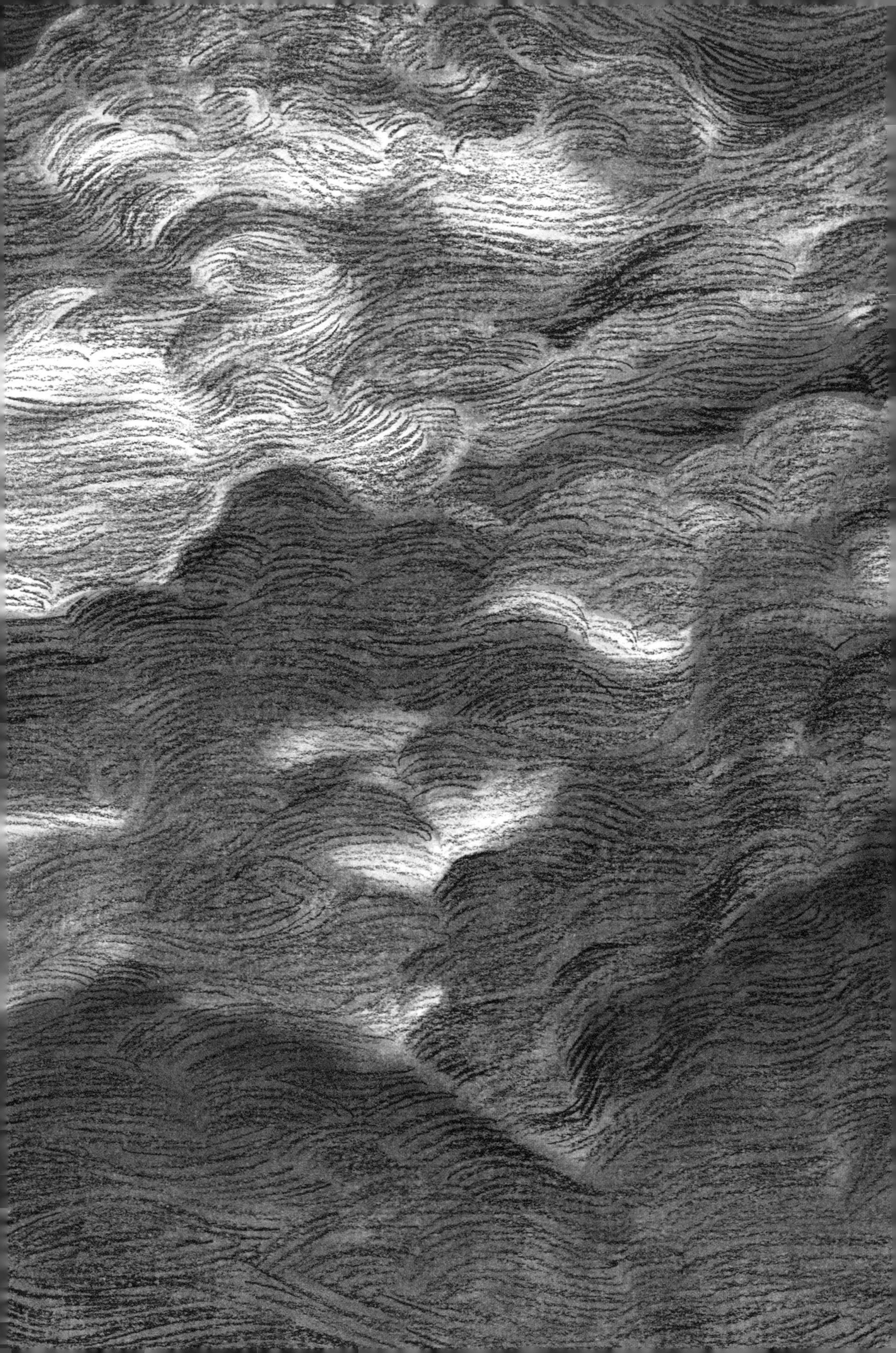

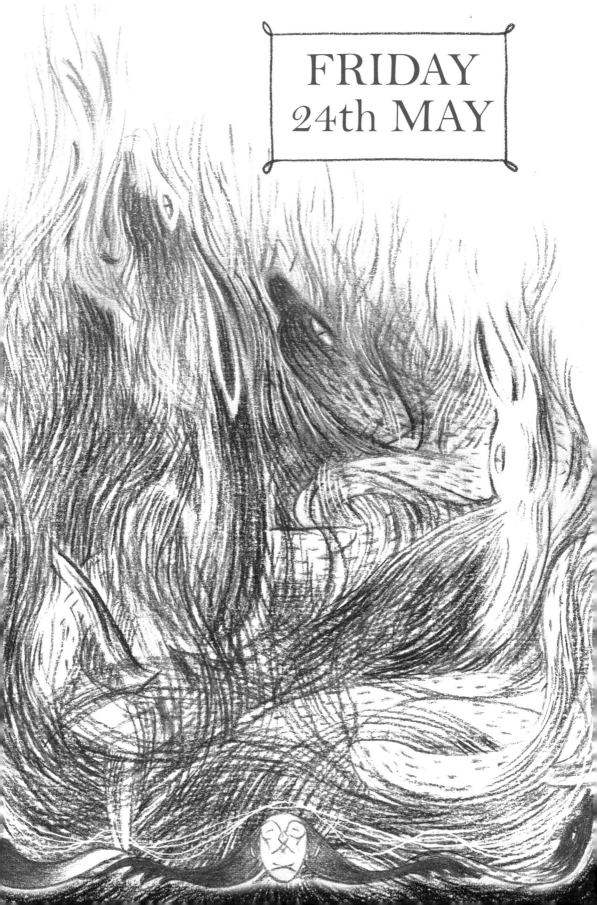

FRIDAY
24th MAY

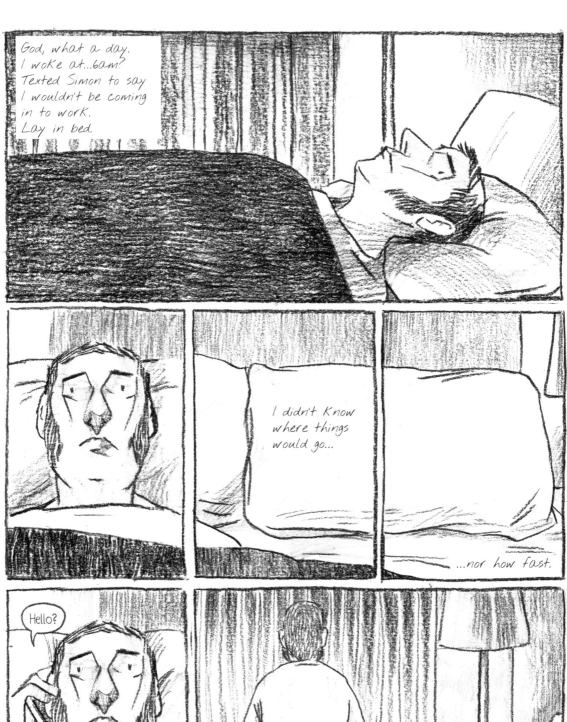

God, what a day.
I woke at...6am?
Texted Simon to say
I wouldn't be coming
in to work.
Lay in bed.

I didn't know
where things
would go...

...nor how fast.

Hello?

I phoned ICU. It seemed
that you were stable.
I think your dad
might have phoned,
although that may
have been later.

I came in to see you,
I can't remember when.

Things didn't seem that bad, but maybe when I arrived, maybe a little later, I was told the surgeon wanted to see me.

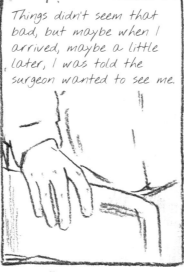

Hello, Dan? Could you wait, the consultant will be here to talk to you soon.

God, my memory is so scrambled, I really can't remember quite how this all happened – the order of it.

I seem to remember I called Karen, who was looking after Tam and Ted. Tilda was still at school.

She told me Kathy and Diana were coming to be with me. And Becky, my sister, called...she was coming up.

Hi, Dan, How is she?

Kathy and Diana arrived before the meeting with the surgeon.

Mr Holtom? Dan?

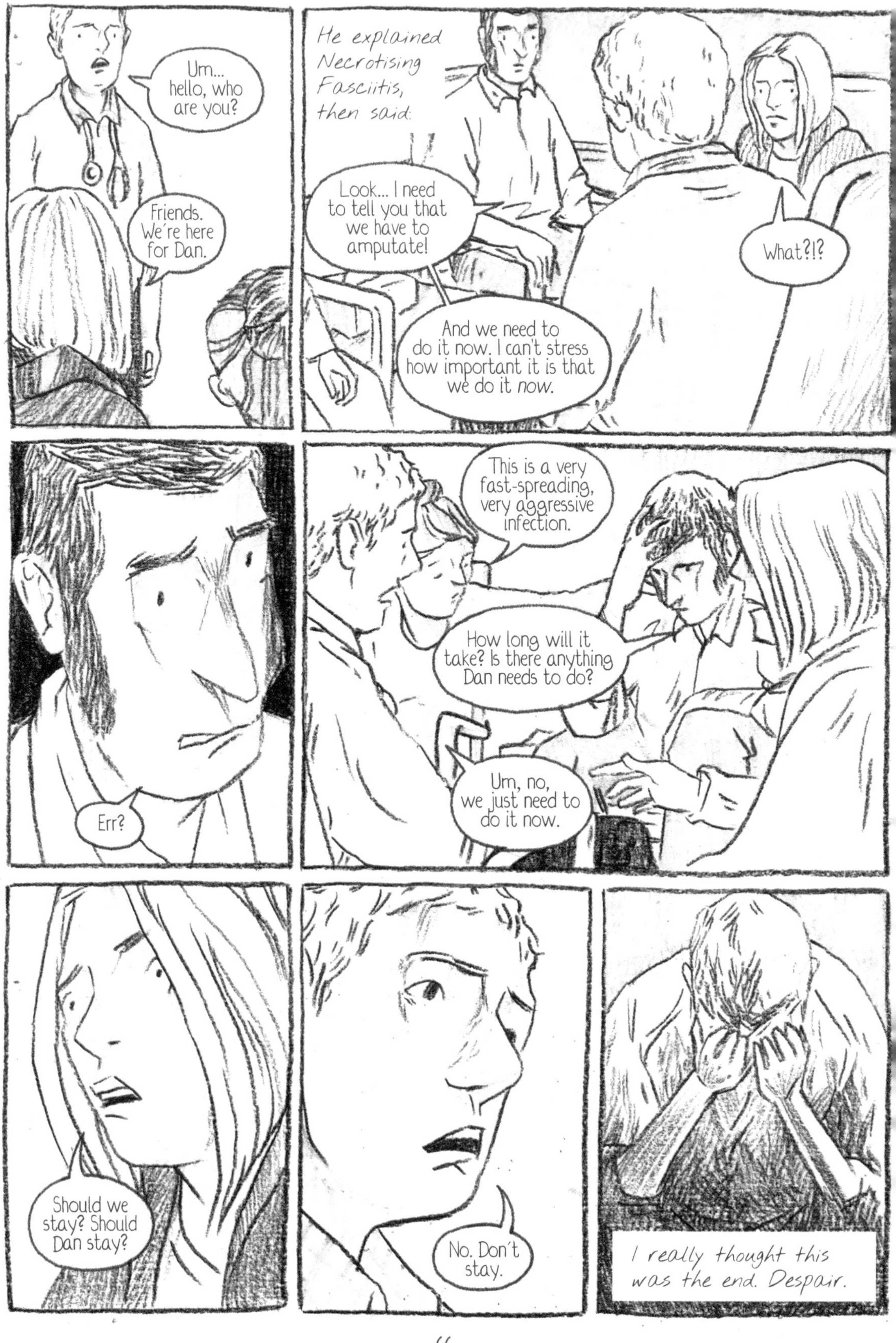

Um... hello, who are you?
Friends. We're here for Dan.
He explained Necrotising Fasciitis, then said:
Look... I need to tell you that we have to amputate!
What?!?
And we need to do it now. I can't stress how important it is that we do it *now*.
Err?
This is a very fast-spreading, very aggressive infection.
How long will it take? Is there anything Dan needs to do?
Um, no, we just need to do it now.
Should we stay? Should Dan stay?
No. Don't stay.
I really thought this was the end. Despair.

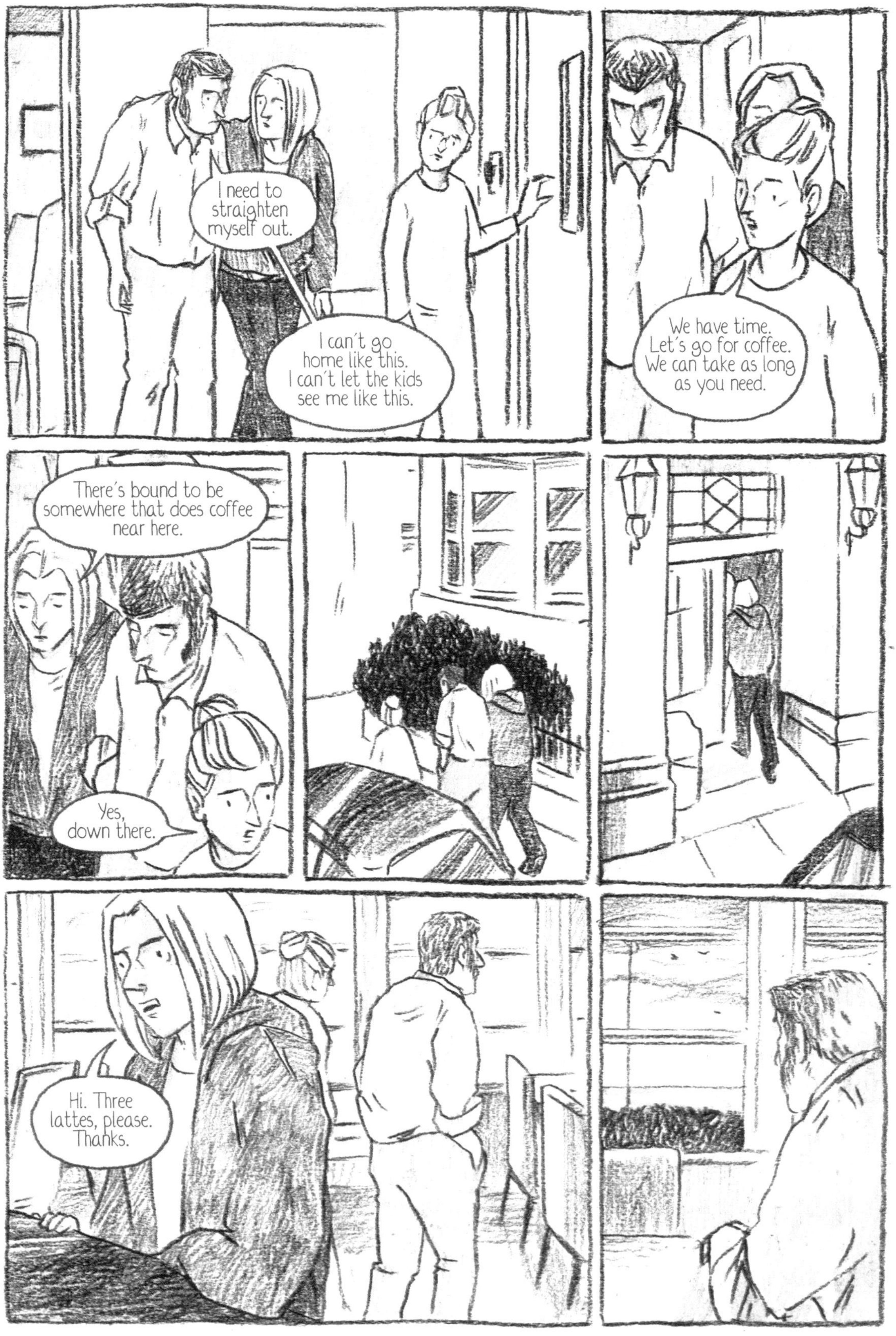
I need to straighten myself out.
I can't go home like this. I can't let the kids see me like this.
We have time. Let's go for coffee. We can take as long as you need.
There's bound to be somewhere that does coffee near here.
Yes, down there.
Hi. Three lattes, please. Thanks.

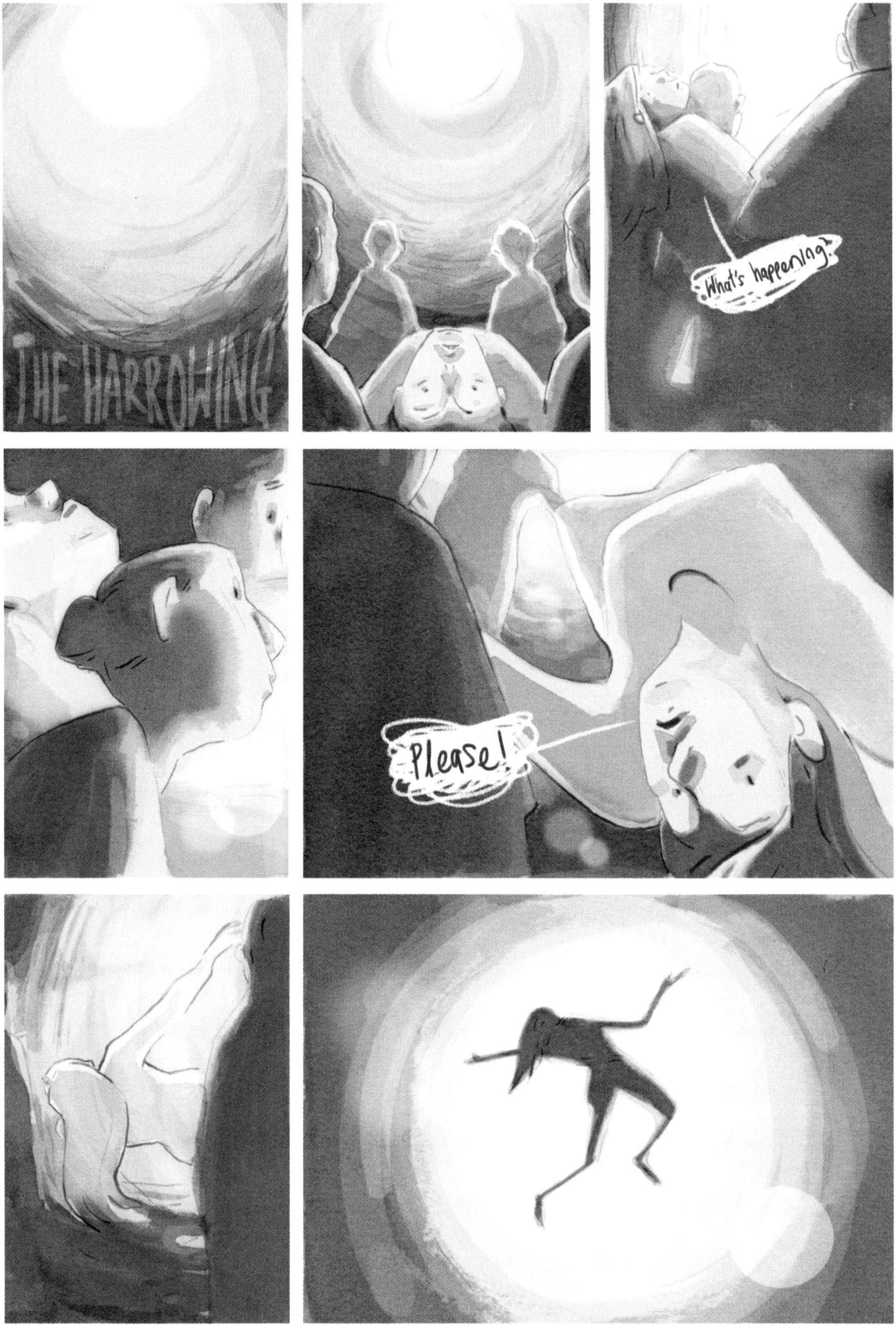
THE HARROWING
What's happening?
Please!

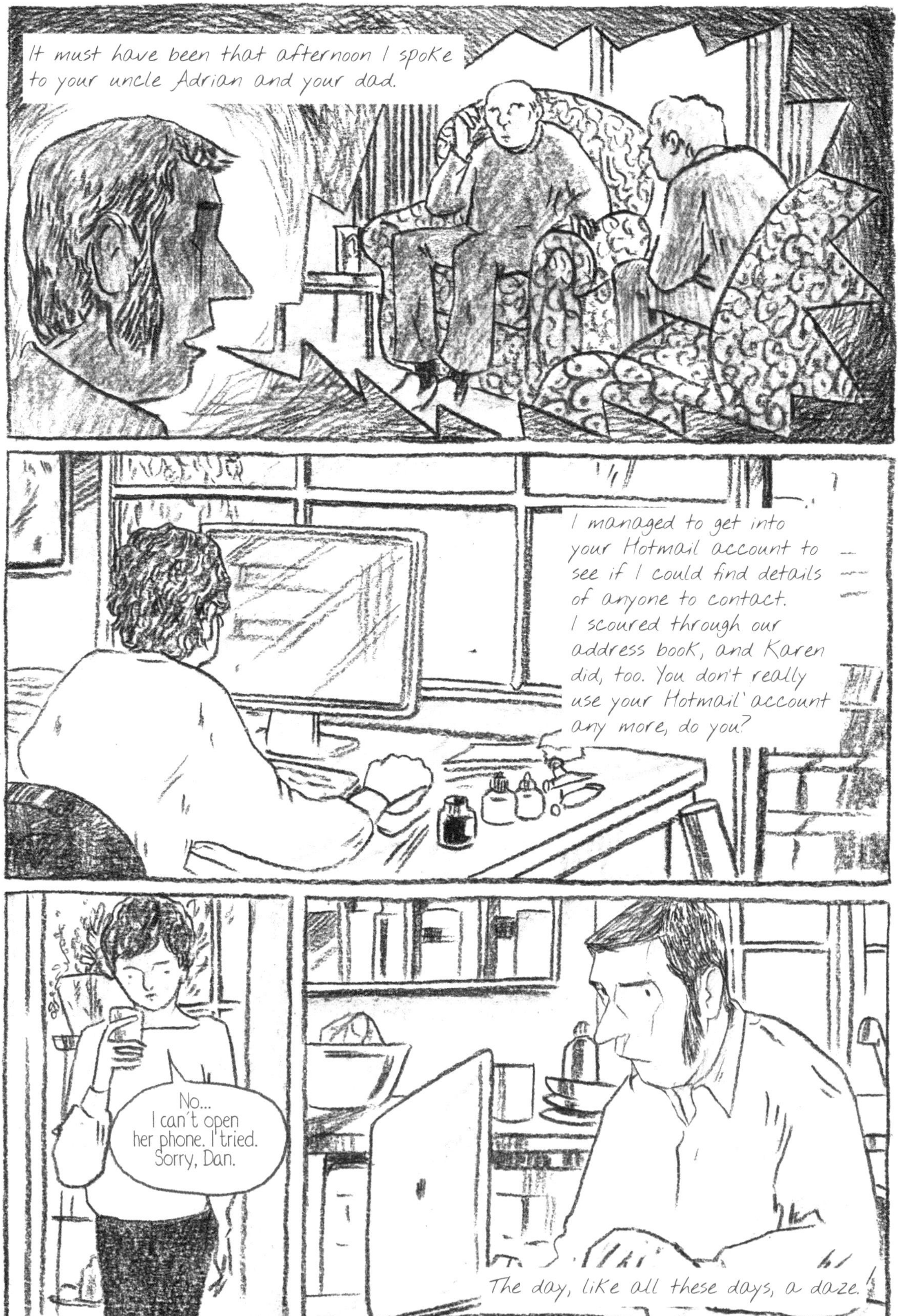
It must have been that afternoon I spoke to your uncle Adrian and your dad.
I managed to get into your Hotmail account to see if I could find details of anyone to contact. I scoured through our address book, and Karen did, too. You don't really use your Hotmail account any more, do you?
No... I can't open her phone. I tried. Sorry, Dan.
The day, like all these days, a daze.

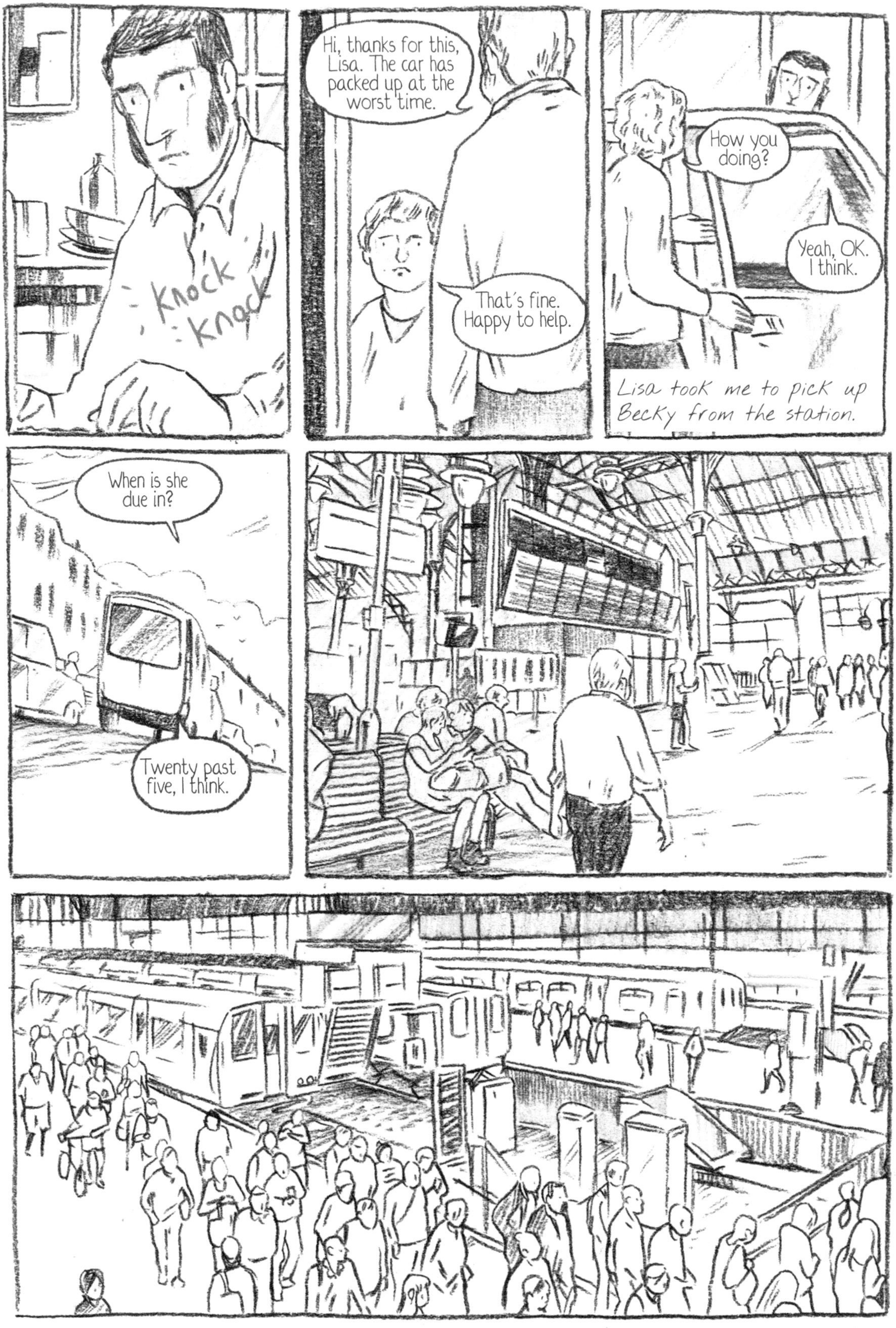
knock
knock
Hi, thanks for this, Lisa. The car has packed up at the worst time.
That's fine. Happy to help.
How you doing?
Yeah, OK. I think.
Lisa took me to pick up Becky from the station.
When is she due in?
Twenty past five, I think.

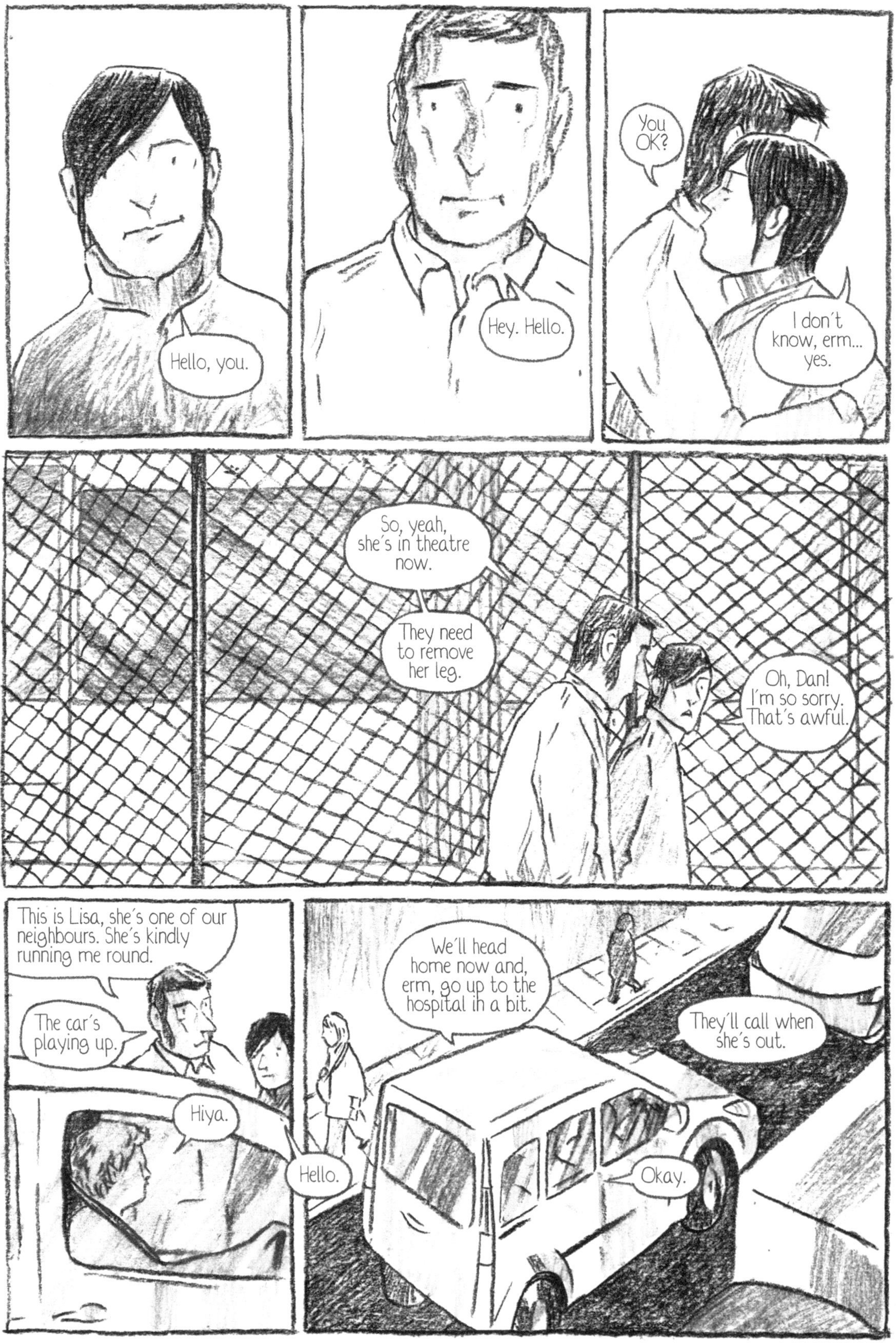
Hello, you.
Hey. Hello.
You OK?
I don't know, erm... yes.
So, yeah, she's in theatre now.
They need to remove her leg.
Oh, Dan! I'm so sorry. That's awful.
This is Lisa, she's one of our neighbours. She's kindly running me round.
The car's playing up.
Hiya.
Hello.
We'll head home now and, erm, go up to the hospital in a bit.
They'll call when she's out.
Okay.

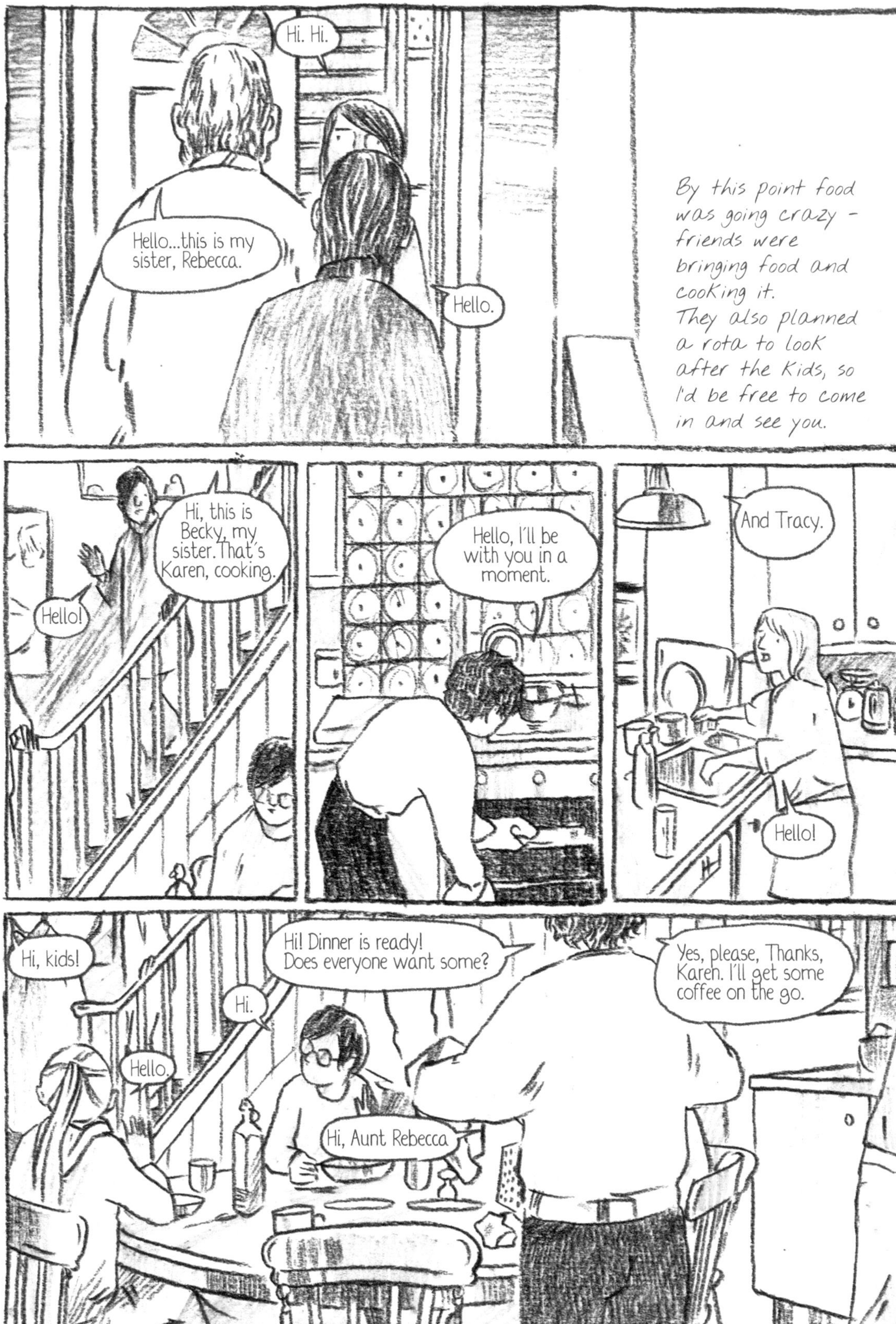
Hi. Hi.
Hello...this is my sister, Rebecca.
Hello.
By this point food was going crazy - friends were bringing food and cooking it. They also planned a rota to look after the kids, so I'd be free to come in and see you.
Hi, this is Becky, my sister. That's Karen, cooking.
Hello!
Hello, I'll be with you in a moment.
And Tracy.
Hello!
Hi, kids!
Hi! Dinner is ready! Does everyone want some?
Yes, please, Thanks, Karen. I'll get some coffee on the go.
Hi.
Hello.
Hi, Aunt Rebecca

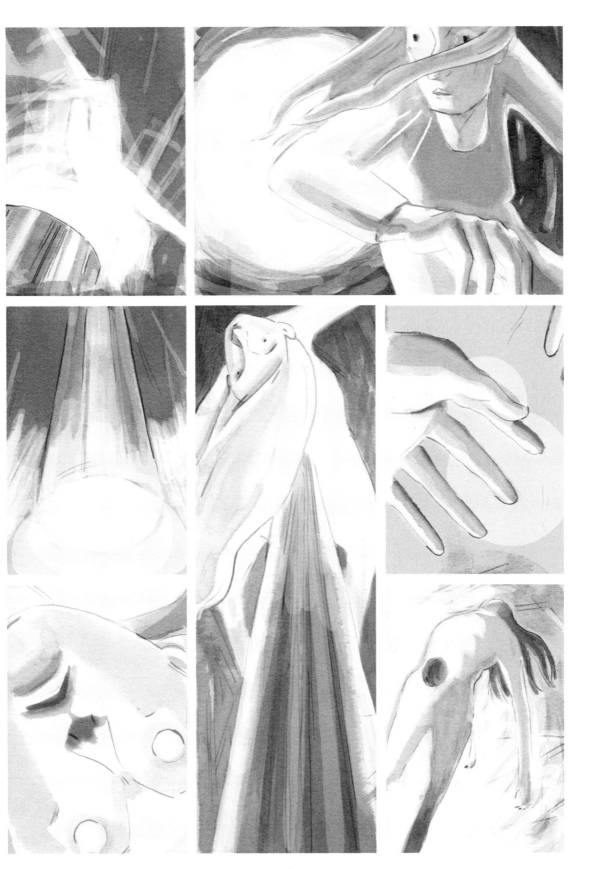

I came in with Becky post-op... Pete, I think, gave us a lift.

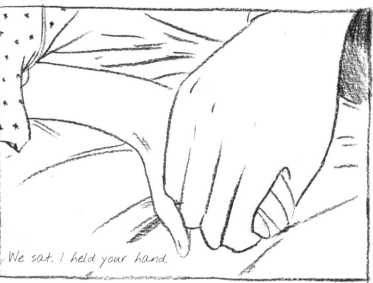

We sat. I held your hand.

I kissed you.

I held your hand, Becky held mine.

It was quiet despair, but not too bad. They kept saying how ill you were. I was sure you would pull through, come back to us, without a leg, but come back to us.

I think the nurse was Nikki that night. Becky paid for a taxi home.

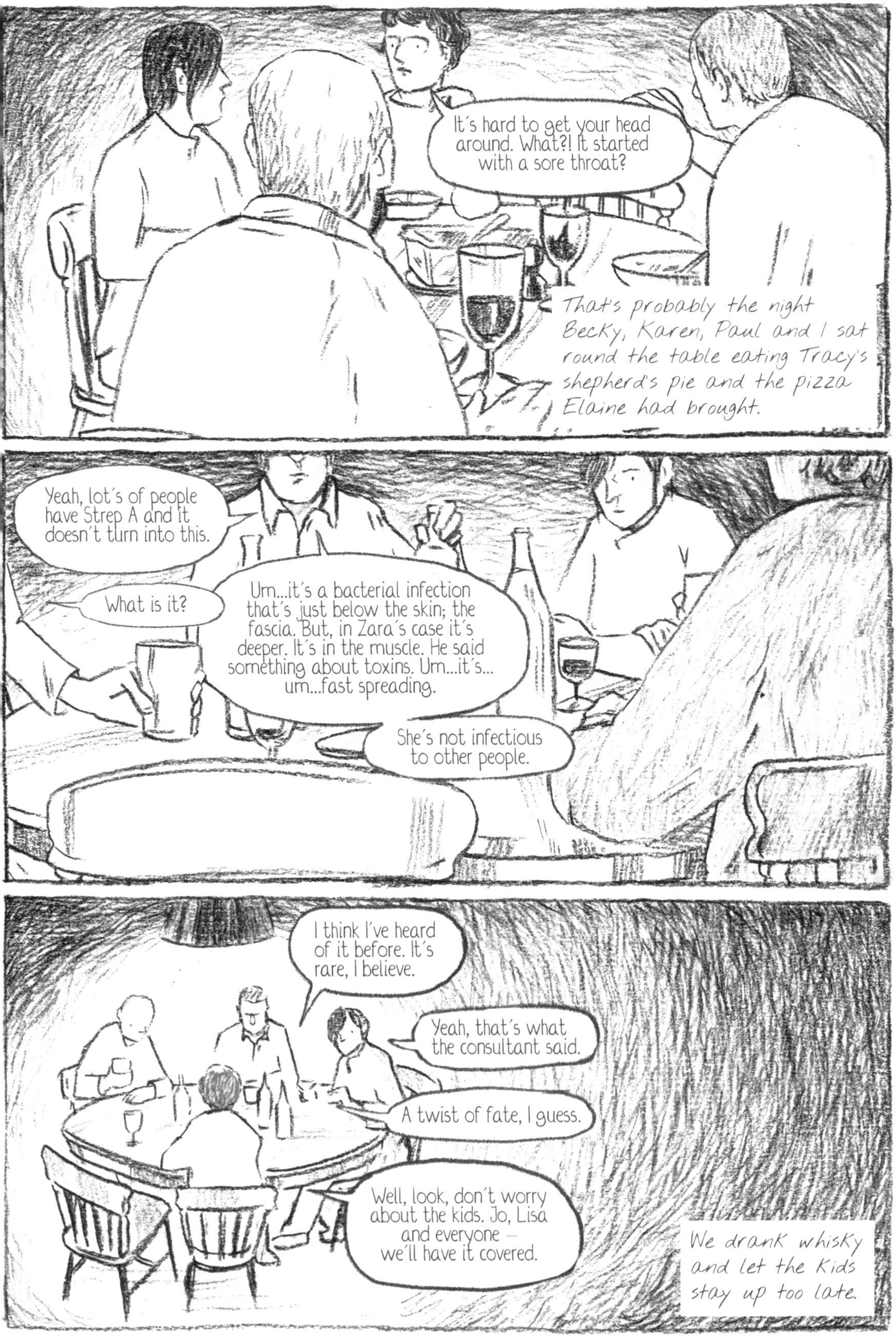
It's hard to get your head around. What?! It started with a sore throat?
That's probably the night Becky, Karen, Paul and I sat round the table eating Tracy's shepherd's pie and the pizza Elaine had brought.
Yeah, lot's of people have Strep A and it doesn't turn into this.
What is it?
Um...it's a bacterial infection that's just below the skin; the fascia. But, in Zara's case it's deeper. It's in the muscle. He said something about toxins. Um...it's... um...fast spreading.
She's not infectious to other people.
I think I've heard of it before. It's rare, I believe.
Yeah, that's what the consultant said.
A twist of fate, I guess.
Well, look, don't worry about the kids. Jo, Lisa and everyone – we'll have it covered.
We drank whisky and let the kids stay up too late.

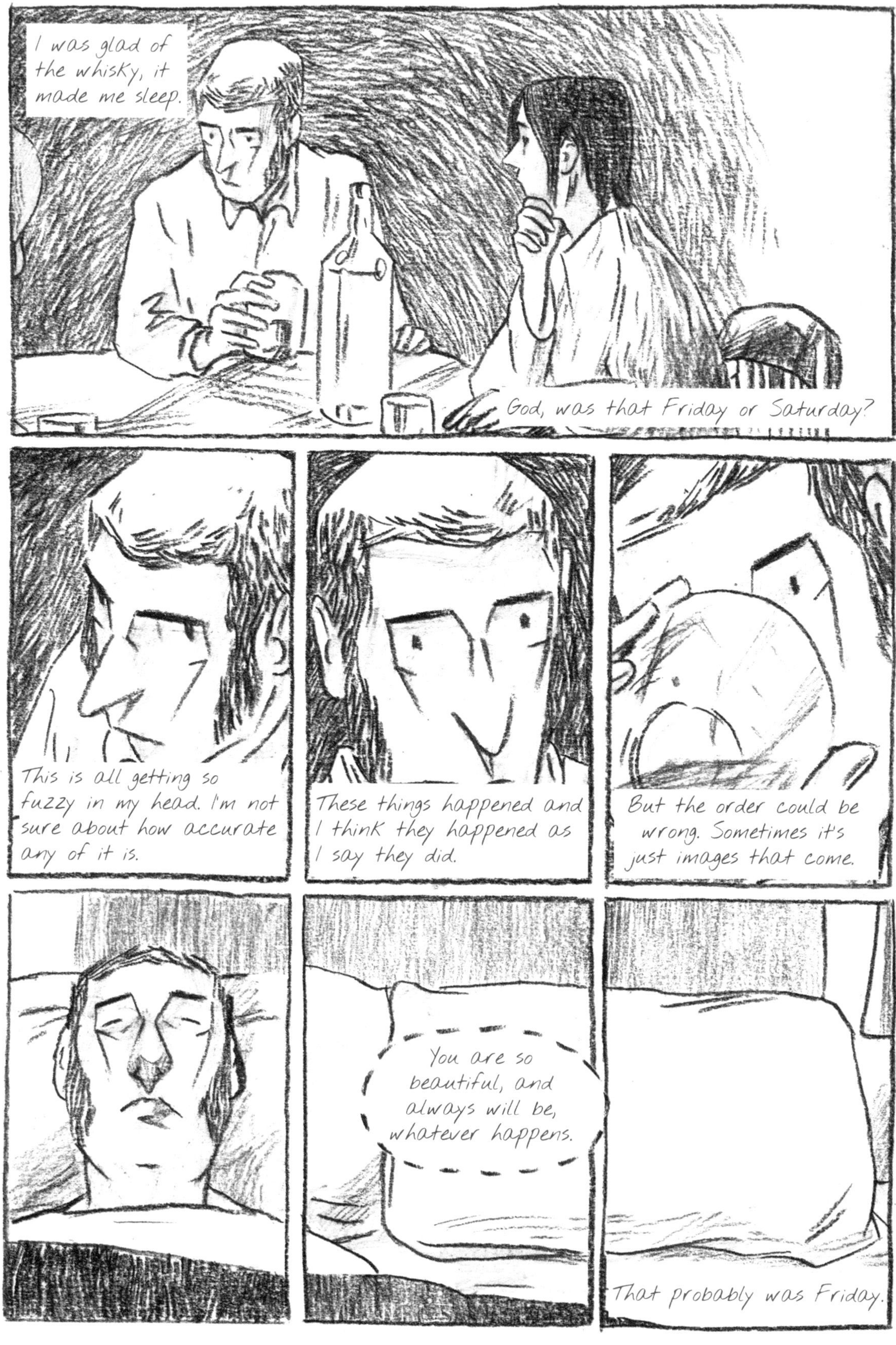
I was glad of the whisky, it made me sleep.
God, was that Friday or Saturday?
This is all getting so fuzzy in my head. I'm not sure about how accurate any of it is.
These things happened and I think they happened as I say they did.
But the order could be wrong. Sometimes it's just images that come.
You are so beautiful, and always will be, whatever happens.
That probably was Friday.

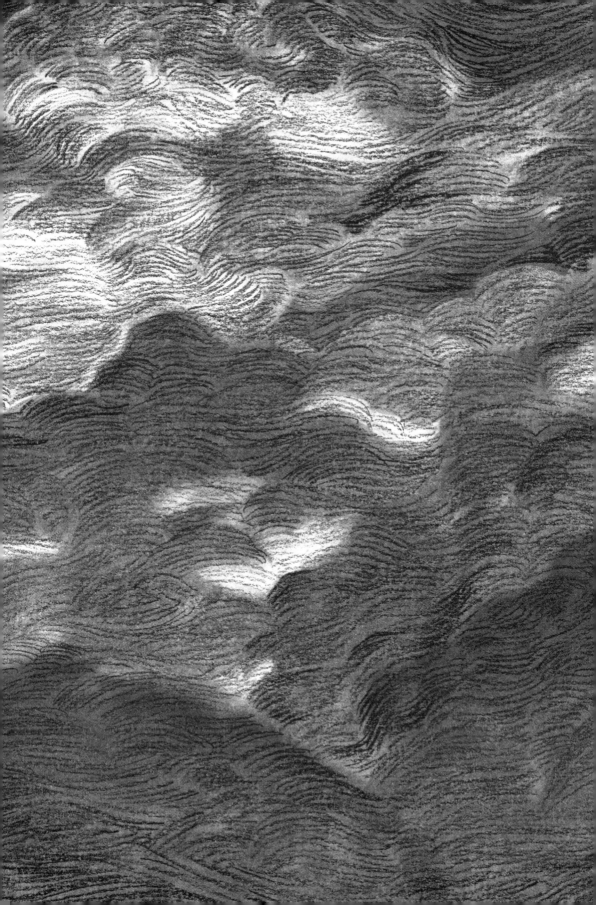

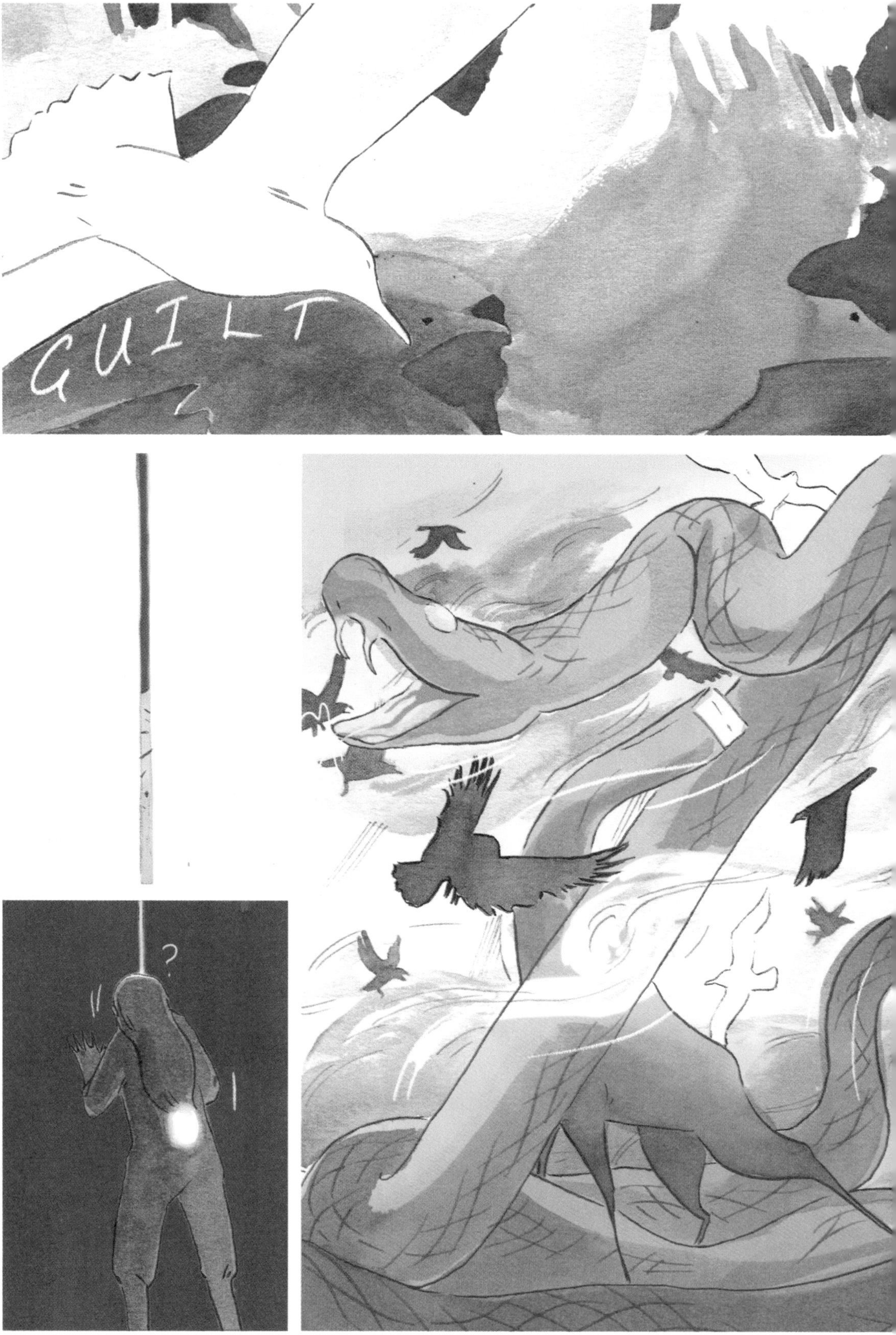
GUILT
?

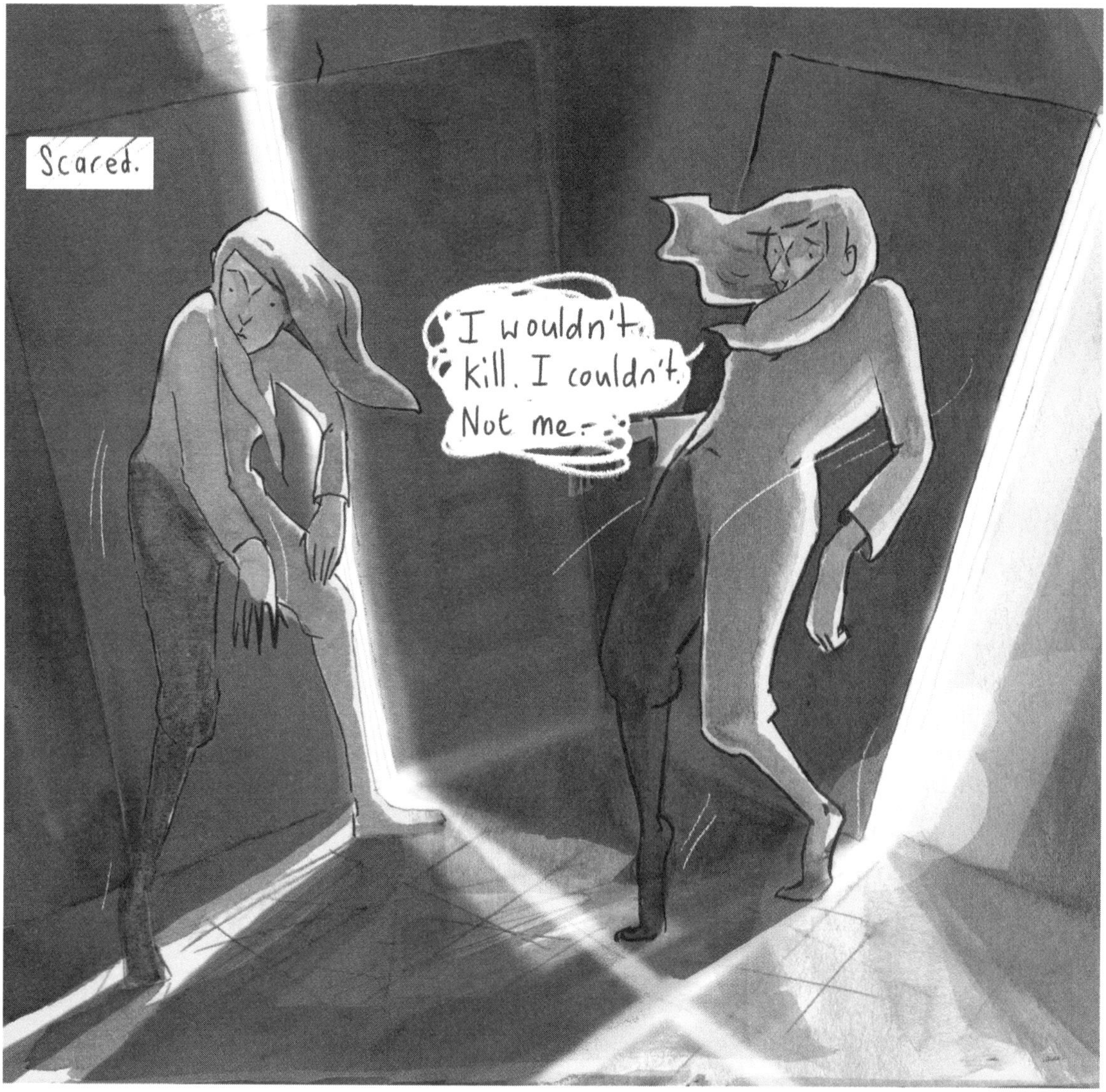
Scared.
I wouldn't kill. I couldn't. Not me.

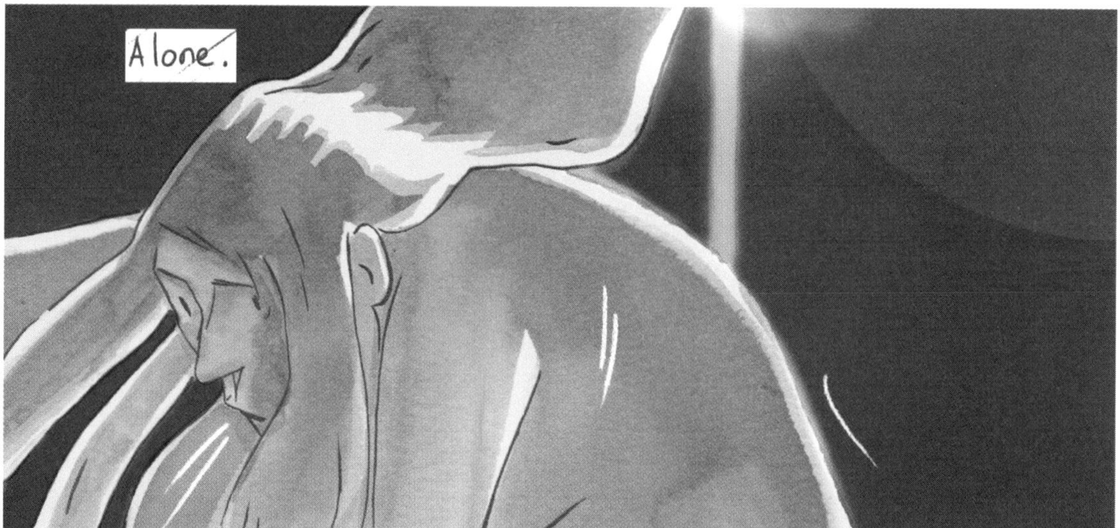
Alone.

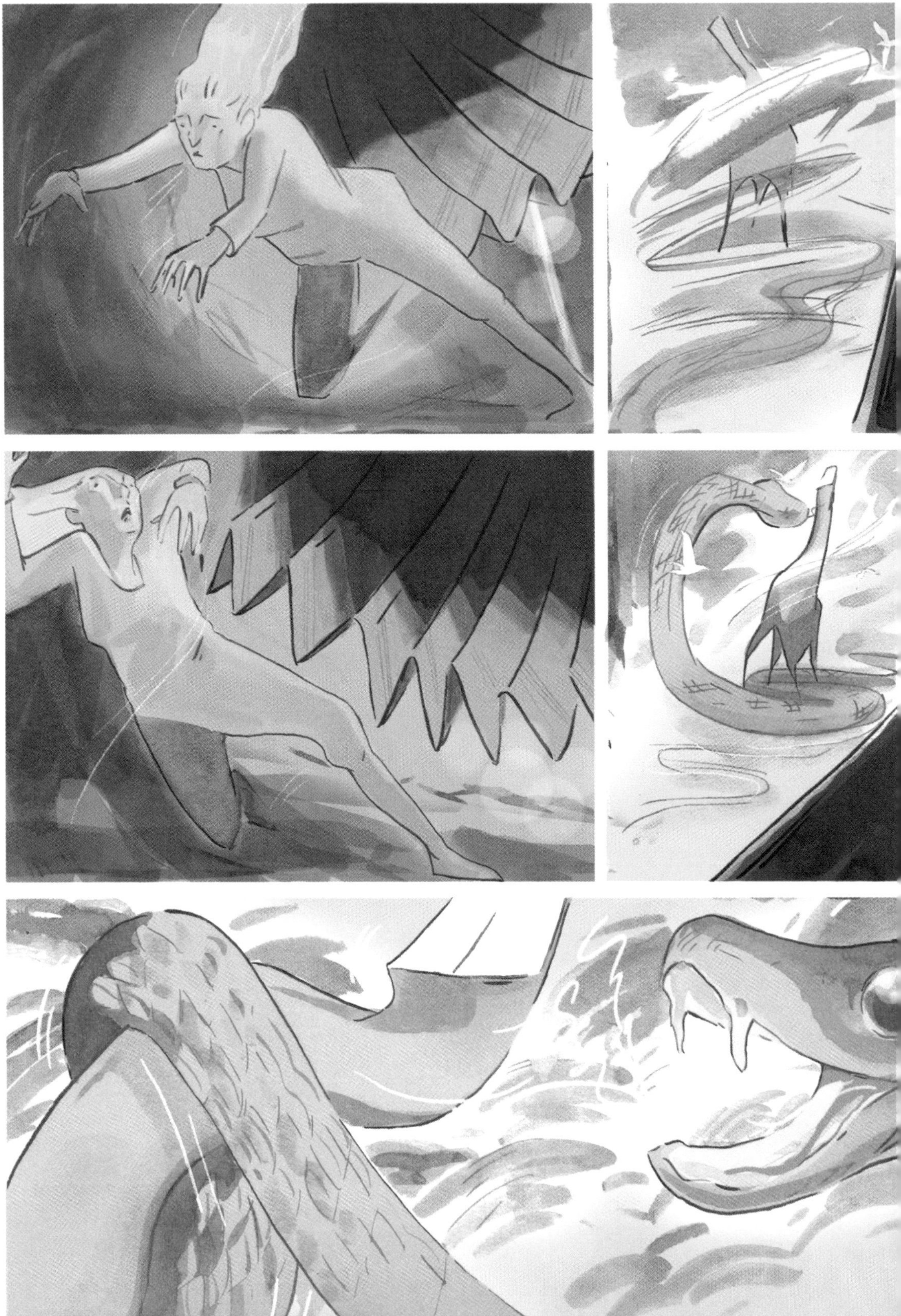

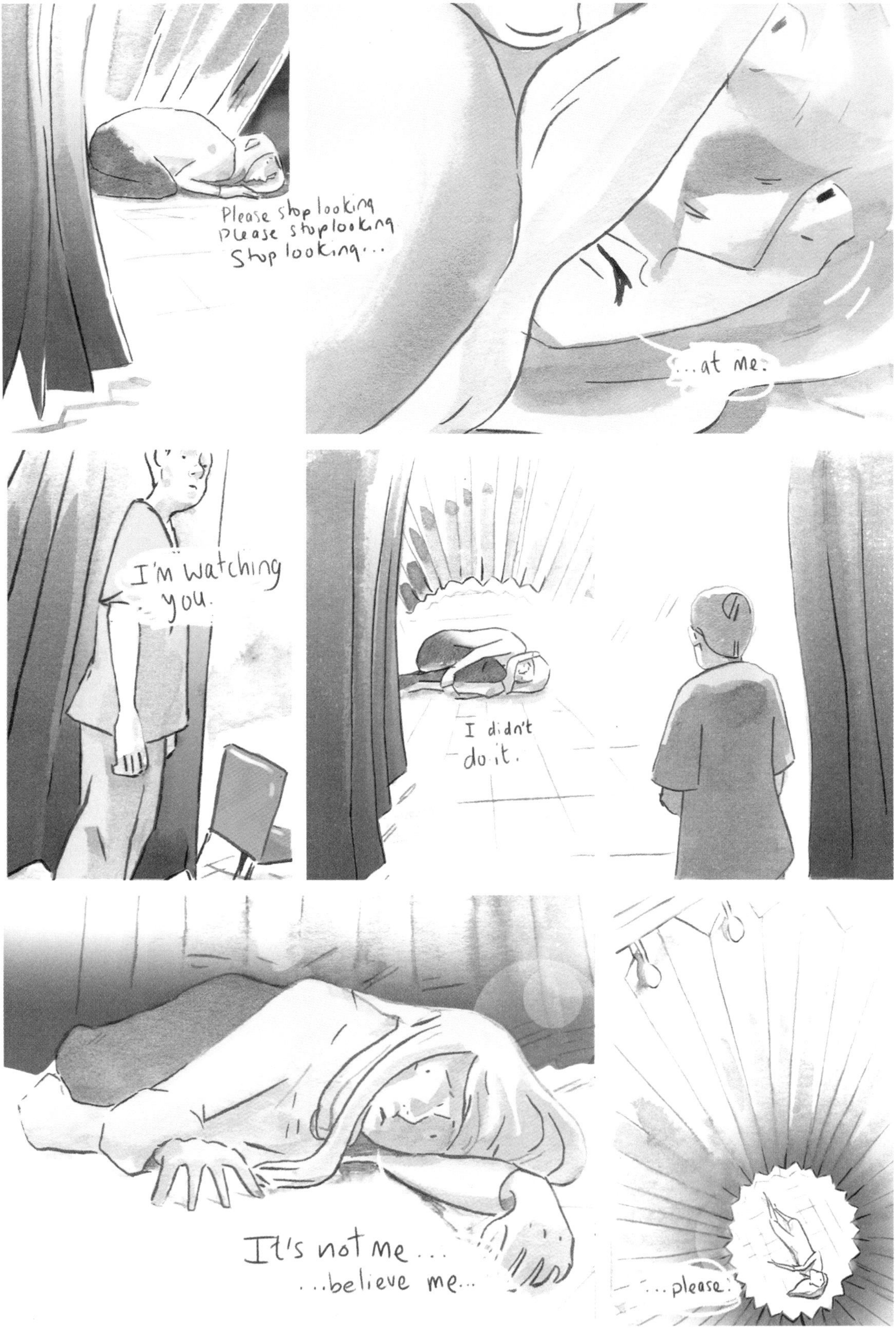
Please stop looking
Please stop looking
Stop looking...
...at me.
I'm watching you.
I didn't do it.
It's not me...
...believe me...
...please.

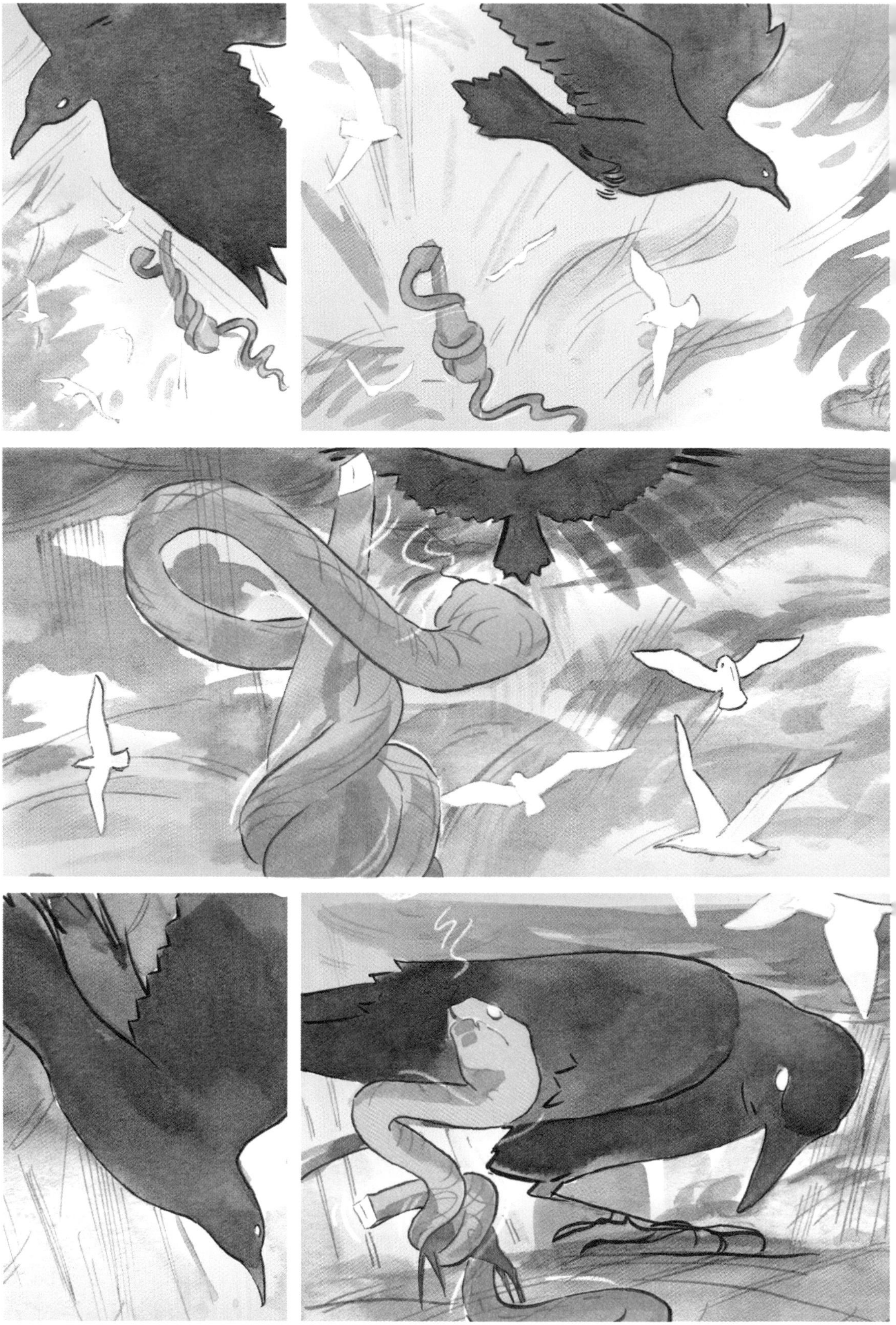

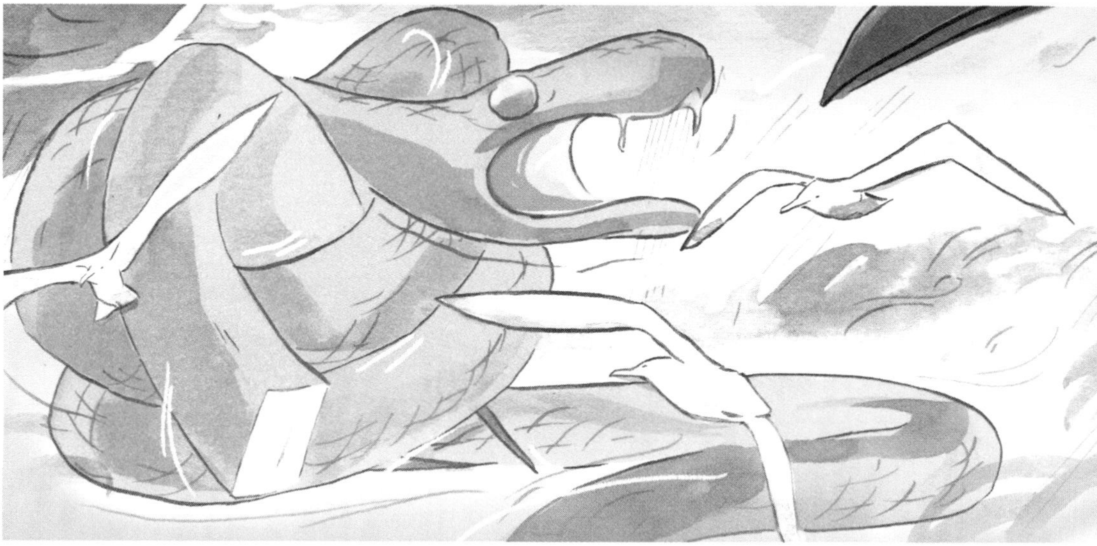

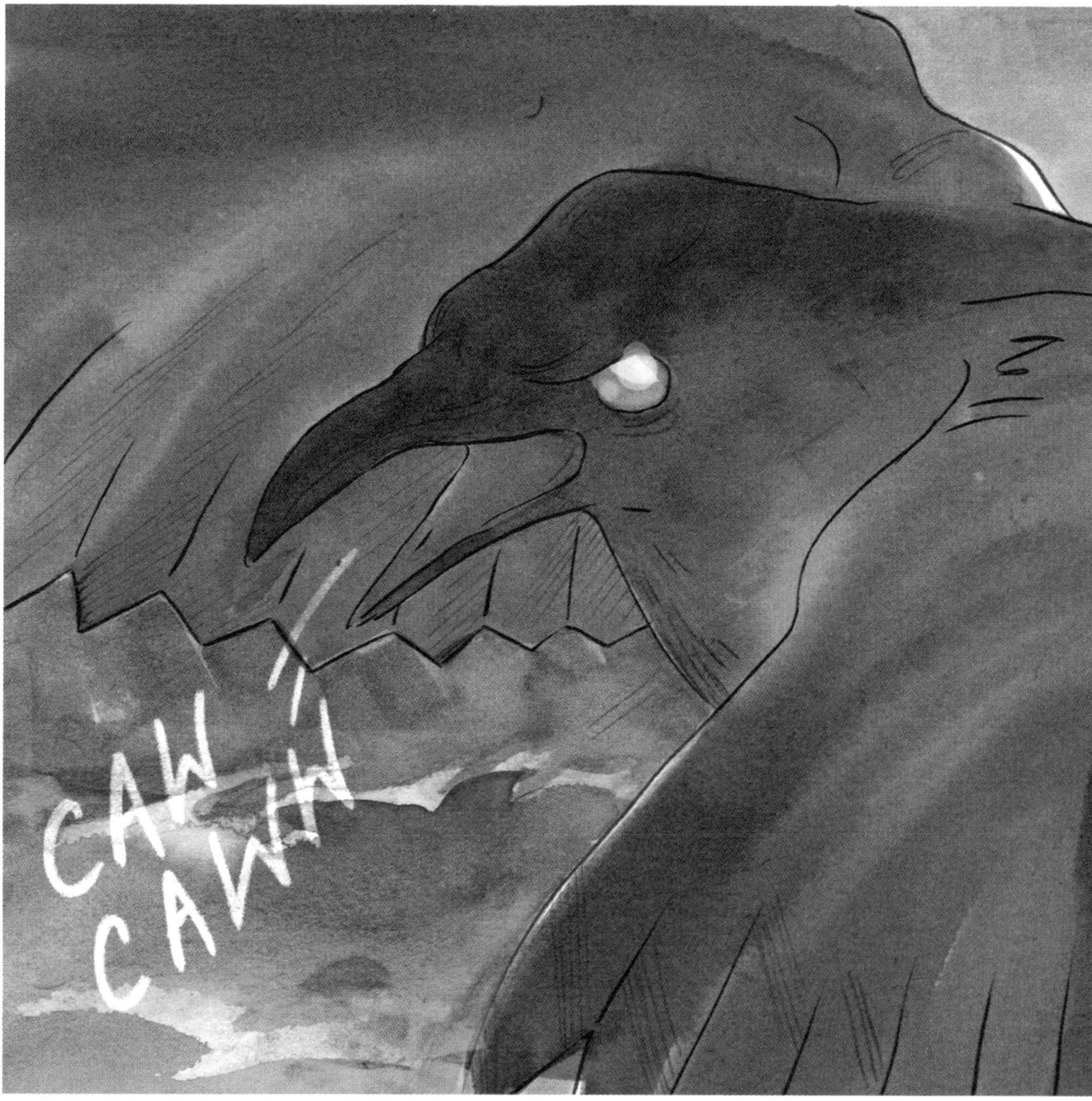
CAW
CAWW

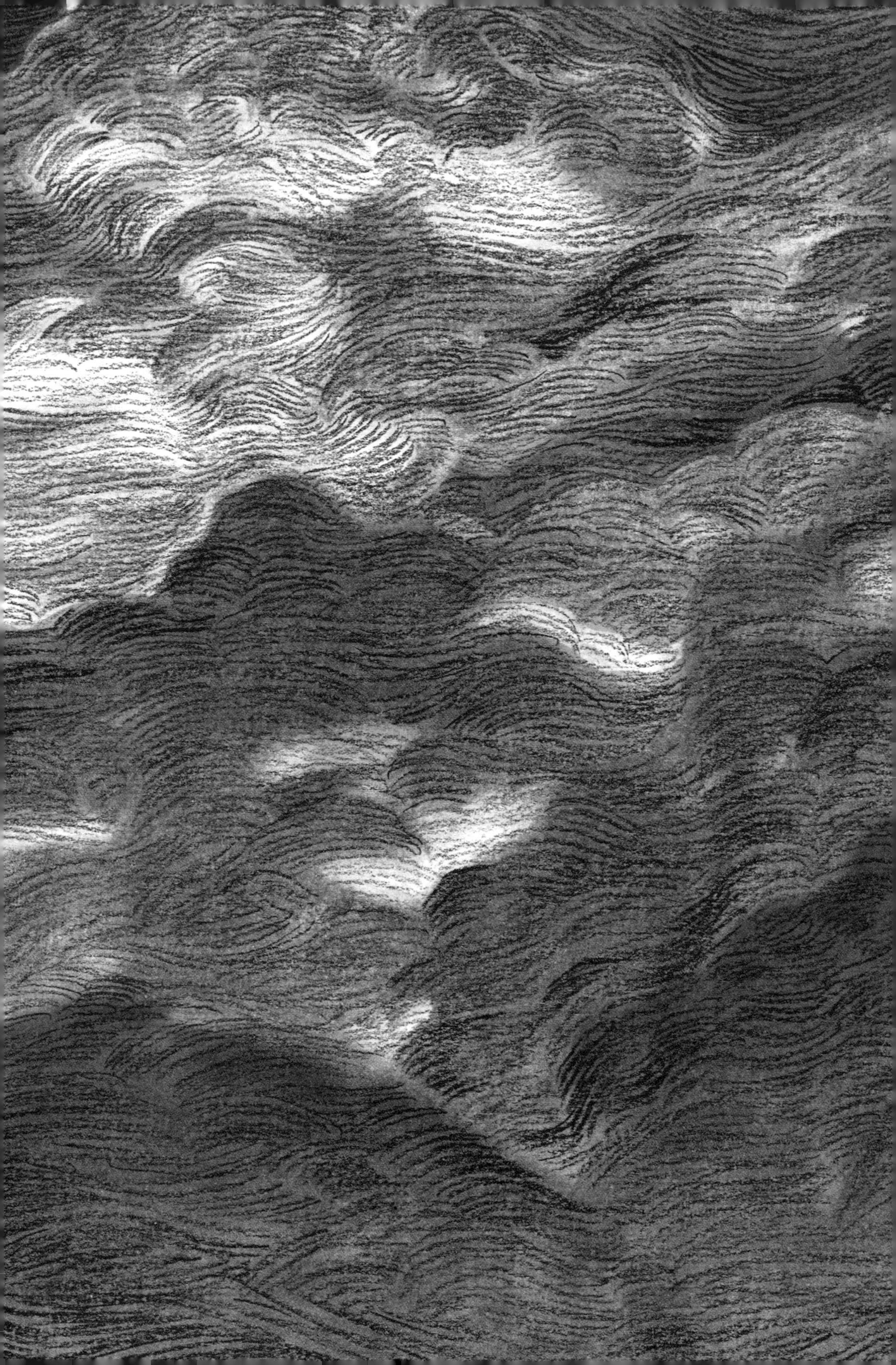

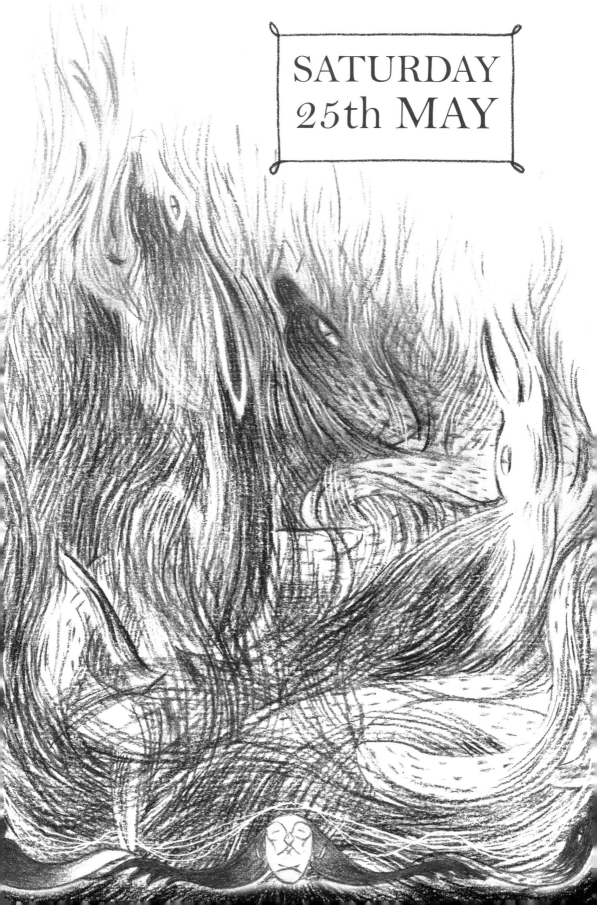

SATURDAY
25th MAY

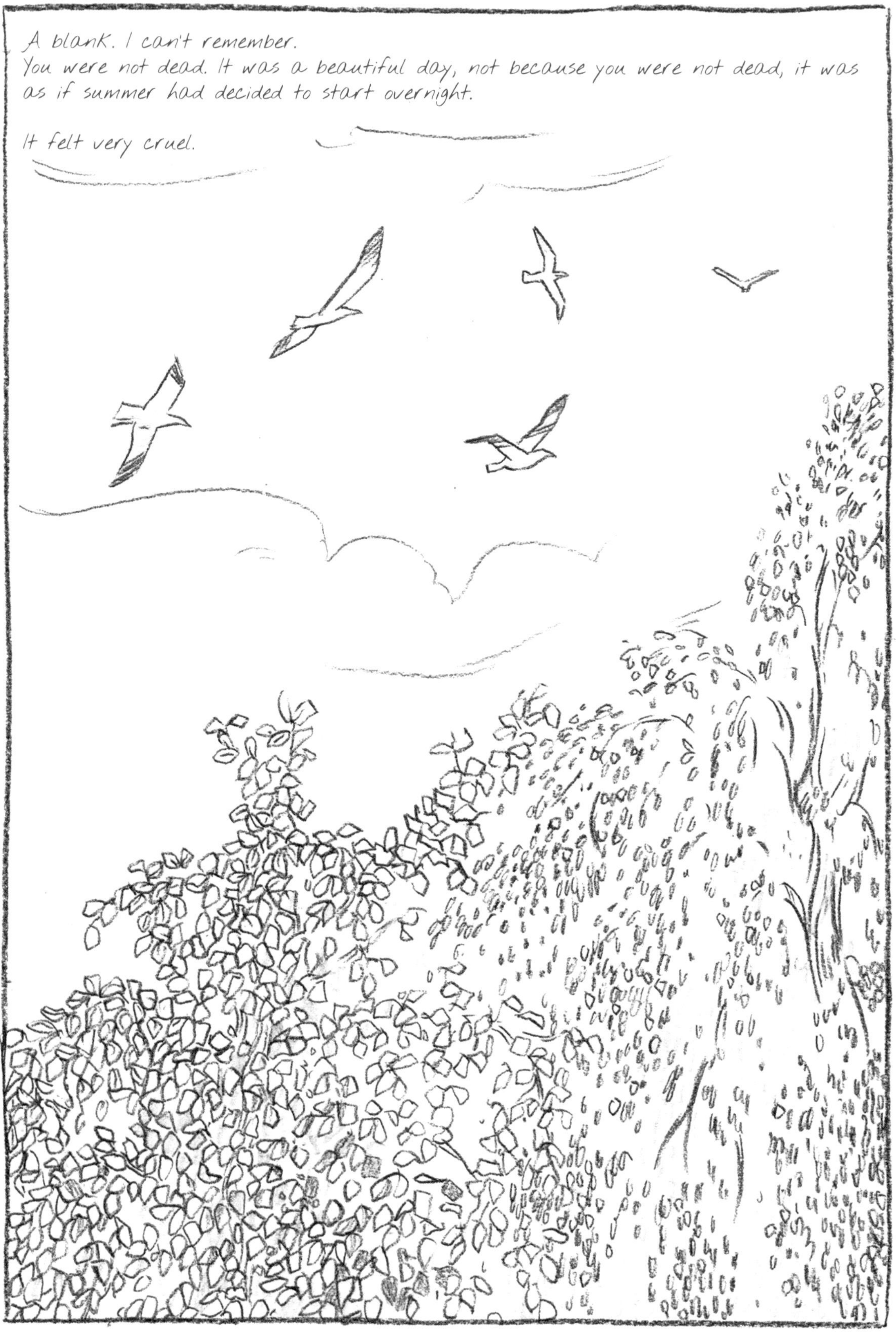
A blank. I can't remember.
You were not dead. It was a beautiful day, not because you were not dead, it was as if summer had decided to start overnight.
It felt very cruel.

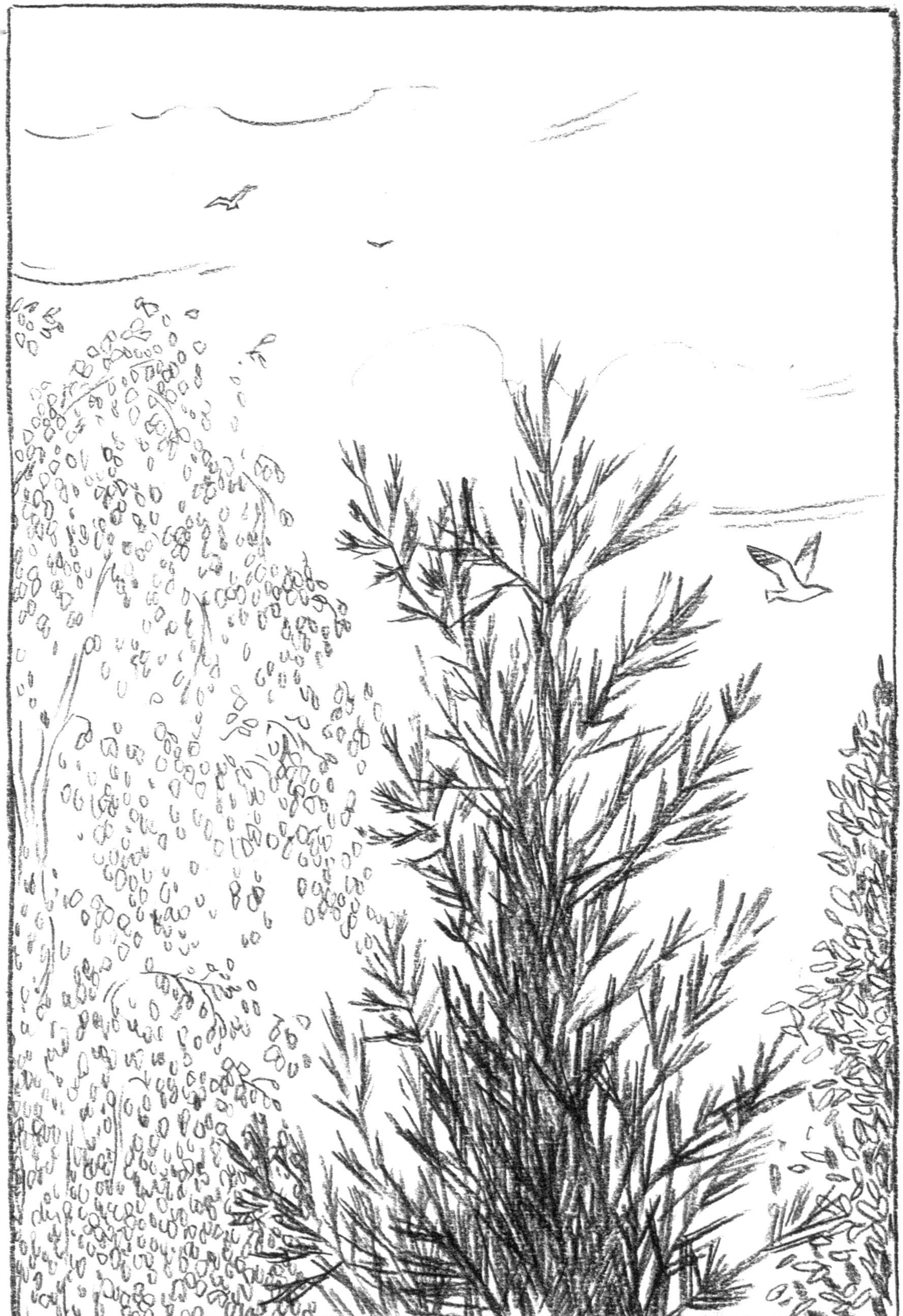

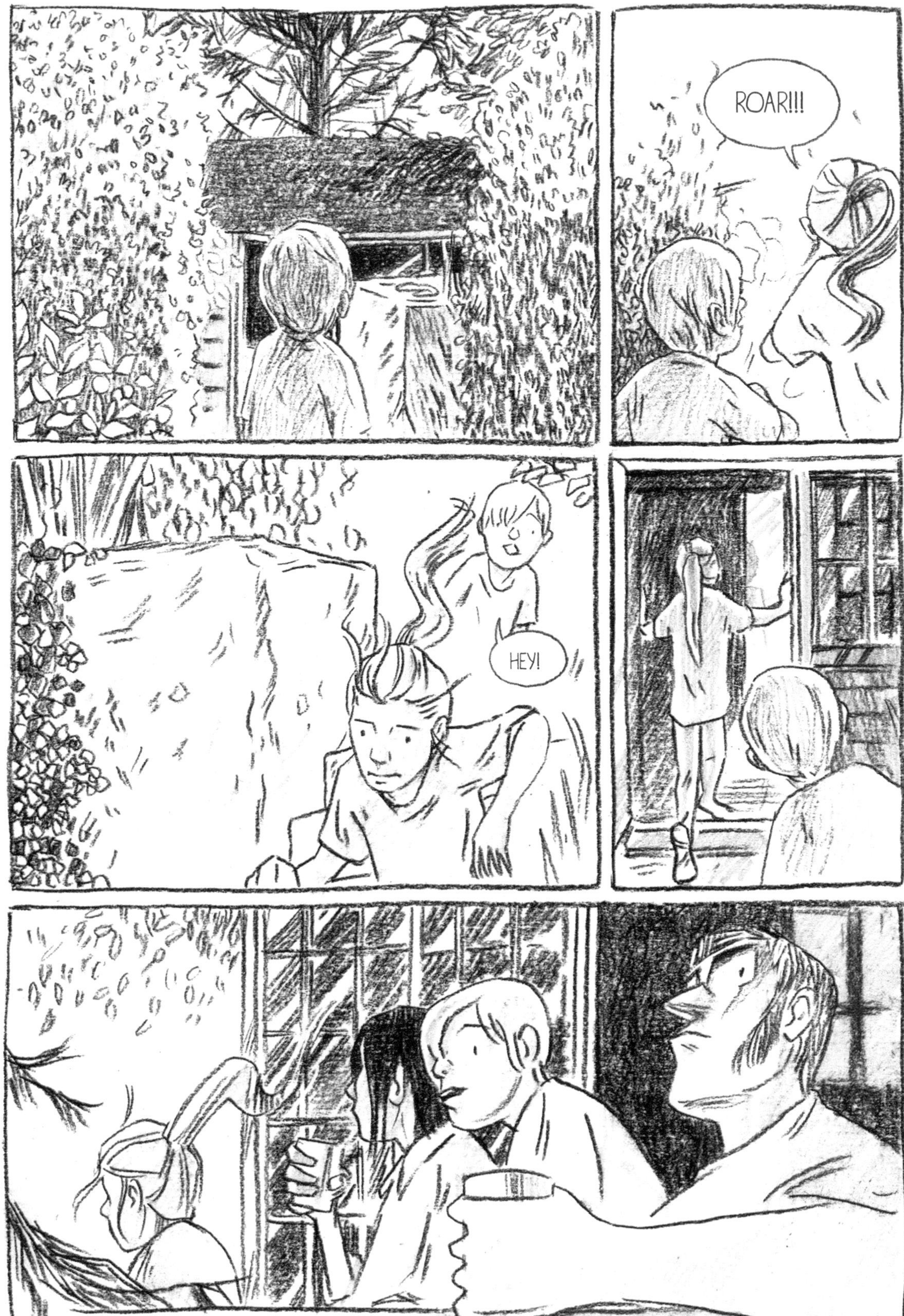
ROAR!!!
HEY!

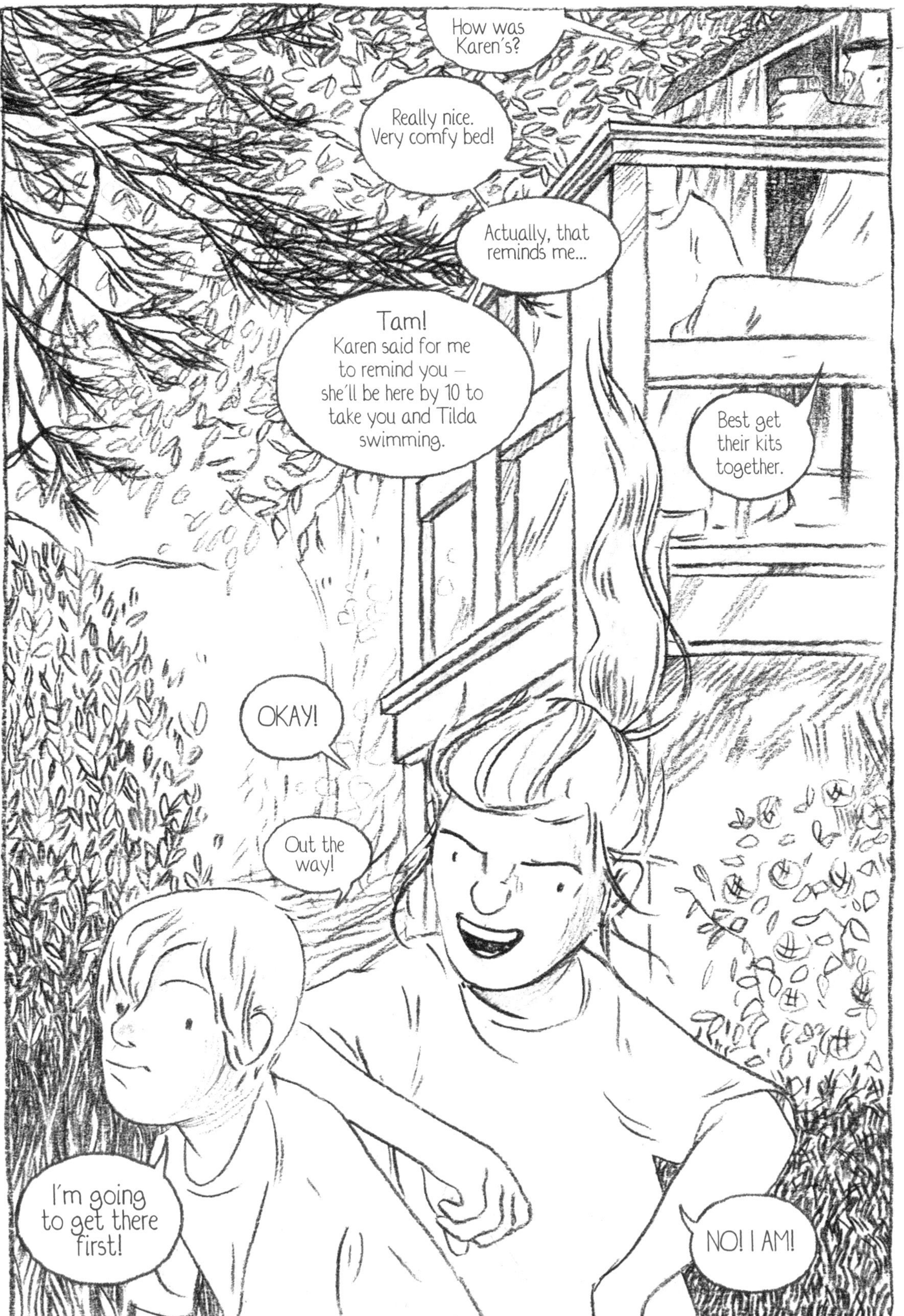
How was Karen's?
Really nice. Very comfy bed!
Actually, that reminds me...
Tam! Karen said for me to remind you – she'll be here by 10 to take you and Tilda swimming.
Best get their kits together.
OKAY!
Out the way!
I'm going to get there first!
NO! I AM!

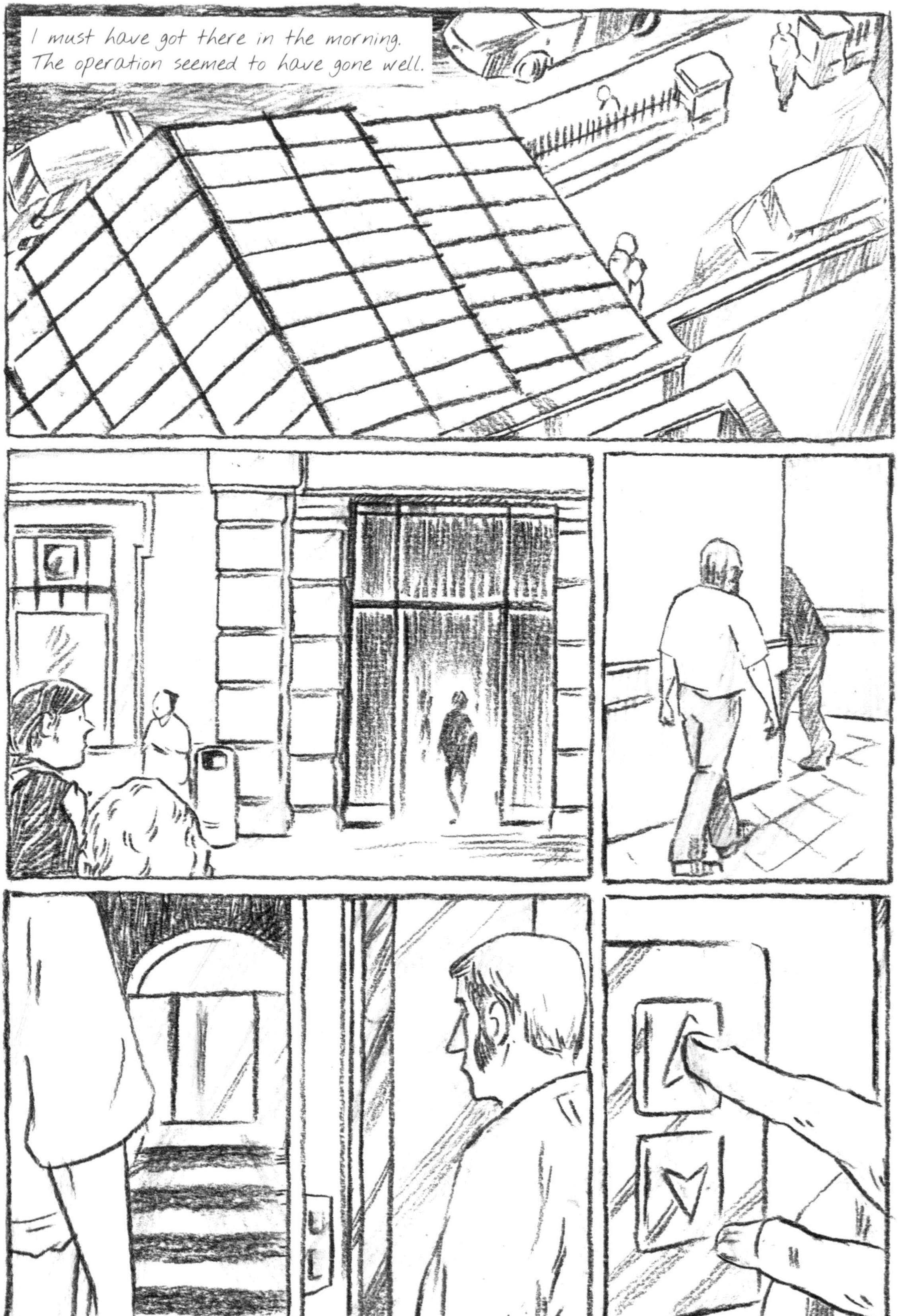
I must have got there in the morning.
The operation seemed to have gone well.

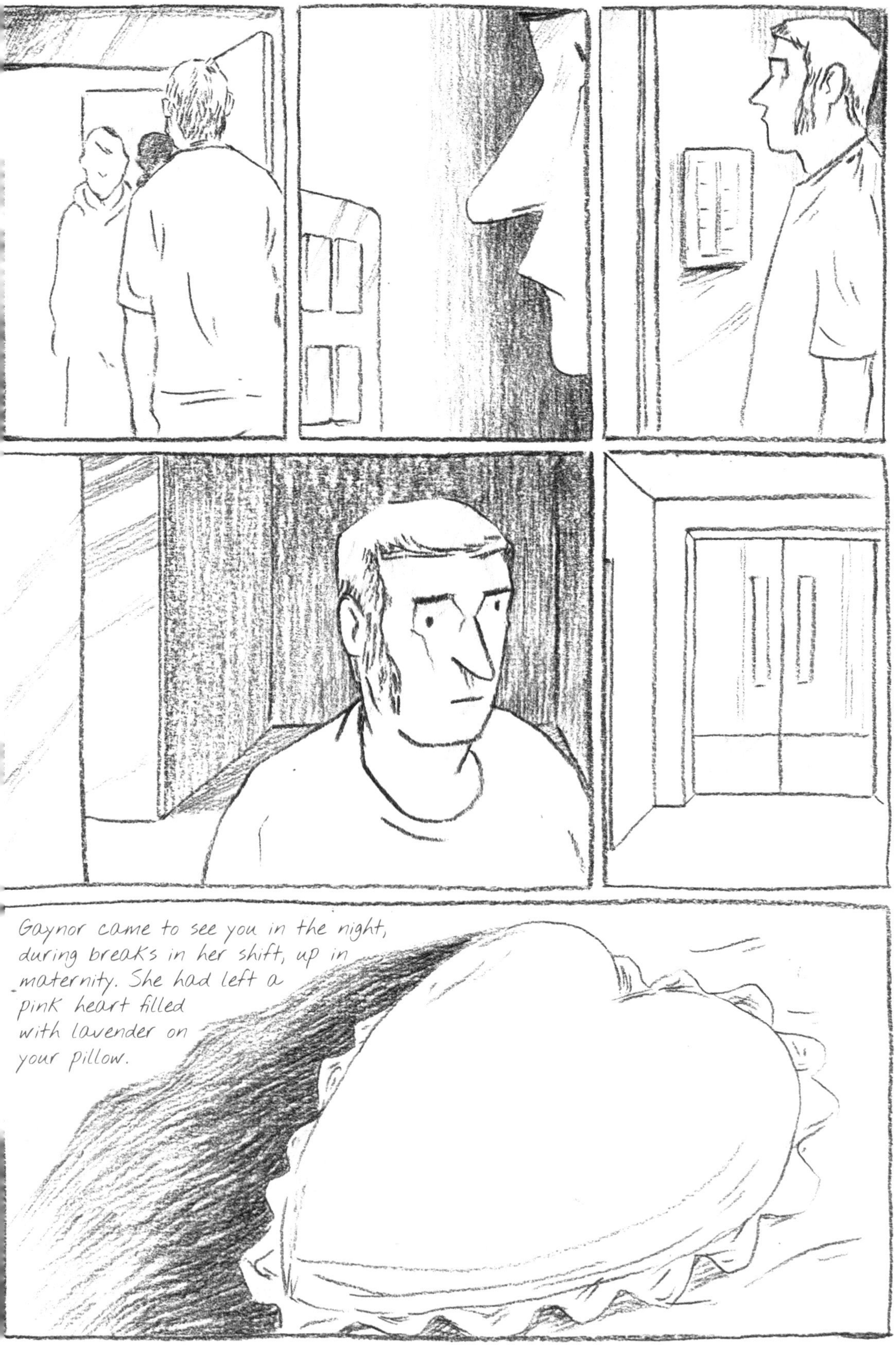
Gaynor came to see you in the night, during breaks in her shift, up in maternity. She had left a pink heart filled with lavender on your pillow.

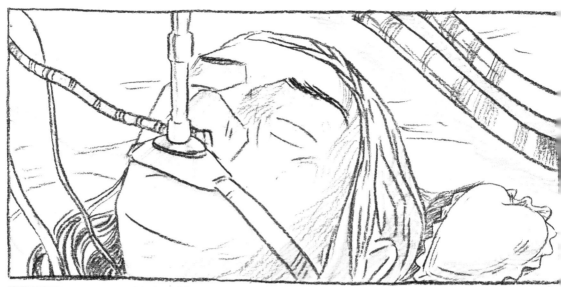

She called me later in the day.

I think you should start writing things down. It'll help you make sense of this, but it'll also help Zara with all her lost days.

This is where I started writing things down.

It's Saturday. I call my Dad to say I won't be coming.

Everyone is sending so much love your way.

92

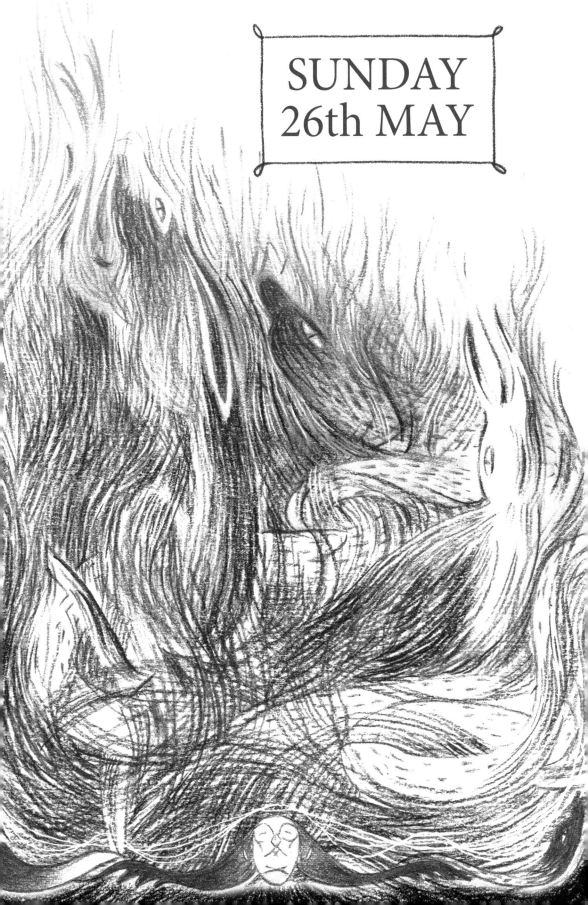

SUNDAY
26th MAY

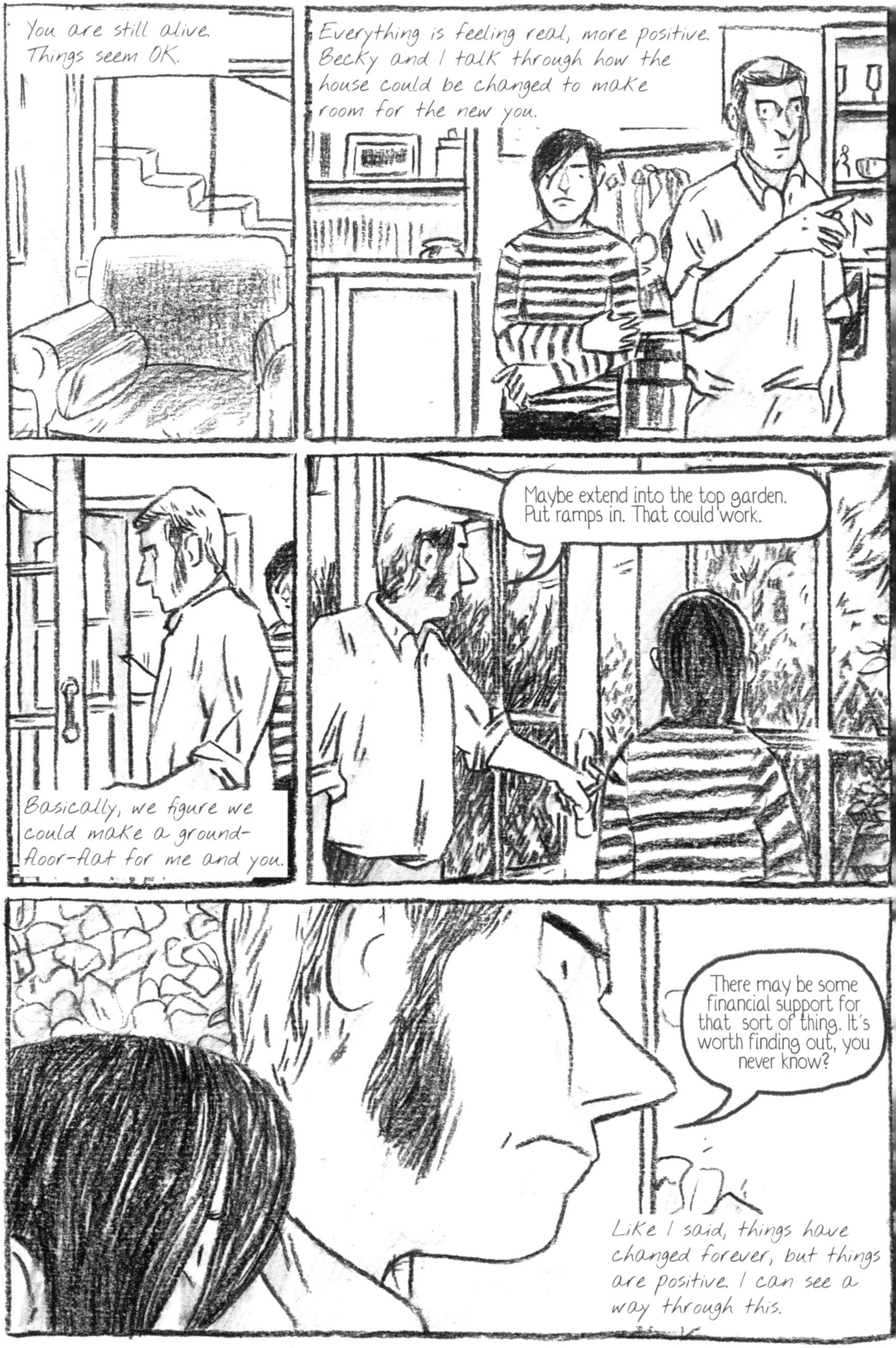
You are still alive. Things seem OK.
Everything is feeling real, more positive. Becky and I talk through how the house could be changed to make room for the new you.
Basically, we figure we could make a ground-floor-flat for me and you.
Maybe extend into the top garden. Put ramps in. That could work.
There may be some financial support for that sort of thing. It's worth finding out, you never know?
Like I said, things have changed forever, but things are positive. I can see a way through this.

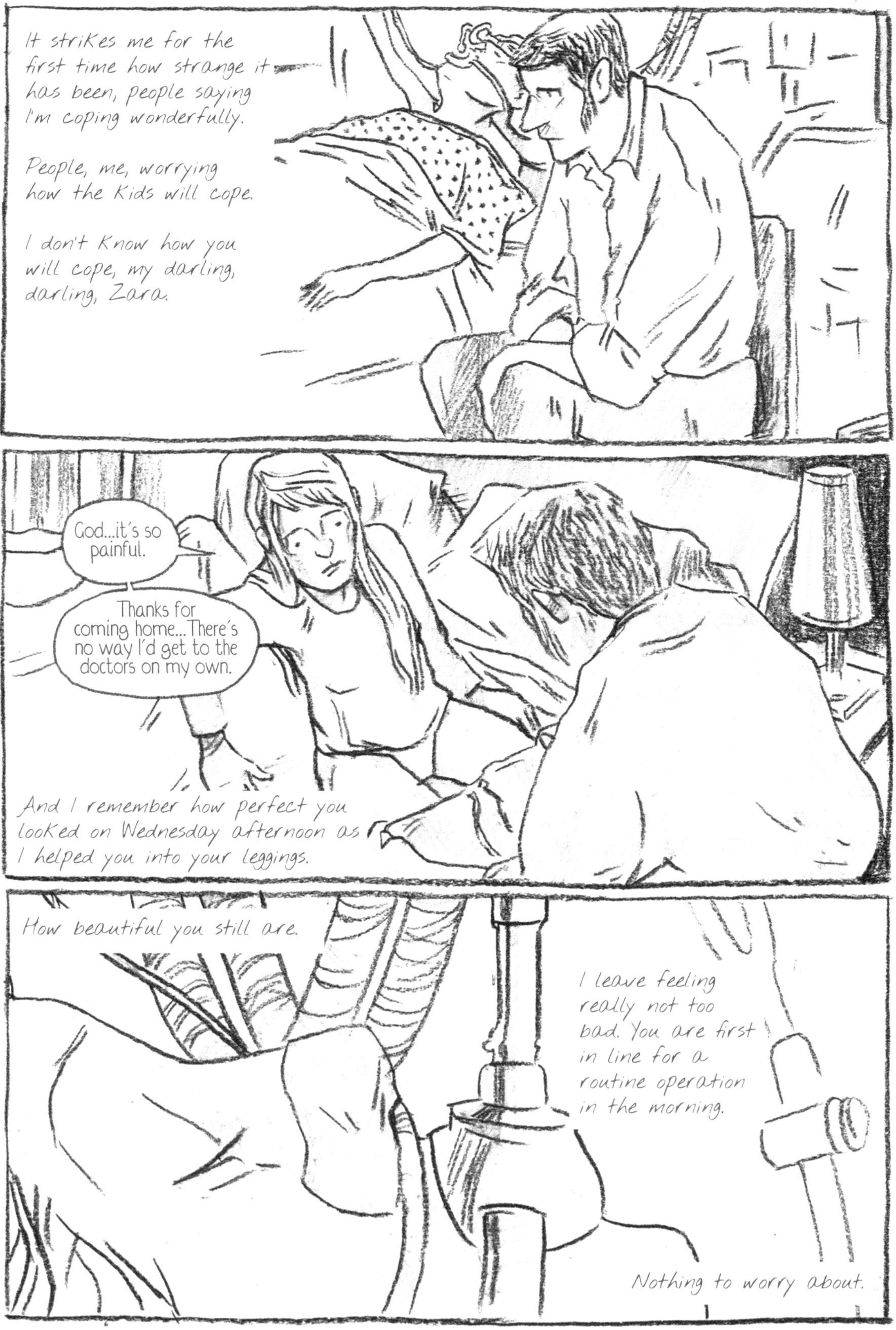
It strikes me for the first time how strange it has been, people saying I'm coping wonderfully.
People, me, worrying how the kids will cope.
I don't know how you will cope, my darling, darling, Zara.
God...it's so painful.
Thanks for coming home...There's no way I'd get to the doctors on my own.
And I remember how perfect you looked on Wednesday afternoon as I helped you into your leggings.
How beautiful you still are.
I leave feeling really not too bad. You are first in line for a routine operation in the morning.
Nothing to worry about.

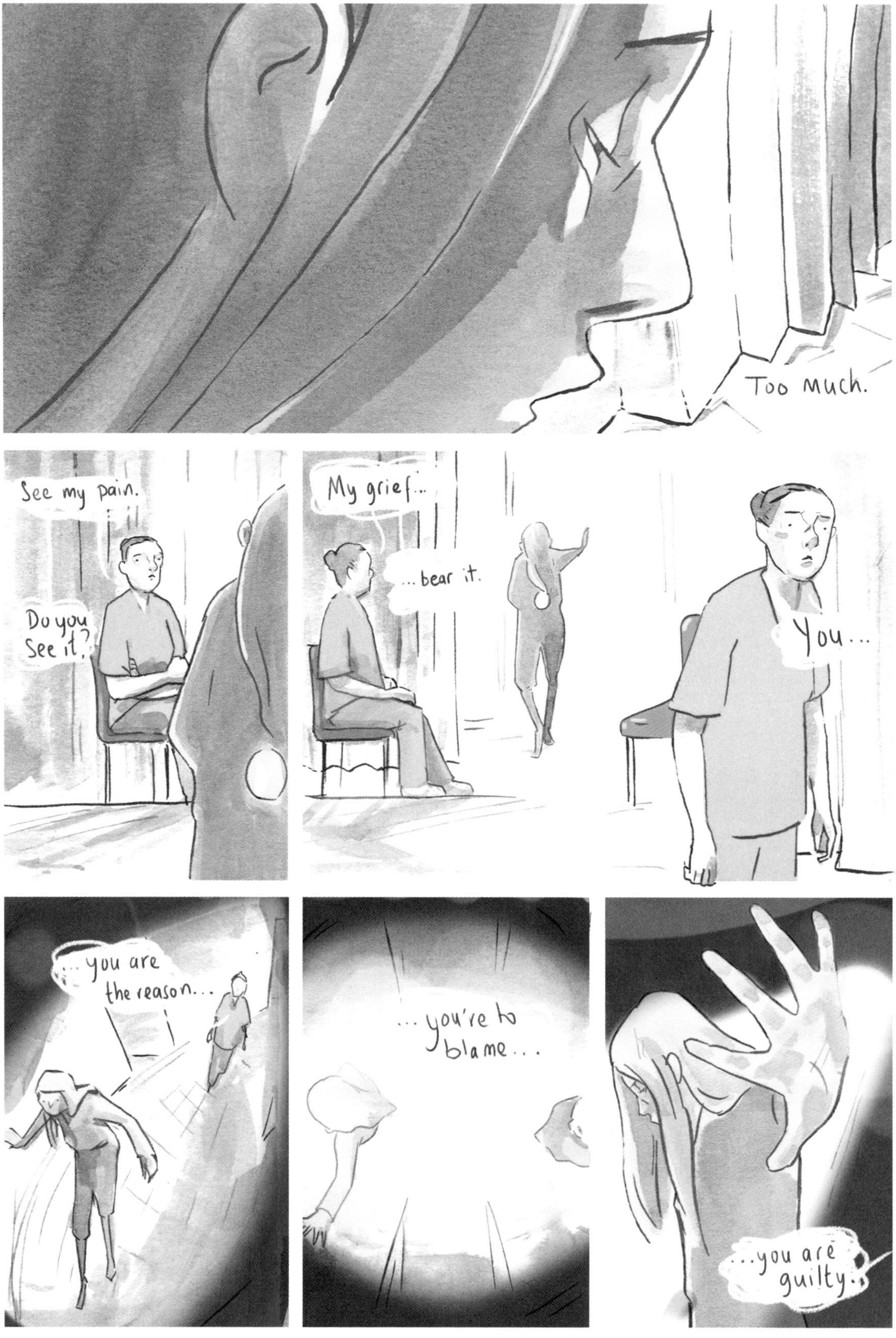
Too much.
See my pain.
Do you See it?
My grief...
...bear it.
You...
...you are the reason...
...you're to blame...
...you are guilty.

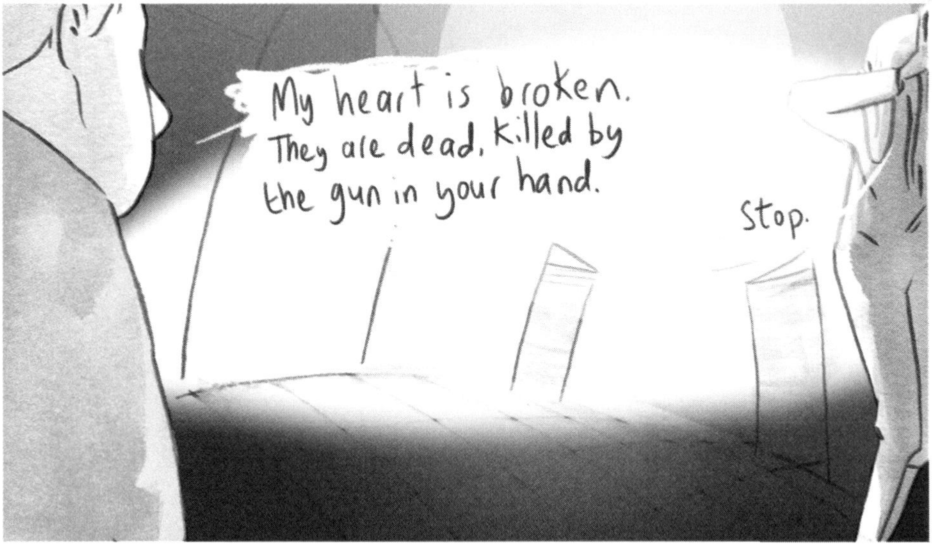
My heart is broken.
They are dead, killed by the gun in your hand.
Stop.

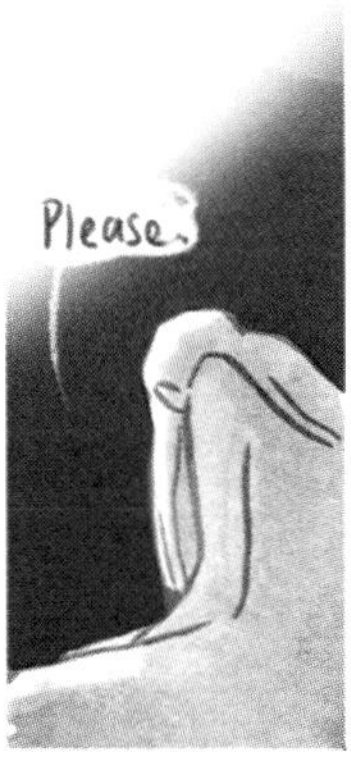
Please.

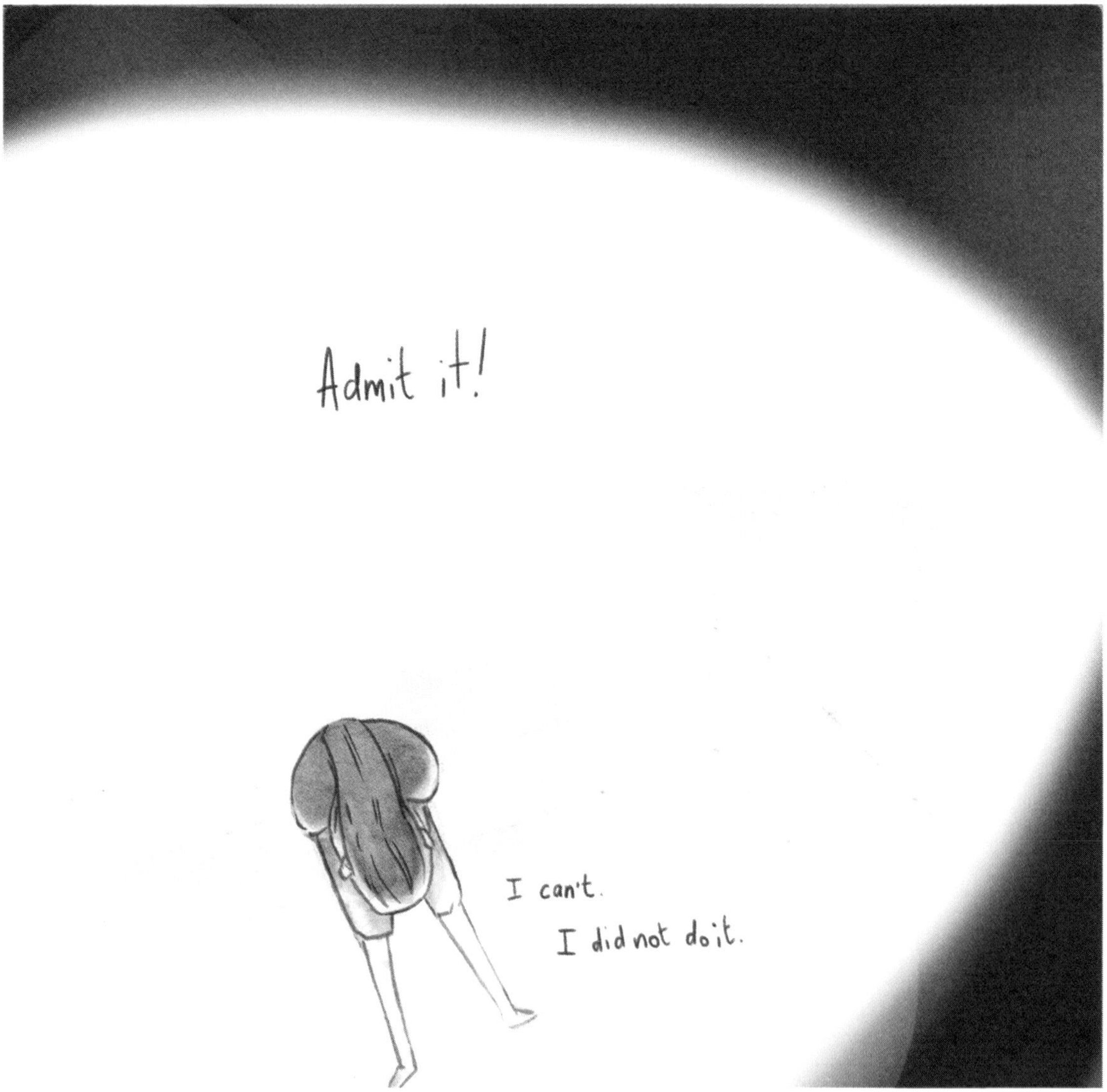
Admit it!
I can't.
I did not do it.

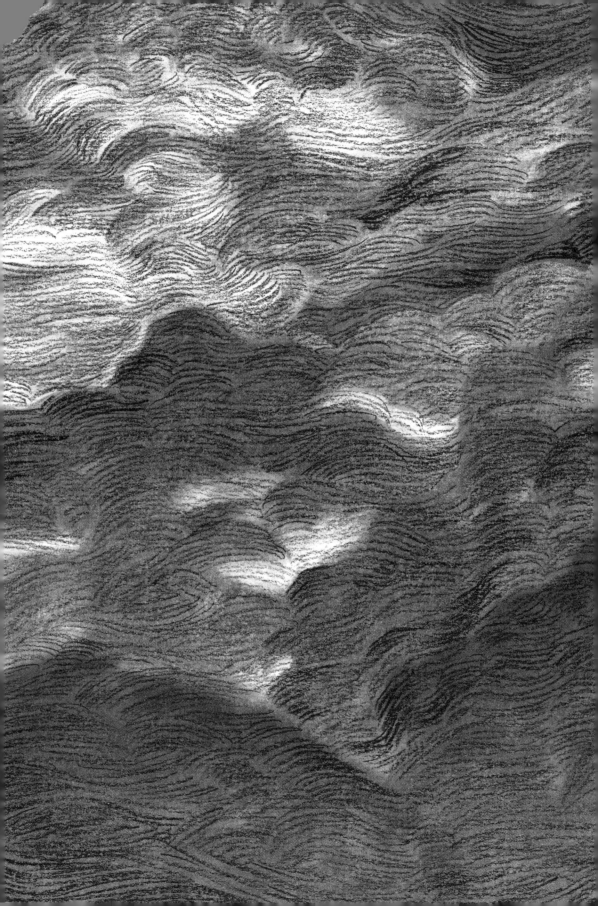

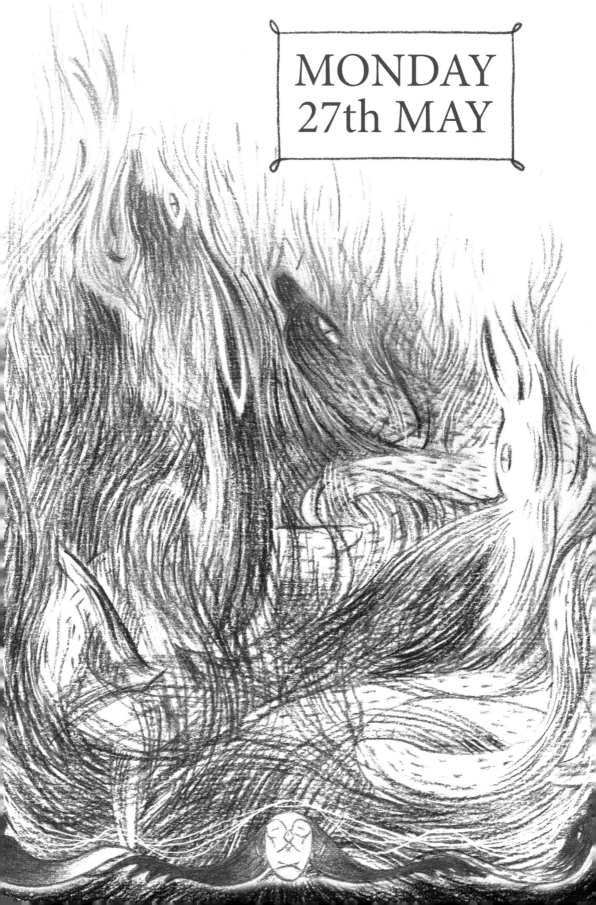

MONDAY
27th MAY

Everything still feels OK, strange but OK. Your VAC dressing will need adjusting, more minor surgery. Still, it seems our major worry is going to be how to deal with your missing leg.

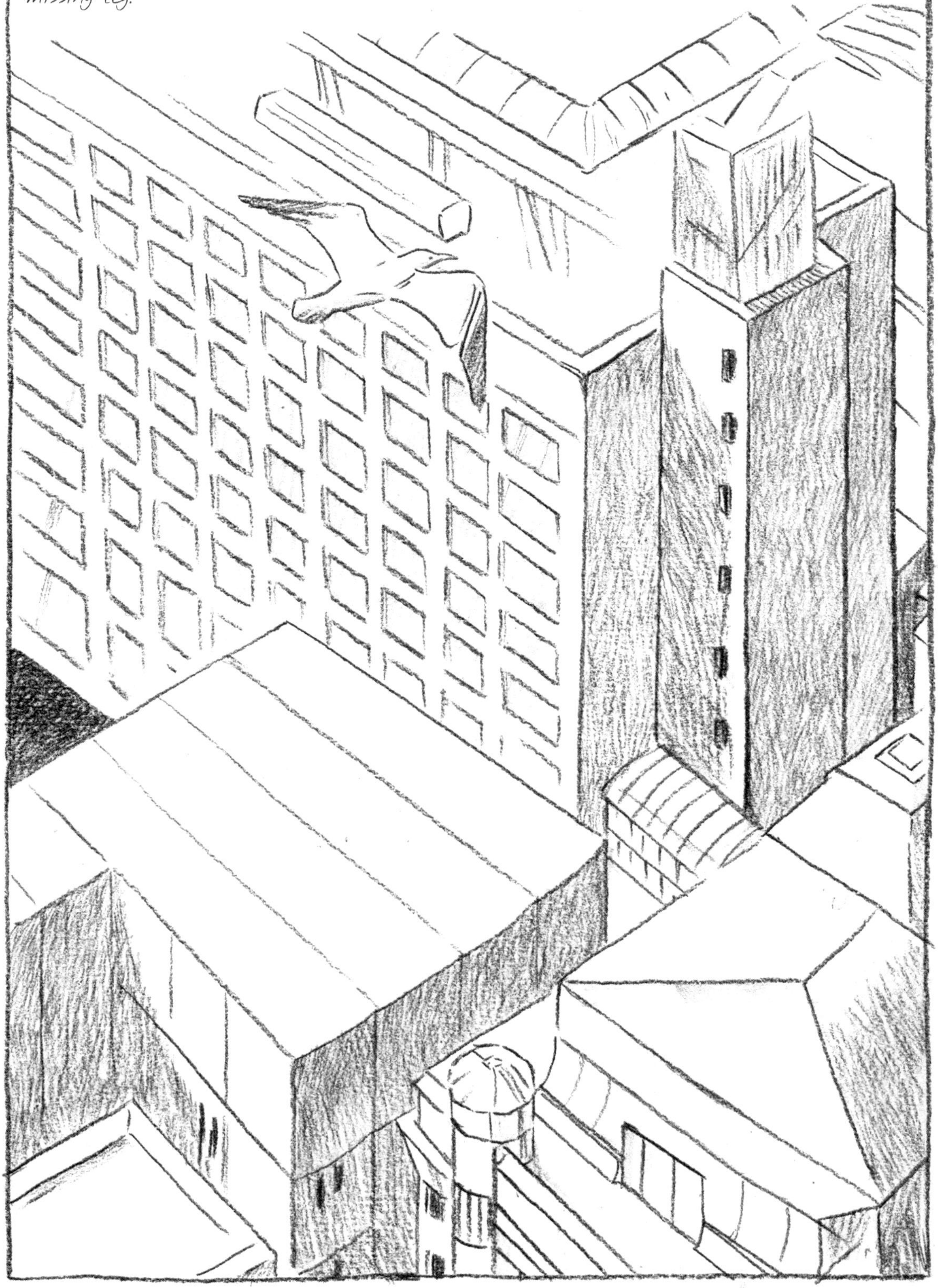

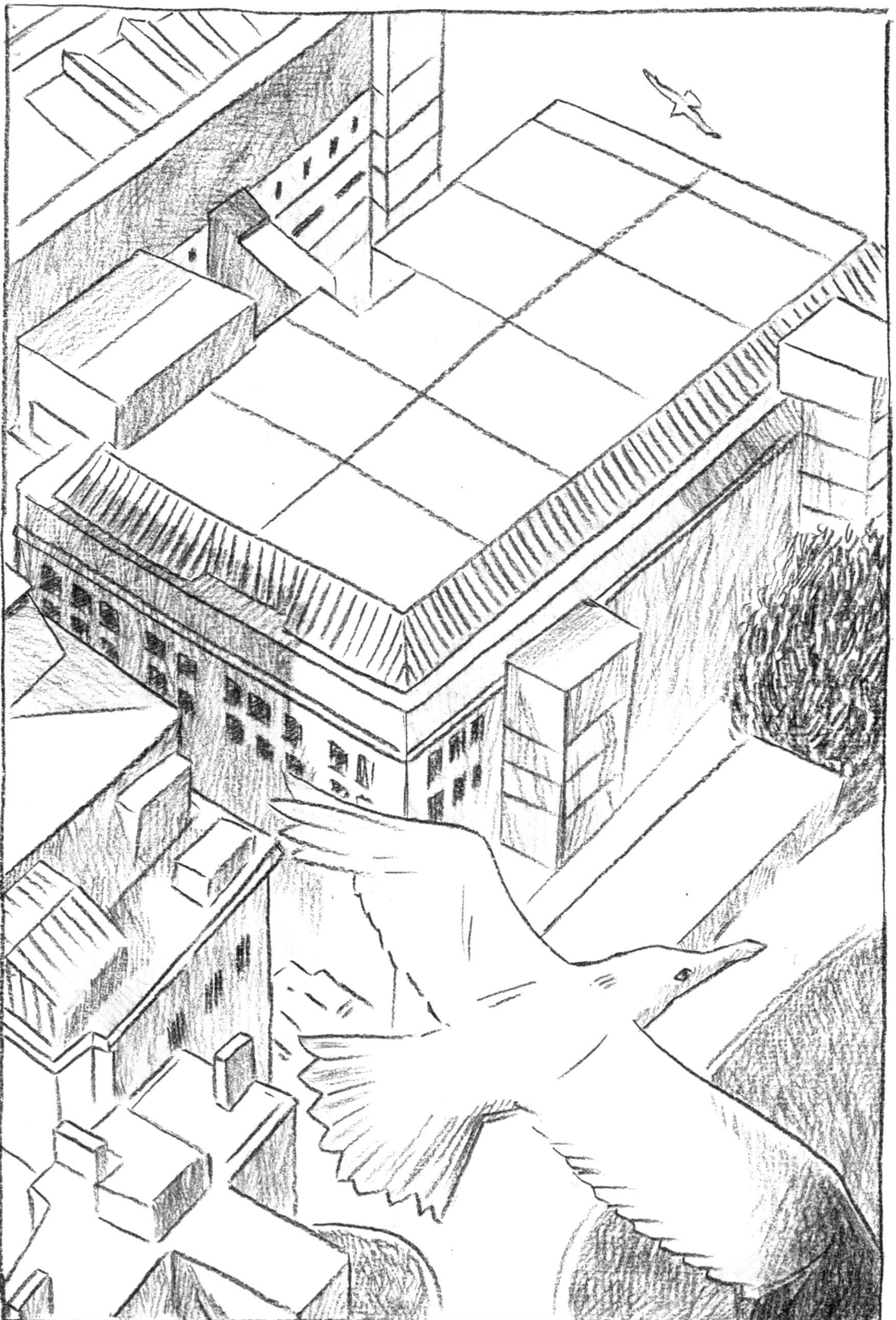

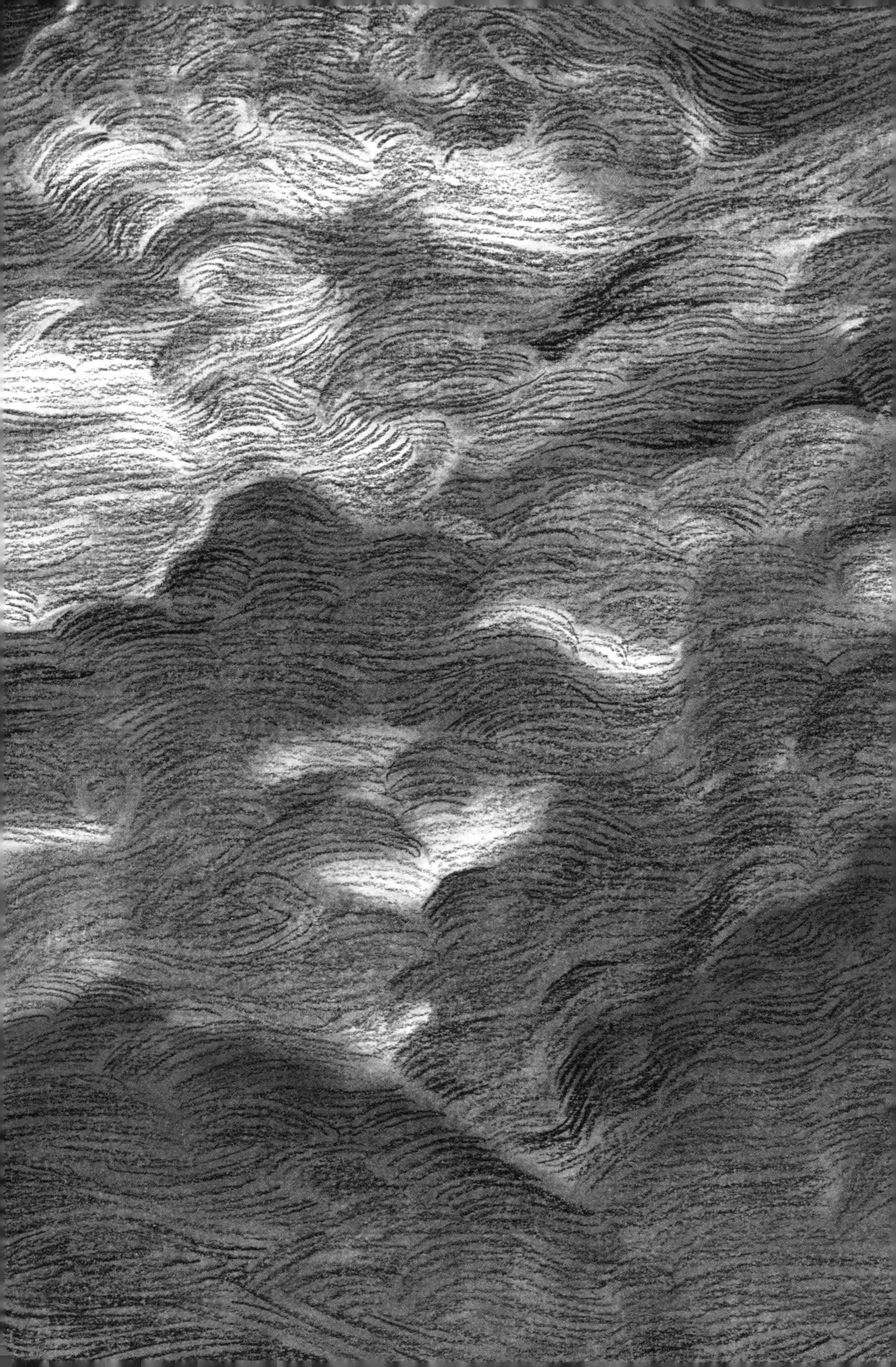

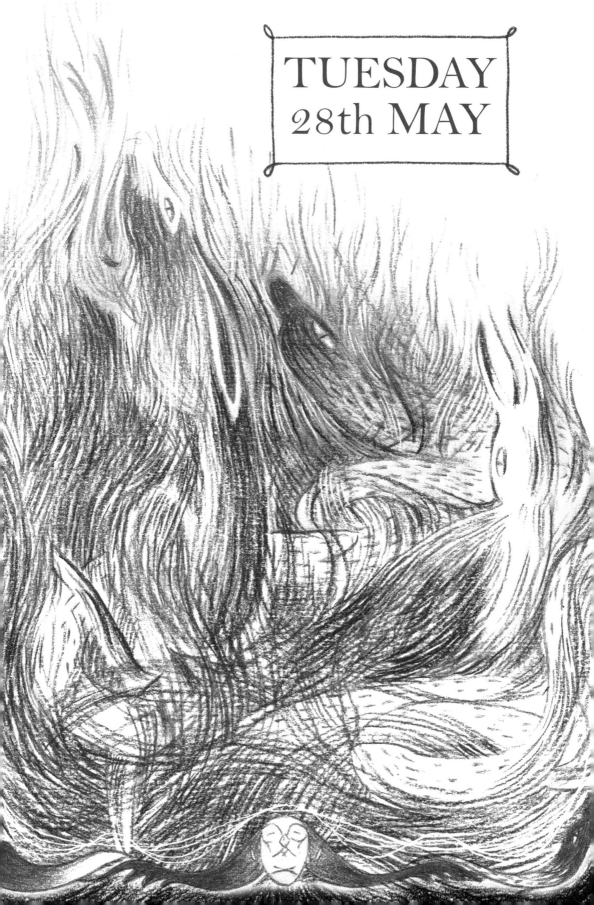

TUESDAY
28th MAY

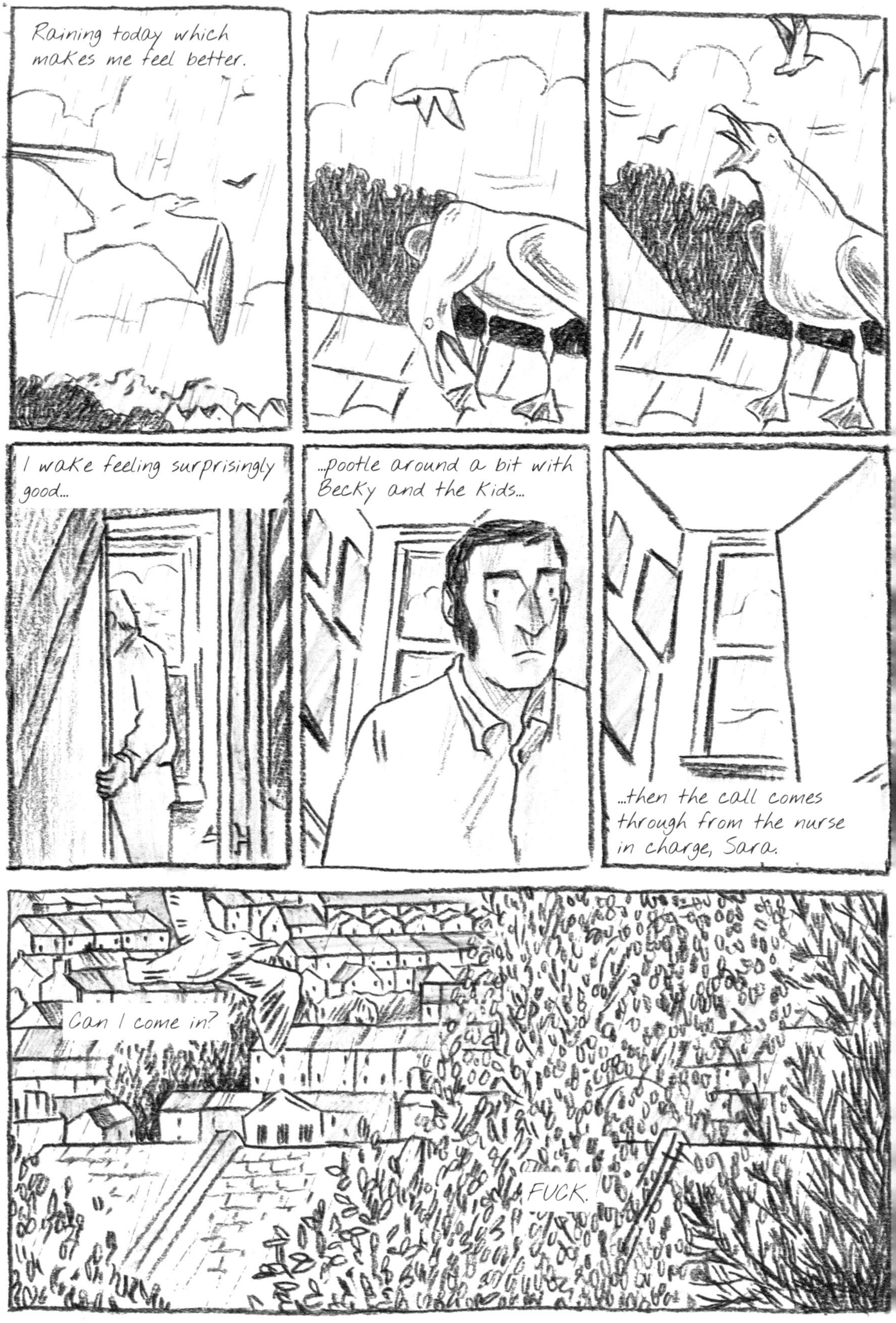

Raining today which makes me feel better.
I wake feeling surprisingly good...
...pootle around a bit with Becky and the Kids...
...then the call comes through from the nurse in charge, Sara.
Can I come in?
FUCK.

Becky is with me.

We sit with you.

She's looking better.

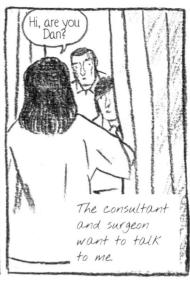

Hi, are you Dan?

The consultant and surgeon want to talk to me.

Stupid, but I still think things really can't be all that bad.

They are.

It's not looking good, I'm afraid.

The last operations were not that straight forward.

More tissue had to be removed each time.

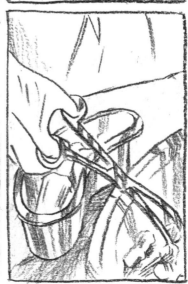

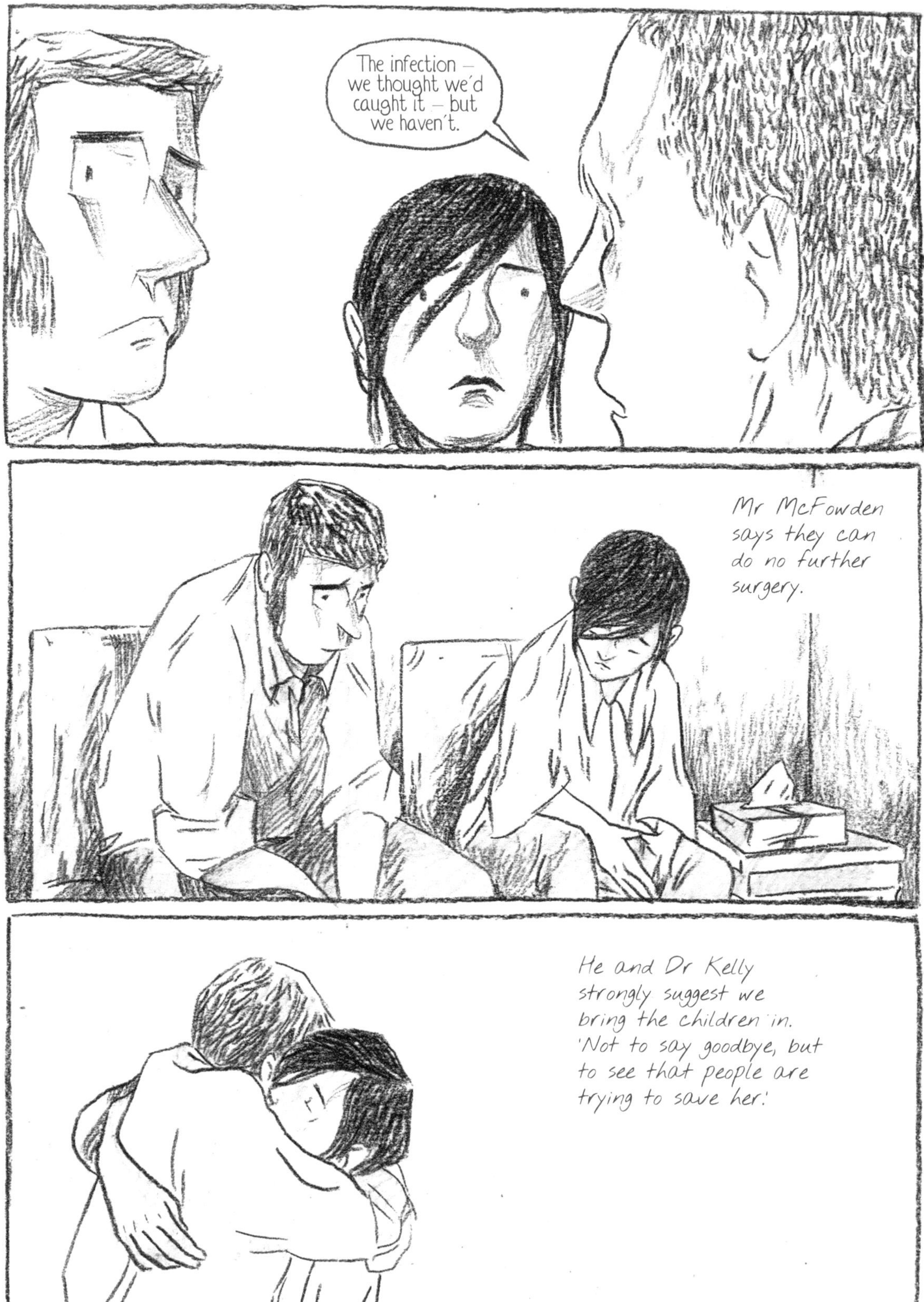
The infection – we thought we'd caught it – but we haven't.
Mr McFowden says they can do no further surgery.
He and Dr Kelly strongly suggest we bring the children in. 'Not to say goodbye, but to see that people are trying to save her.'
I reel again... Becky is there.

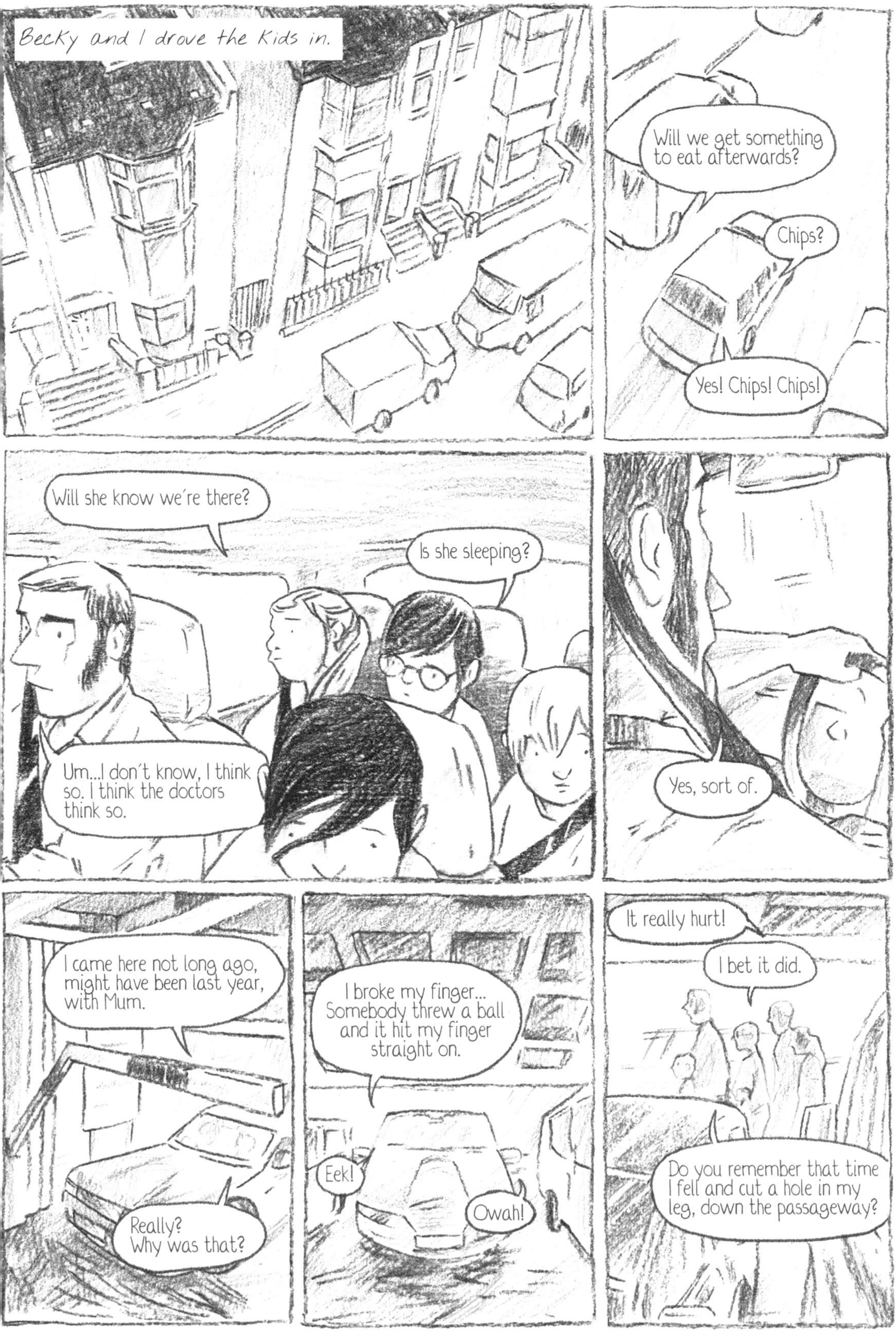
Becky and I drove the kids in.
Will we get something to eat afterwards?
Chips?
Yes! Chips! Chips!
Will she know we're there?
Is she sleeping?
Um...I don't know, I think so. I think the doctors think so.
Yes, sort of.
I came here not long ago, might have been last year, with Mum.
Really? Why was that?
I broke my finger... Somebody threw a ball and it hit my finger straight on.
Eek!
Owah!
It really hurt!
I bet it did.
Do you remember that time I fell and cut a hole in my leg, down the passageway?

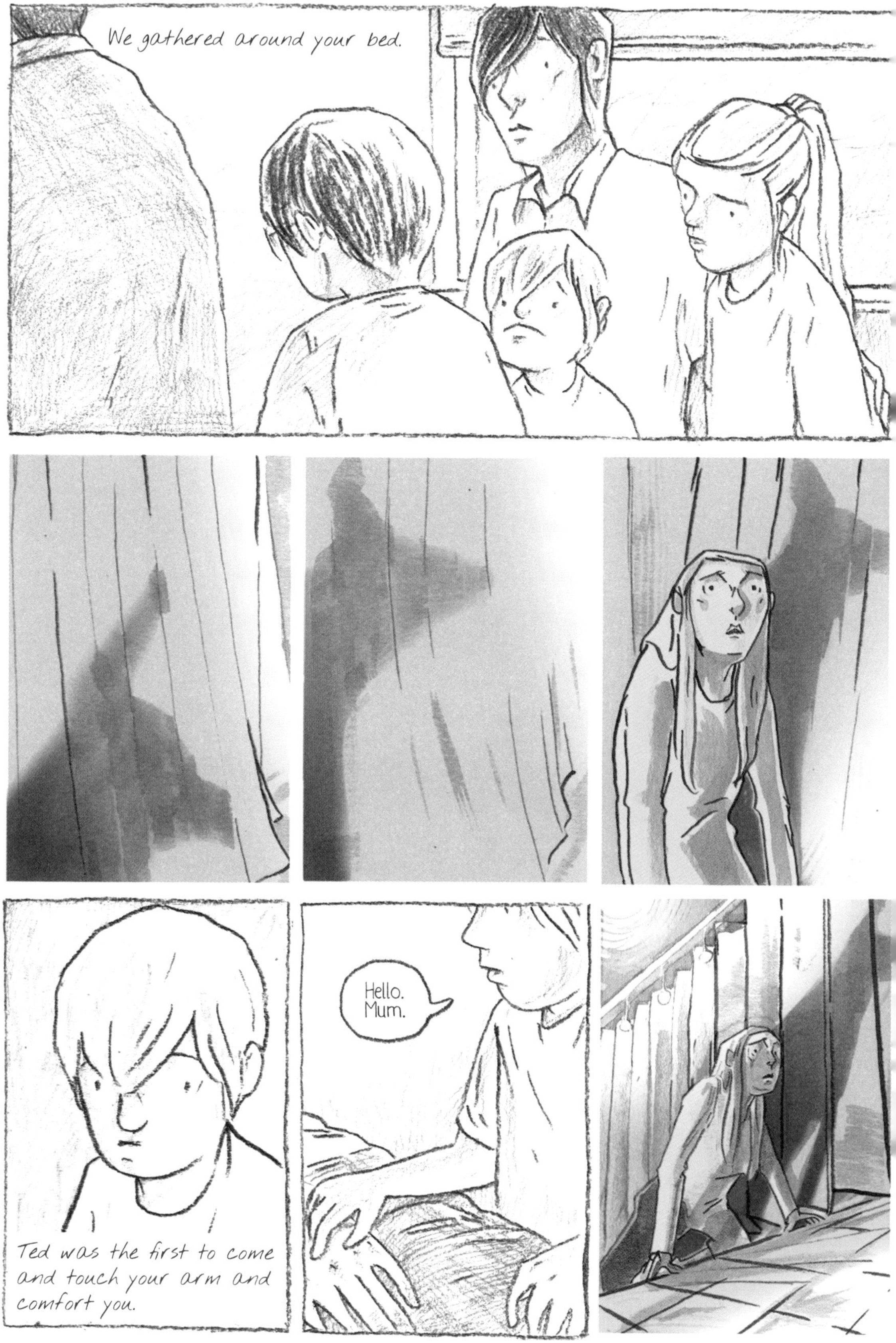
We gathered around your bed.
Ted was the first to come and touch your arm and comfort you.
Hello. Mum.

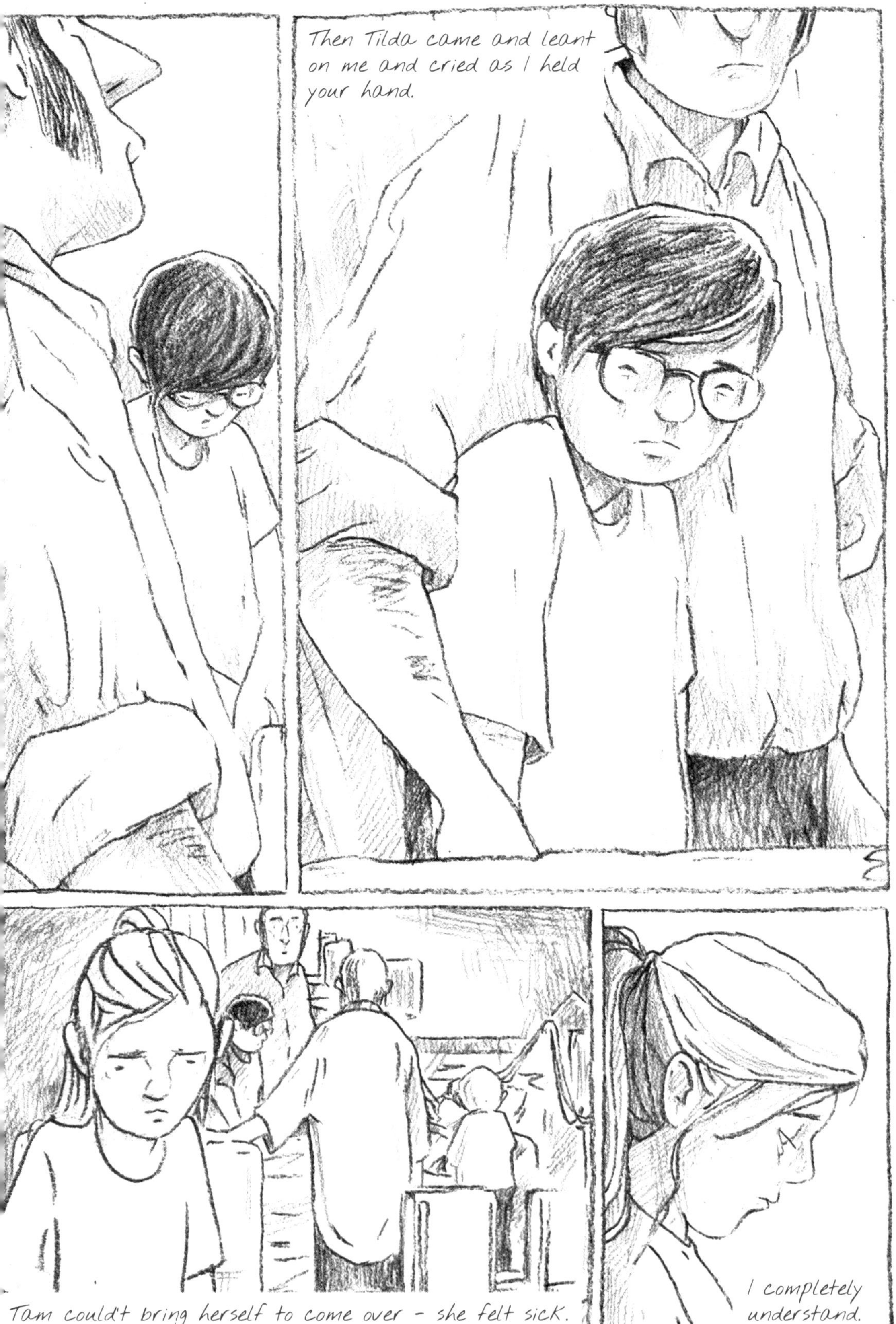
Then Tilda came and leant on me and cried as I held your hand.
Tam could't bring herself to come over - she felt sick.
I completely understand.

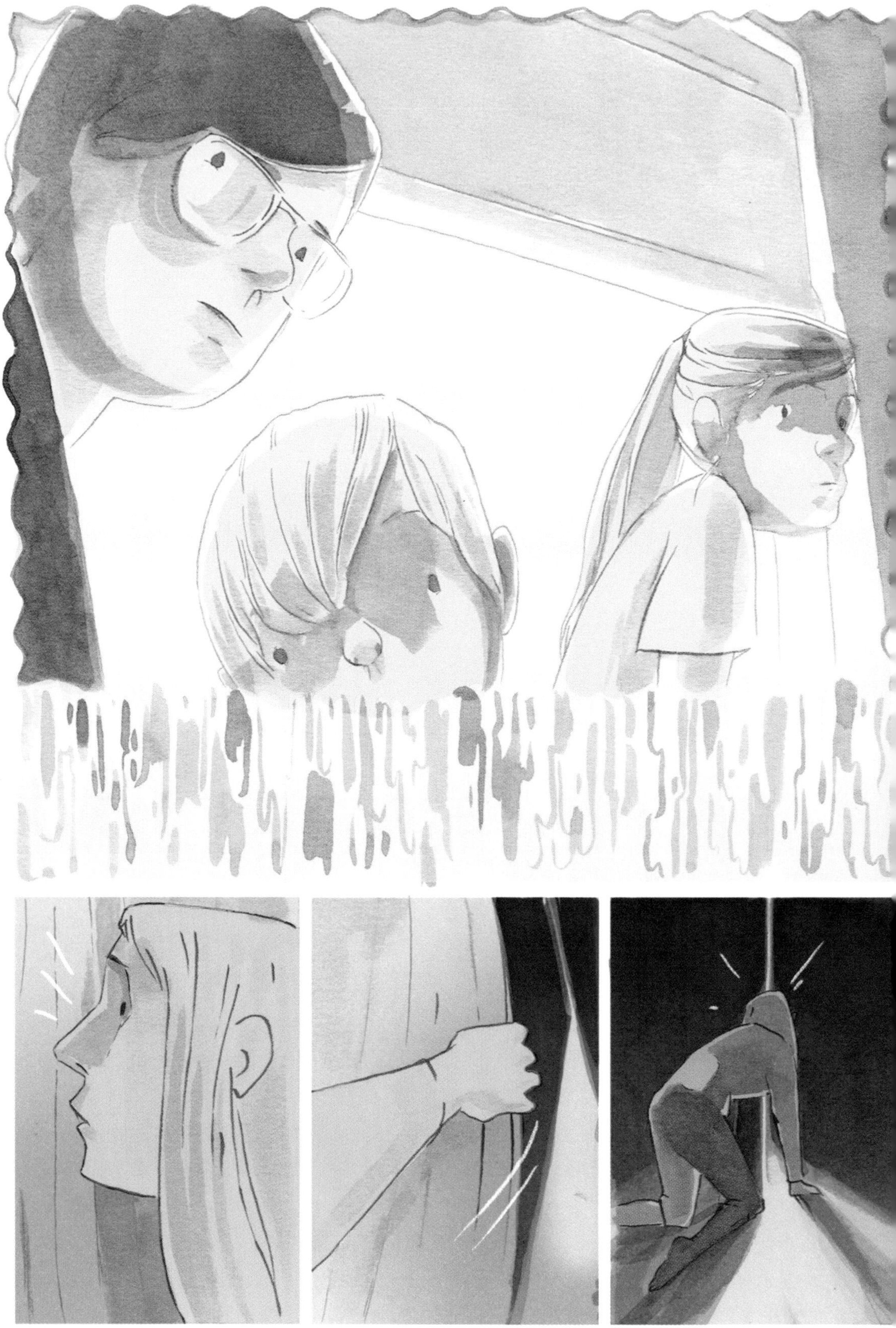

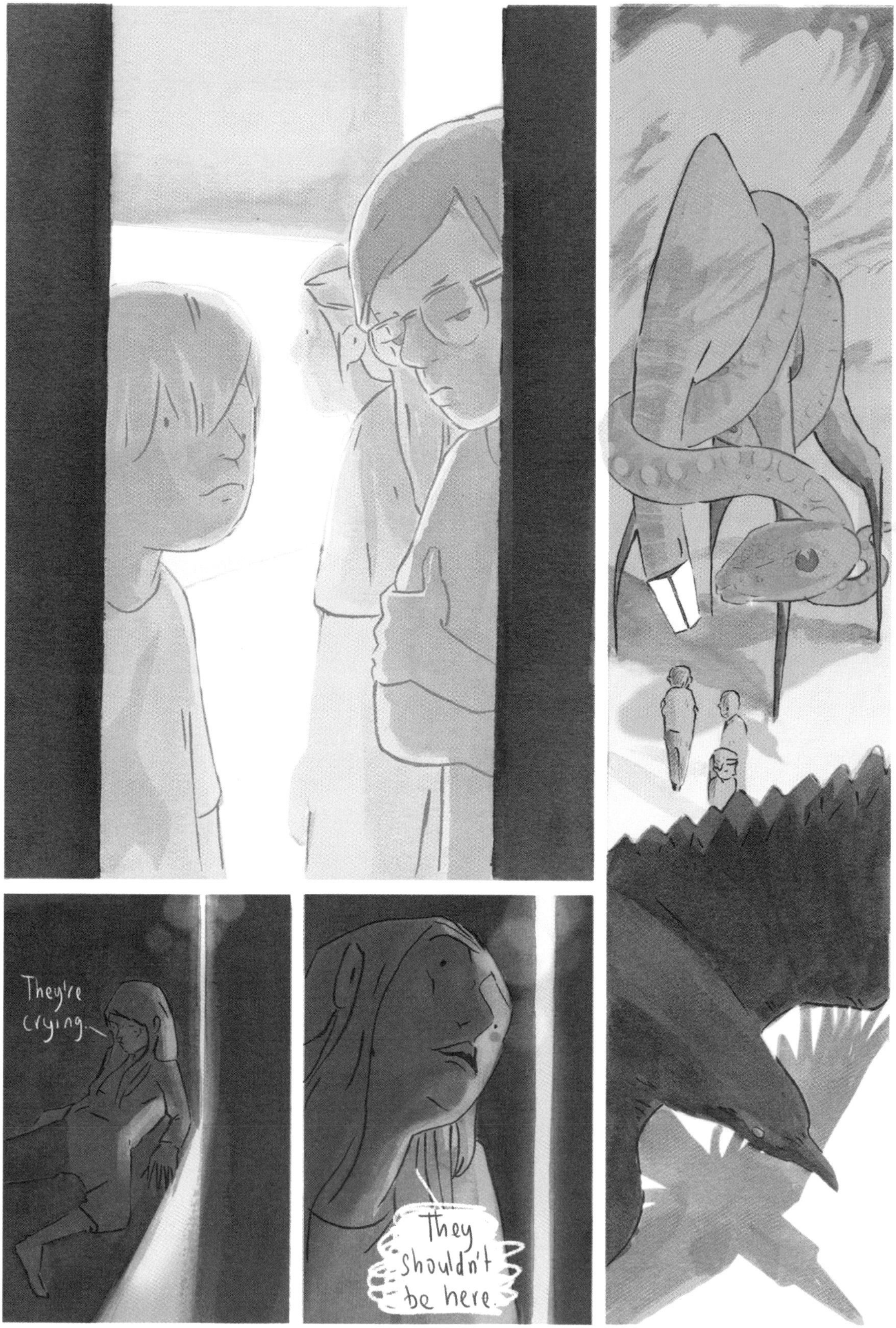
They're crying.
They shouldn't be here.

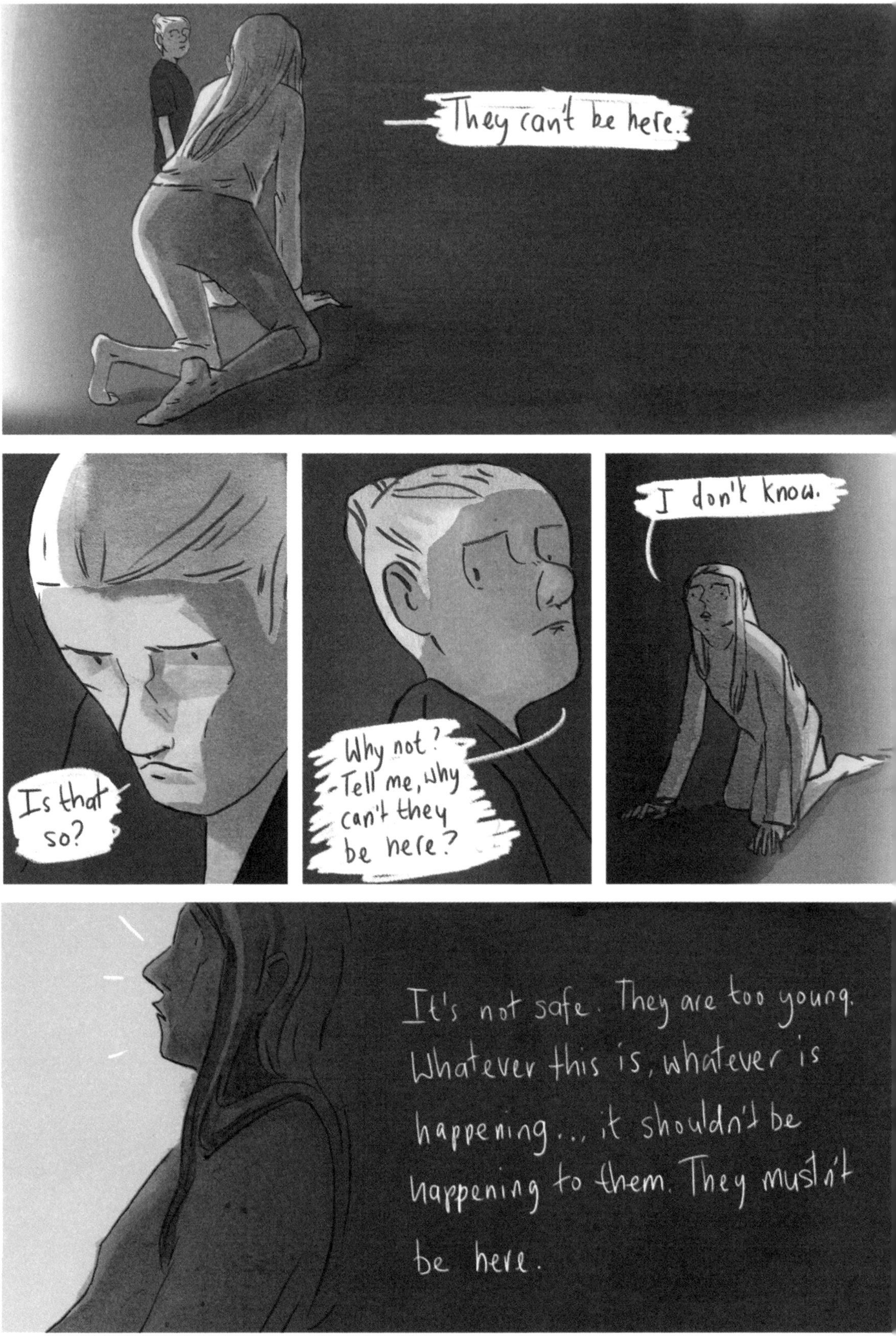
They can't be here.
Is that so?
Why not? Tell me, why can't they be here?
I don't know.
It's not safe. They are too young. Whatever this is, whatever is happening... it shouldn't be happening to them. They mustn't be here.

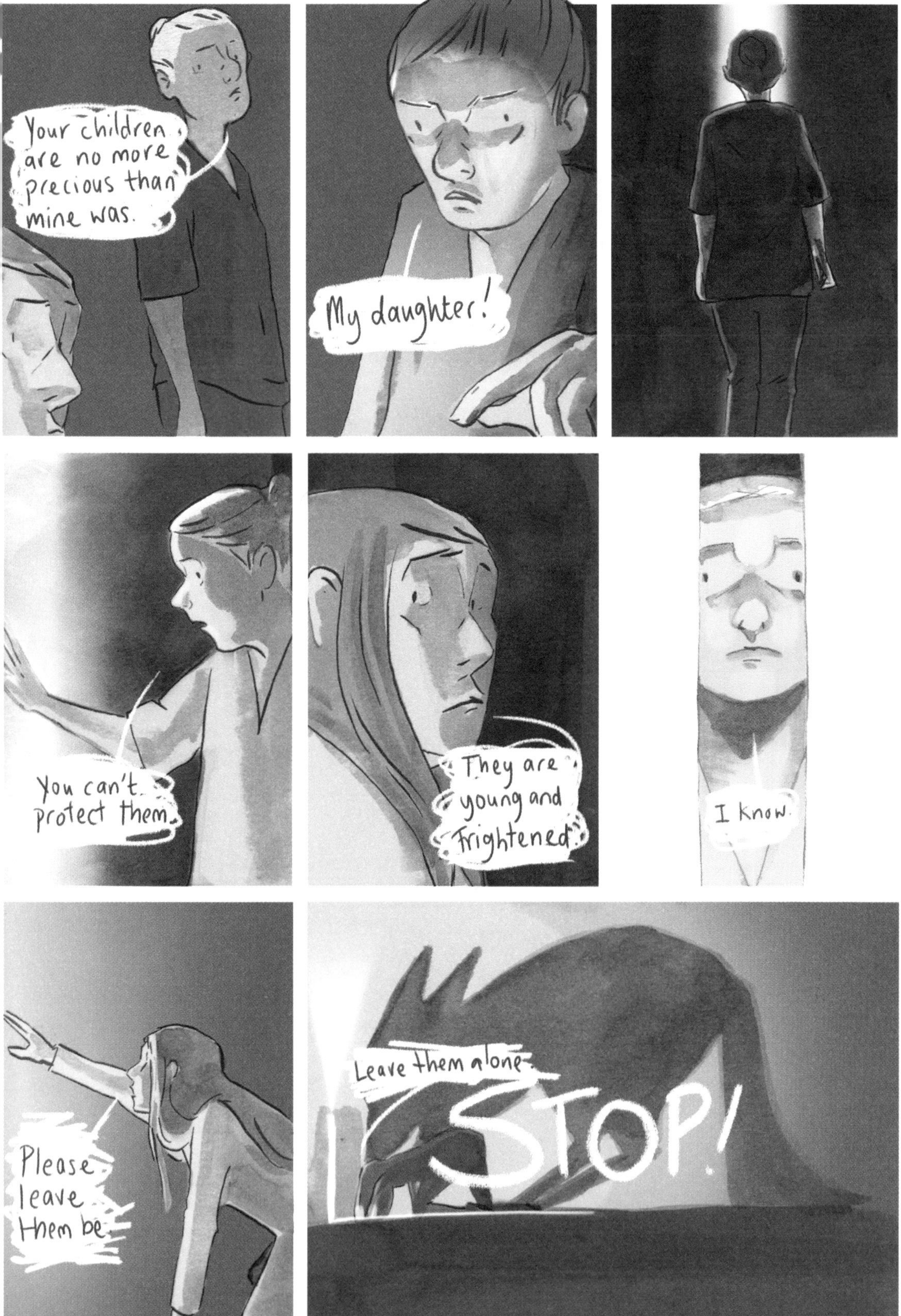
Your children are no more precious than mine was.
My daughter!
You can't protect them.
They are young and frightened.
I know.
Please leave them be.
Leave them alone.
STOP!

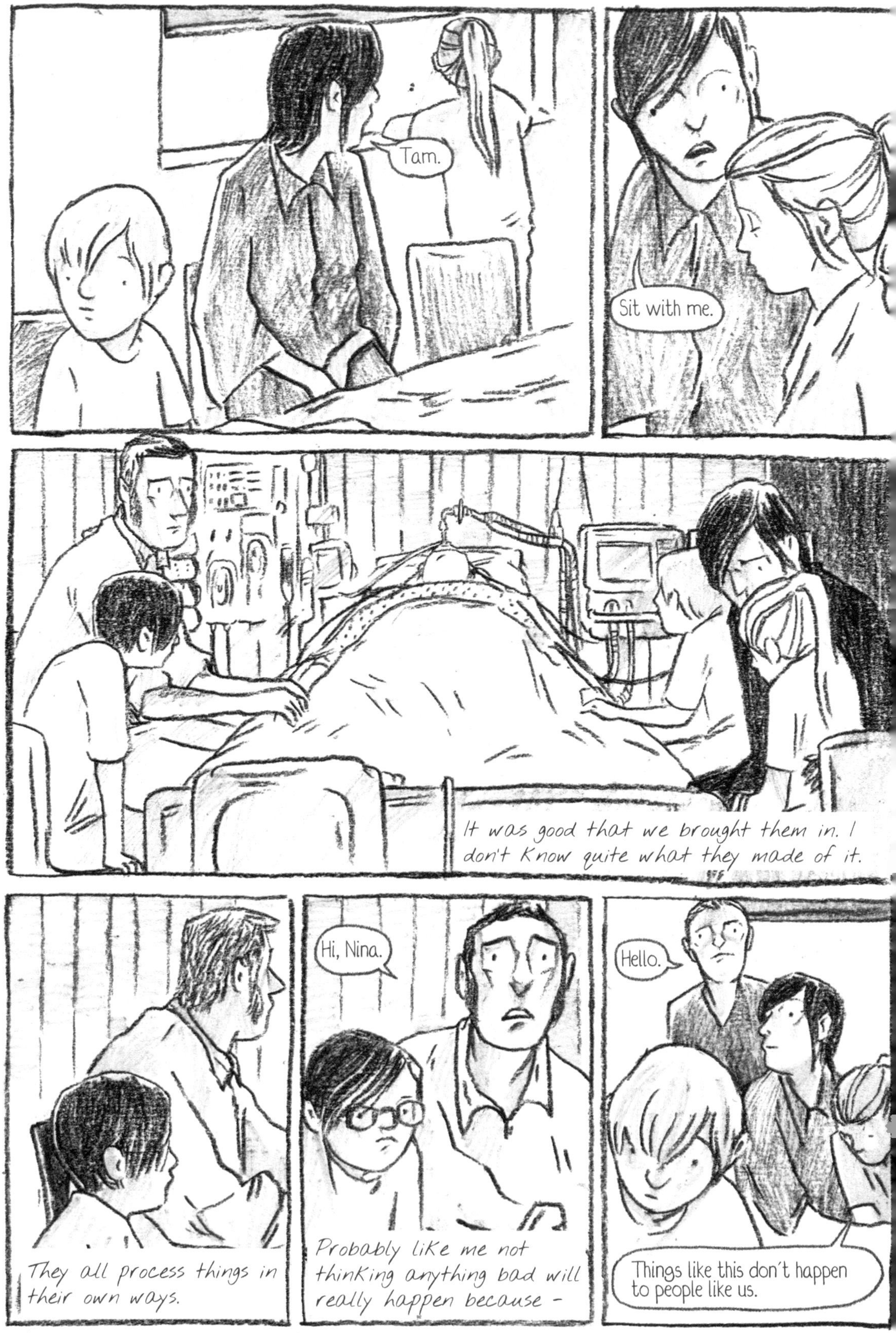
Tam.
Sit with me.
It was good that we brought them in. I don't know quite what they made of it.
They all process things in their own ways.
Hi, Nina.
Probably like me not thinking anything bad will really happen because -
Hello.
Things like this don't happen to people like us.

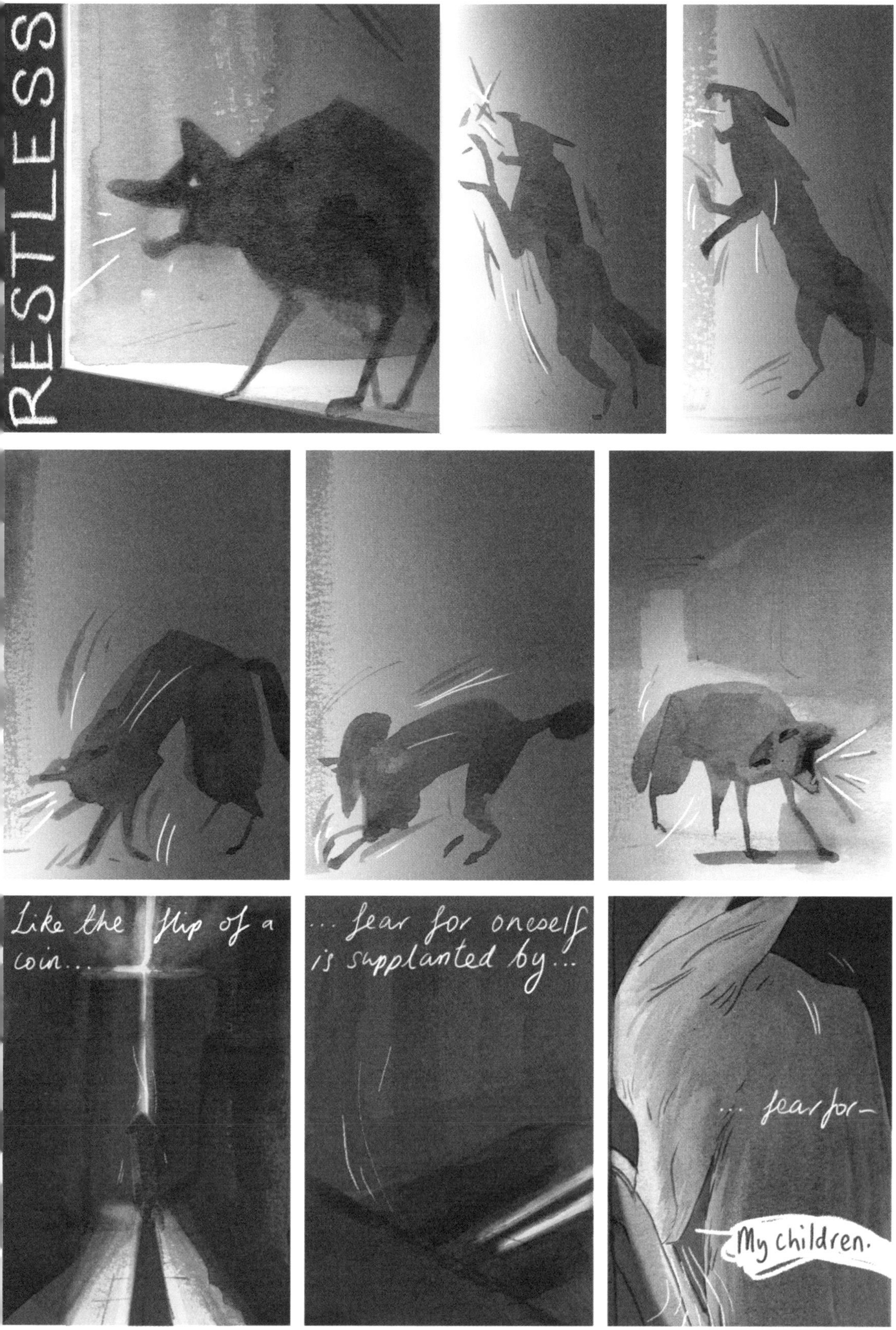
RESTLESS
Like the flip of a coin...
... fear for oneself is supplanted by...
... fear for—
—My children.

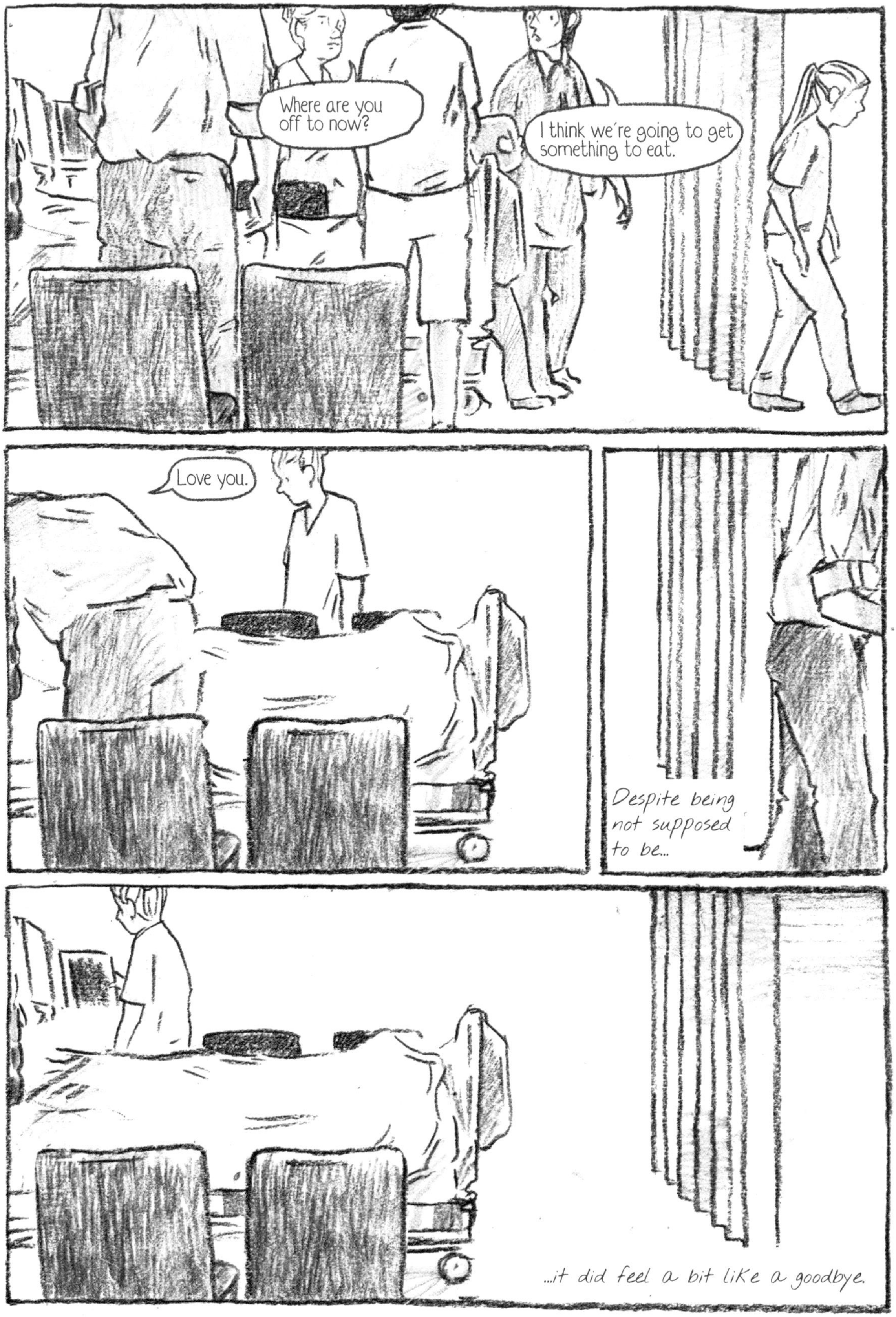
Where are you off to now?
I think we're going to get something to eat.
Love you.
Despite being not supposed to be...
...it did feel a bit like a goodbye.

NO

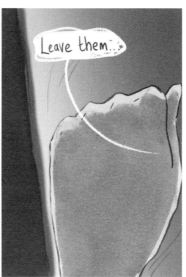

Leave them...

... alone.

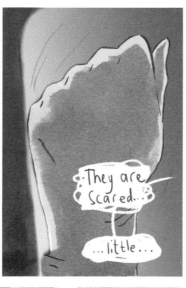

They are scared...

...little...

... and Ted only eats fish fingers.

117

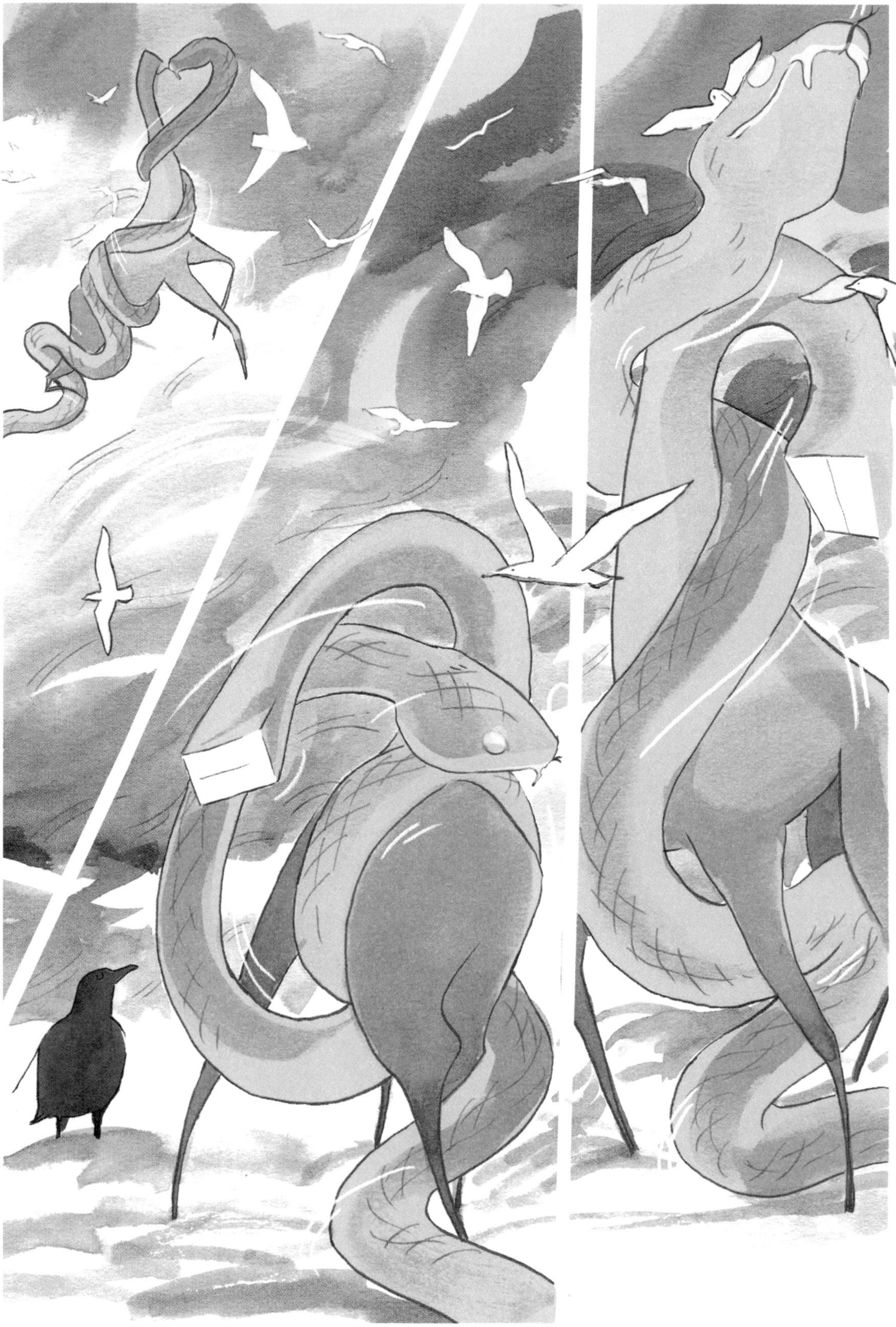

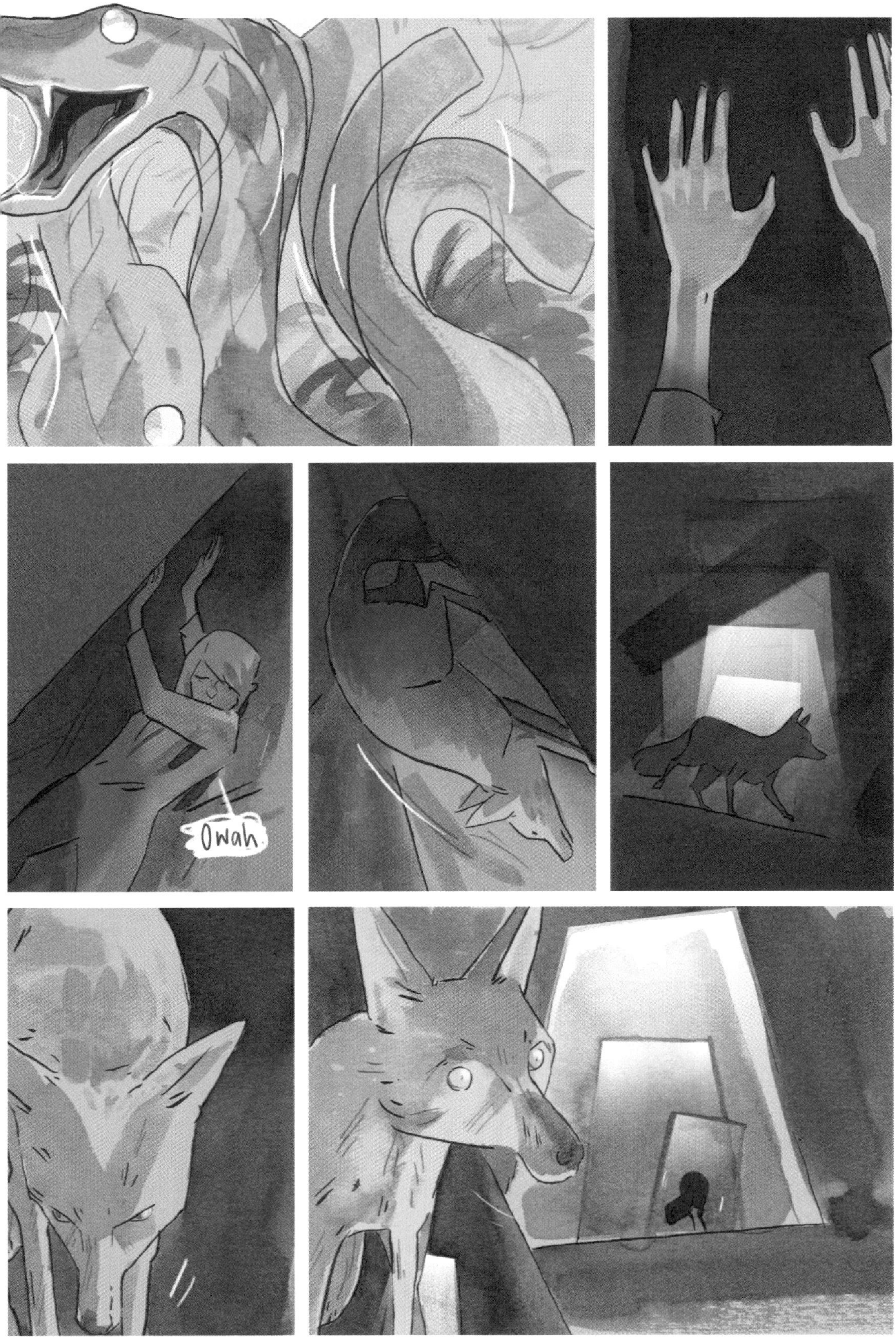
Owah

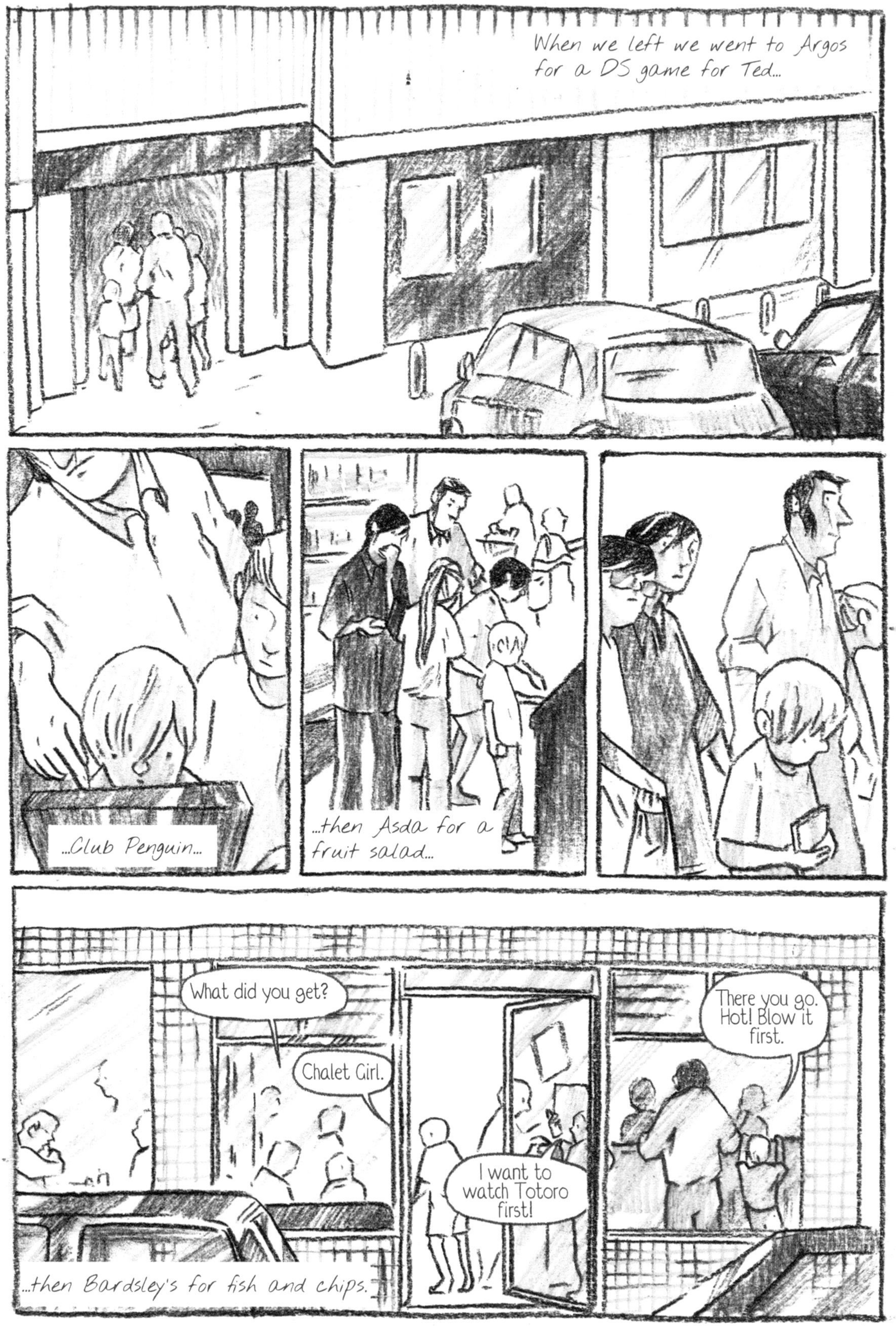
When we left we went to Argos for a DS game for Ted...
...Club Penguin...
...then Asda for a fruit salad...
What did you get?
Chalet Girl.
I want to watch Totoro first!
There you go. Hot! Blow it first.
...then Bardsley's for fish and chips.

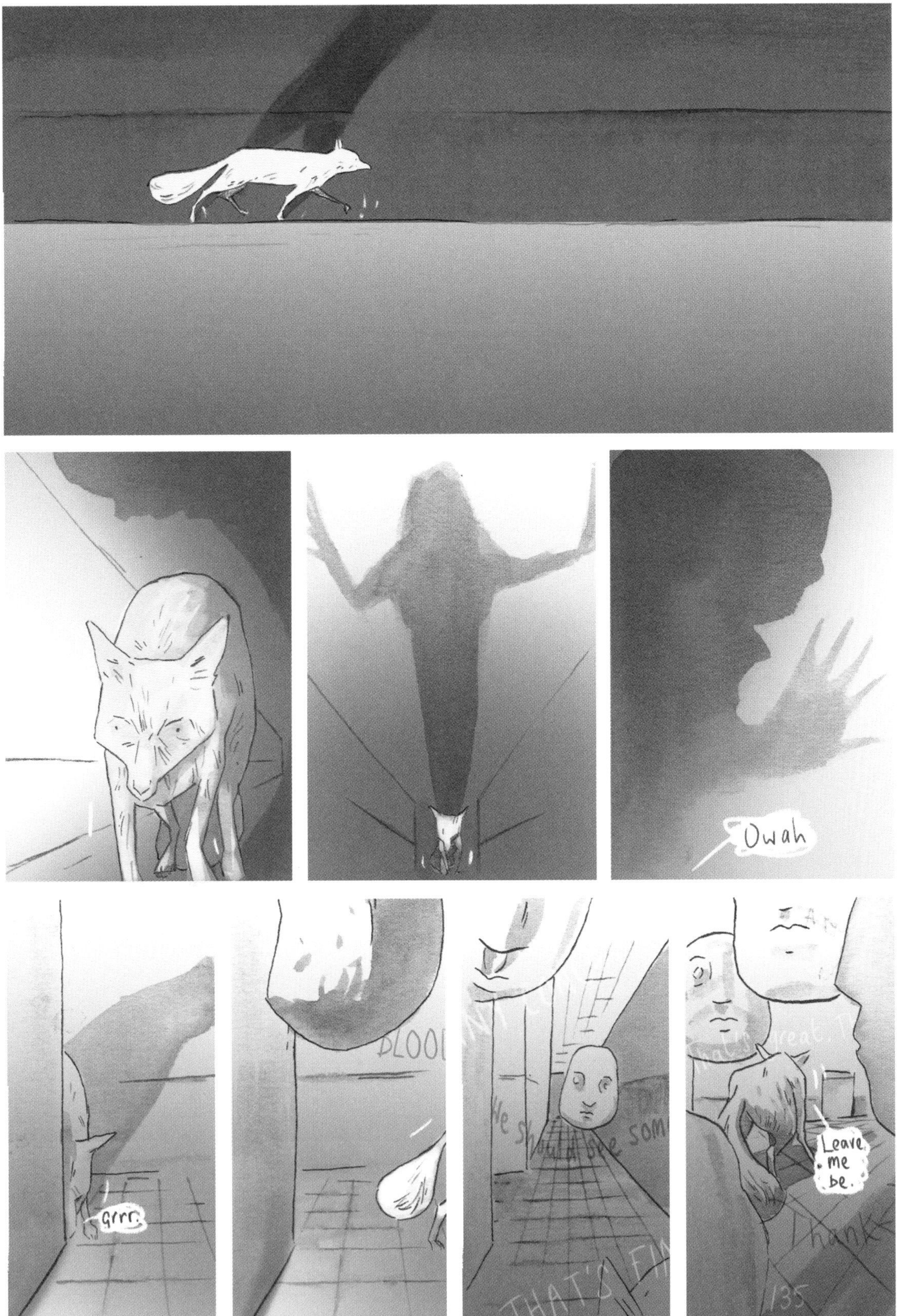
Owah
grrr.
Leave me be.

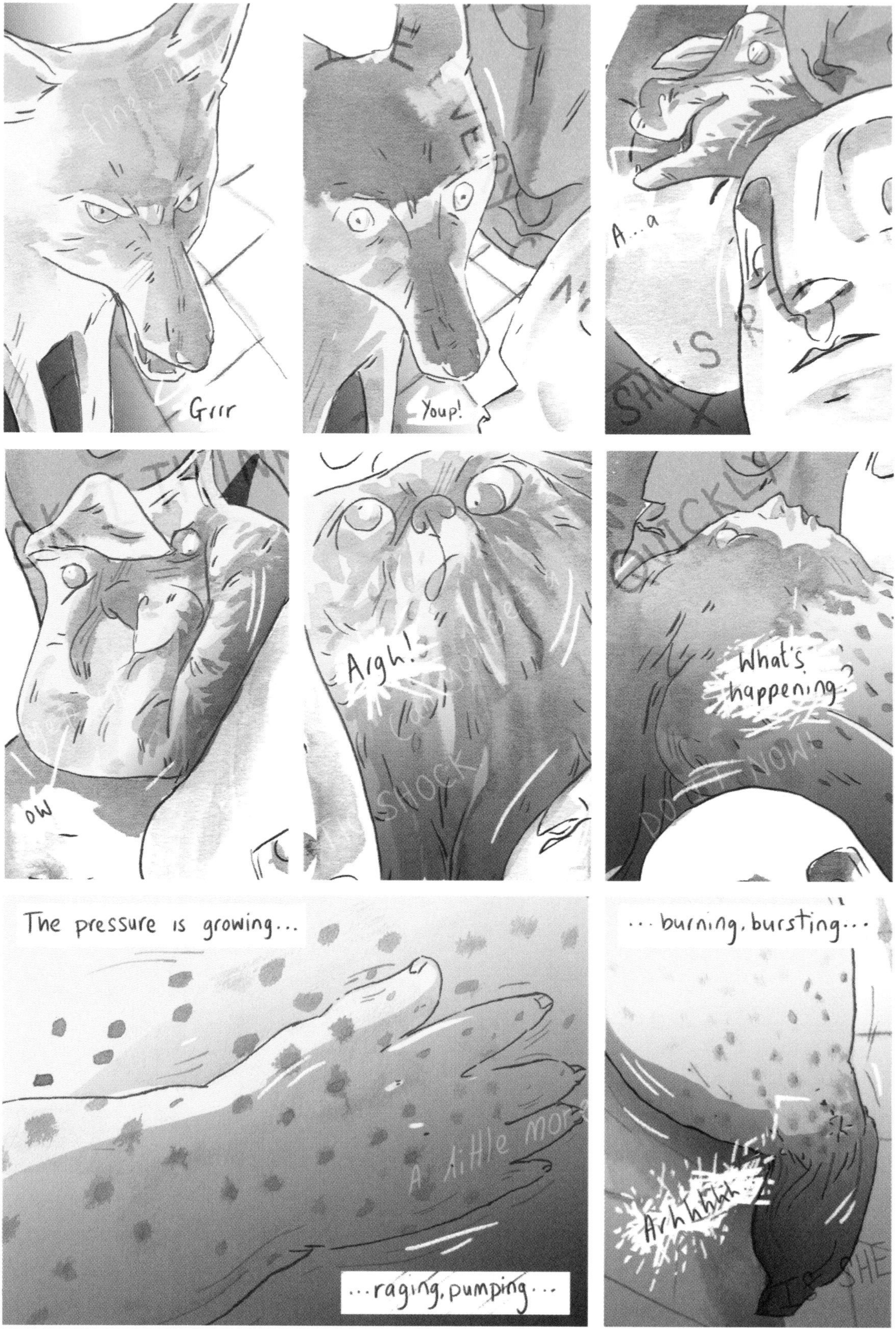
Grrr
Youp!
A...a
ow
Argh!
What's happening?
The pressure is growing...
A little more
...raging, pumping...
...burning, bursting...
Arhhhhh

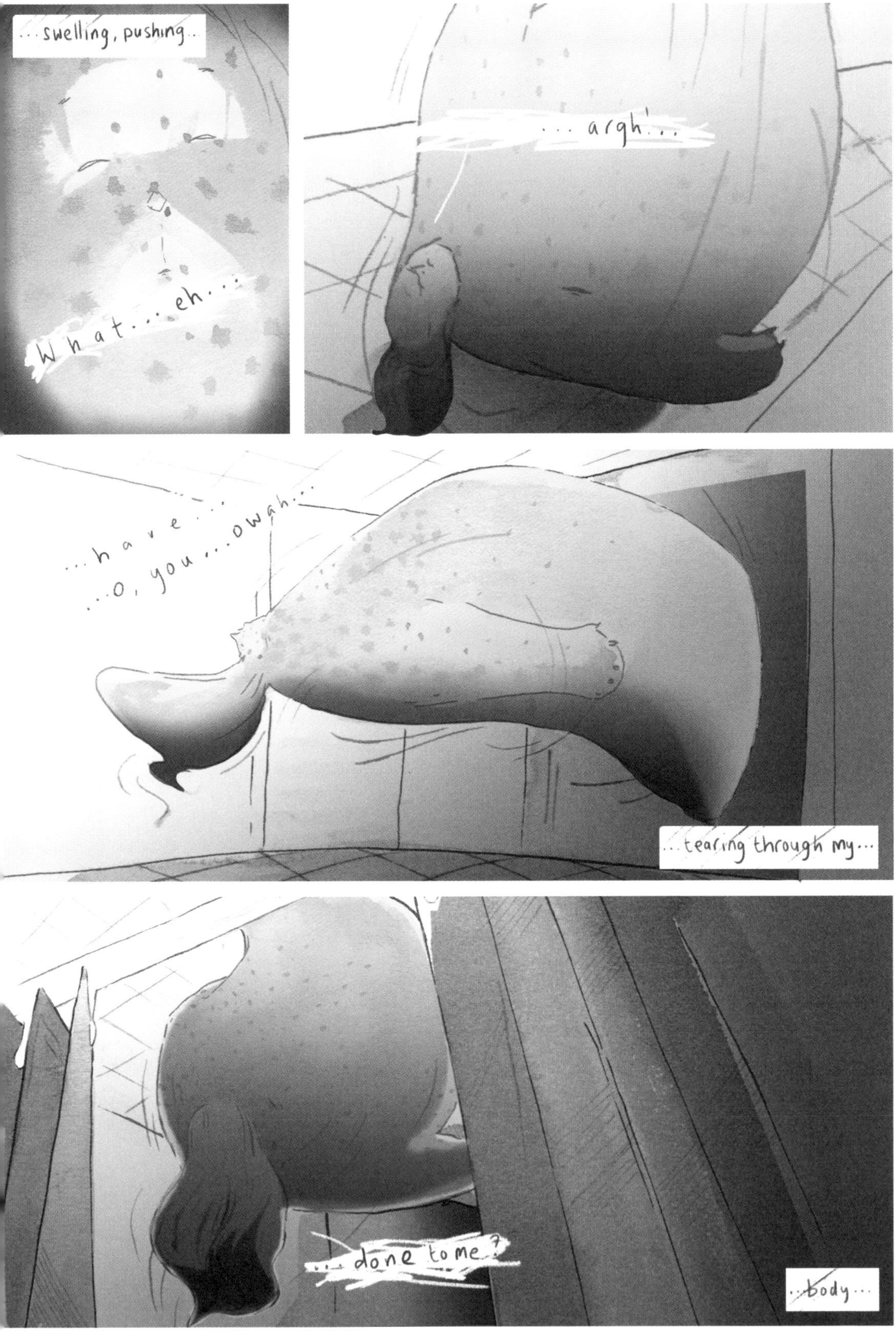
...swelling, pushing...
What...eh...
...argh!...
...have...
...o, you...owah...
...tearing through my...
...done to me?
...body...

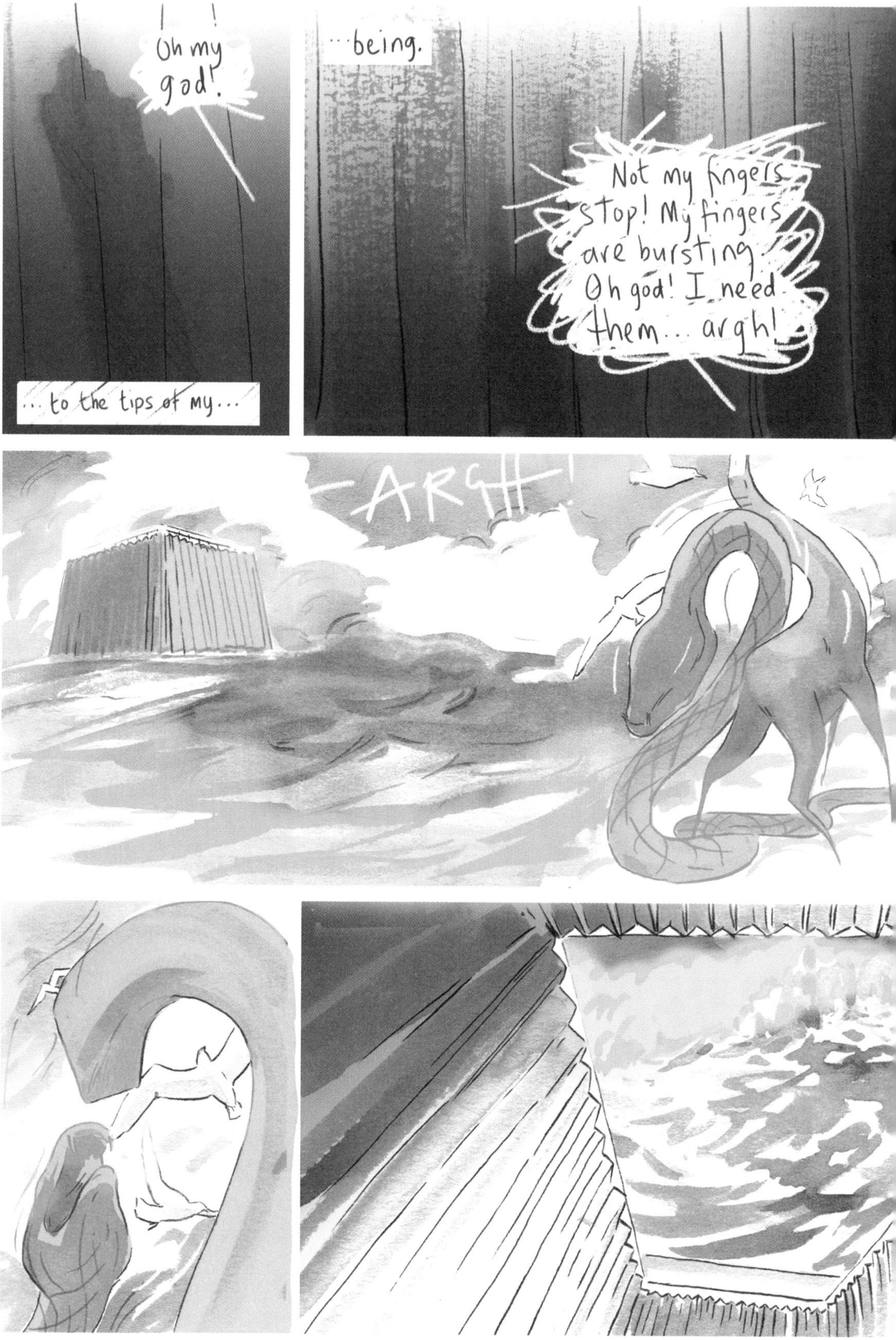

Oh my god!
... to the tips of my...
...being.
Not my fingers stop! My fingers are bursting. Oh god! I need them... argh!
ARGH!

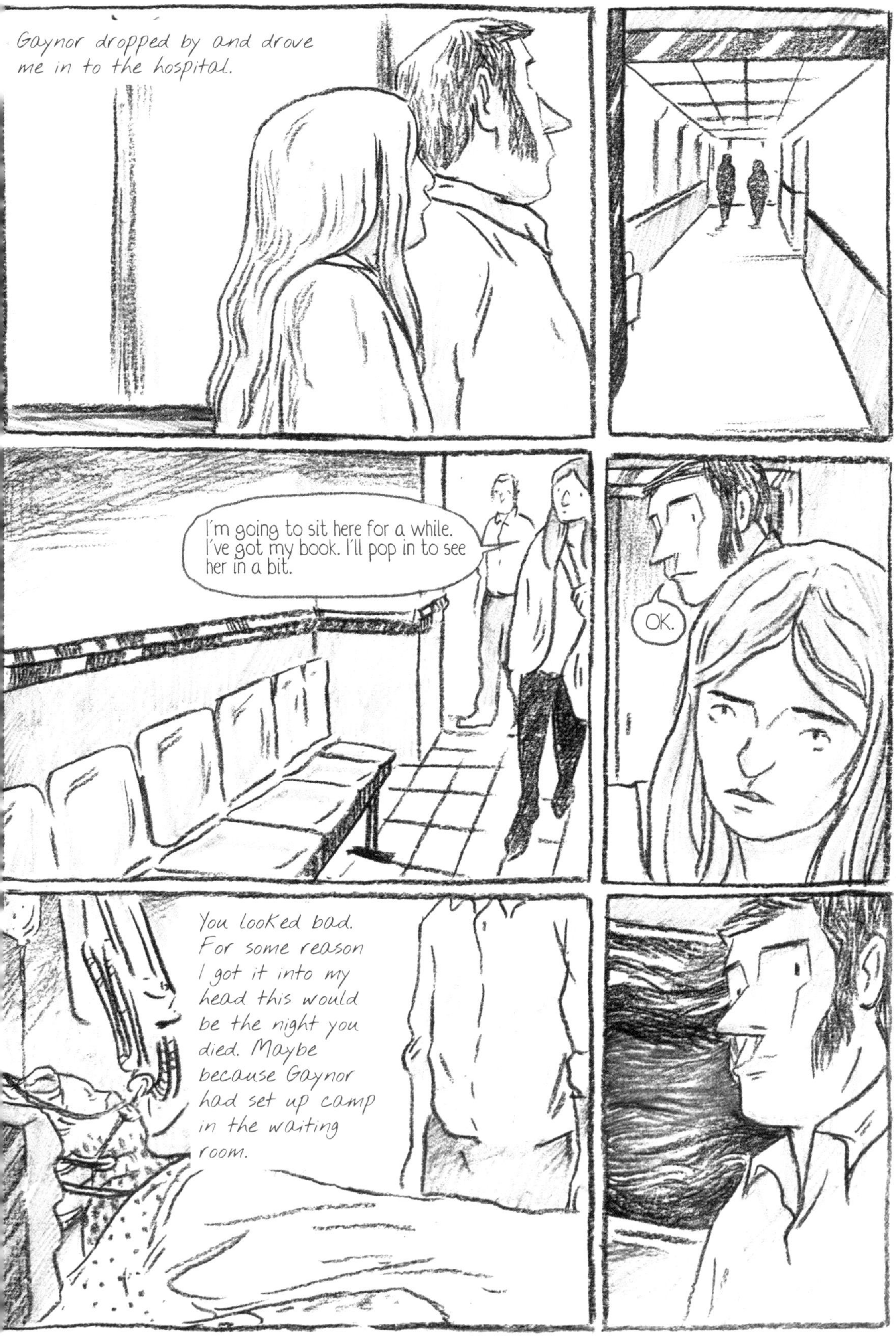

Gaynor dropped by and drove me in to the hospital.
I'm going to sit here for a while. I've got my book. I'll pop in to see her in a bit.
OK.
You looked bad. For some reason I got it into my head this would be the night you died. Maybe because Gaynor had set up camp in the waiting room.

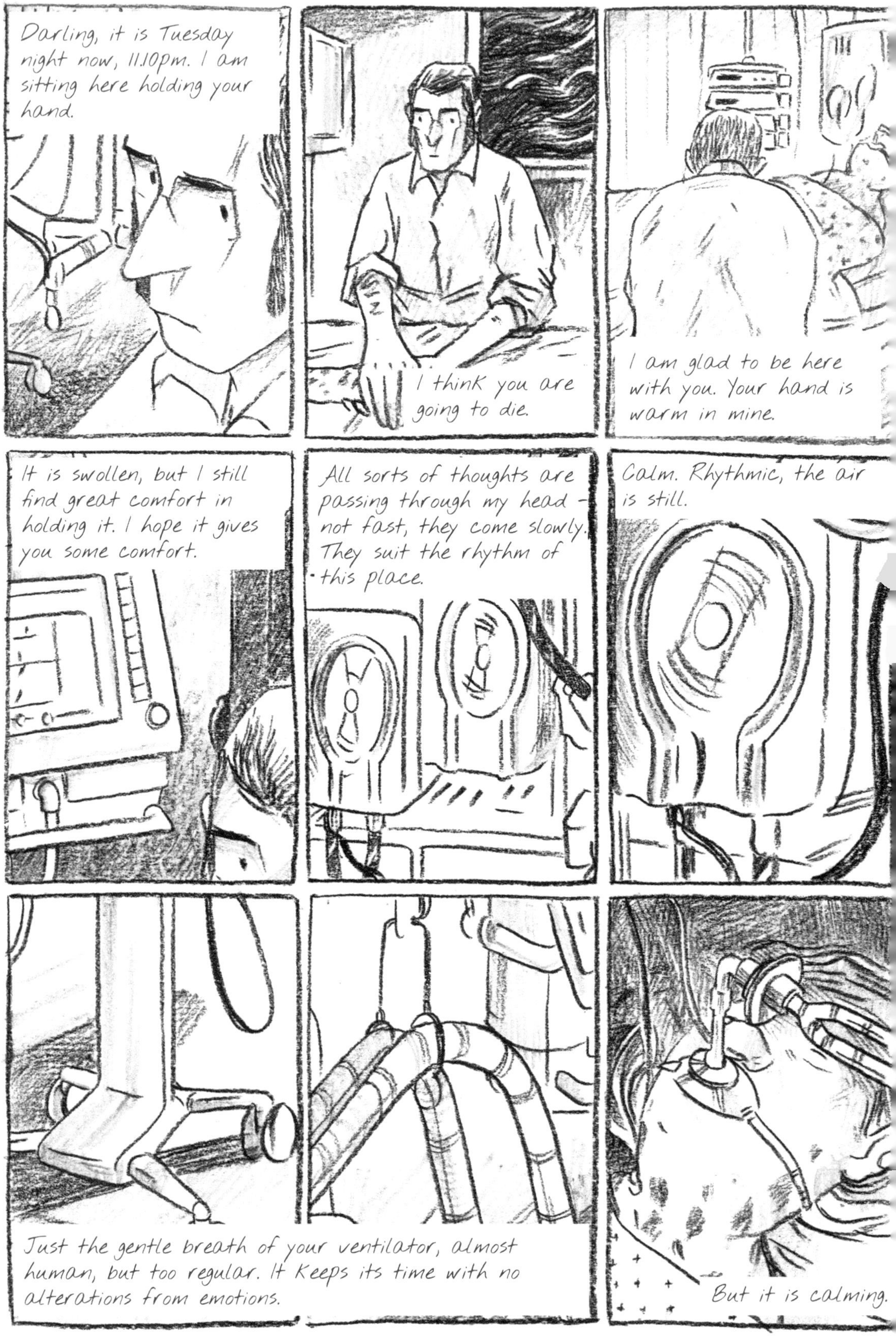
Darling, it is Tuesday night now, 11.10pm. I am sitting here holding your hand.
I think you are going to die.
I am glad to be here with you. Your hand is warm in mine.
It is swollen, but I still find great comfort in holding it. I hope it gives you some comfort.
All sorts of thoughts are passing through my head - not fast, they come slowly. They suit the rhythm of this place.
Calm. Rhythmic, the air is still.
Just the gentle breath of your ventilator, almost human, but too regular. It keeps its time with no alterations from emotions.
But it is calming.

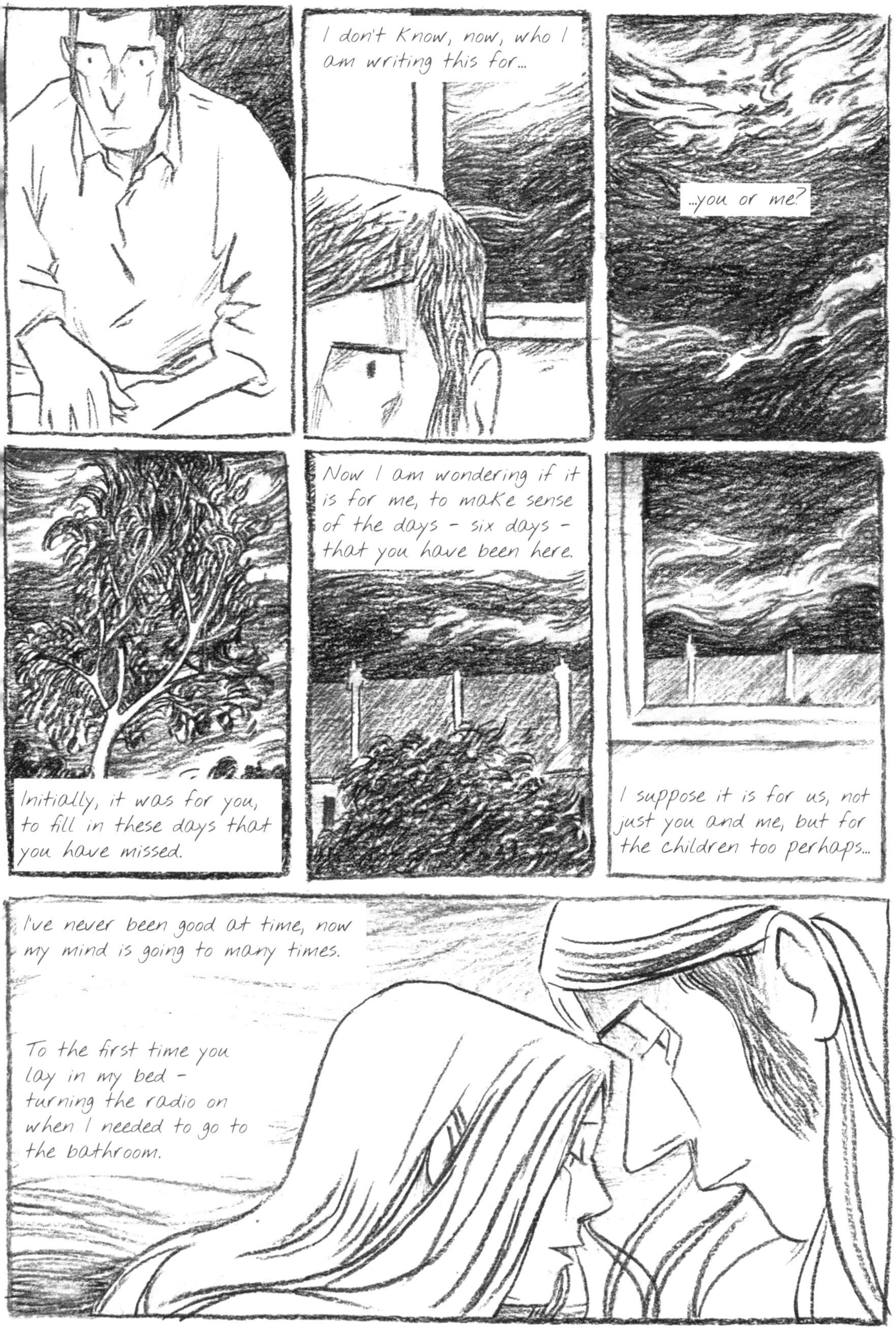
I don't know, now, who I am writing this for...
...you or me?
Initially, it was for you, to fill in these days that you have missed.
Now I am wondering if it is for me, to make sense of the days - six days - that you have been here.
I suppose it is for us, not just you and me, but for the children too perhaps...
I've never been good at time, now my mind is going to many times.
To the first time you lay in my bed - turning the radio on when I needed to go to the bathroom.

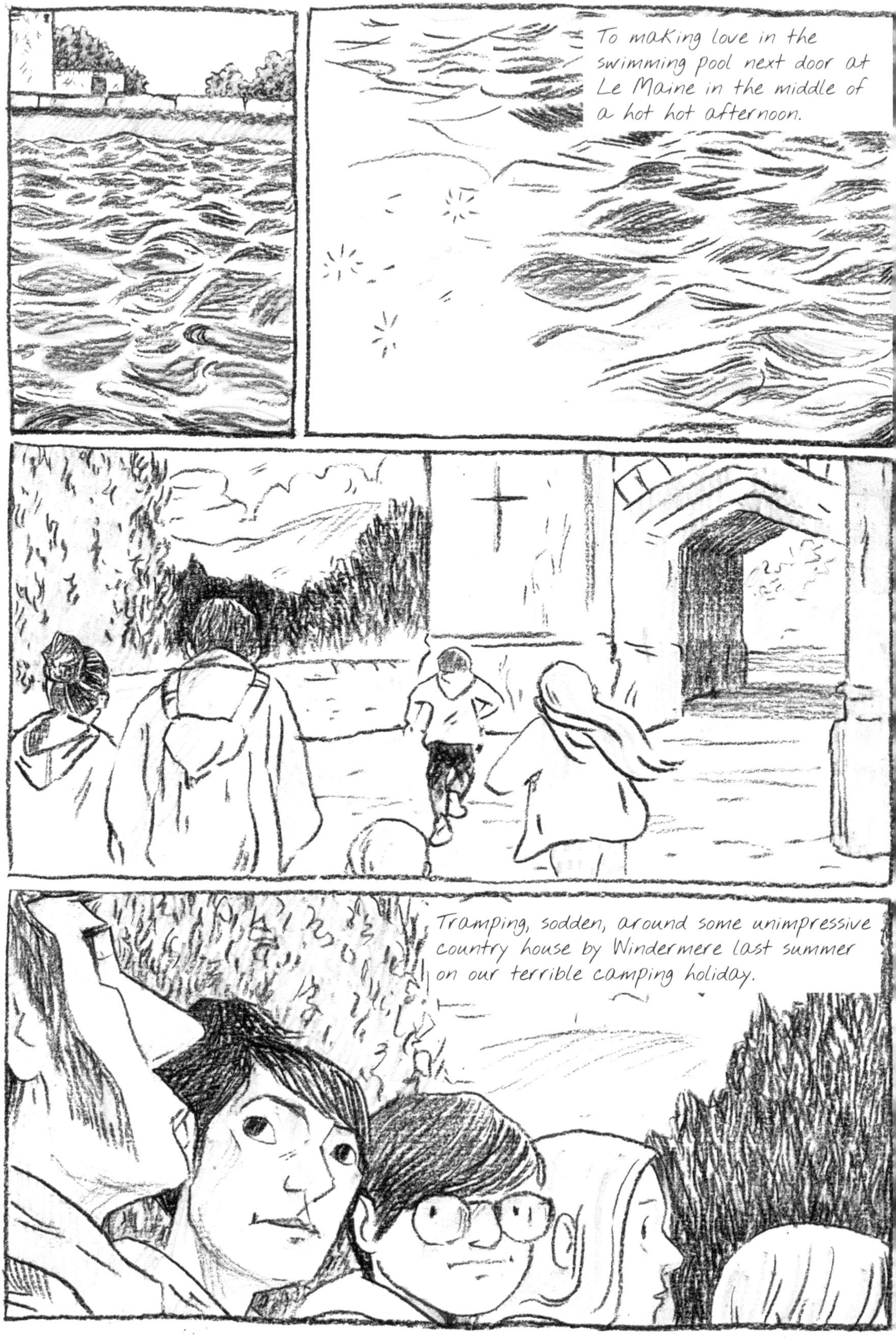

To making love in the swimming pool next door at Le Maine in the middle of a hot hot afternoon.
Tramping, sodden, around some unimpressive country house by Windermere last summer on our terrible camping holiday.

To this afternoon, waiting for the consultant surgeon and doctor and nurse, knowing things were badly wrong, not despairing any more. I did that last Friday, almost knowing what they were going to say, not the details, obviously, but knowing it was going to be bad, not really life-changing – our lives changed already. Last Friday? Last Thursday? Wednesday? Who knows when our lives were changed, we'll never know quite when.

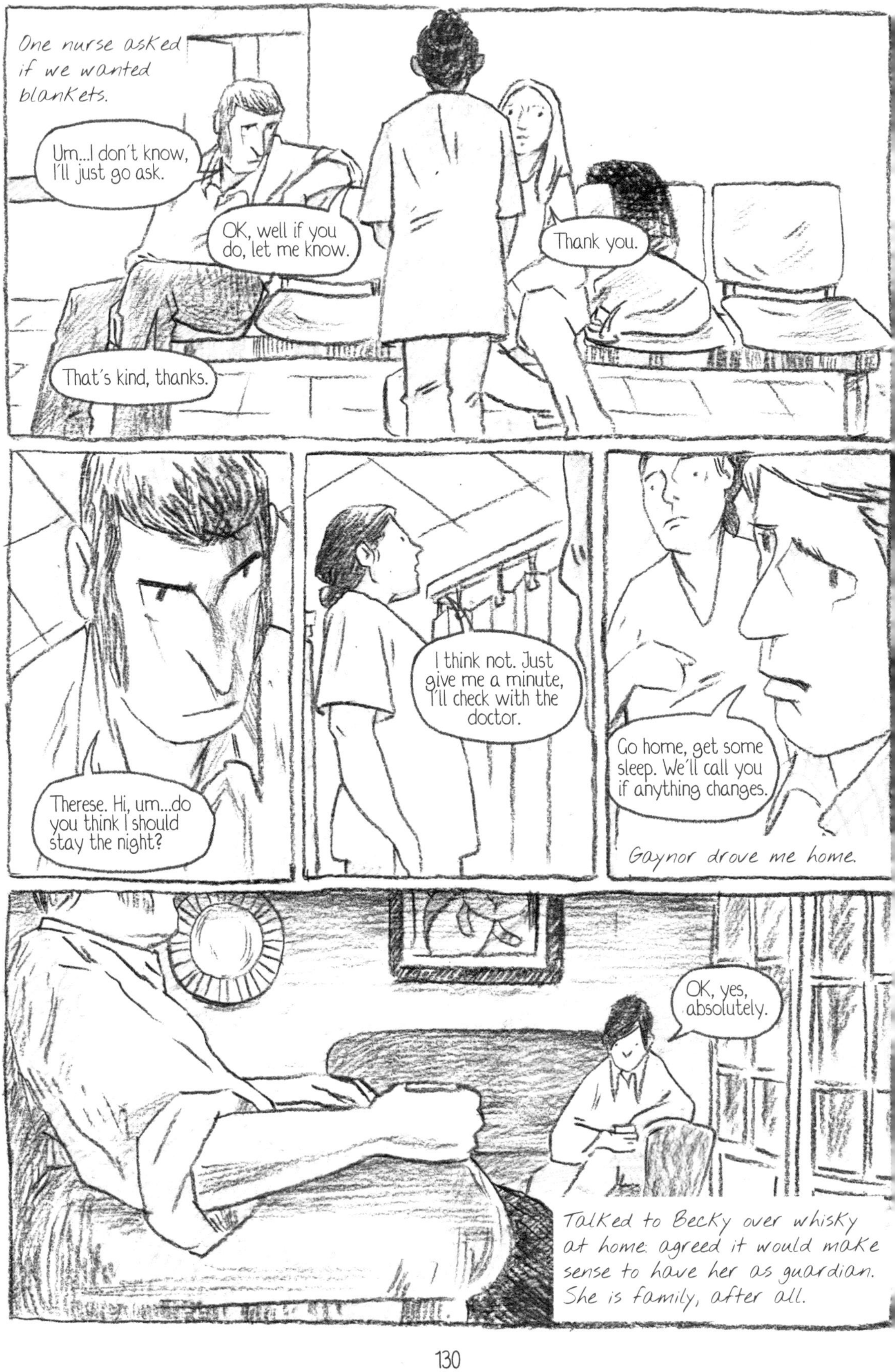
One nurse asked if we wanted blankets.
Um...I don't know, I'll just go ask.
OK, well if you do, let me know.
Thank you.
That's kind, thanks.
Therese. Hi, um...do you think I should stay the night?
I think not. Just give me a minute, I'll check with the doctor.
Go home, get some sleep. We'll call you if anything changes.
Gaynor drove me home.
OK, yes, absolutely.
Talked to Becky over whisky at home: agreed it would make sense to have her as guardian. She is family, after all.

WEDNESDAY 29th MAY

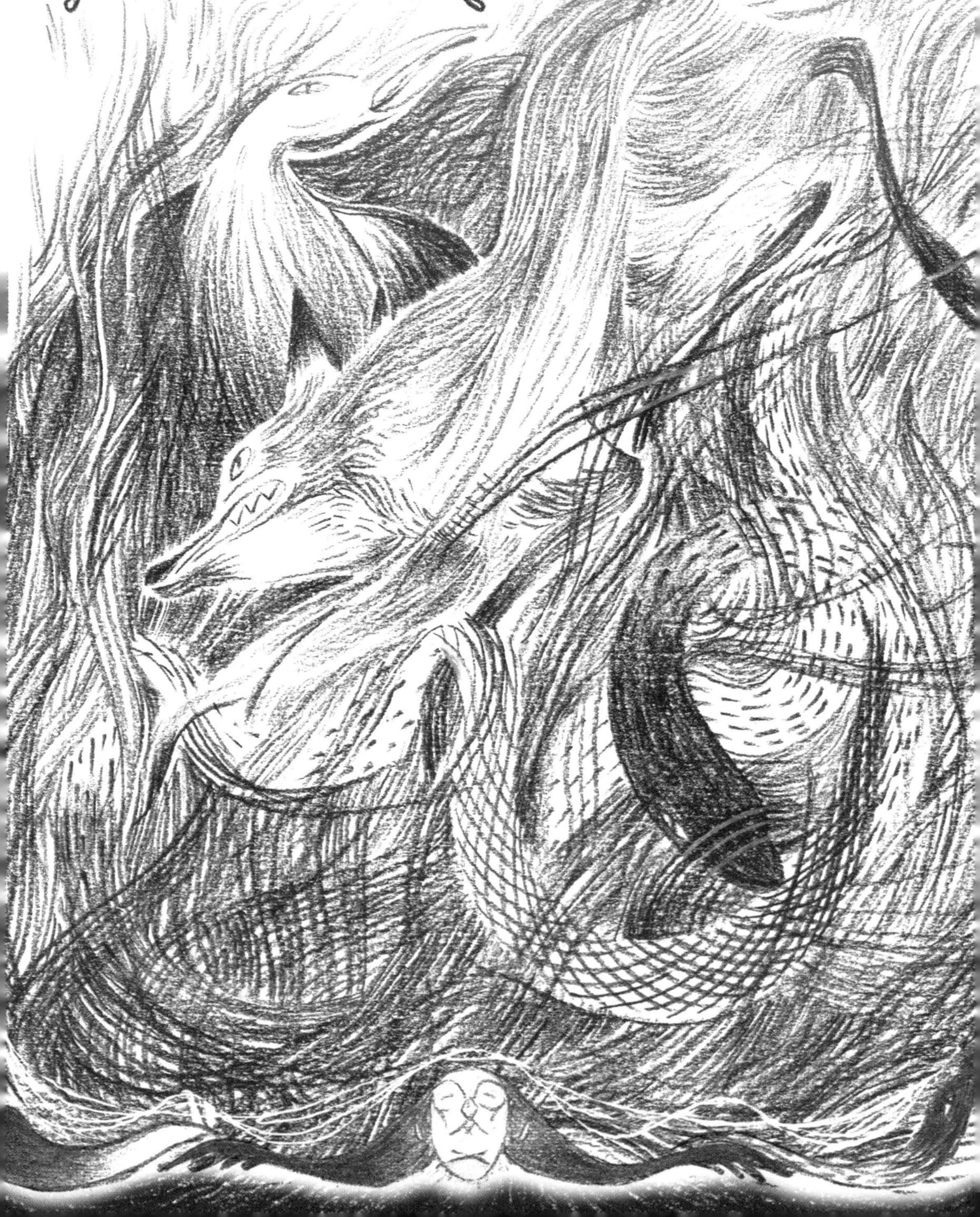

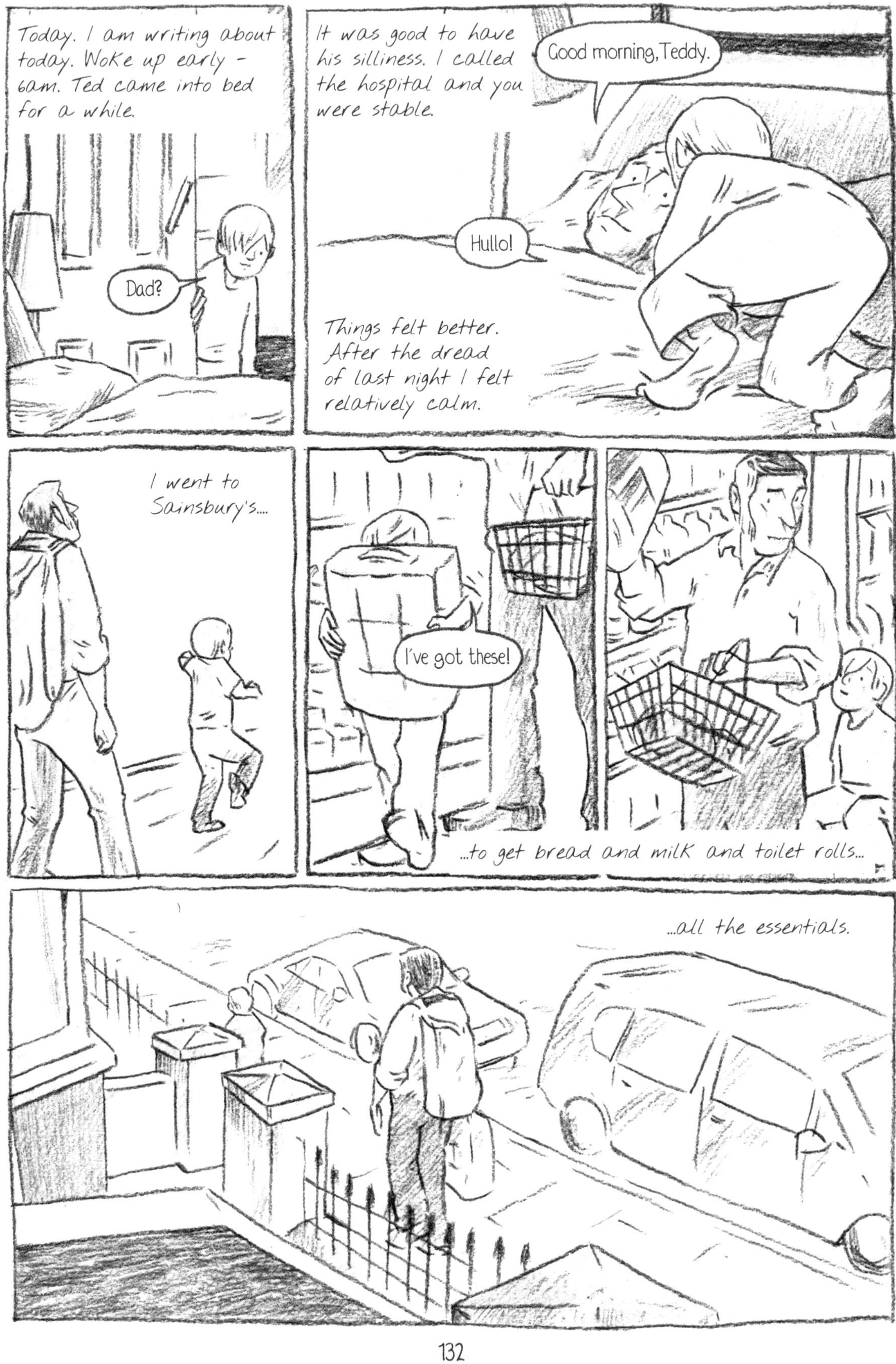

Today. I am writing about today. Woke up early - 6am. Ted came into bed for a while.
Dad?
It was good to have his silliness. I called the hospital and you were stable.
Good morning, Teddy.
Hullo!
Things felt better. After the dread of last night I felt relatively calm.
I went to Sainsbury's....
I've got these!
...to get bread and milk and toilet rolls...
...all the essentials.

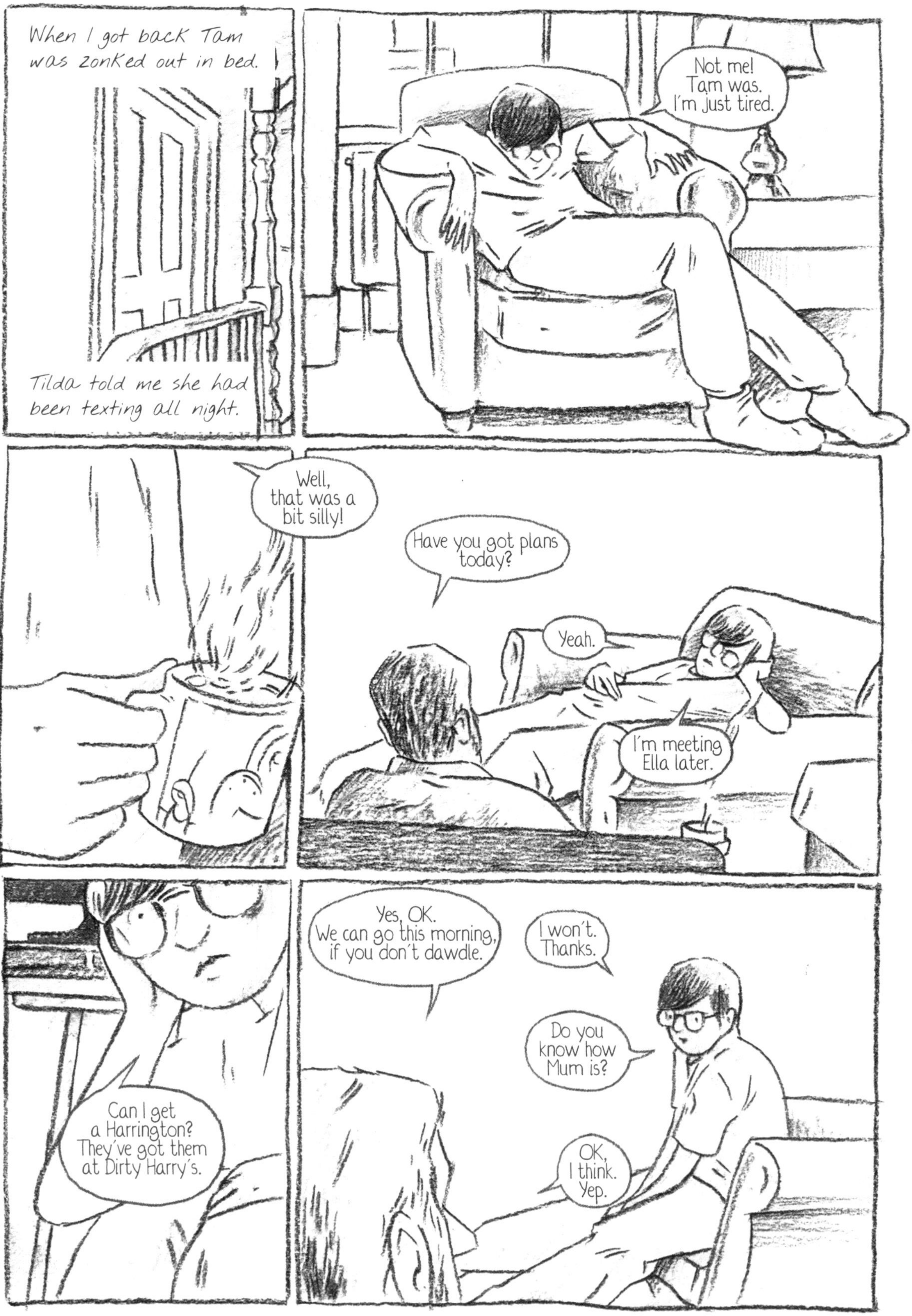
When I got back Tam was zonked out in bed.
Tilda told me she had been texting all night.
Not me! Tam was. I'm just tired.
Well, that was a bit silly!
Have you got plans today?
Yeah.
I'm meeting Ella later.
Can I get a Harrington? They've got them at Dirty Harry's.
Yes, OK. We can go this morning, if you don't dawdle.
I won't. Thanks.
Do you know how Mum is?
OK, I think. Yep.

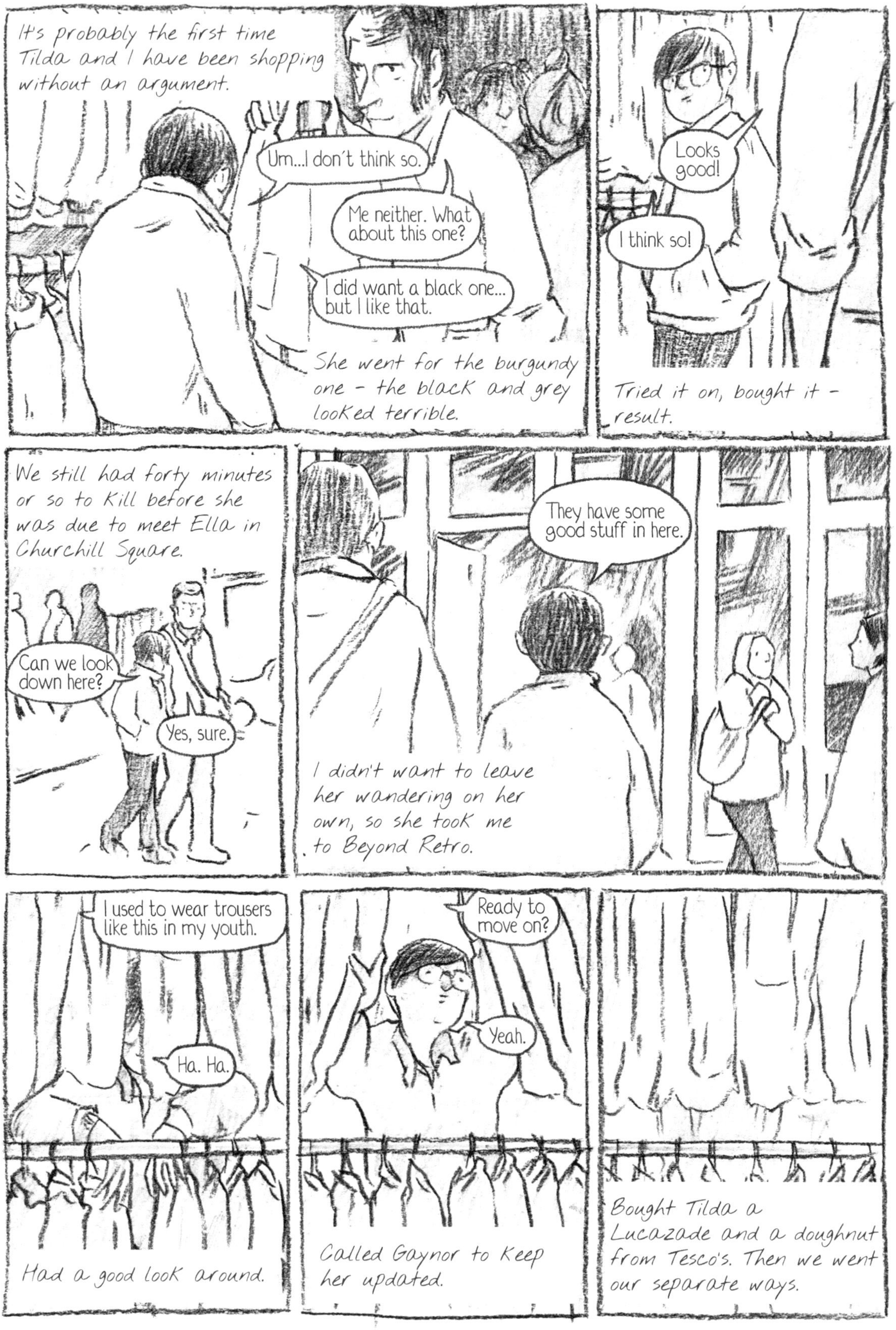
It's probably the first time Tilda and I have been shopping without an argument.
Um...I don't think so.
Me neither. What about this one?
I did want a black one... but I like that.
She went for the burgundy one - the black and grey looked terrible.
Looks good!
I think so!
Tried it on, bought it - result.
We still had forty minutes or so to kill before she was due to meet Ella in Churchill Square.
Can we look down here?
Yes, sure.
They have some good stuff in here.
I didn't want to leave her wandering on her own, so she took me to Beyond Retro.
I used to wear trousers like this in my youth.
Ha. Ha.
Had a good look around.
Ready to move on?
Yeah.
Called Gaynor to keep her updated.
Bought Tilda a Lucazade and a doughnut from Tesco's. Then we went our separate ways.

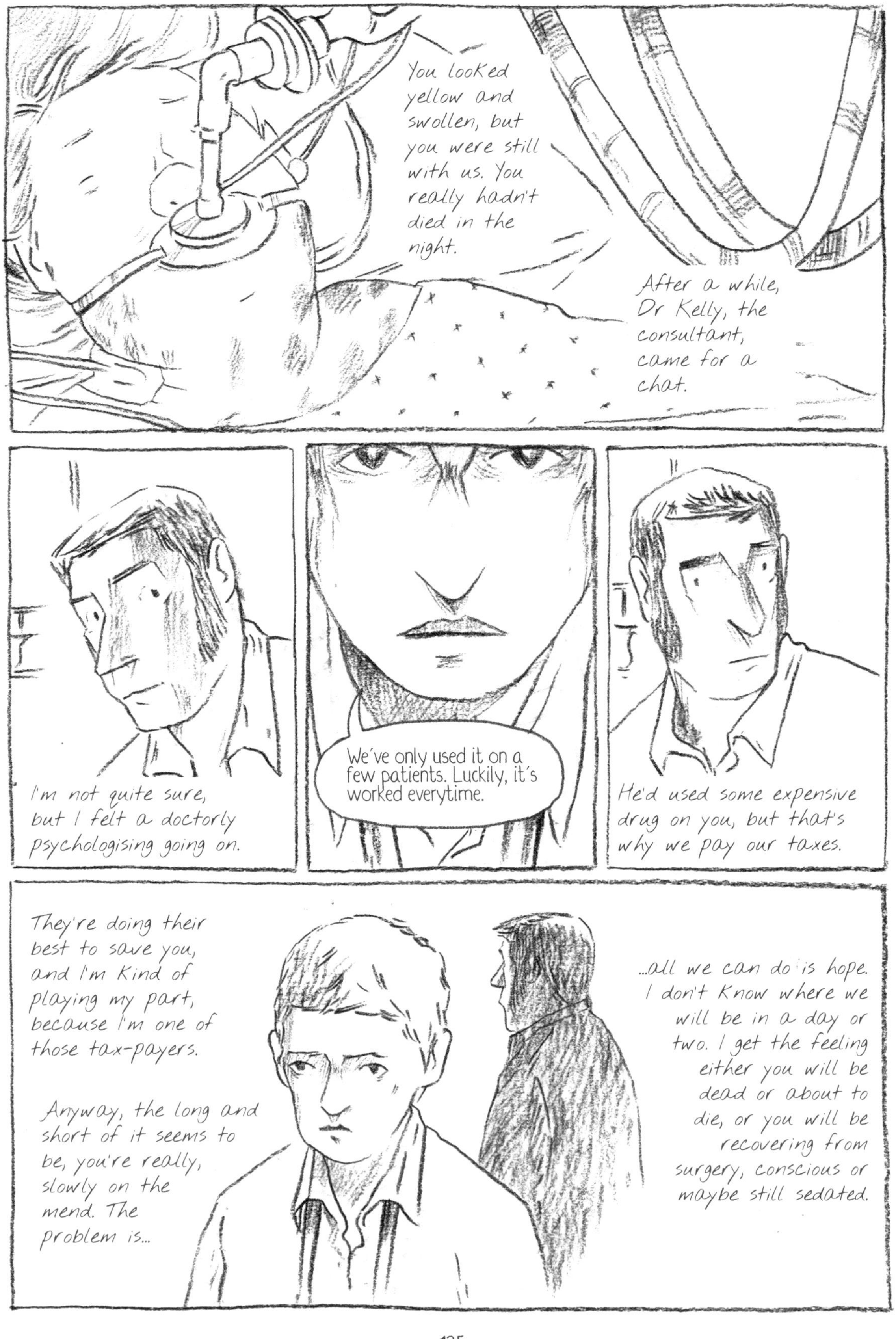

You looked yellow and swollen, but you were still with us. You really hadn't died in the night.
After a while, Dr Kelly, the consultant, came for a chat.
I'm not quite sure, but I felt a doctorly psychologising going on.
We've only used it on a few patients. Luckily, it's worked everytime.
He'd used some expensive drug on you, but that's why we pay our taxes.
They're doing their best to save you, and I'm kind of playing my part, because I'm one of those tax-payers.
Anyway, the long and short of it seems to be, you're really, slowly on the mend. The problem is...
...all we can do is hope. I don't know where we will be in a day or two. I get the feeling either you will be dead or about to die, or you will be recovering from surgery, conscious or maybe still sedated.

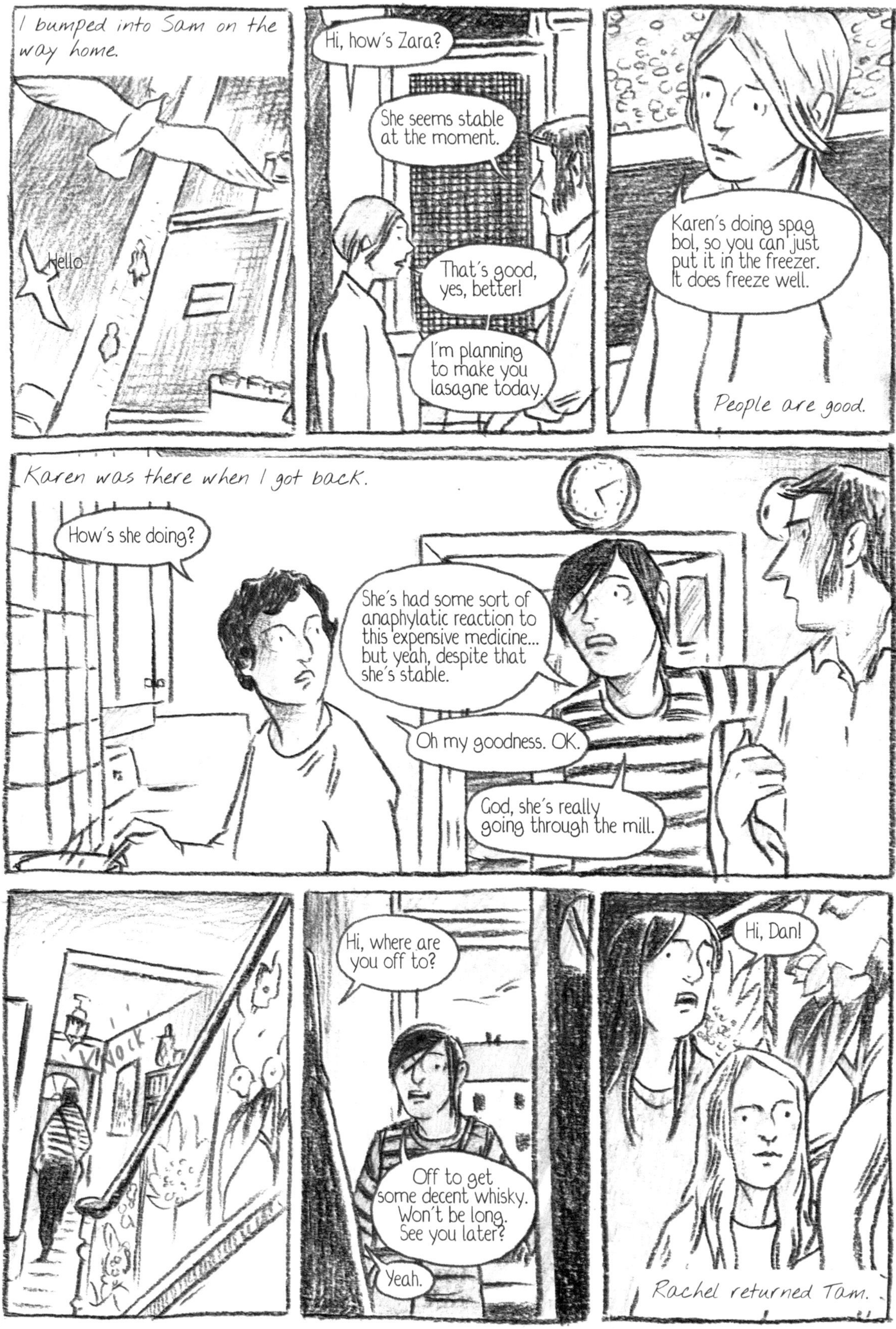
I bumped into Sam on the way home.
Hello
Hi, how's Zara?
She seems stable at the moment.
That's good, yes, better!
I'm planning to make you lasagne today.
Karen's doing spag bol, so you can just put it in the freezer. It does freeze well.
People are good.
Karen was there when I got back.
How's she doing?
She's had some sort of anaphylatic reaction to this expensive medicine... but yeah, despite that she's stable.
Oh my goodness. OK.
God, she's really going through the mill.
Hi, where are you off to?
Off to get some decent whisky. Won't be long. See you later?
Yeah.
Hi, Dan!
Rachel returned Tam.

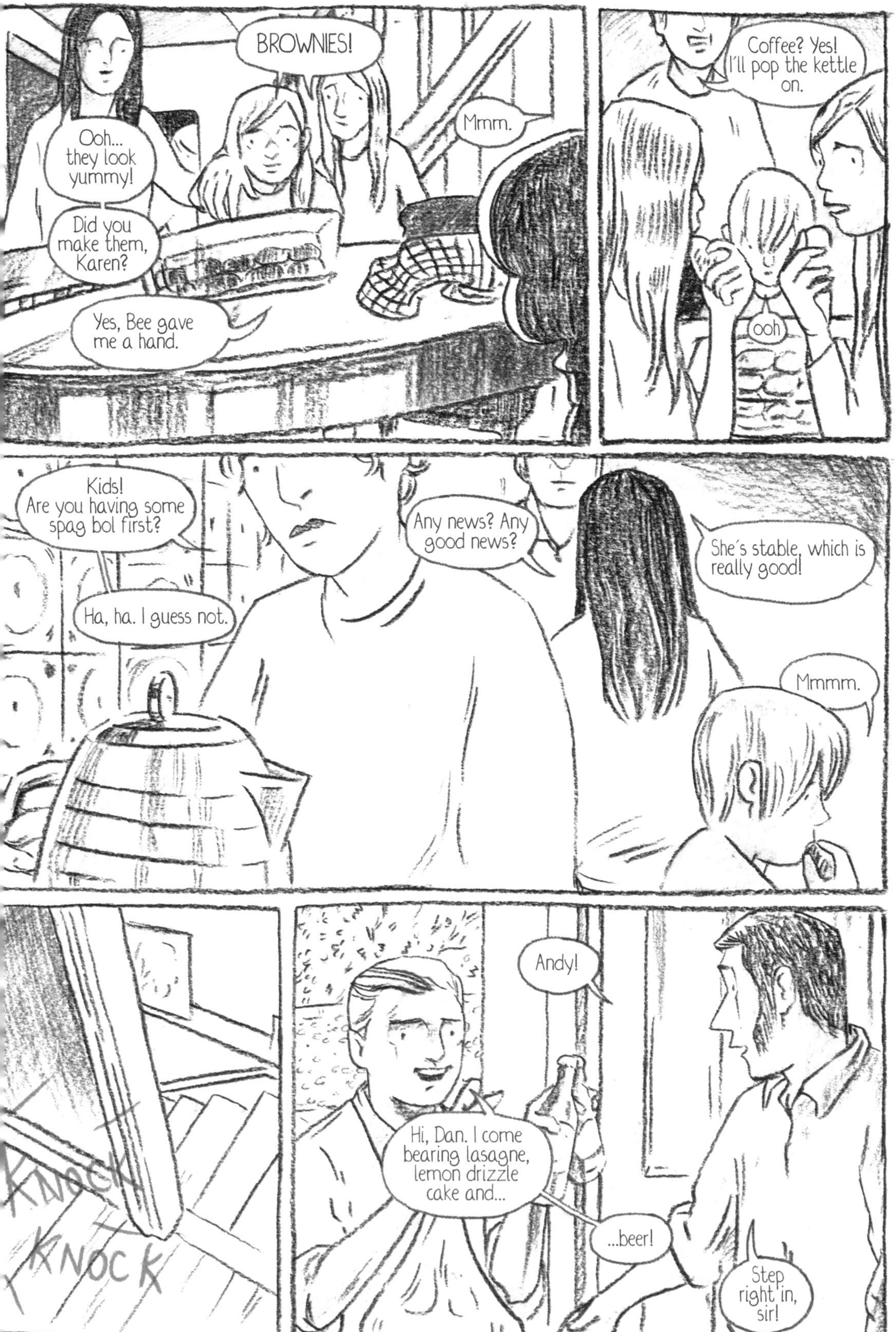
BROWNIES!
Ooh... they look yummy!
Did you make them, Karen?
Mmm.
Yes, Bee gave me a hand.
Coffee? Yes! I'll pop the kettle on.
ooh
Kids! Are you having some spag bol first?
Ha, ha. I guess not.
Any news? Any good news?
She's stable, which is really good!
Mmmm.
KNOCK KNOCK
Andy!
Hi, Dan. I come bearing lasagne, lemon drizzle cake and...
...beer!
Step right in, sir!

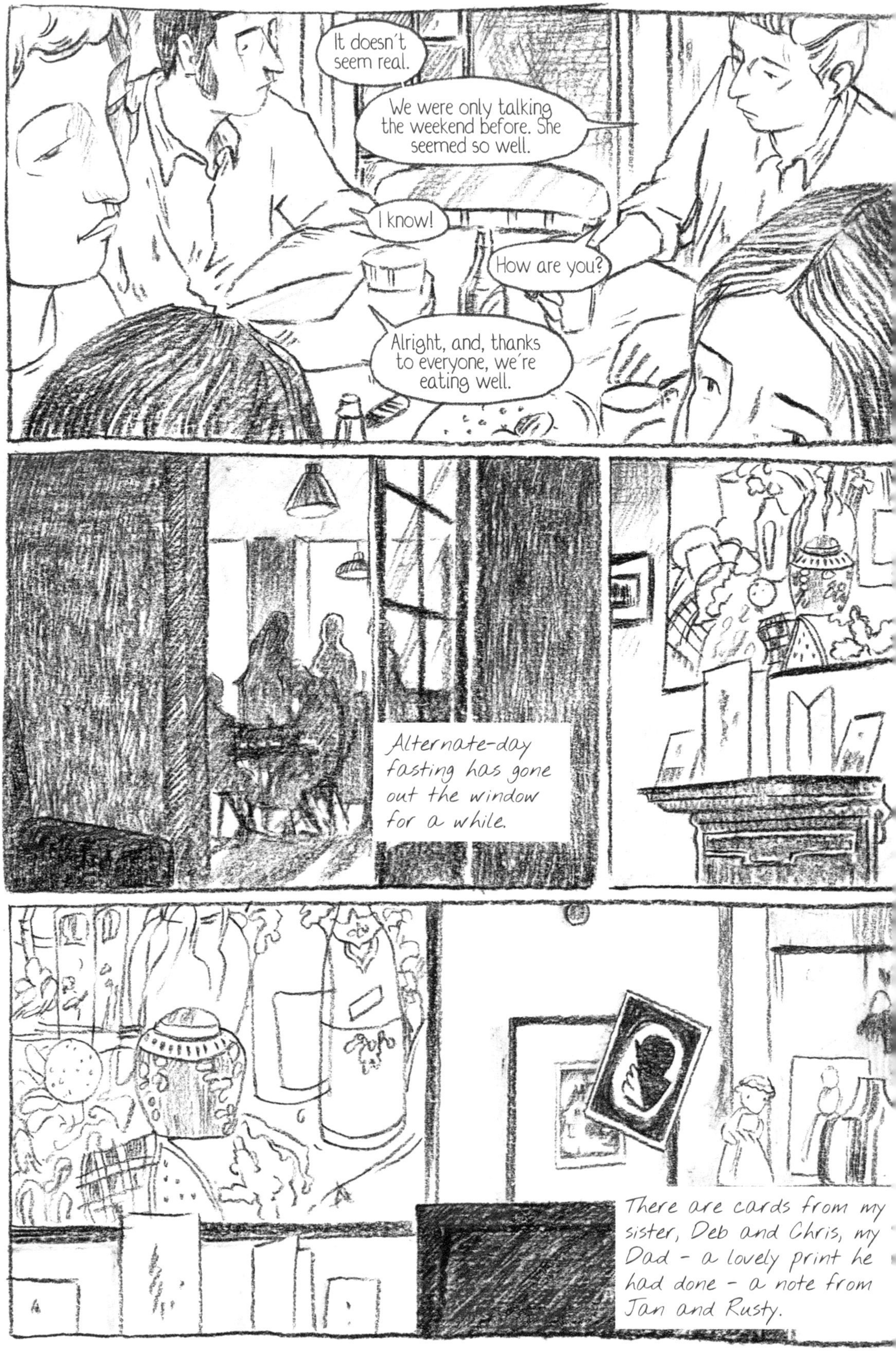
It doesn't seem real.
We were only talking the weekend before. She seemed so well.
I know!
How are you?
Alright, and, thanks to everyone, we're eating well.
Alternate-day fasting has gone out the window for a while.
There are cards from my sister, Deb and Chris, my Dad - a lovely print he had done - a note from Jan and Rusty.

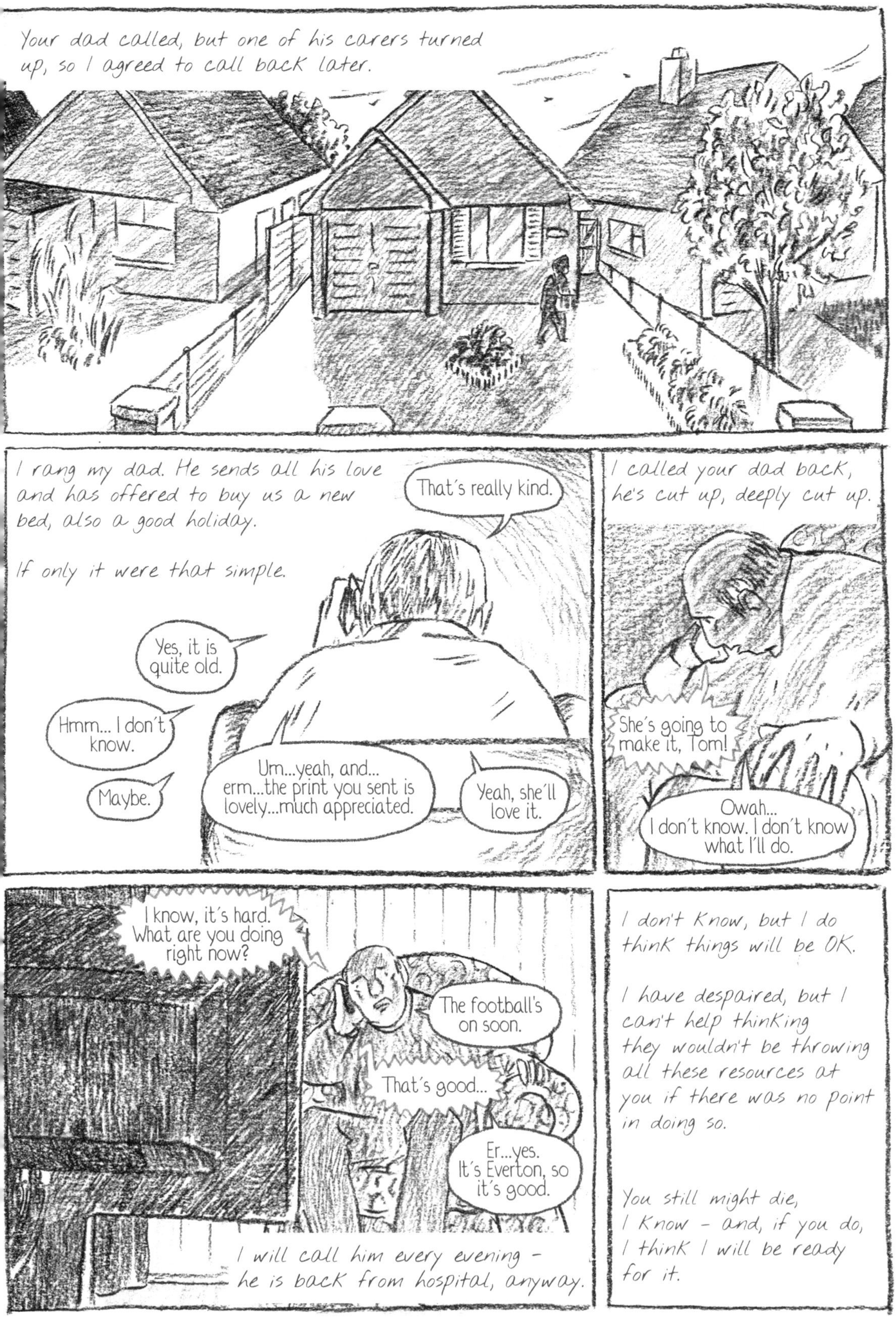
Your dad called, but one of his carers turned up, so I agreed to call back later.
I rang my dad. He sends all his love and has offered to buy us a new bed, also a good holiday.
If only it were that simple.
That's really kind.
Yes, it is quite old.
Hmm... I don't know.
Maybe.
Um...yeah, and... erm...the print you sent is lovely...much appreciated.
Yeah, she'll love it.
I called your dad back, he's cut up, deeply cut up.
She's going to make it, Tom!
Owah... I don't know. I don't know what I'll do.
I know, it's hard. What are you doing right now?
The football's on soon.
That's good...
Er...yes. It's Everton, so it's good.
I will call him every evening – he is back from hospital, anyway.
I don't know, but I do think things will be OK.
I have despaired, but I can't help thinking they wouldn't be throwing all these resources at you if there was no point in doing so.
You still might die, I know – and, if you do, I think I will be ready for it.

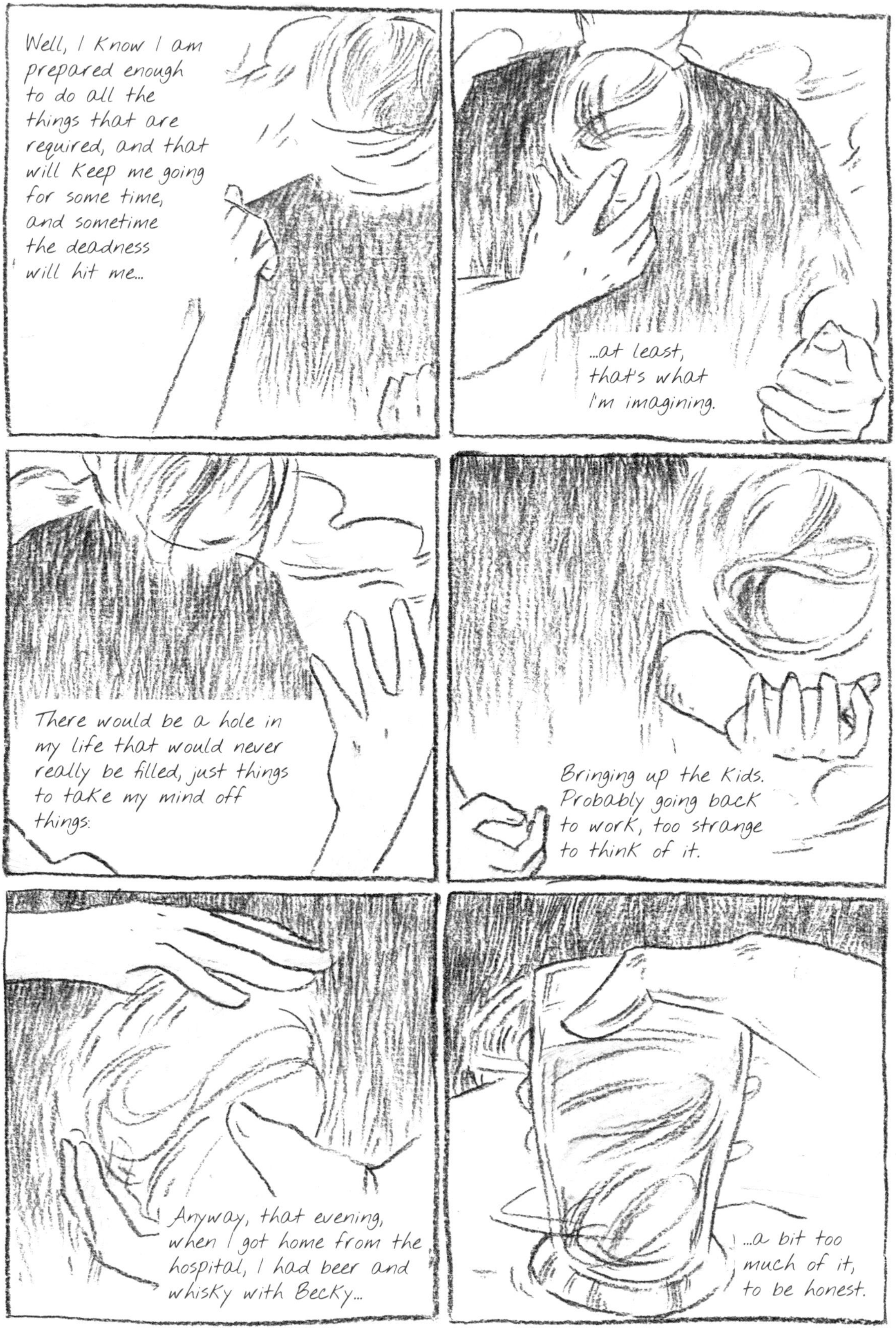
Well, I know I am prepared enough to do all the things that are required, and that will keep me going for some time, and sometime the deadness will hit me...
...at least, that's what I'm imagining.
There would be a hole in my life that would never really be filled, just things to take my mind off things.
Bringing up the kids. Probably going back to work, too strange to think of it.
Anyway, that evening, when I got home from the hospital, I had beer and whisky with Becky...
...a bit too much of it, to be honest.

THURSDAY 30th MAY

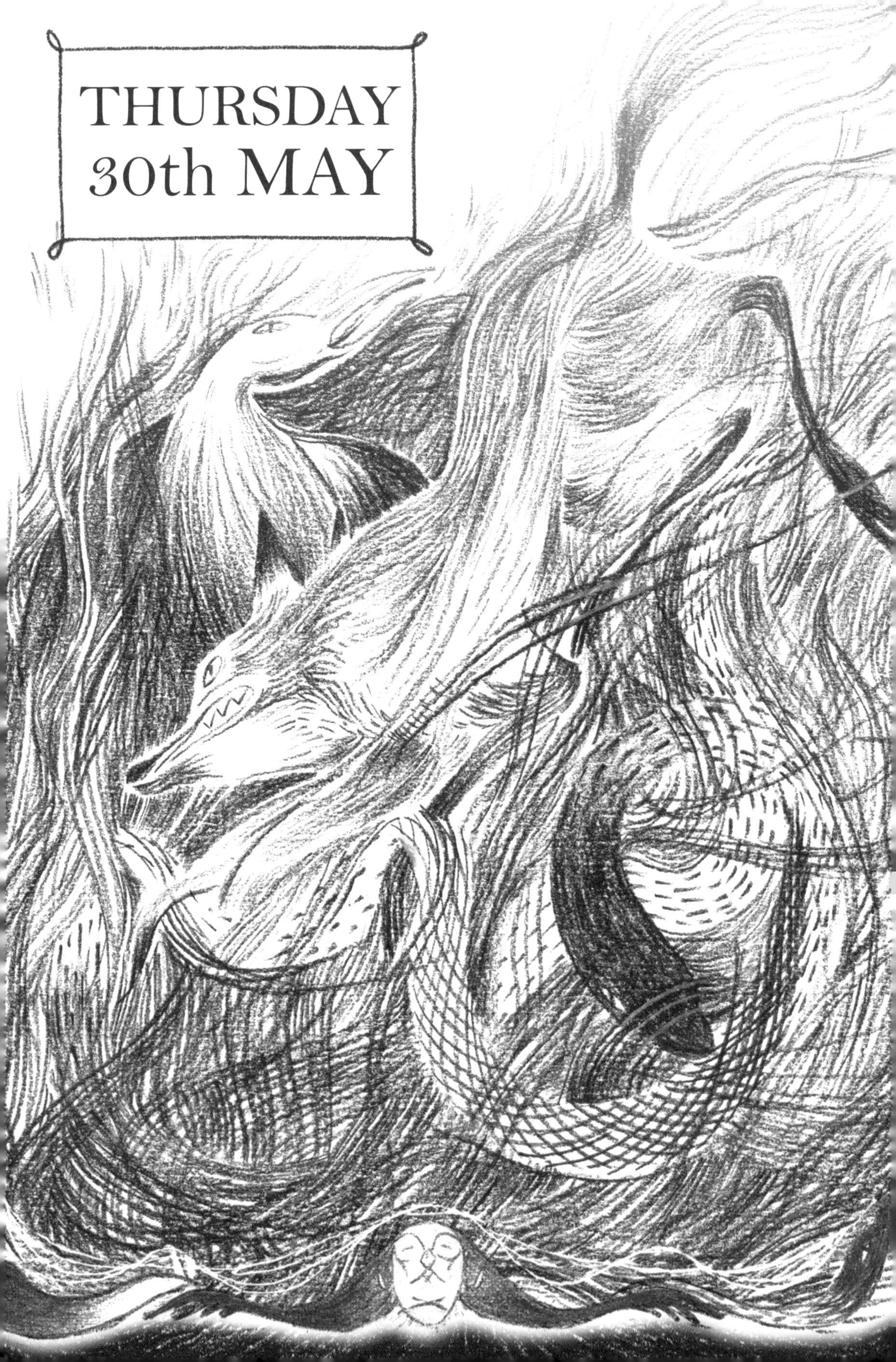

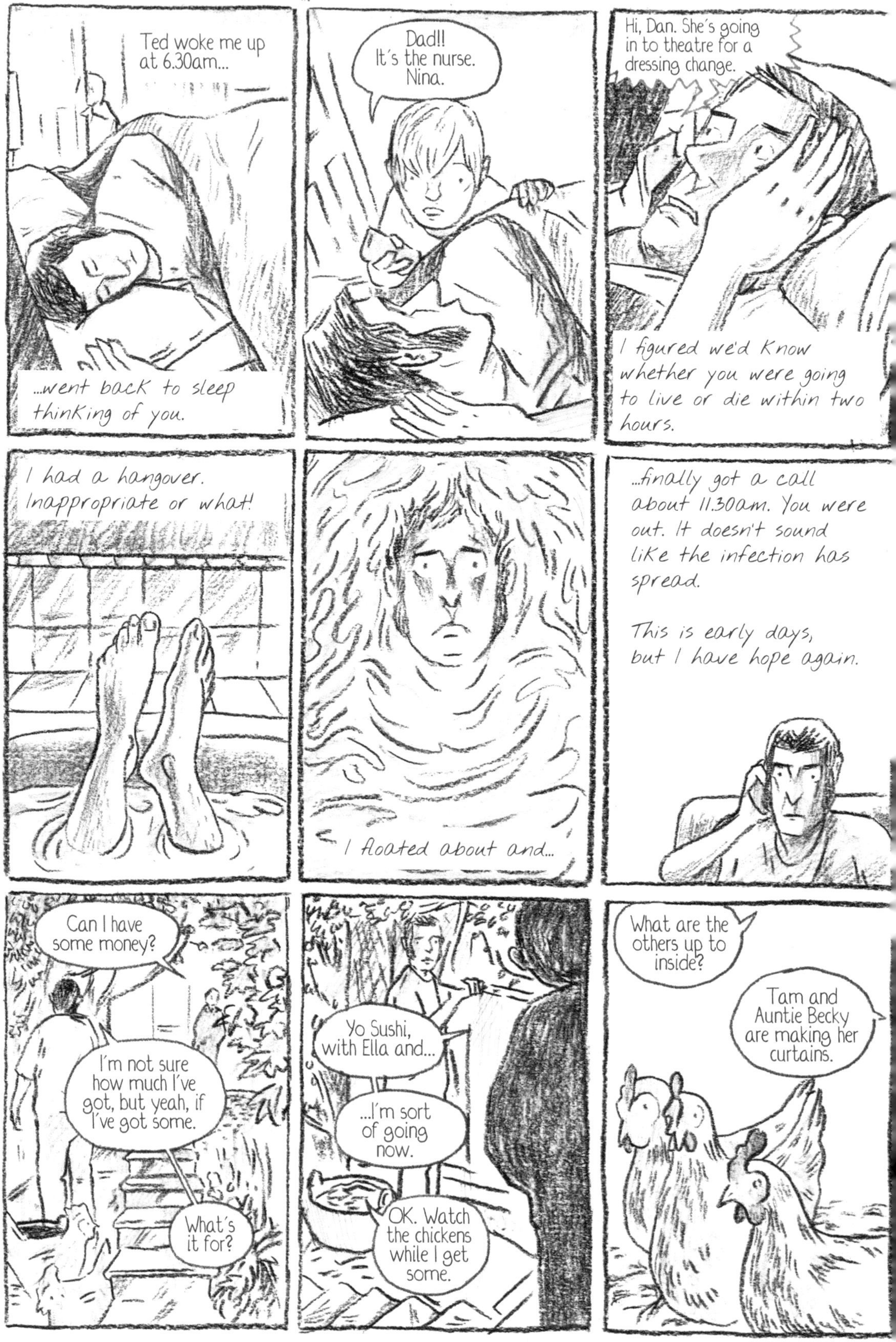
Ted woke me up at 6.30am...
...went back to sleep thinking of you.
Dad!! It's the nurse. Nina.
Hi, Dan. She's going in to theatre for a dressing change.
I figured we'd know whether you were going to live or die within two hours.
I had a hangover. Inappropriate or what!
I floated about and...
...finally got a call about 11.30am. You were out. It doesn't sound like the infection has spread.
This is early days, but I have hope again.
Can I have some money?
I'm not sure how much I've got, but yeah, if I've got some.
What's it for?
Yo Sushi, with Ella and...
...I'm sort of going now.
OK. Watch the chickens while I get some.
What are the others up to inside?
Tam and Auntie Becky are making her curtains.

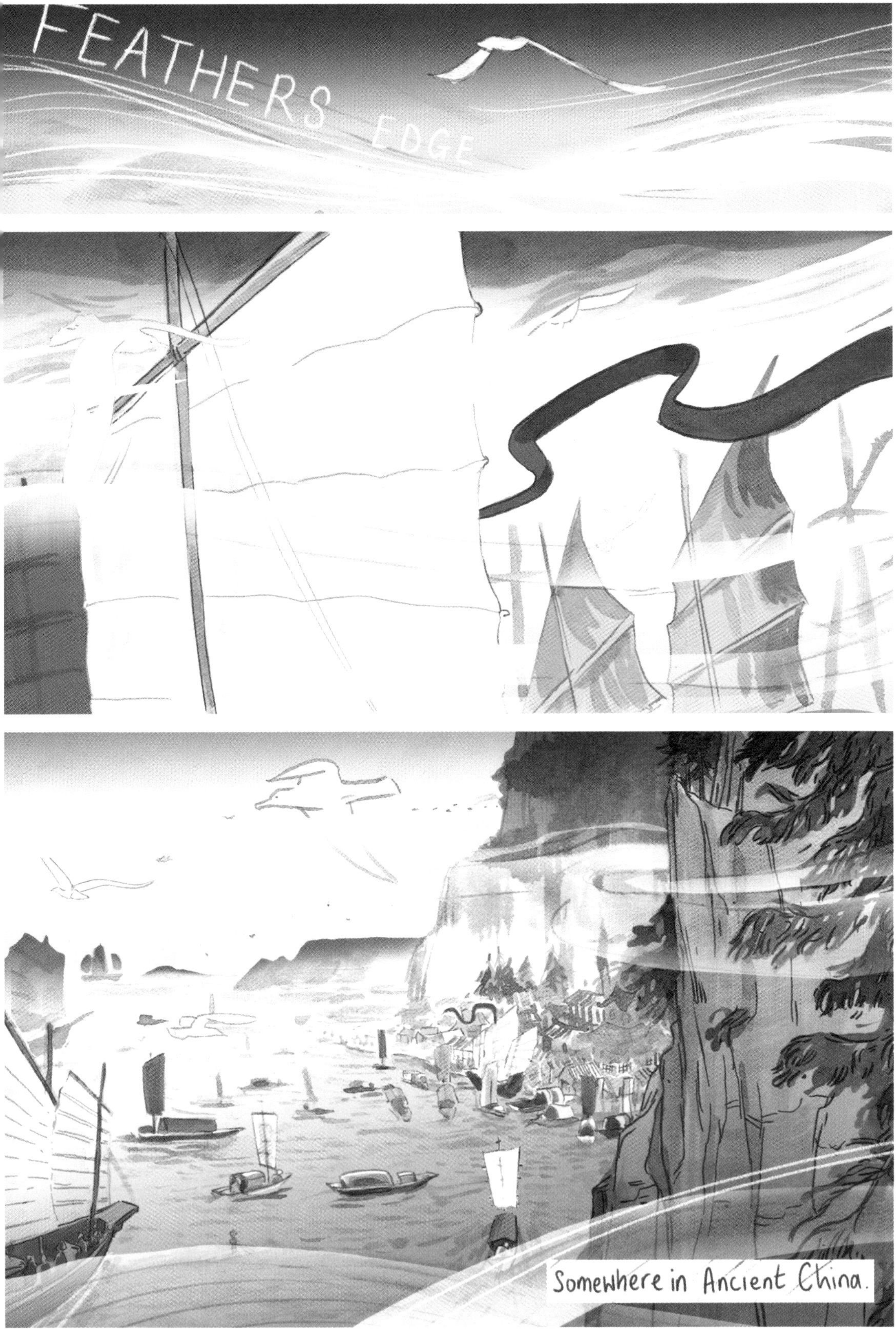
FEATHERS EDGE
Somewhere in Ancient China.

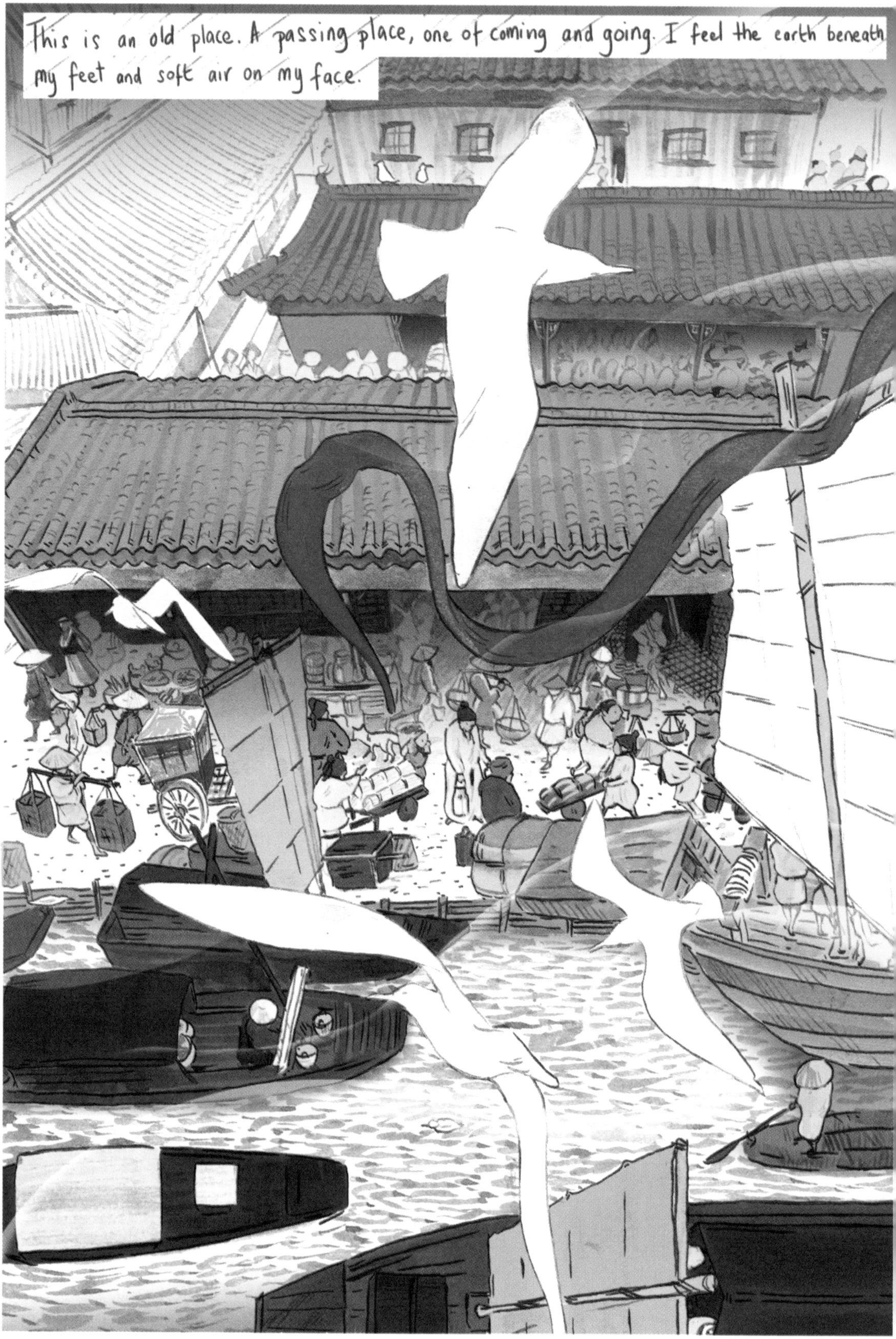
This is an old place. A passing place, one of coming and going. I feel the earth beneath my feet and soft air on my face.

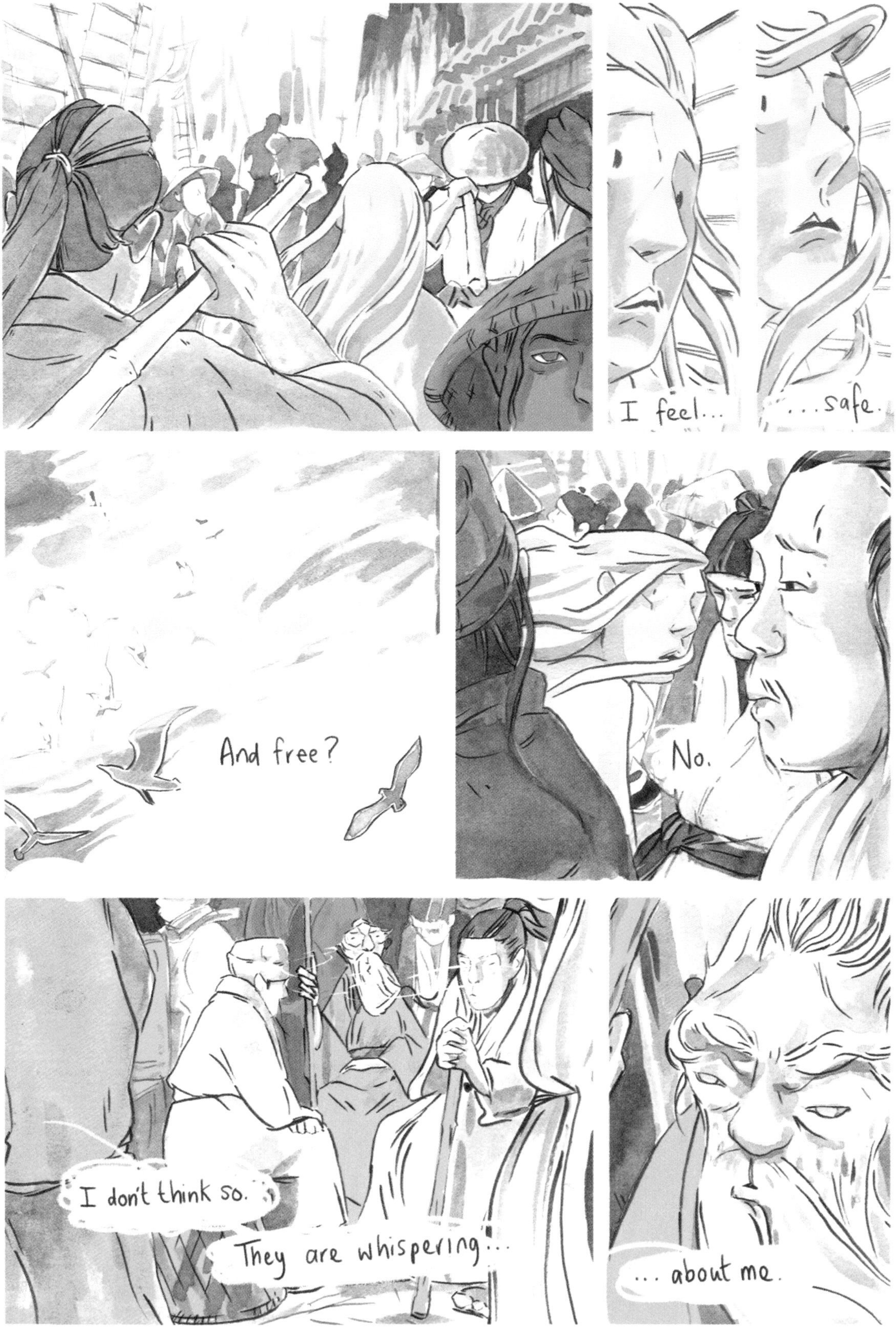
I feel...
...safe.
And free?
No.
I don't think so.
They are whispering...
... about me.

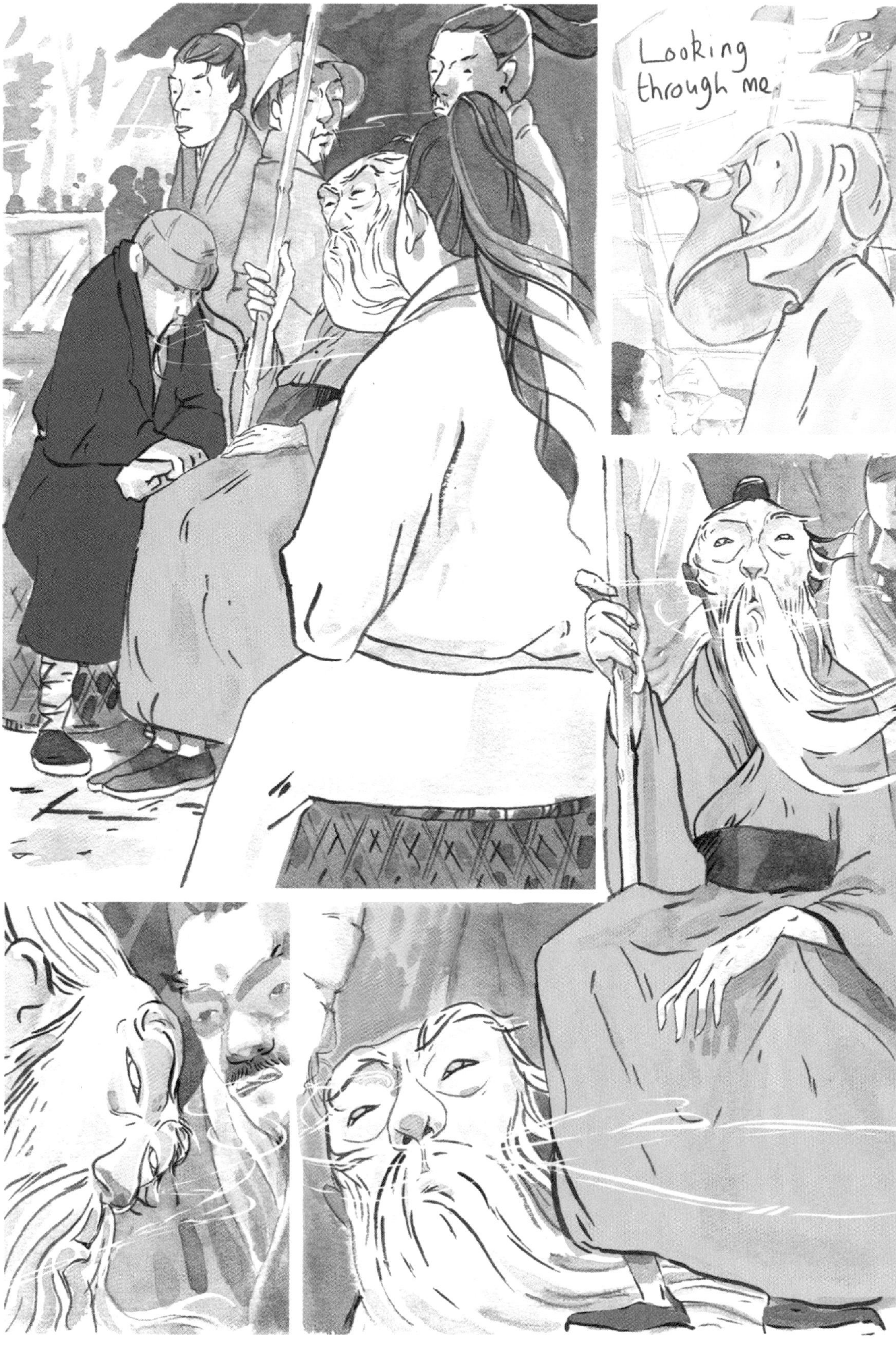
Looking through me

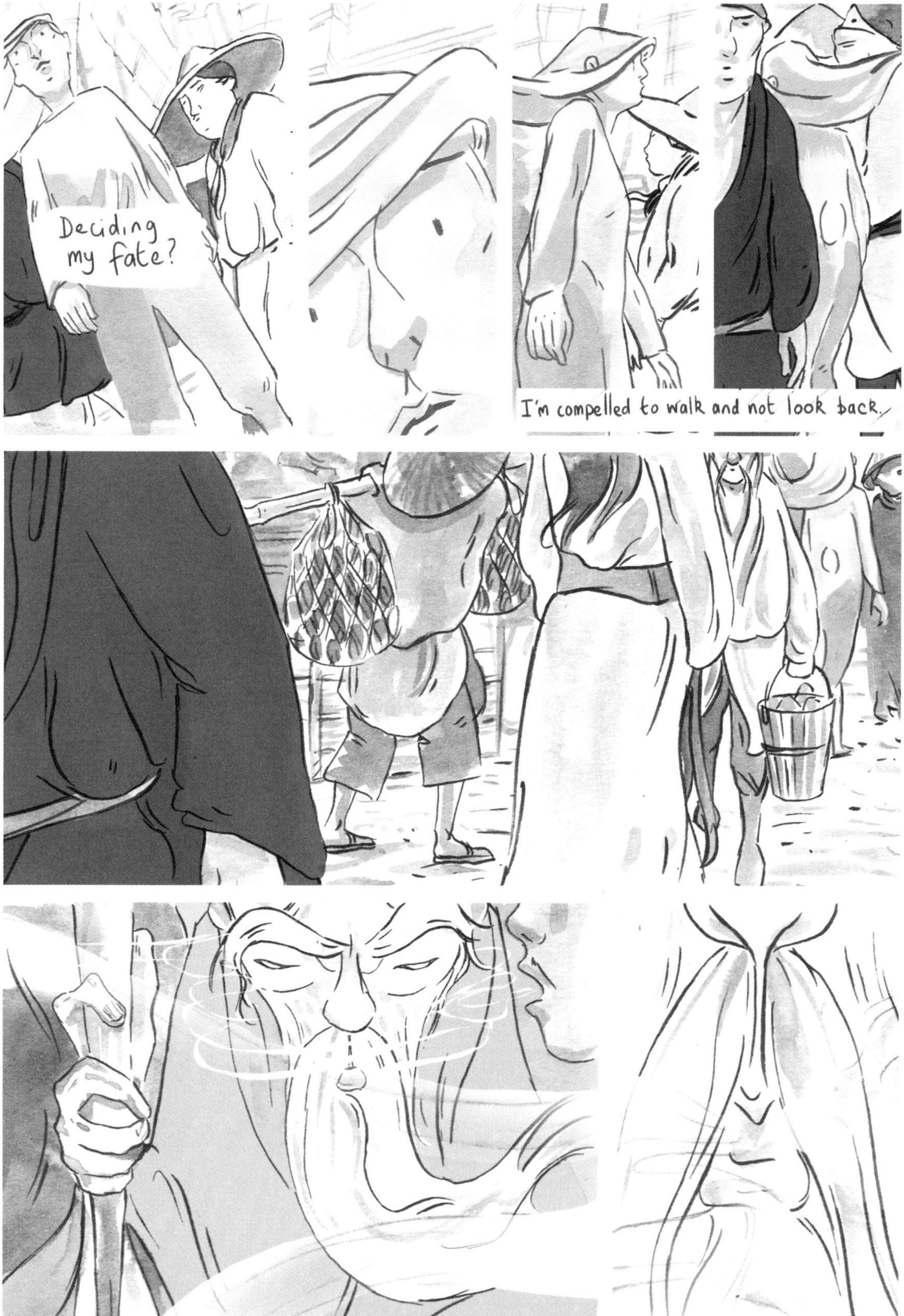
Deciding my fate?
I'm compelled to walk and not look back.

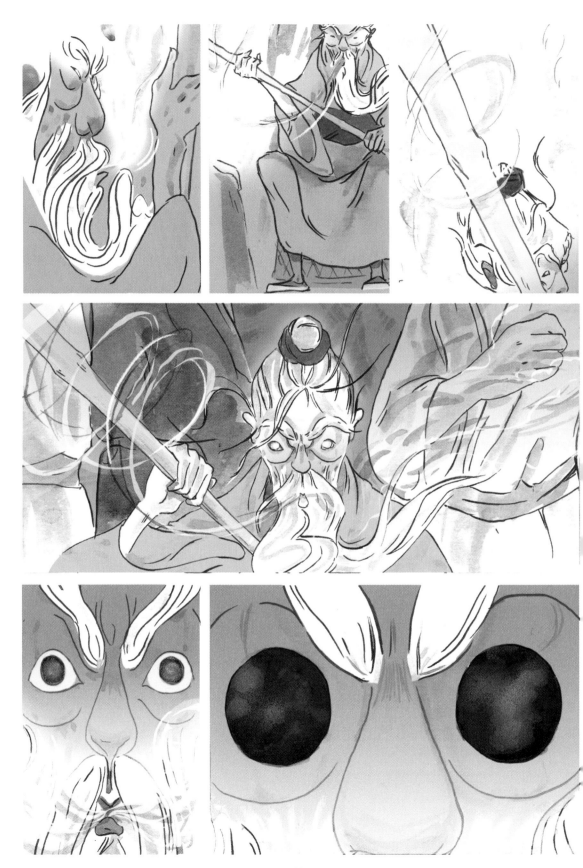

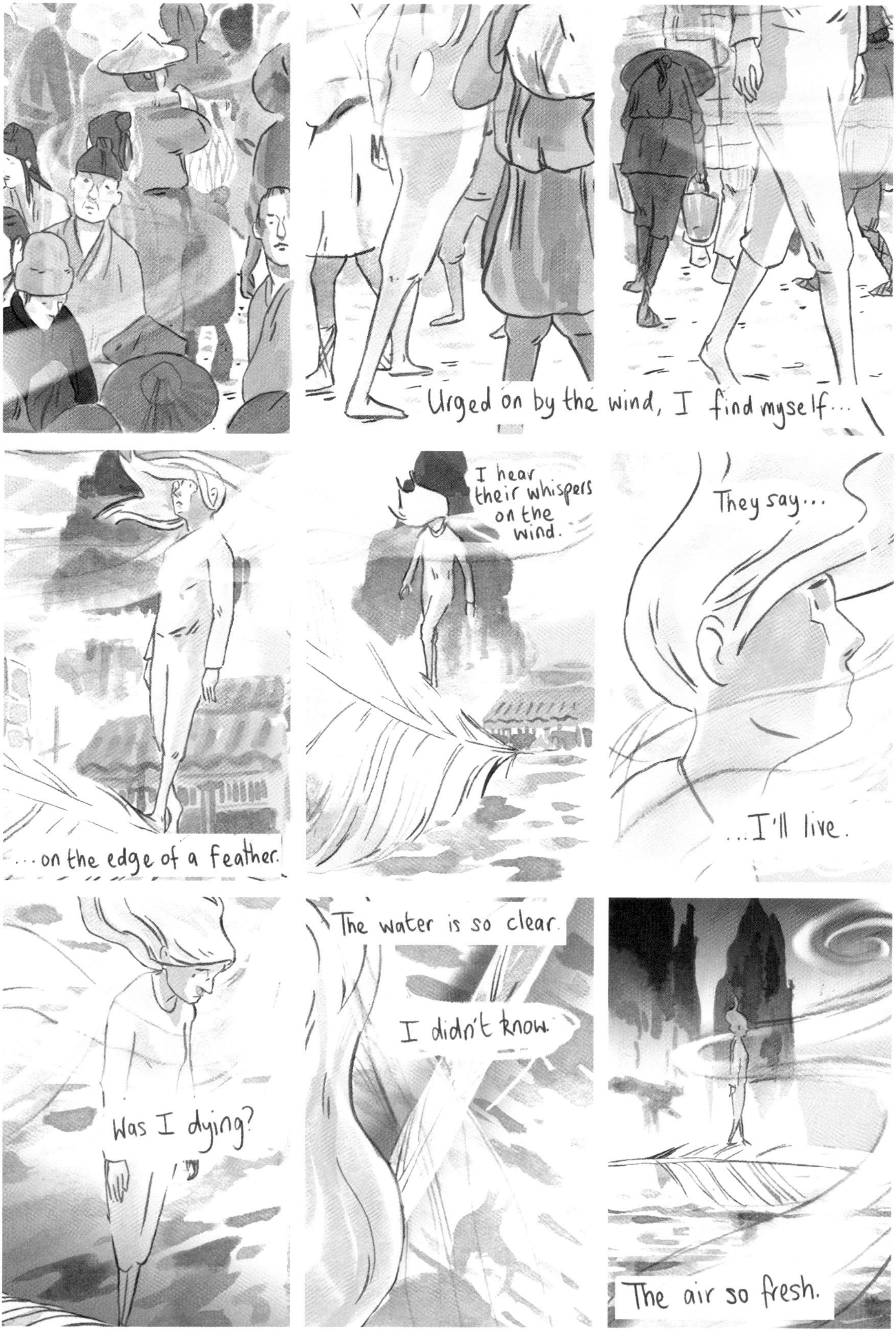
Urged on by the wind, I find myself...
...on the edge of a feather.
I hear their whispers on the wind.
They say...
...I'll live.
Was I dying?
The water is so clear.
I didn't know.
The air so fresh.

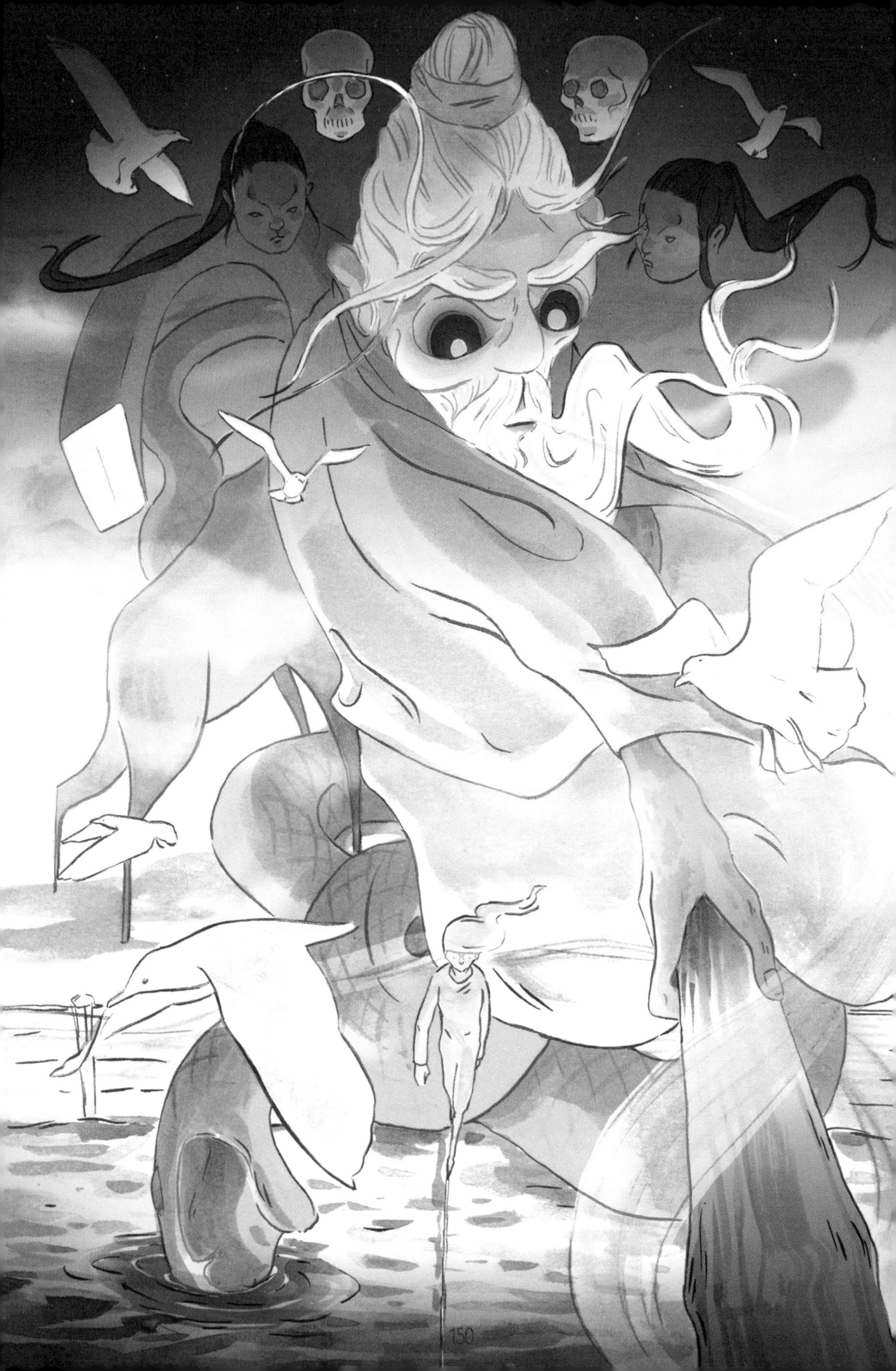

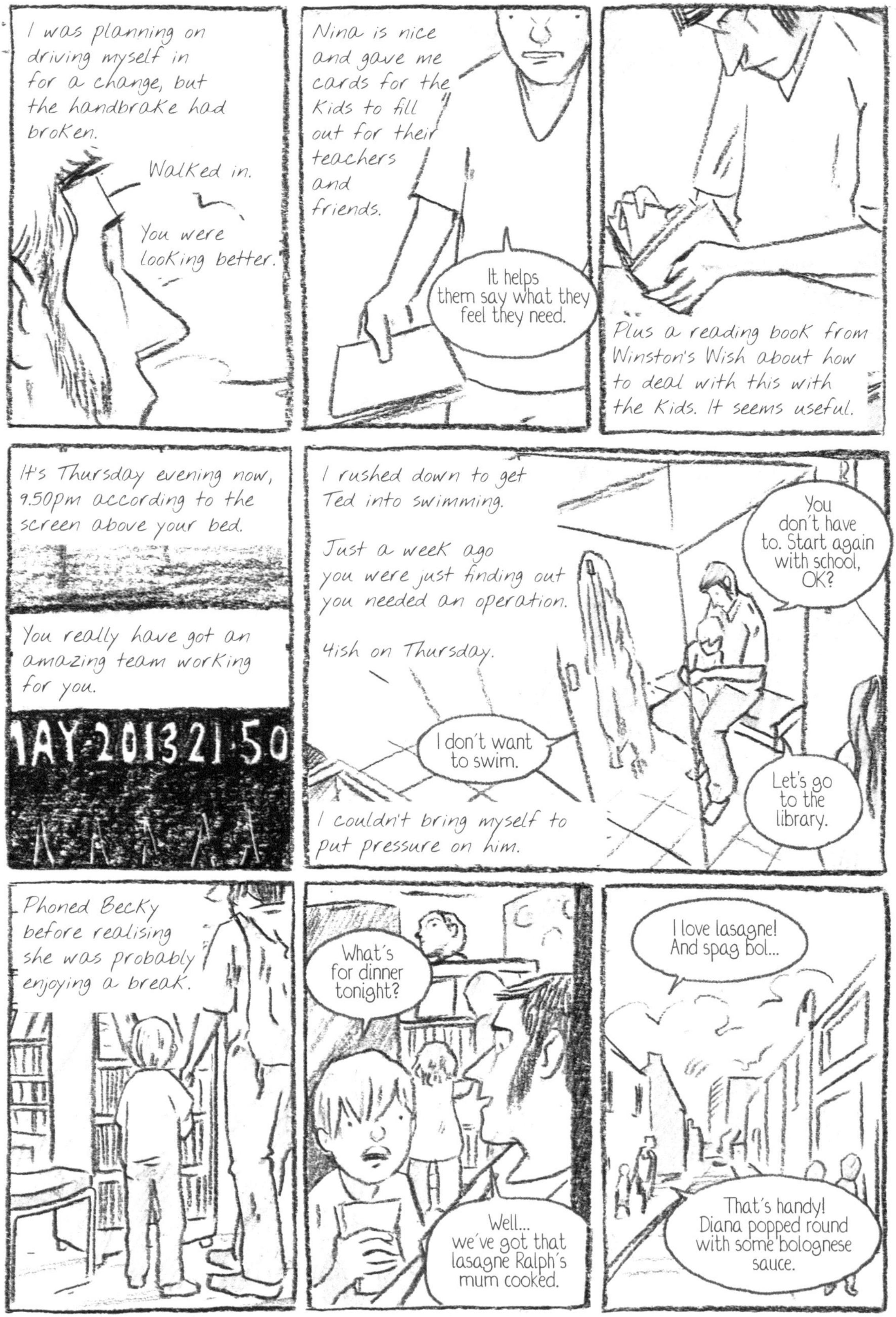
I was planning on driving myself in for a change, but the handbrake had broken.
Walked in.
You were looking better.
Nina is nice and gave me cards for the kids to fill out for their teachers and friends.
It helps them say what they feel they need.
Plus a reading book from Winston's Wish about how to deal with this with the kids. It seems useful.
It's Thursday evening now, 9.50pm according to the screen above your bed.
You really have got an amazing team working for you.
MAY 2013 21:50
I rushed down to get Ted into swimming.
Just a week ago you were just finding out you needed an operation.
4ish on Thursday.
I don't want to swim.
You don't have to. Start again with school, OK?
Let's go to the library.
I couldn't bring myself to put pressure on him.
Phoned Becky before realising she was probably enjoying a break.
What's for dinner tonight?
Well... we've got that lasagne Ralph's mum cooked.
I love lasagne! And spag bol...
That's handy! Diana popped round with some bolognese sauce.

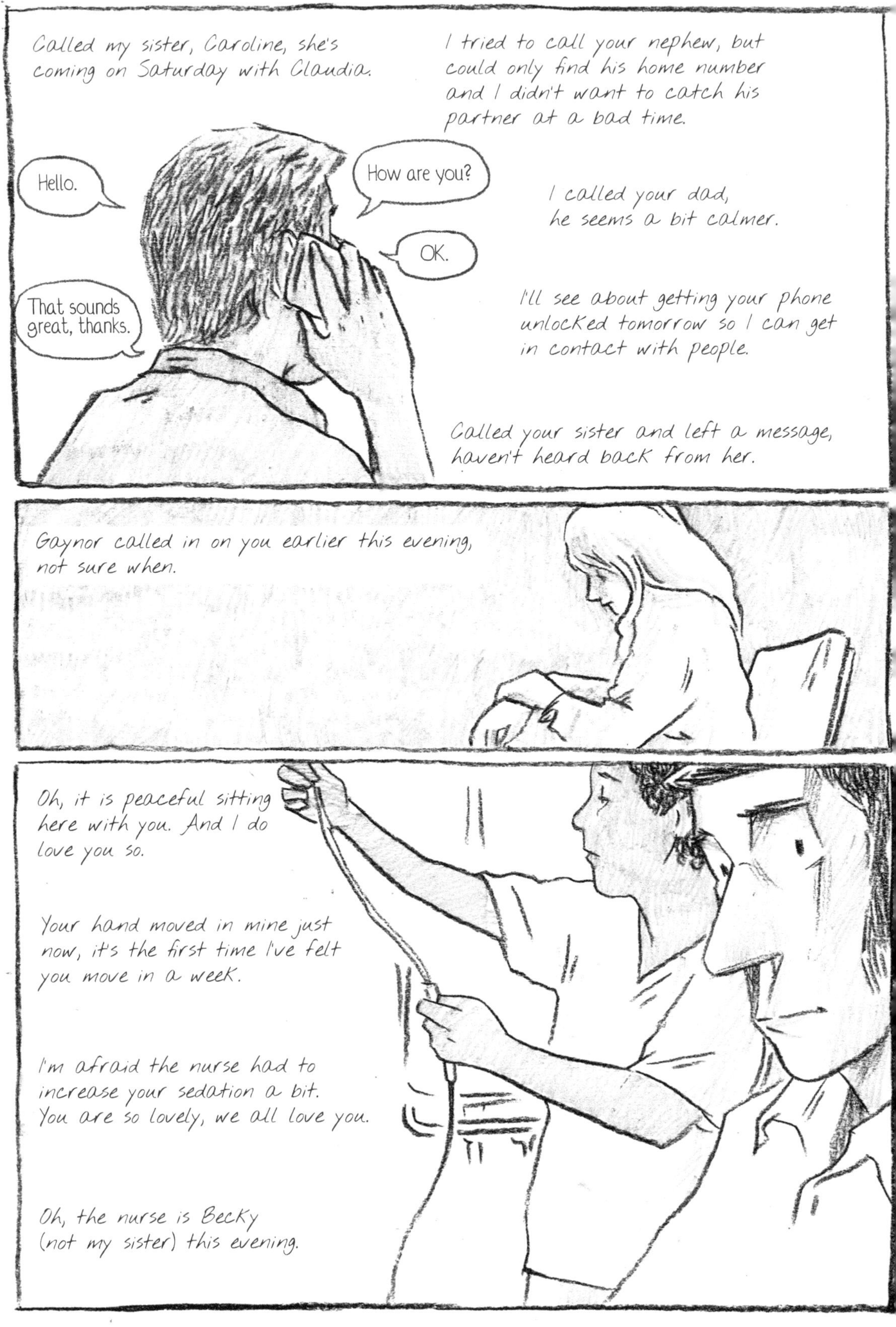
Called my sister, Caroline, she's coming on Saturday with Claudia.
I tried to call your nephew, but could only find his home number and I didn't want to catch his partner at a bad time.
Hello.
How are you?
OK.
That sounds great, thanks.
I called your dad, he seems a bit calmer.
I'll see about getting your phone unlocked tomorrow so I can get in contact with people.
Called your sister and left a message, haven't heard back from her.
Gaynor called in on you earlier this evening, not sure when.
Oh, it is peaceful sitting here with you. And I do love you so.
Your hand moved in mine just now, it's the first time I've felt you move in a week.
I'm afraid the nurse had to increase your sedation a bit. You are so lovely, we all love you.
Oh, the nurse is Becky (not my sister) this evening.

FRIDAY 31st MAY

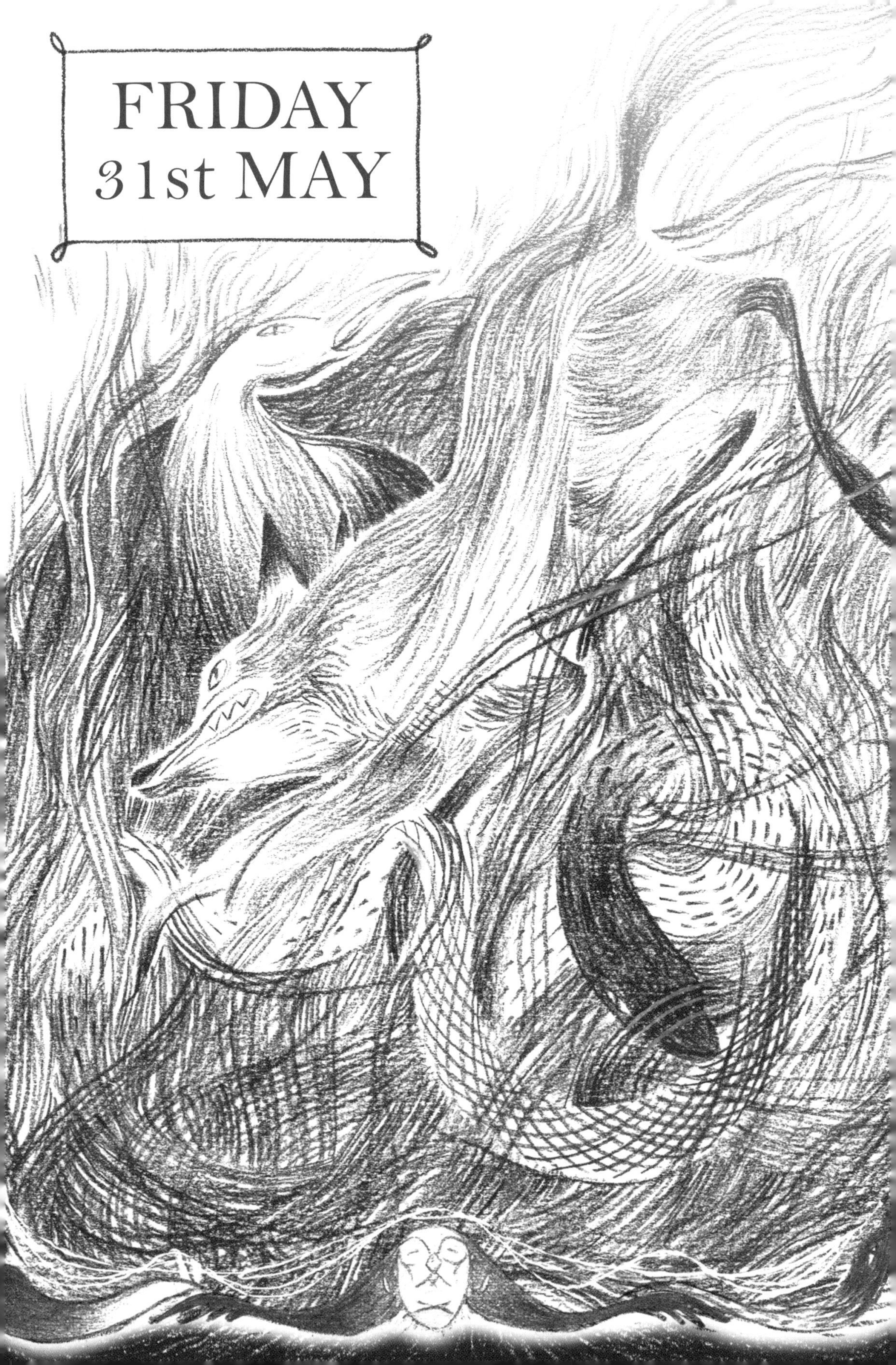

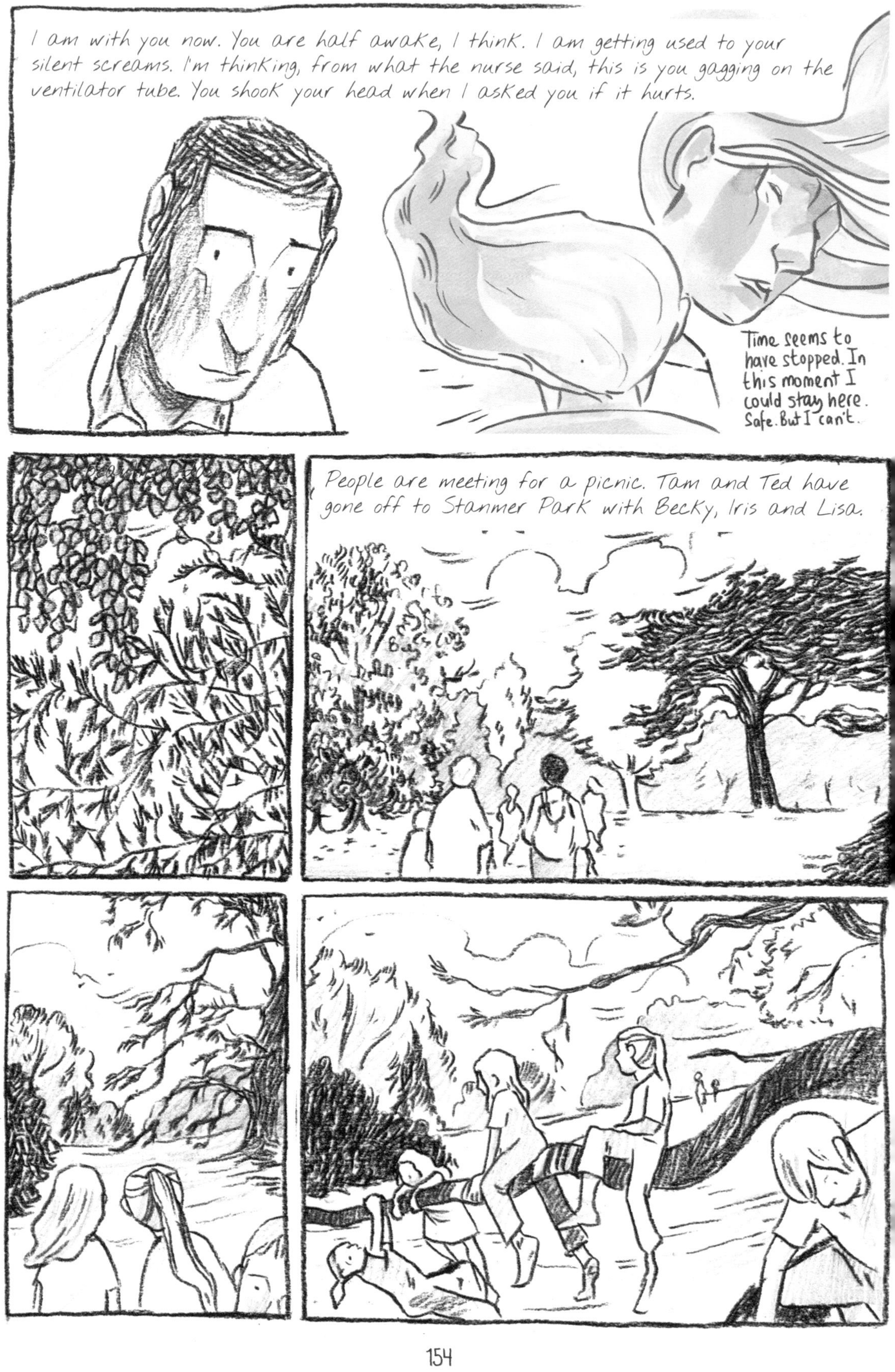
I am with you now. You are half awake, I think. I am getting used to your silent screams. I'm thinking, from what the nurse said, this is you gagging on the ventilator tube. You shook your head when I asked you if it hurts.
Time seems to have stopped. In this moment I could stay here. Safe. But I can't.
People are meeting for a picnic. Tam and Ted have gone off to Stanmer Park with Becky, Iris and Lisa.

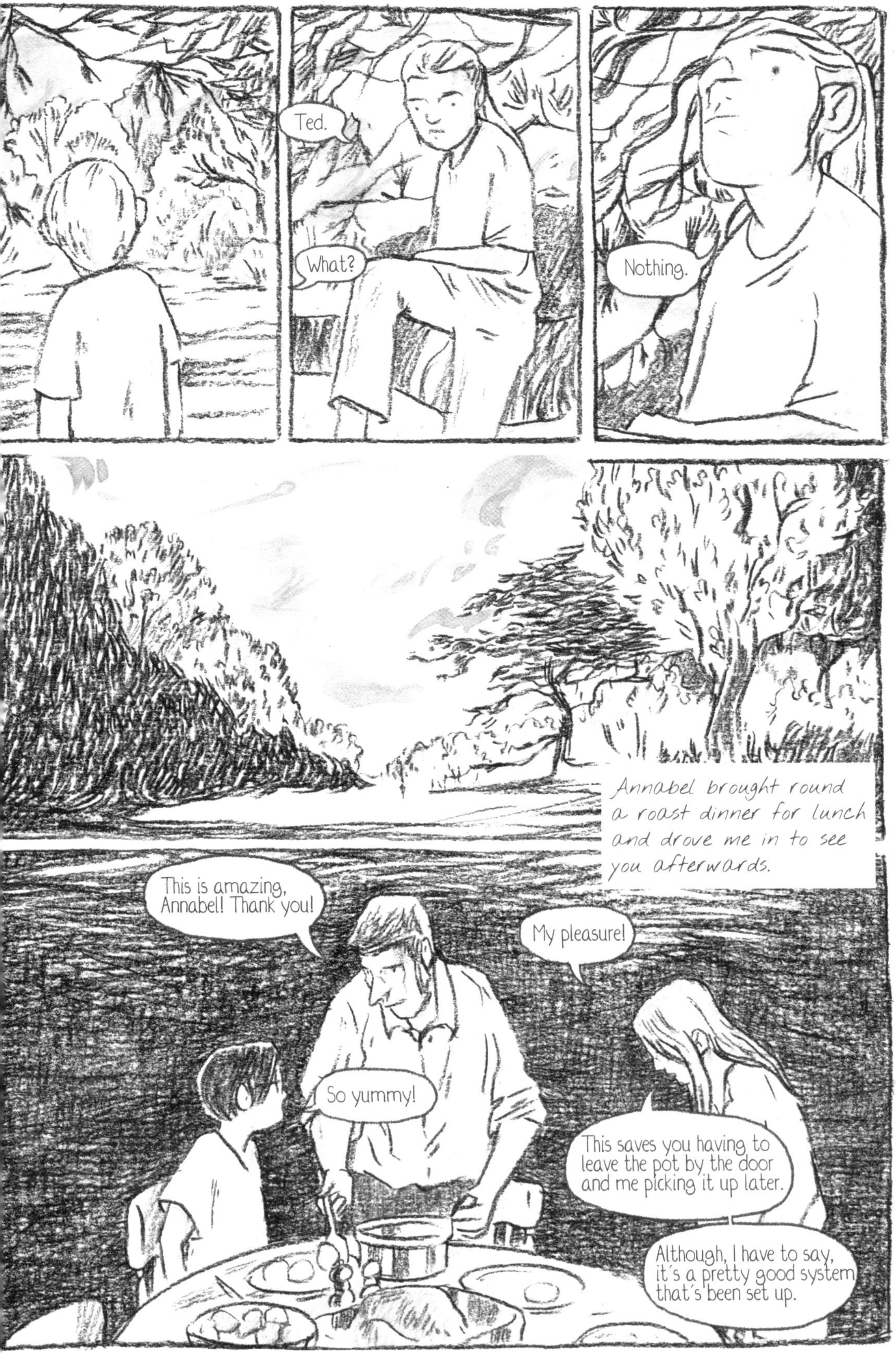
Ted.
What?
Nothing.
Annabel brought round a roast dinner for lunch and drove me in to see you afterwards.
This is amazing, Annabel! Thank you!
My pleasure!
So yummy!
This saves you having to leave the pot by the door and me picking it up later.
Although, I have to say, it's a pretty good system that's been set up.

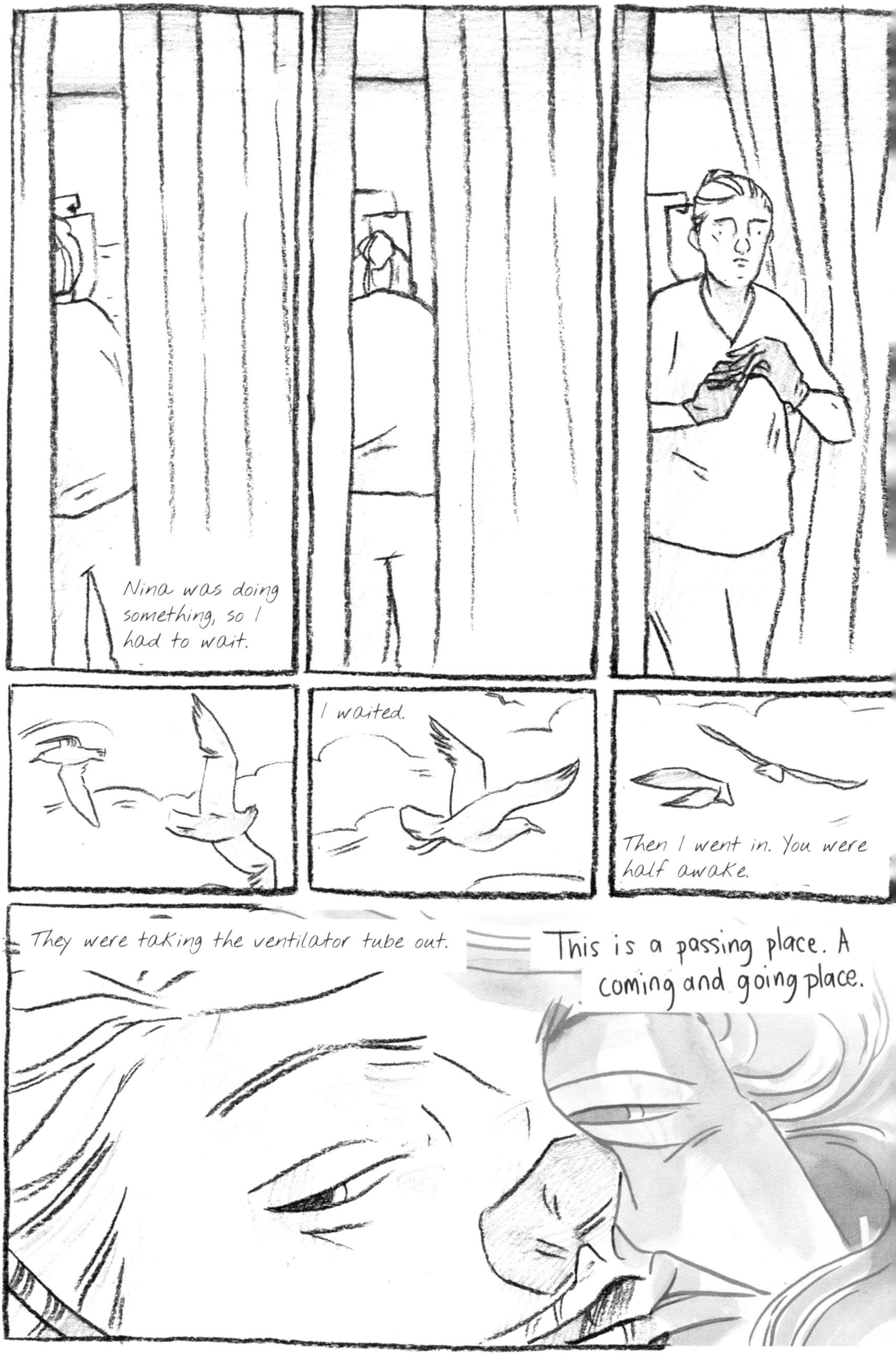
Nina was doing something, so I had to wait.
I waited.
Then I went in. You were half awake.
They were taking the ventilator tube out.
This is a passing place. A coming and going place.

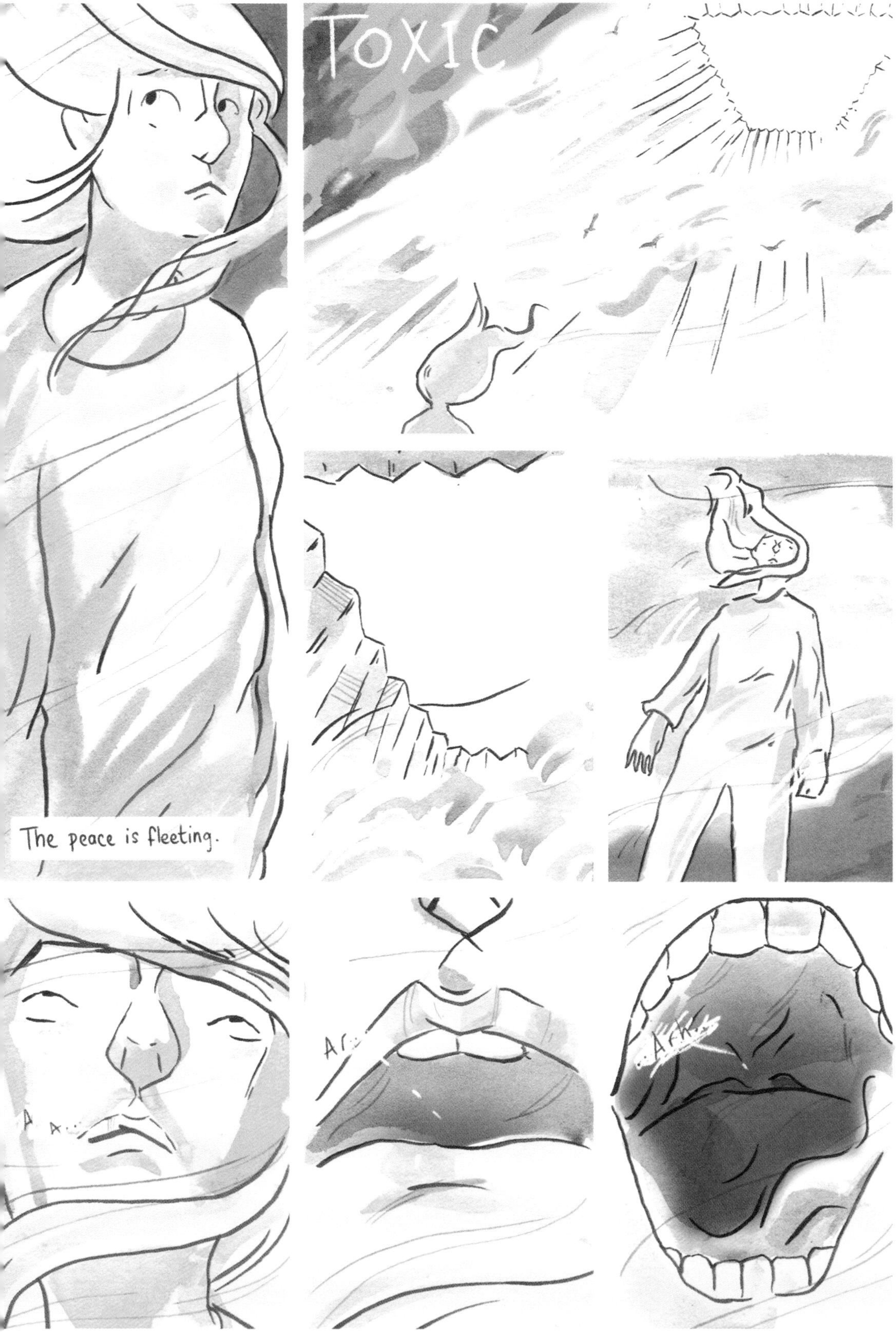
The peace is fleeting.
TOXIC
A A...
Ar...
..Ark..

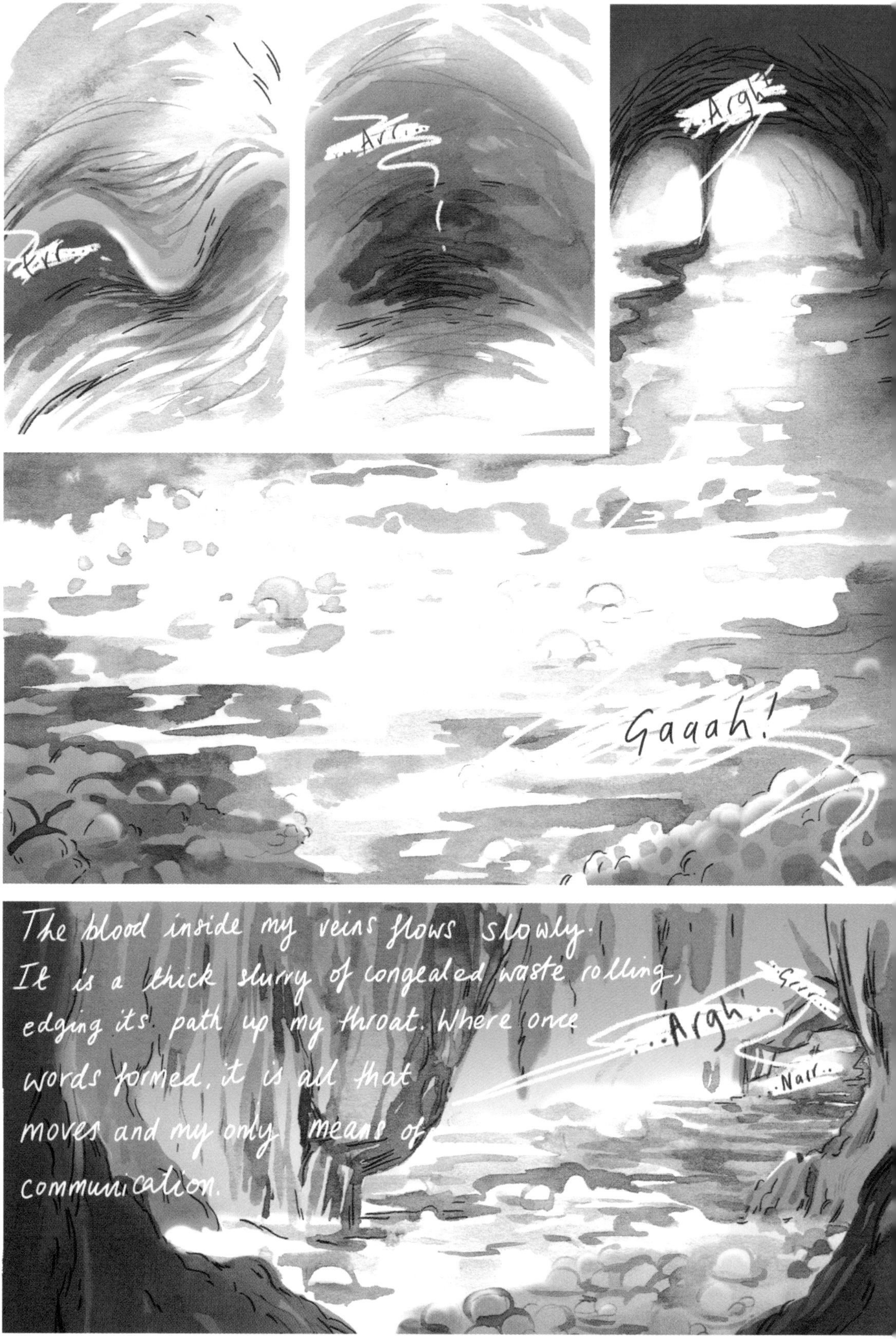
Ar...
..Argh
Gaaah!
The blood inside my veins flows slowly.
It is a thick slurry of congealed waste rolling,
edging its path up my throat. Where once
words formed, it is all that
moves and my only means of
communication.
...Argh...
..Grr..
.Nair..

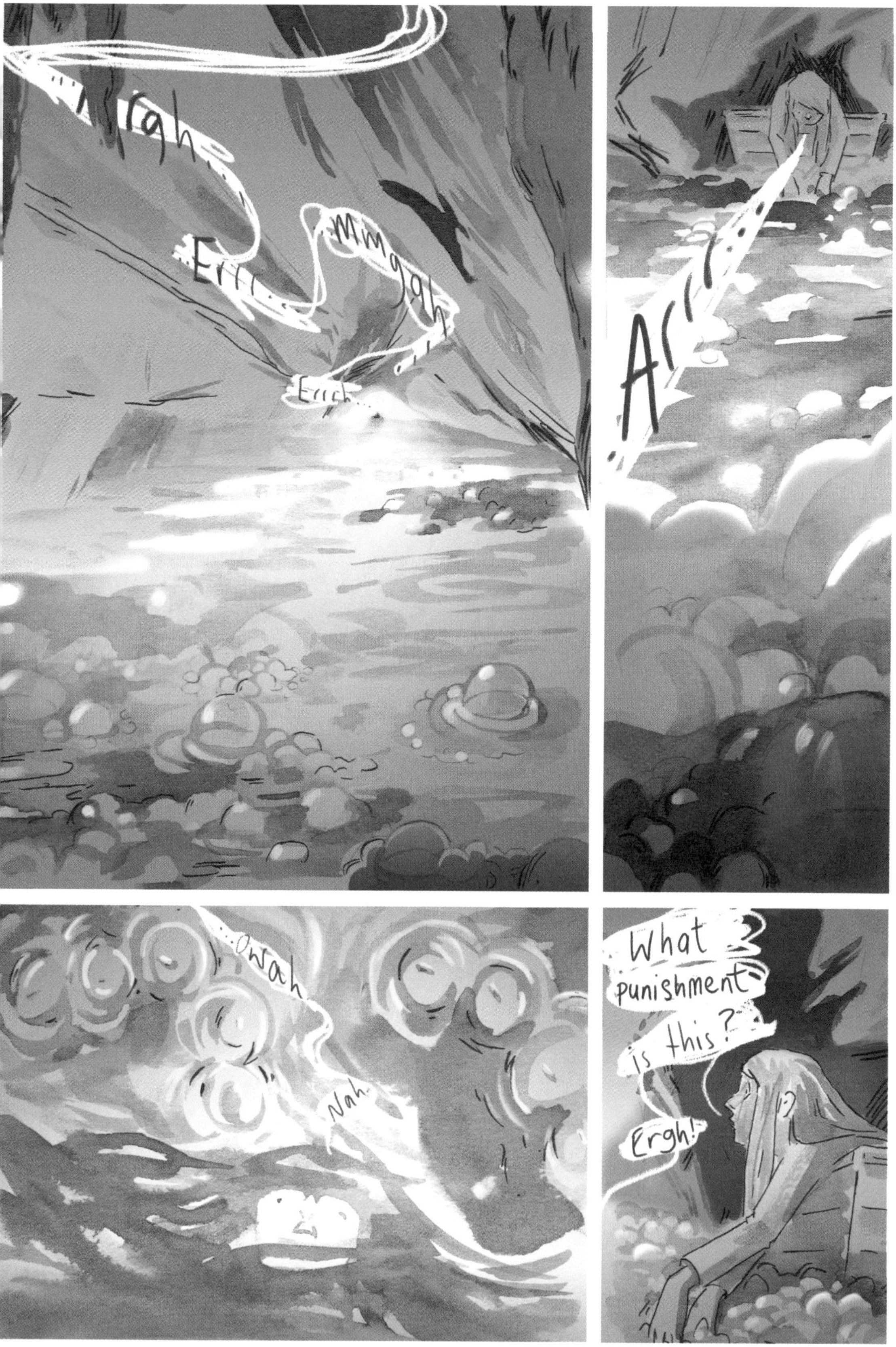
...Argh...
Errr...
...Mmggh...
Errch...
Arrr...
...Owah...
Nah
What punishment is this?
Ergh!

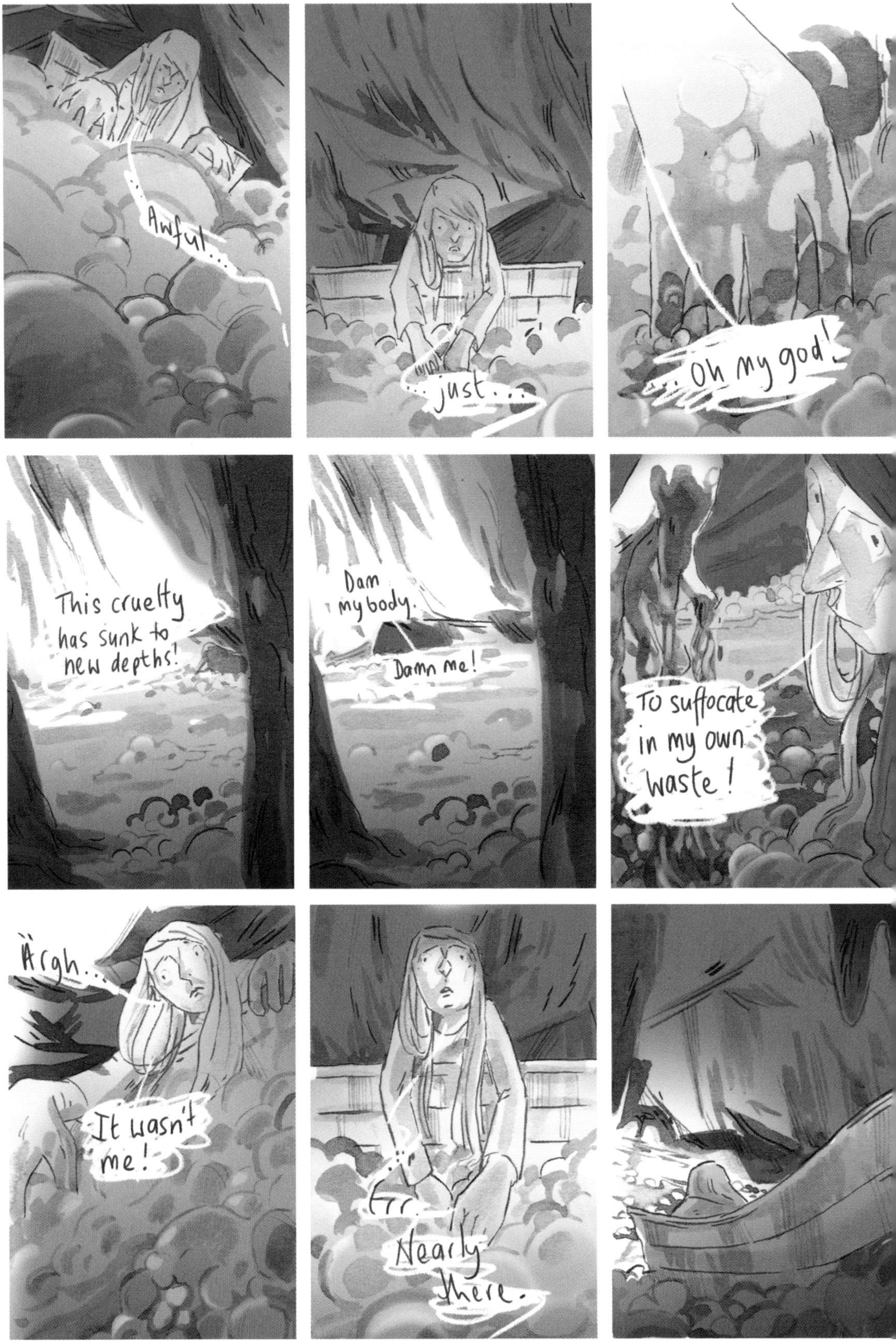

Awful...
... just ...
... Oh my god!
This cruelty has sunk to new depths!
Dam my body.
Damn me!
To suffocate in my own waste!
Argh...
It wasn't me!
...rr
Grr.
Nearly there.

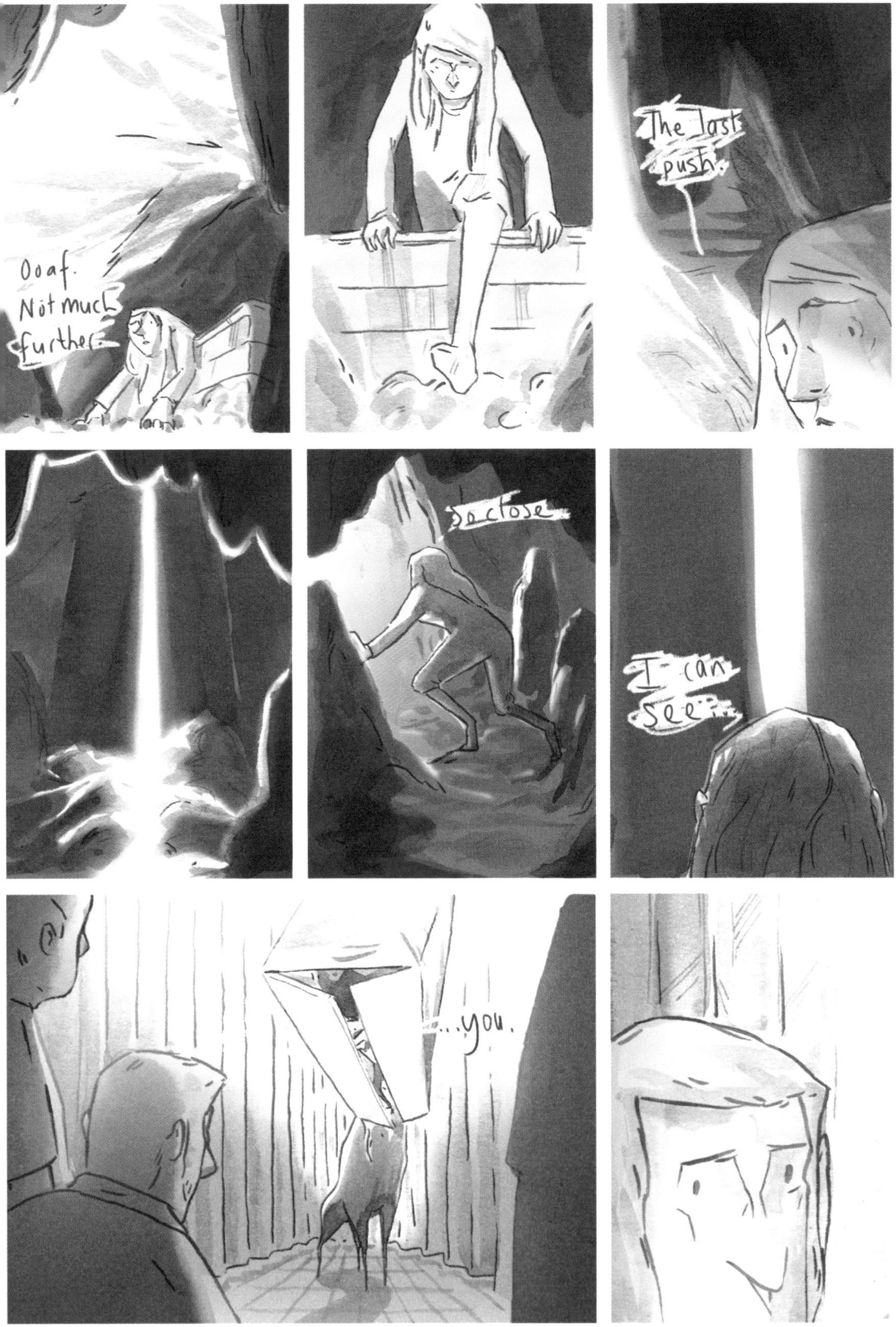
Ooaf. Not much further.
The last push.
So close
I can see...
...you.

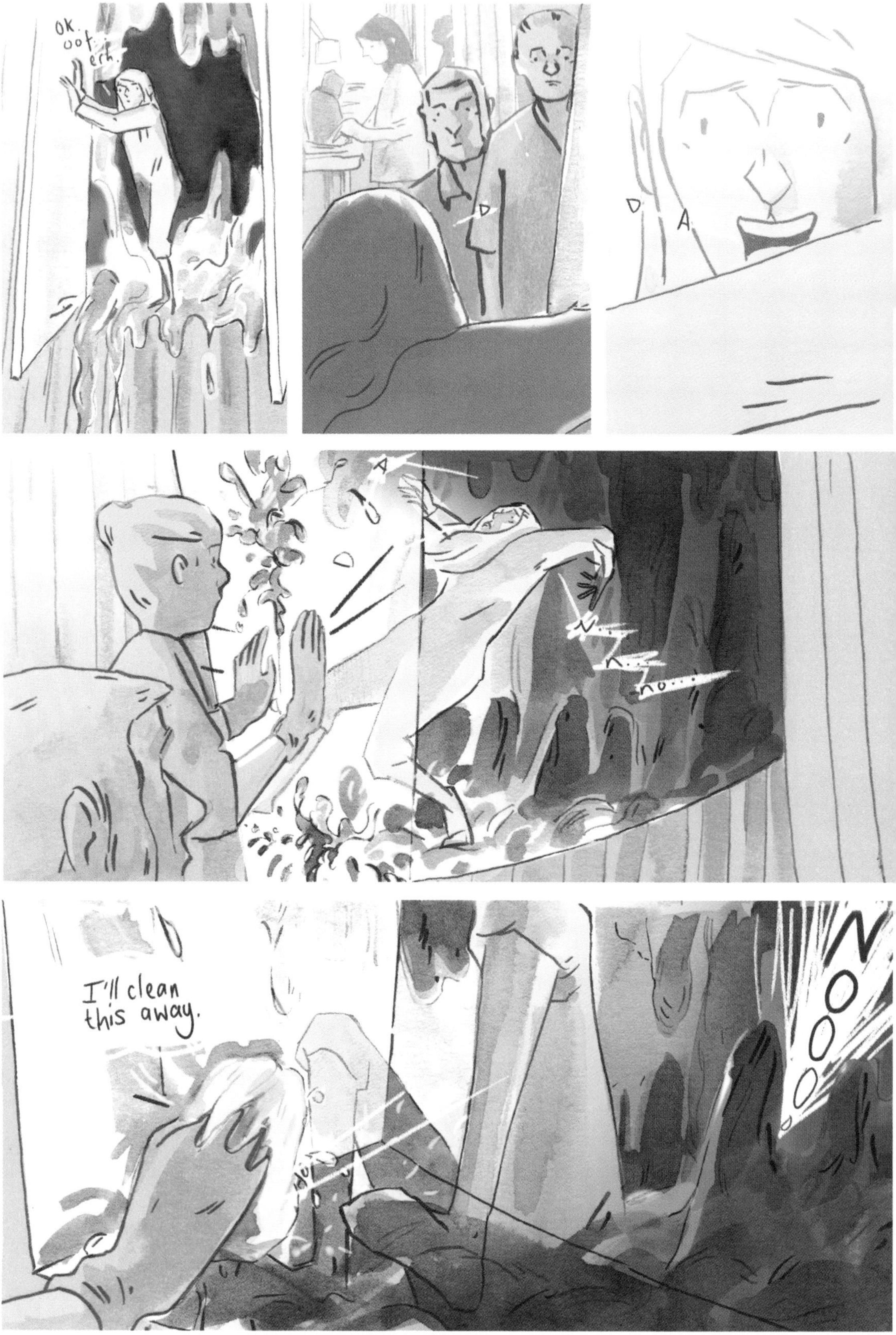
ok. oof. erh.
D
D A
A
n... n... no...
I'll clean this away.
NOOOO

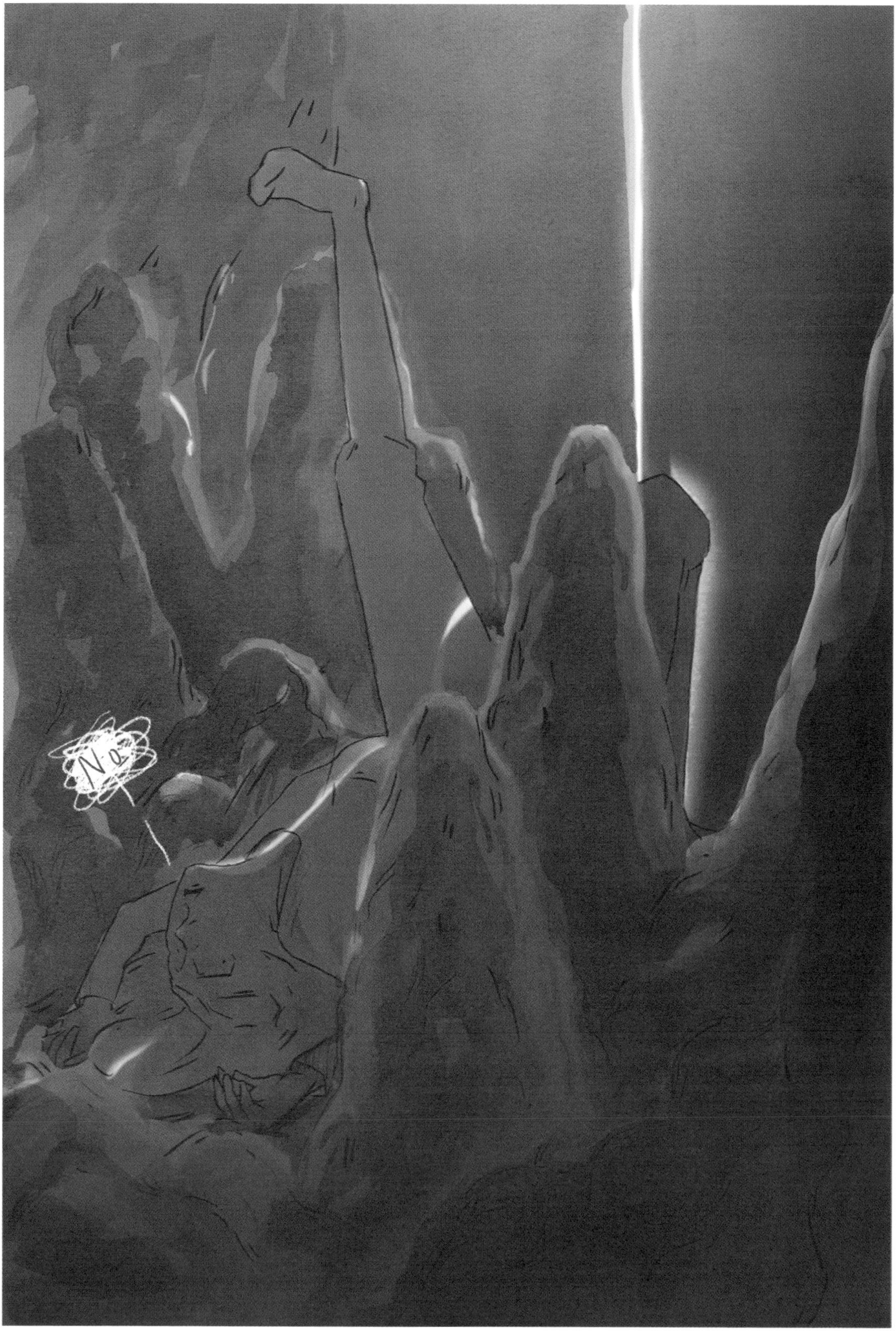
No

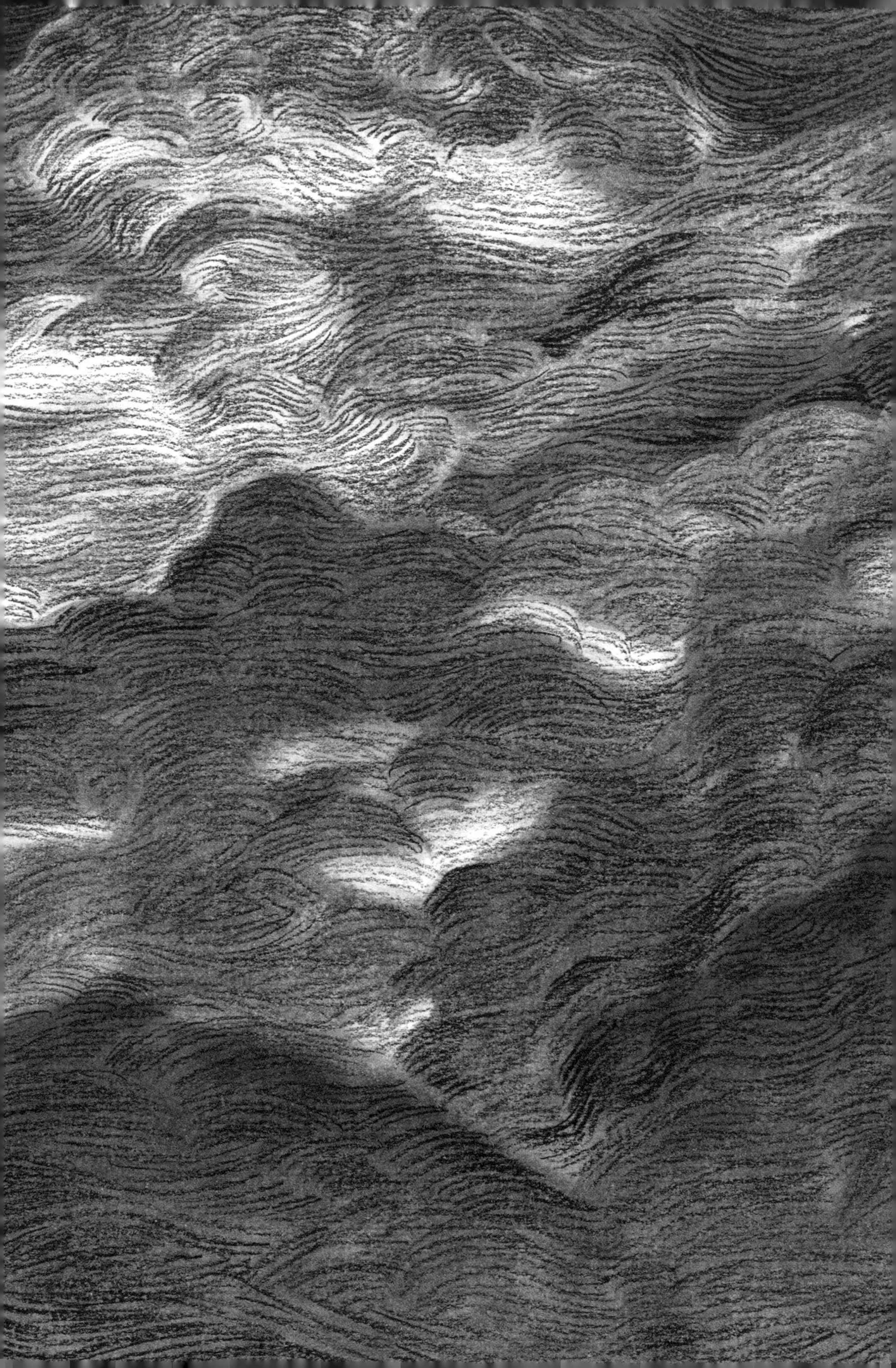

It's Friday evening, about 9.30pm.

Diana's spag bol for tea, Molly and Bee sleeping over with Tam.

Andy Bennett drove me in. Kat the Navy nurse is on tonight.

You are half in and out of a dream.

Your dad is fine. He is planning to call. I told you so.

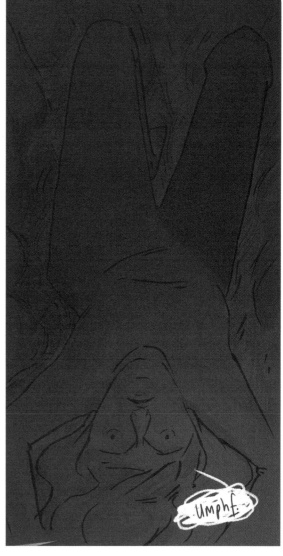

Umph.

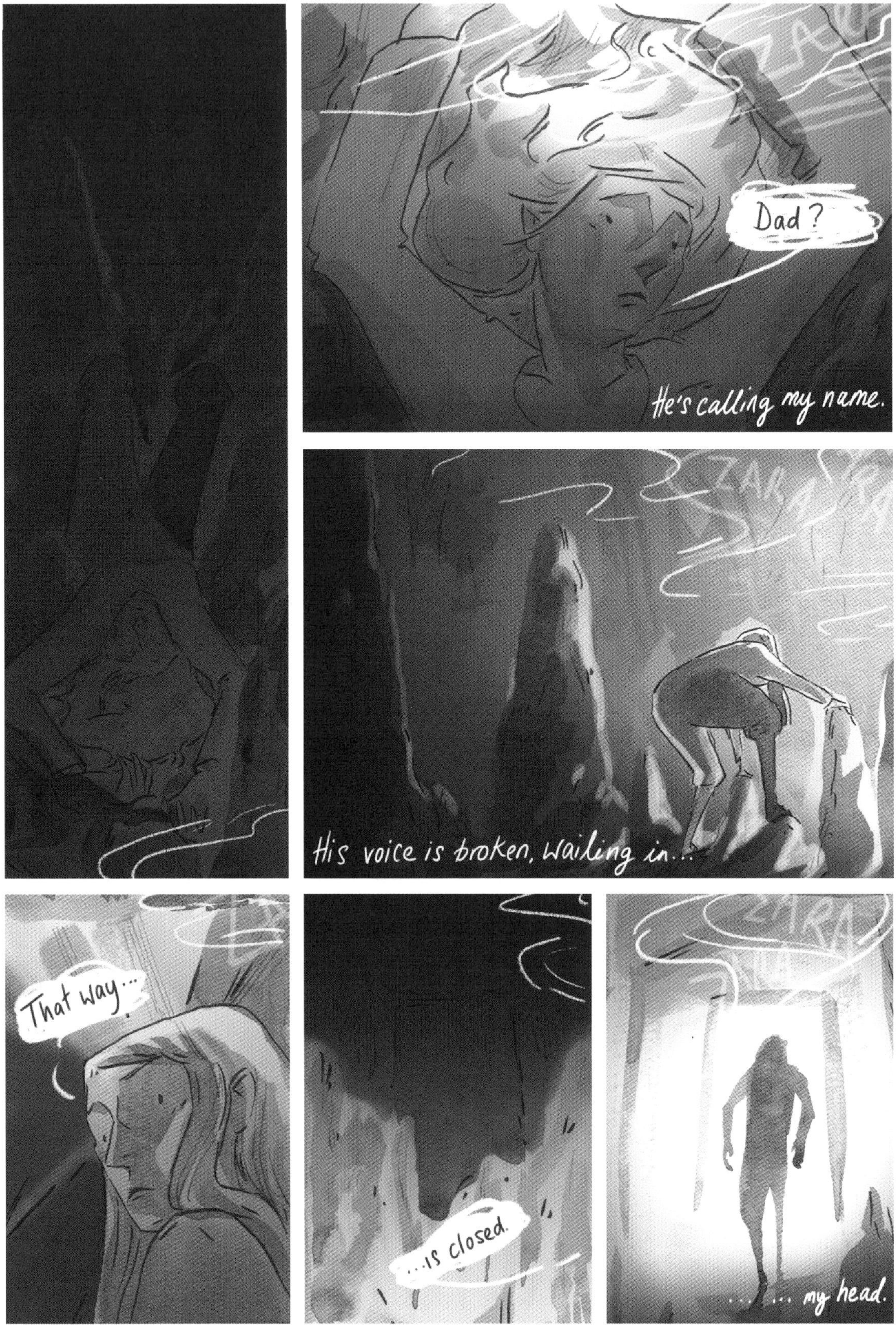
Dad?
He's calling my name.
ZARA
His voice is broken, wailing in...
That way...
...is closed.
ZARA
... ... my head.

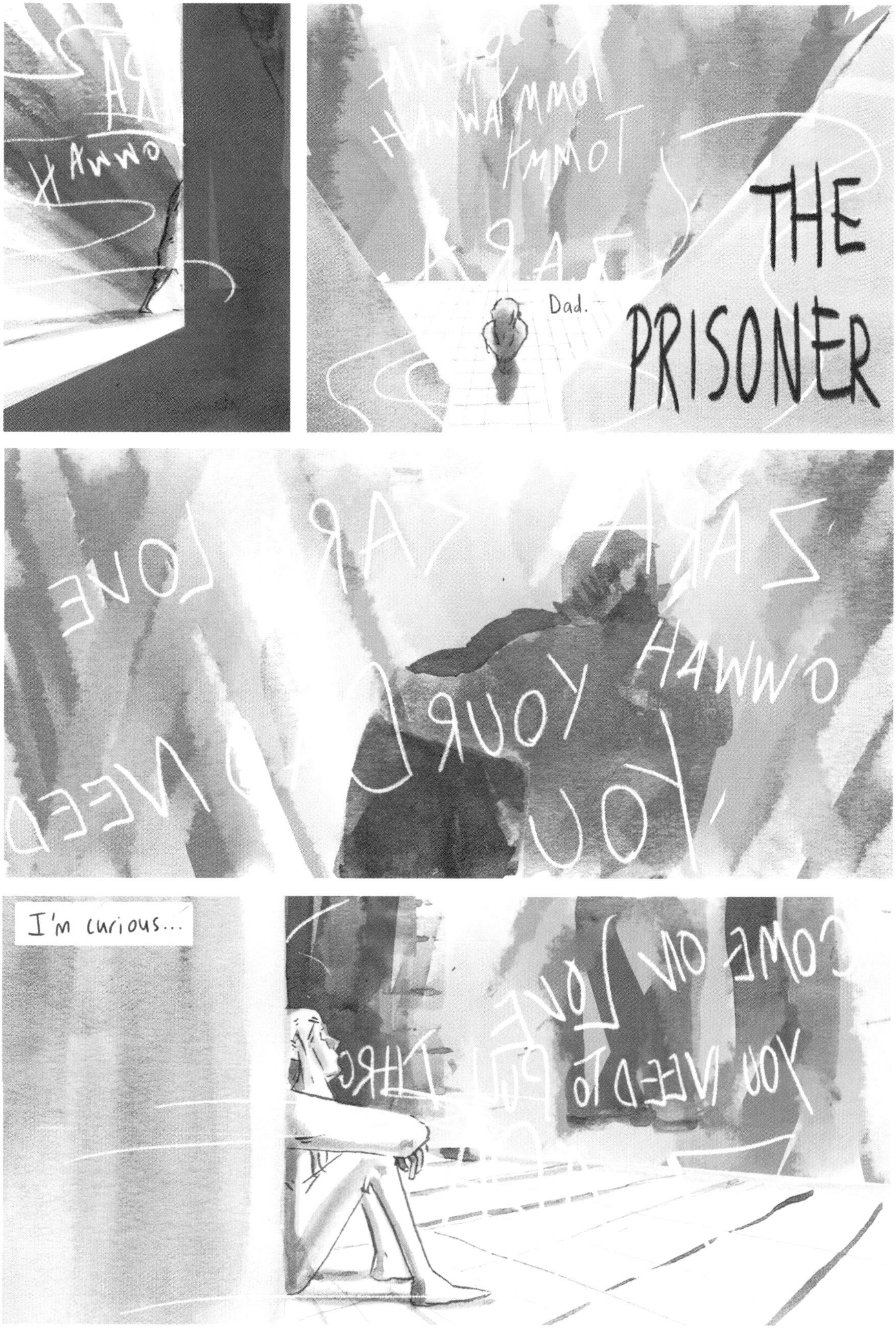
Dad.
THE PRISONER
I'm curious...

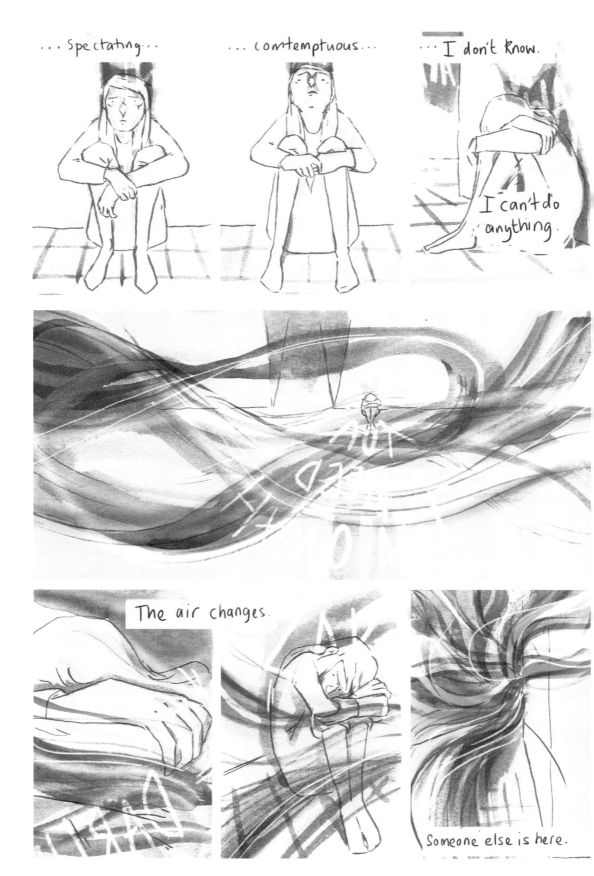

... Spectating...

... comtemptuous...

...I don't know.

I can't do anything.

The air changes.

Someone else is here.

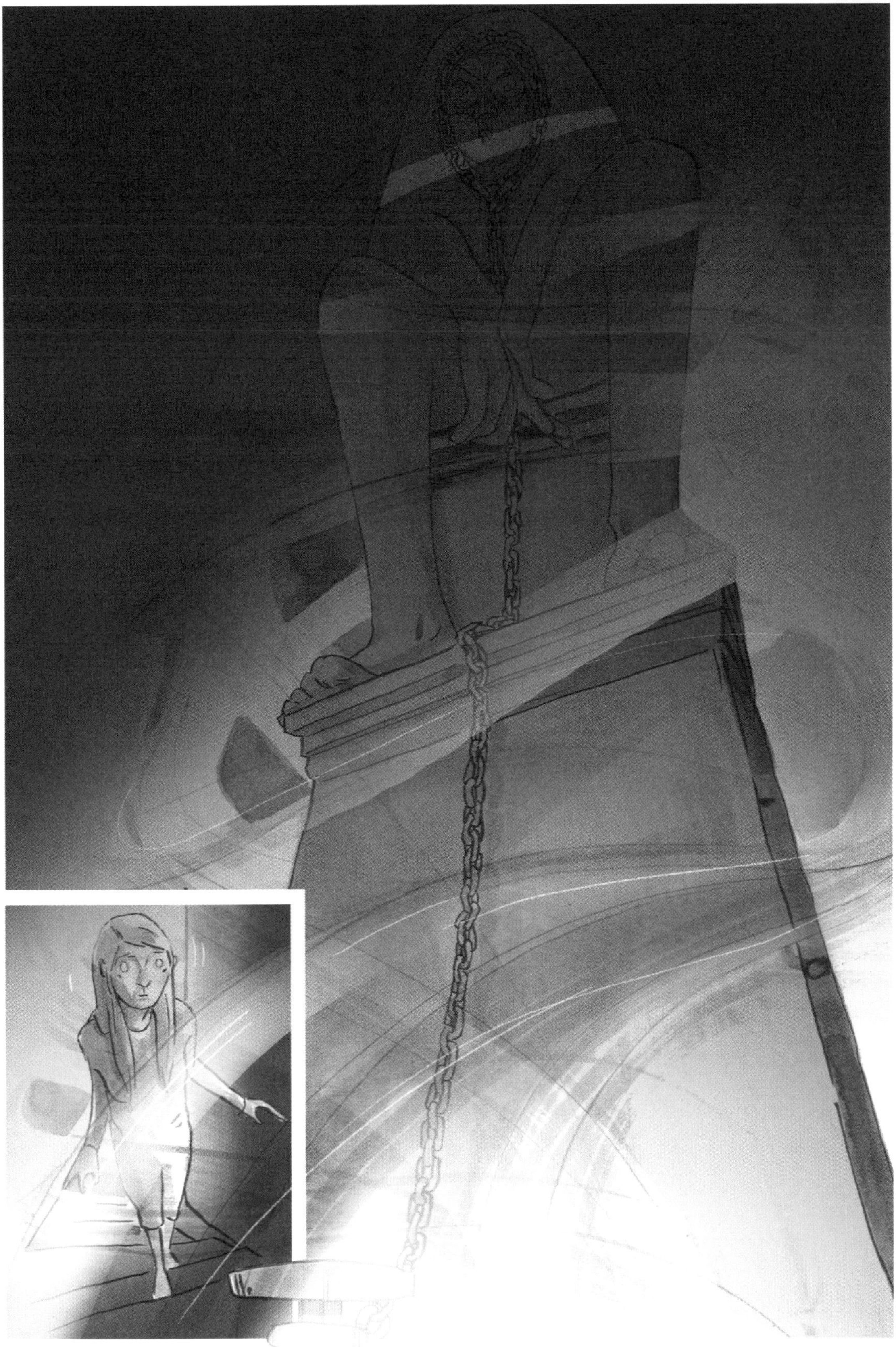

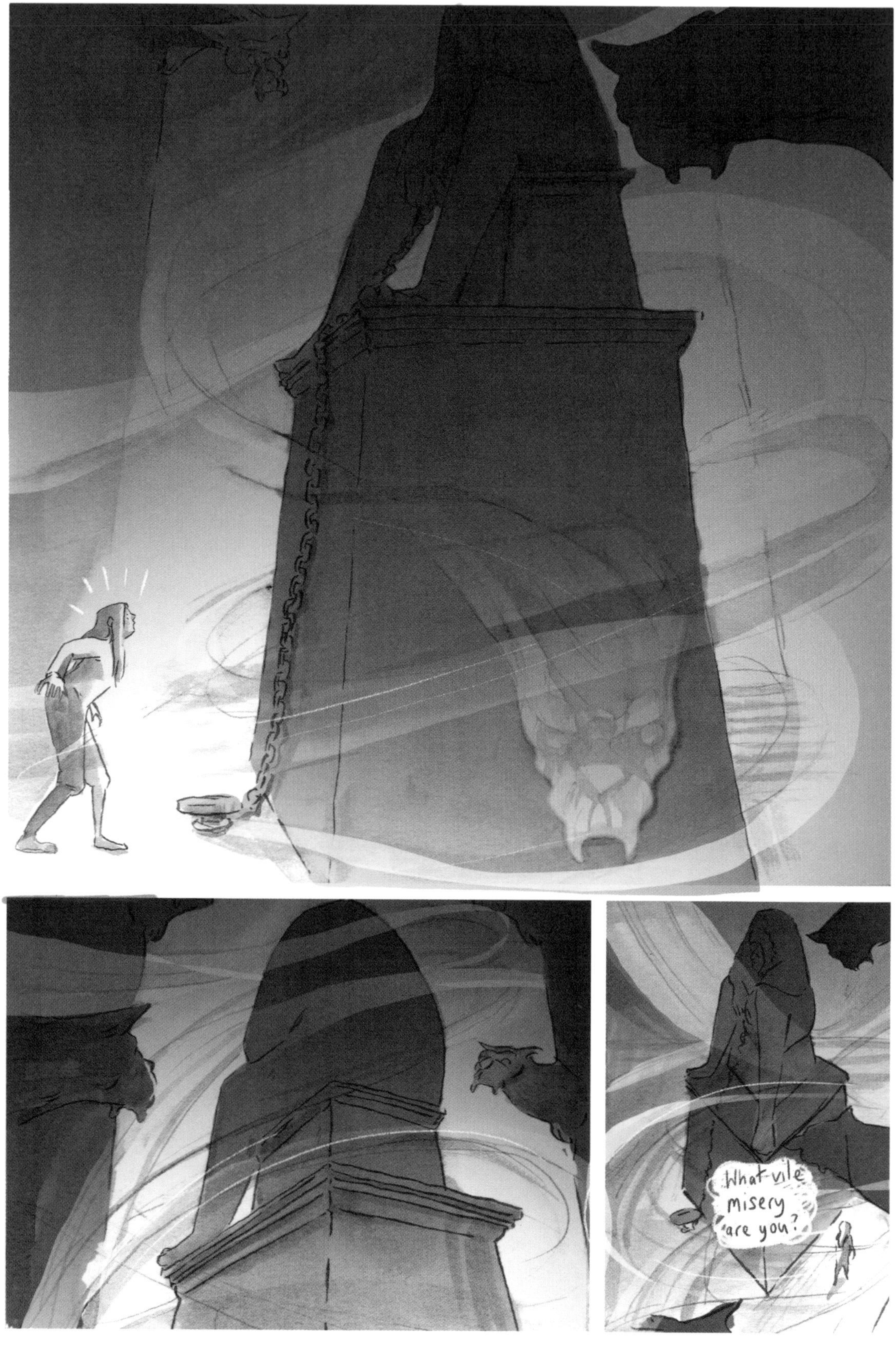
What vile misery are you?

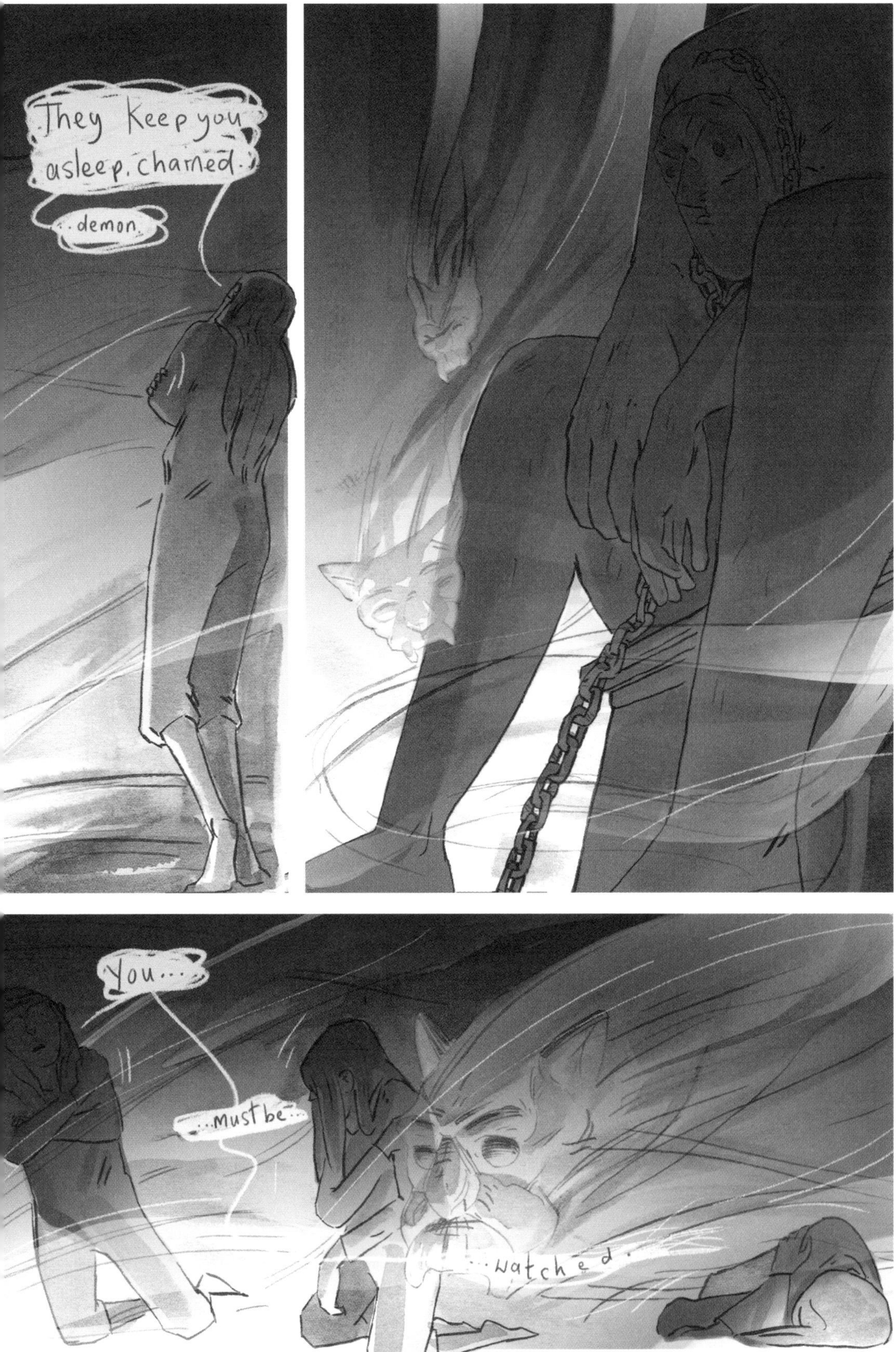
They keep you asleep, charmed.
...demon.
You...
...must be...
...watched.

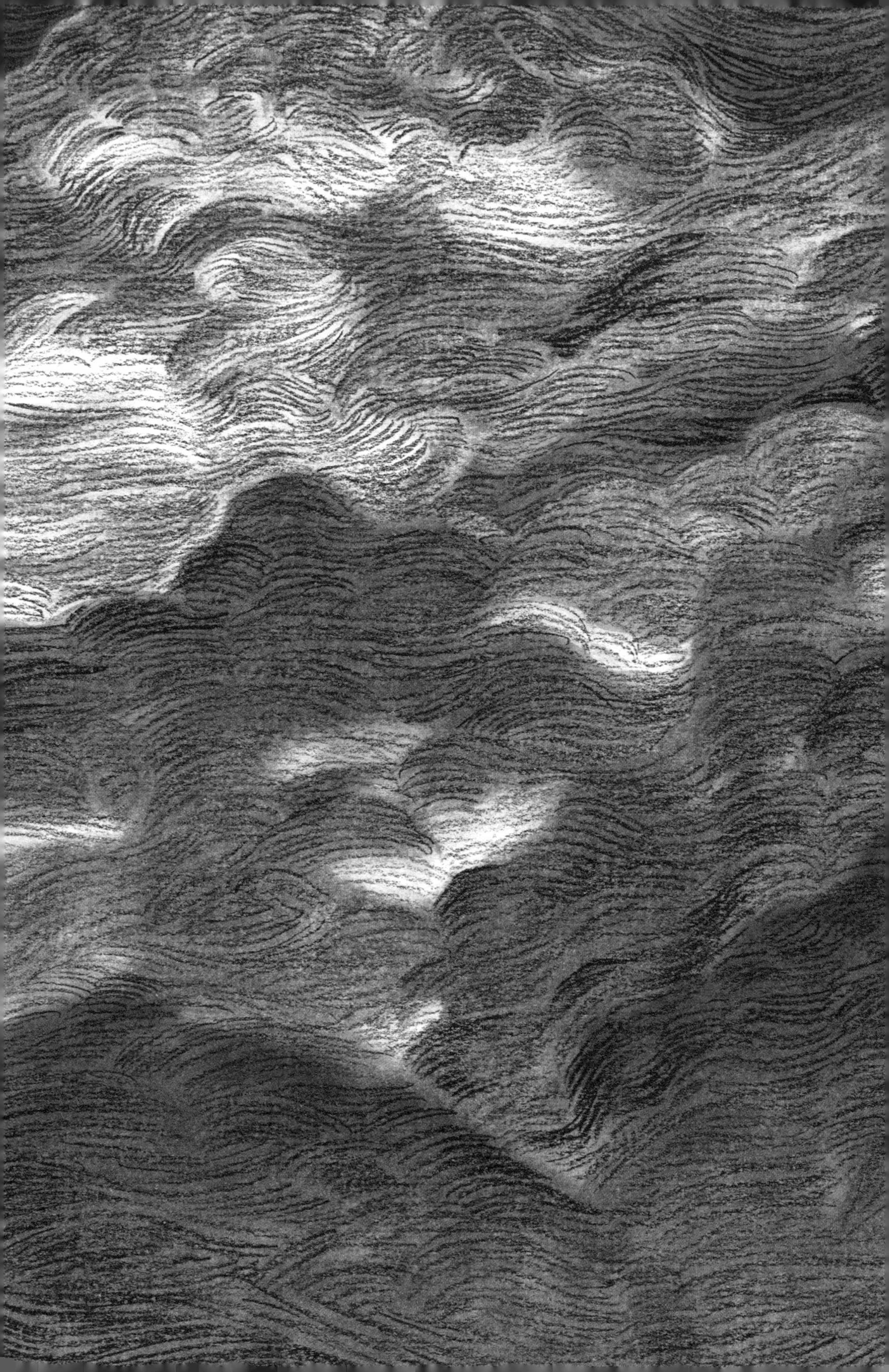

SATURDAY 1st JUNE

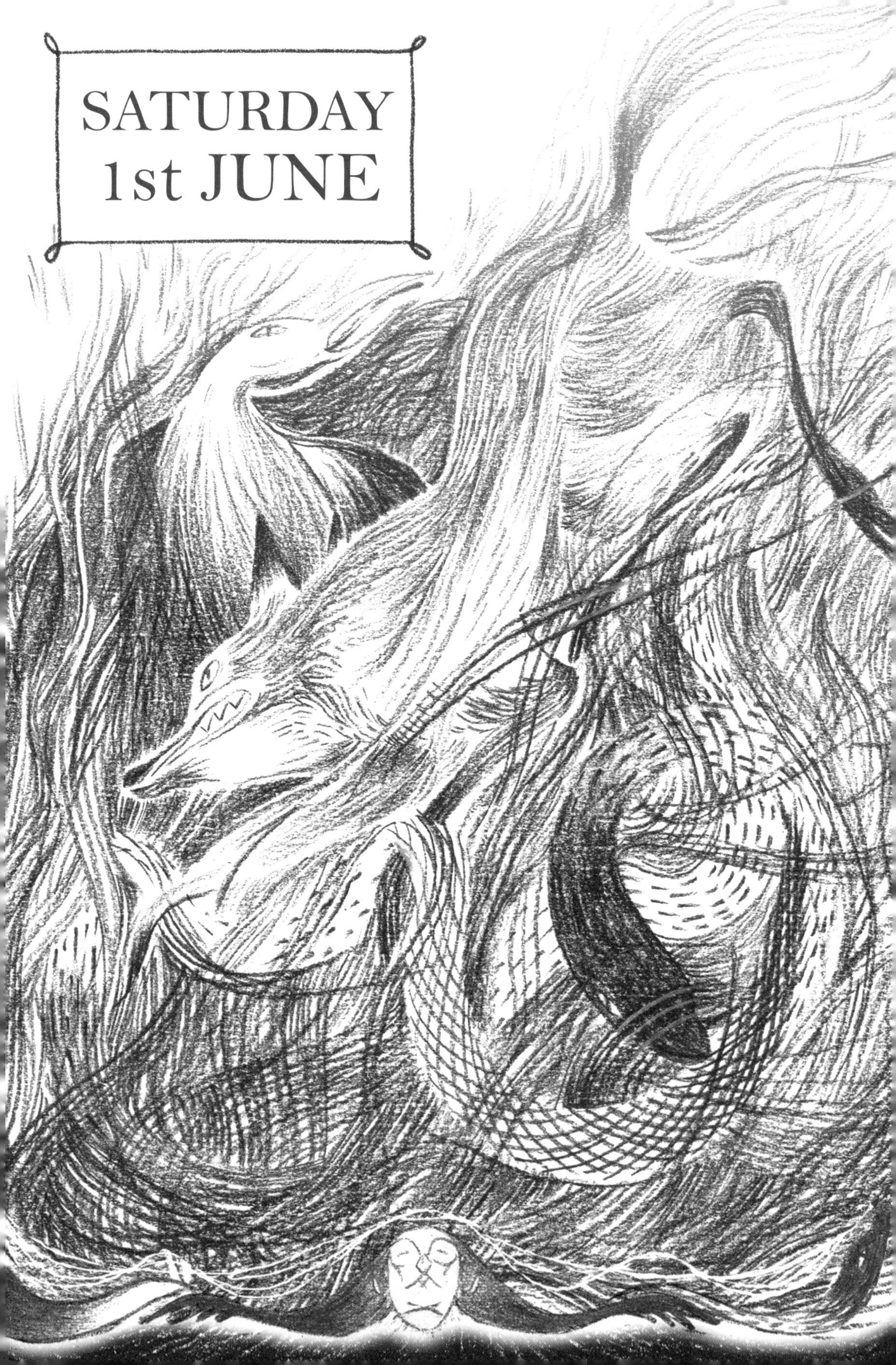

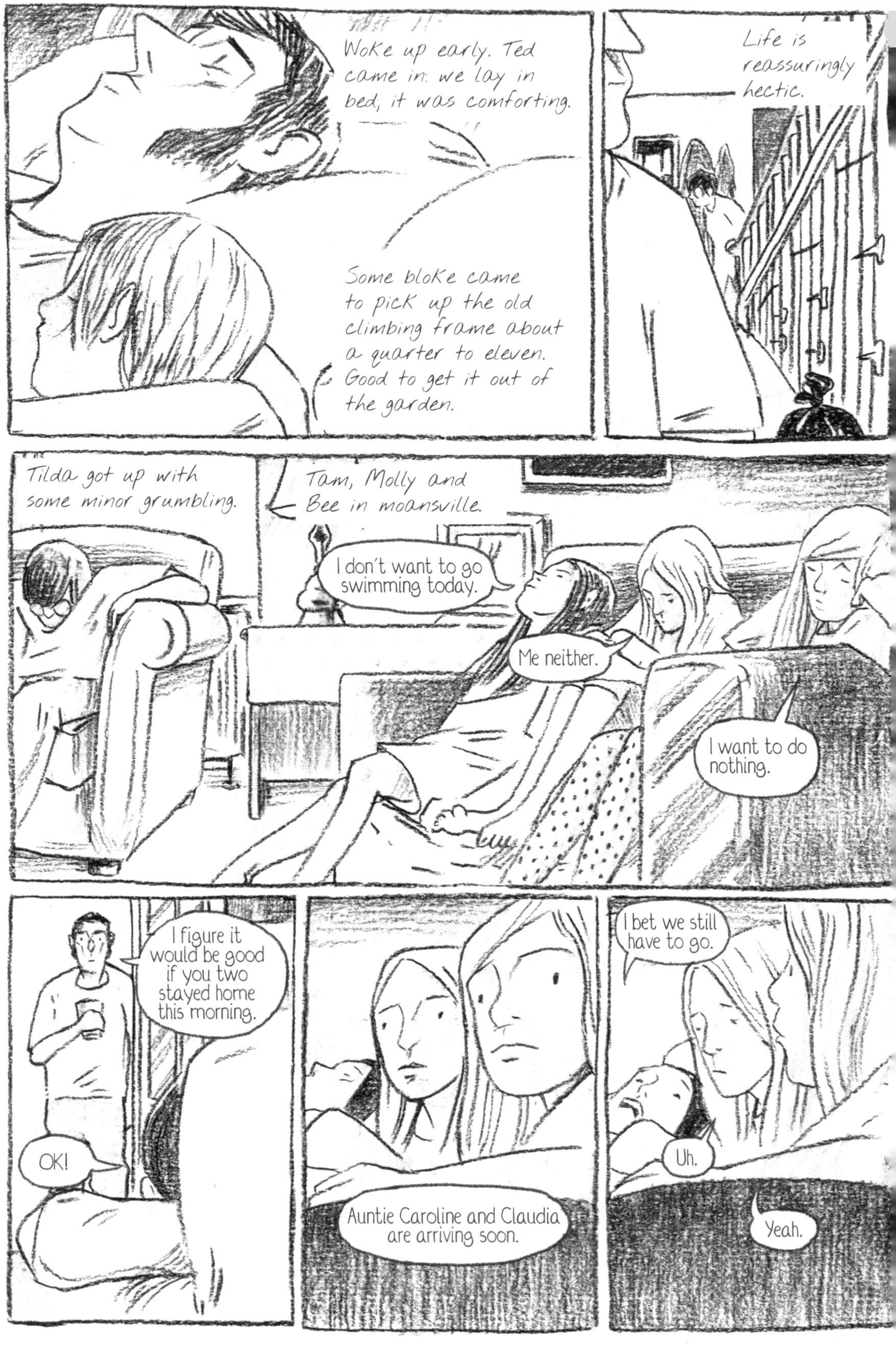
Woke up early. Ted came in: we lay in bed, it was comforting.
Some bloke came to pick up the old climbing frame about a quarter to eleven. Good to get it out of the garden.
Life is reassuringly hectic.
Tilda got up with some minor grumbling.
Tam, Molly and Bee in moansville.
I don't want to go swimming today.
Me neither.
I want to do nothing.
I figure it would be good if you two stayed home this morning.
OK!
Auntie Caroline and Claudia are arriving soon.
I bet we still have to go.
Uh.
Yeah.

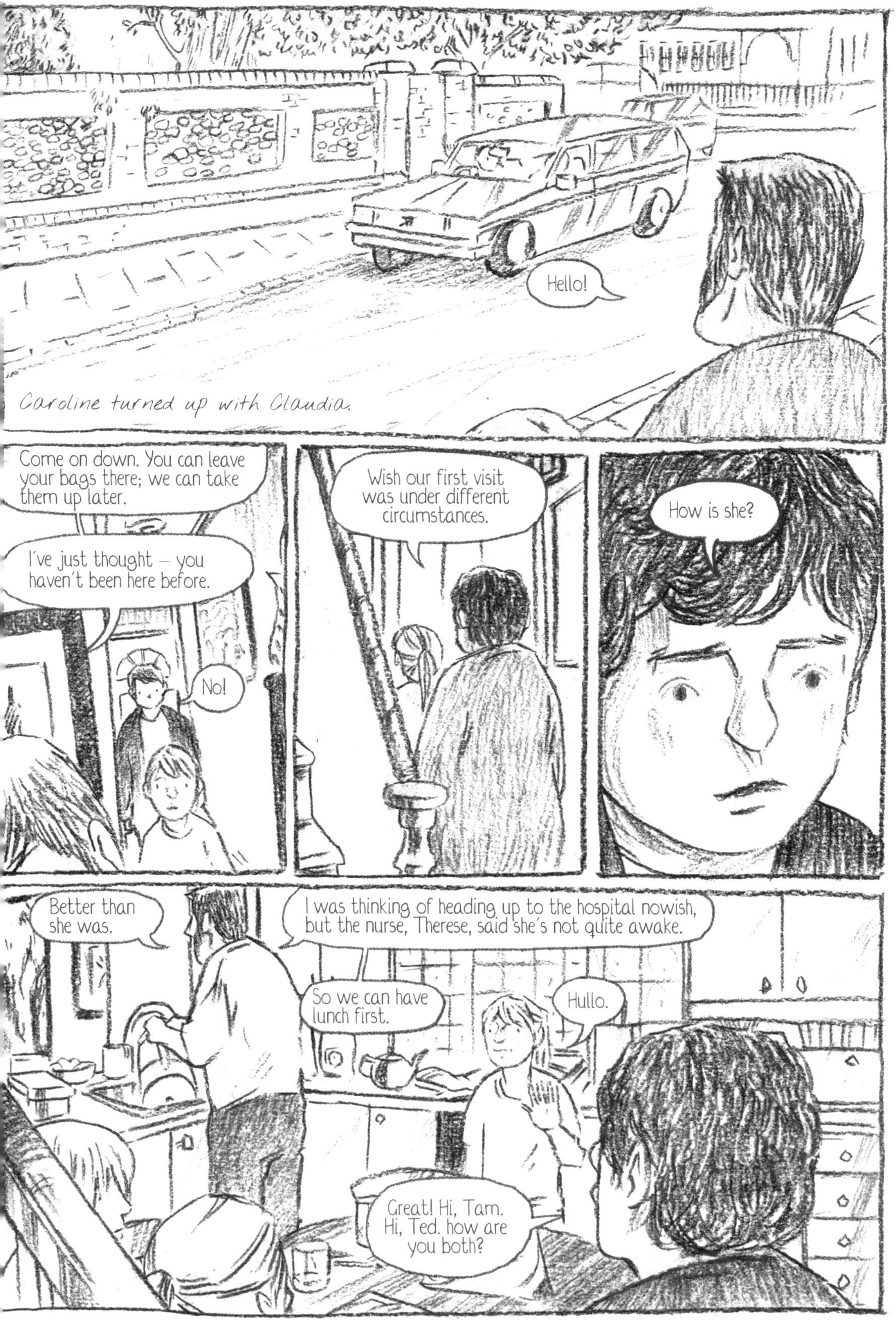

Hello!
Caroline turned up with Claudia.
Come on down. You can leave your bags there; we can take them up later.
I've just thought – you haven't been here before.
No!
Wish our first visit was under different circumstances.
How is she?
Better than she was.
I was thinking of heading up to the hospital nowish, but the nurse, Therese, said she's not quite awake.
So we can have lunch first.
Hullo.
Great! Hi, Tam. Hi, Ted. how are you both?

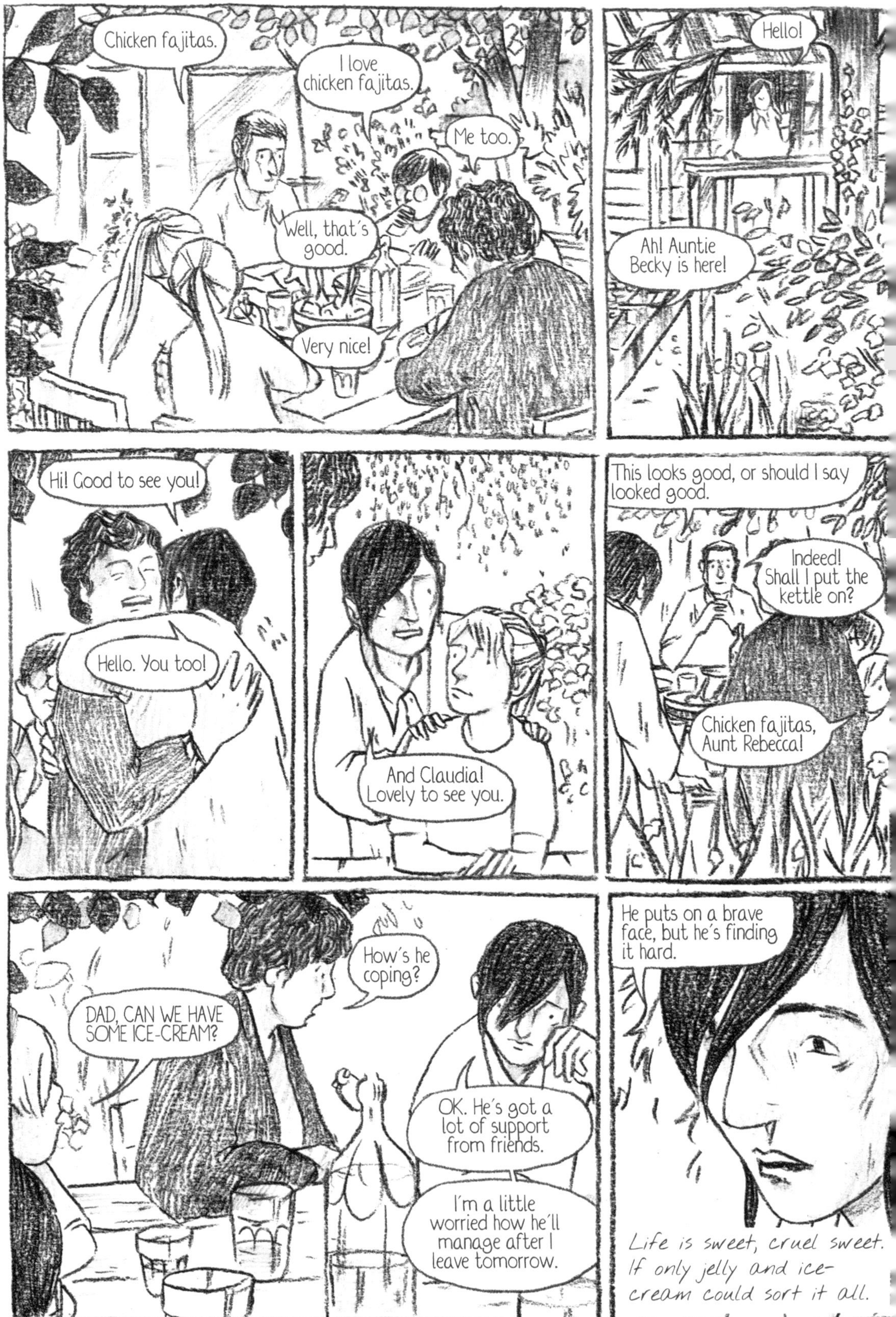
Chicken fajitas.
I love chicken fajitas.
Me too.
Well, that's good.
Very nice!
Hello!
Ah! Auntie Becky is here!
Hi! Good to see you!
Hello. You too!
And Claudia! Lovely to see you.
This looks good, or should I say looked good.
Indeed! Shall I put the kettle on?
Chicken fajitas, Aunt Rebecca!
DAD, CAN WE HAVE SOME ICE-CREAM?
How's he coping?
OK. He's got a lot of support from friends.
I'm a little worried how he'll manage after I leave tomorrow.
He puts on a brave face, but he's finding it hard.
Life is sweet, cruel sweet. If only jelly and ice-cream could sort it all.

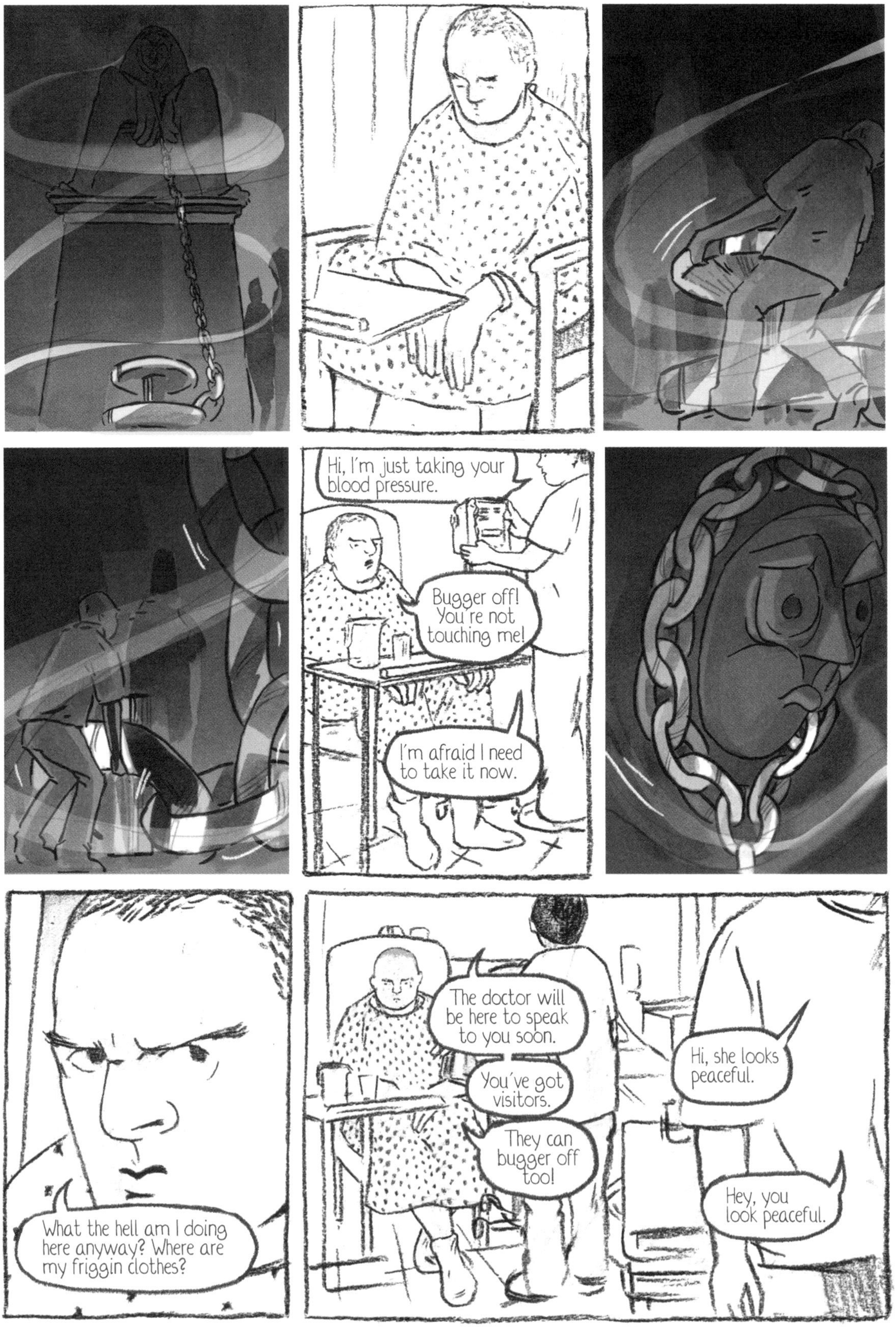
Hi, I'm just taking your blood pressure.
Bugger off! You're not touching me!
I'm afraid I need to take it now.
What the hell am I doing here anyway? Where are my friggin clothes?
The doctor will be here to speak to you soon.
You've got visitors.
They can bugger off too!
Hi, she looks peaceful.
Hey, you look peaceful.

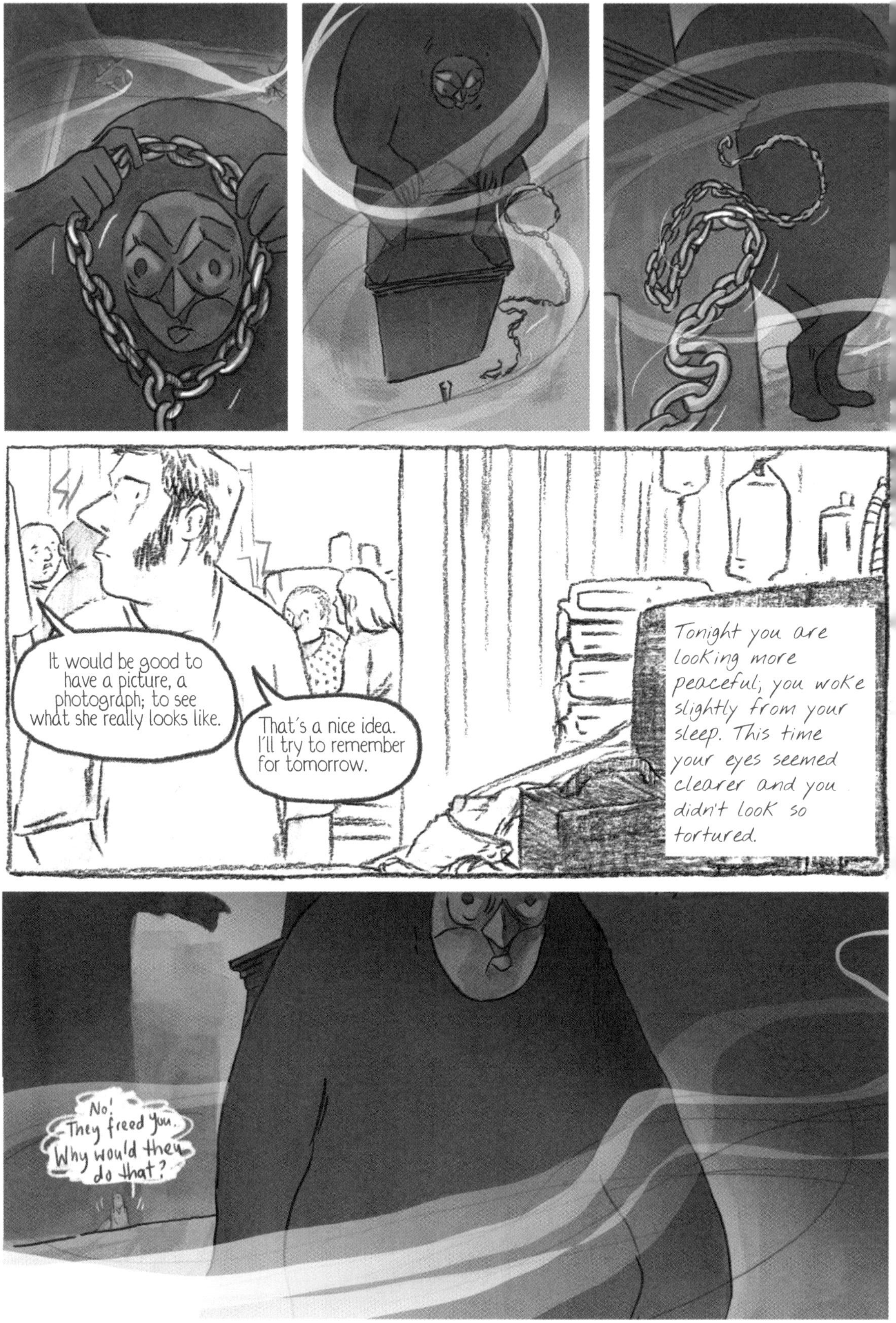
It would be good to have a picture, a photograph; to see what she really looks like.
That's a nice idea. I'll try to remember for tomorrow.
Tonight you are looking more peaceful; you woke slightly from your sleep. This time your eyes seemed clearer and you didn't look so tortured.
No! They freed you. Why would they do that?

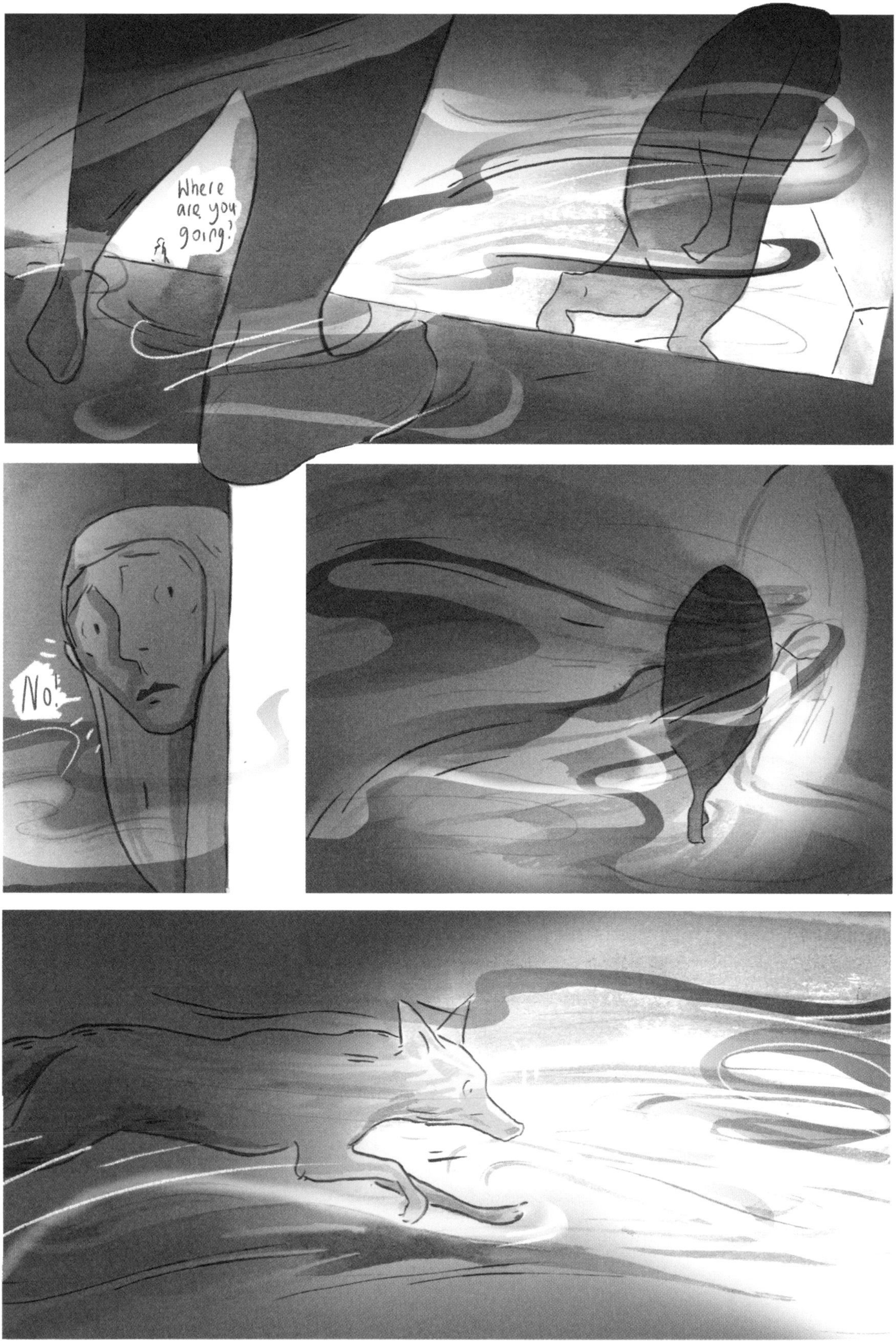
Where are you going?
No!

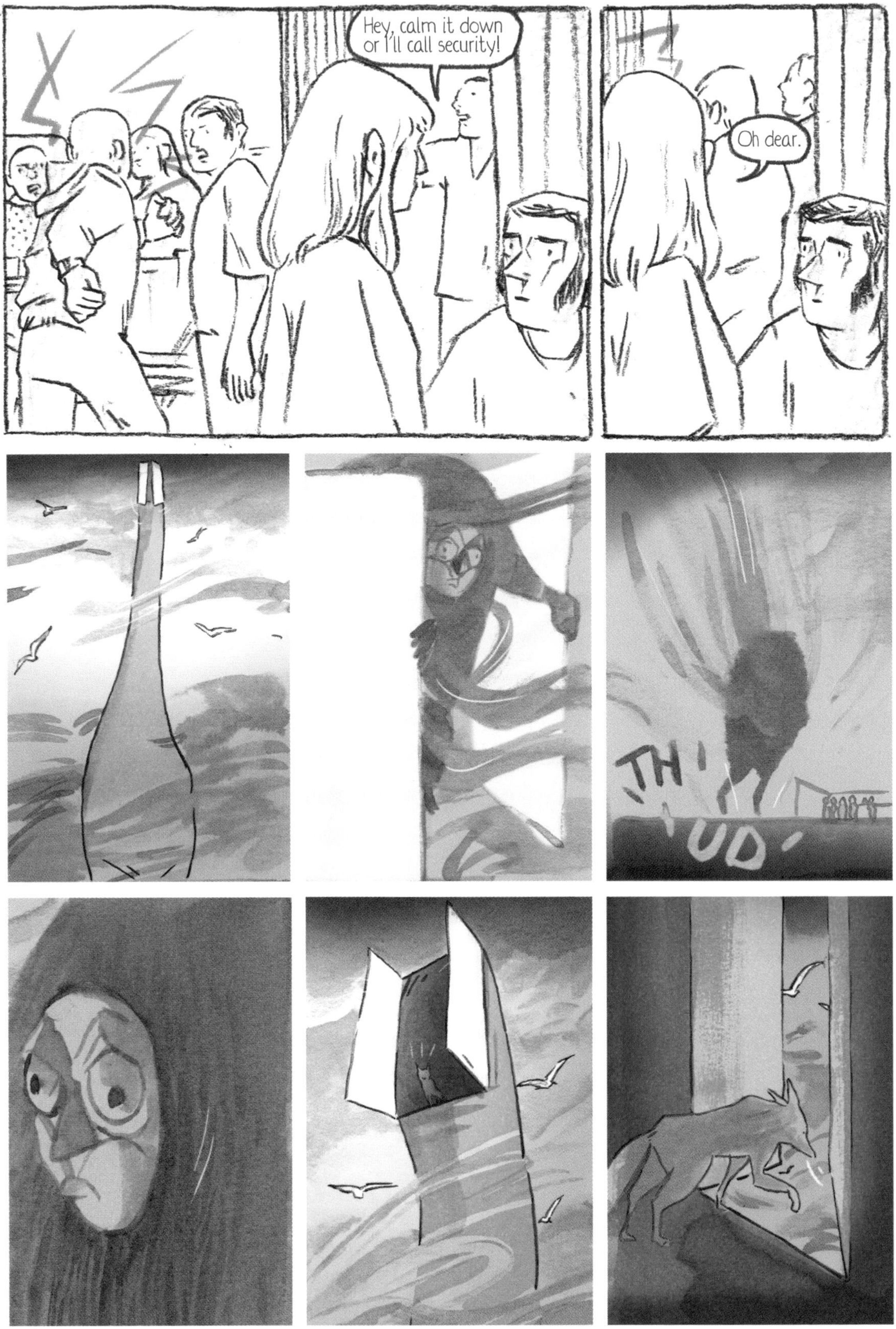
Hey, calm it down or I'll call security!
Oh dear.
THUD

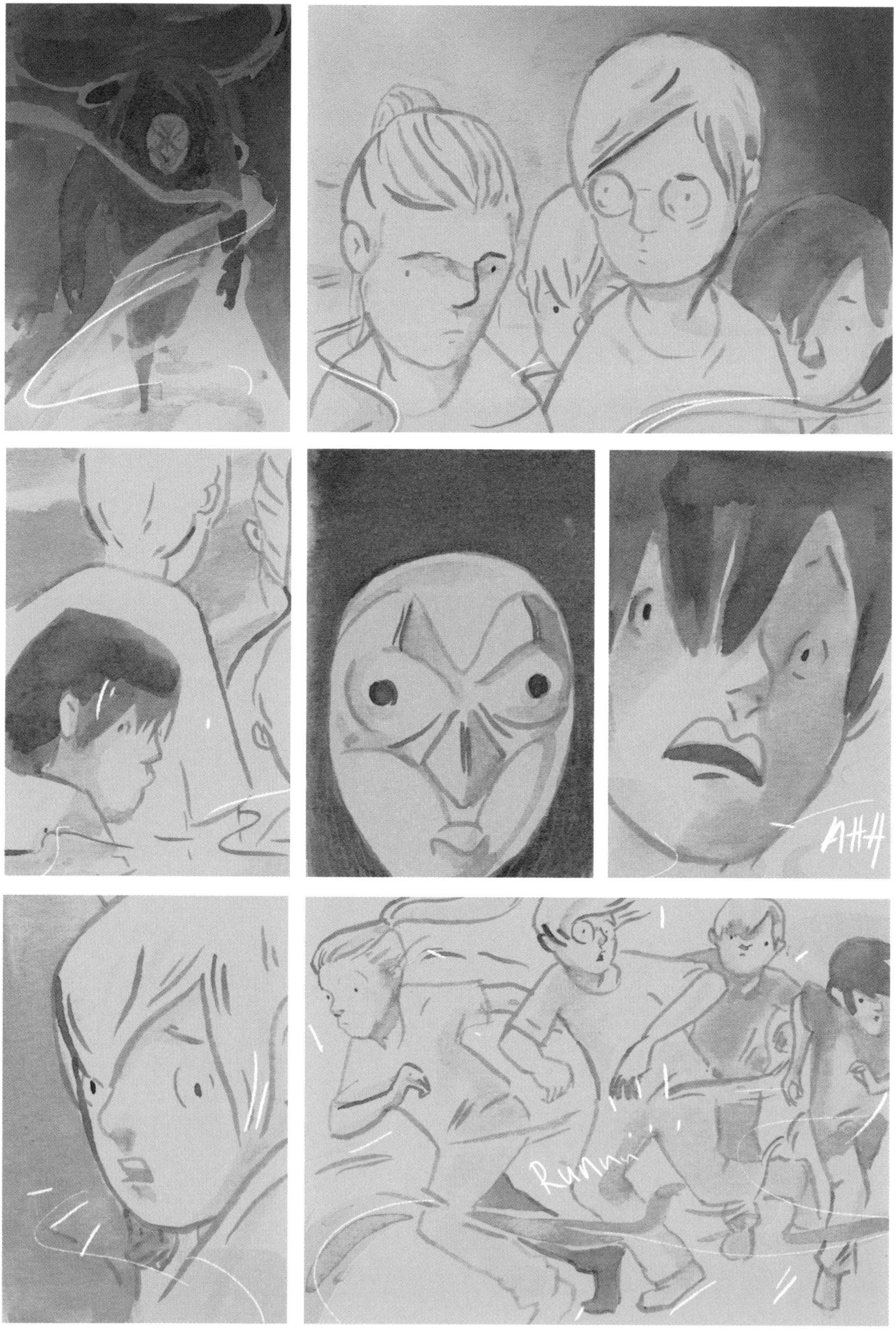
AHH
Runn

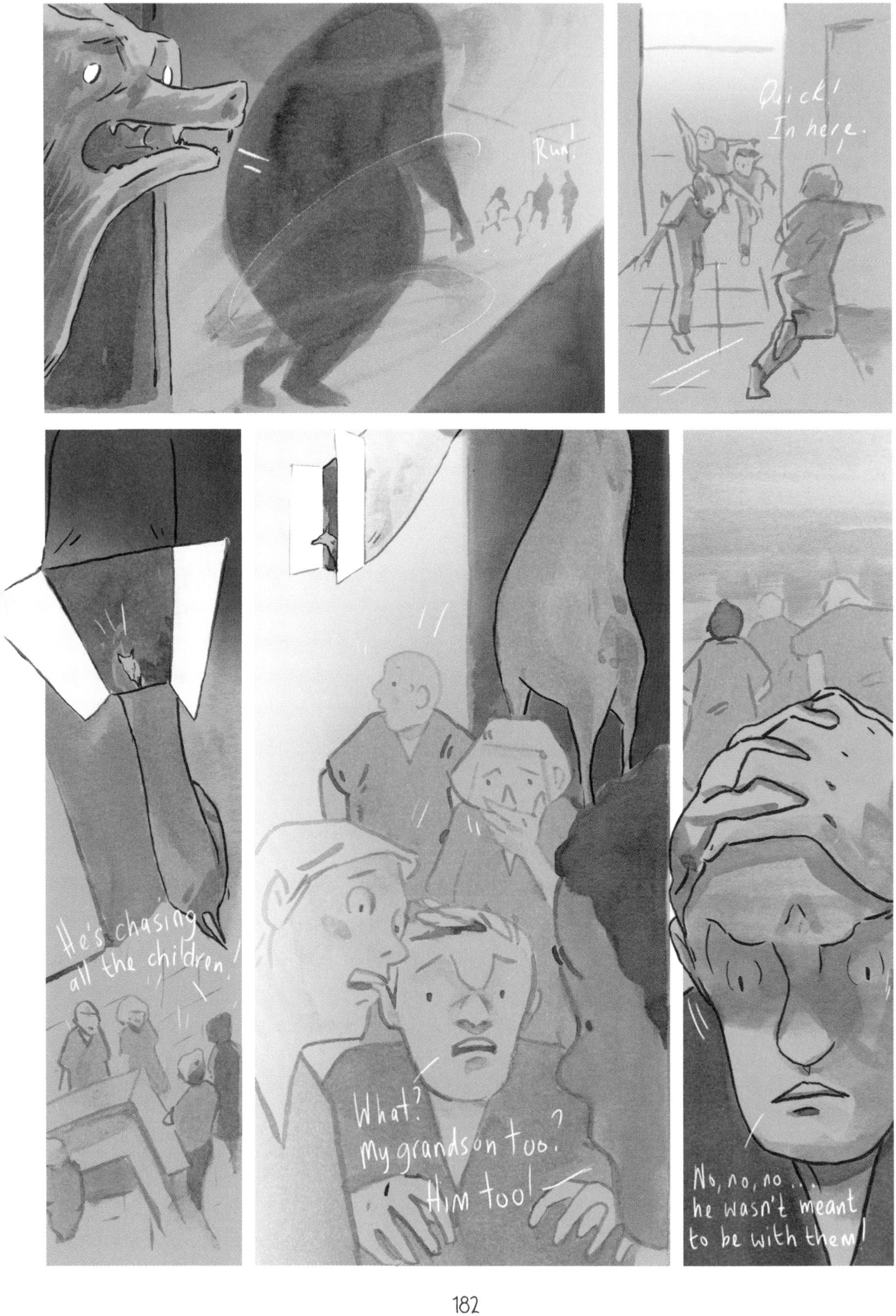

Run!
Quick! In here.
He's chasing all the children!
What? My grandson too? Him too!
No, no, no... he wasn't meant to be with them!

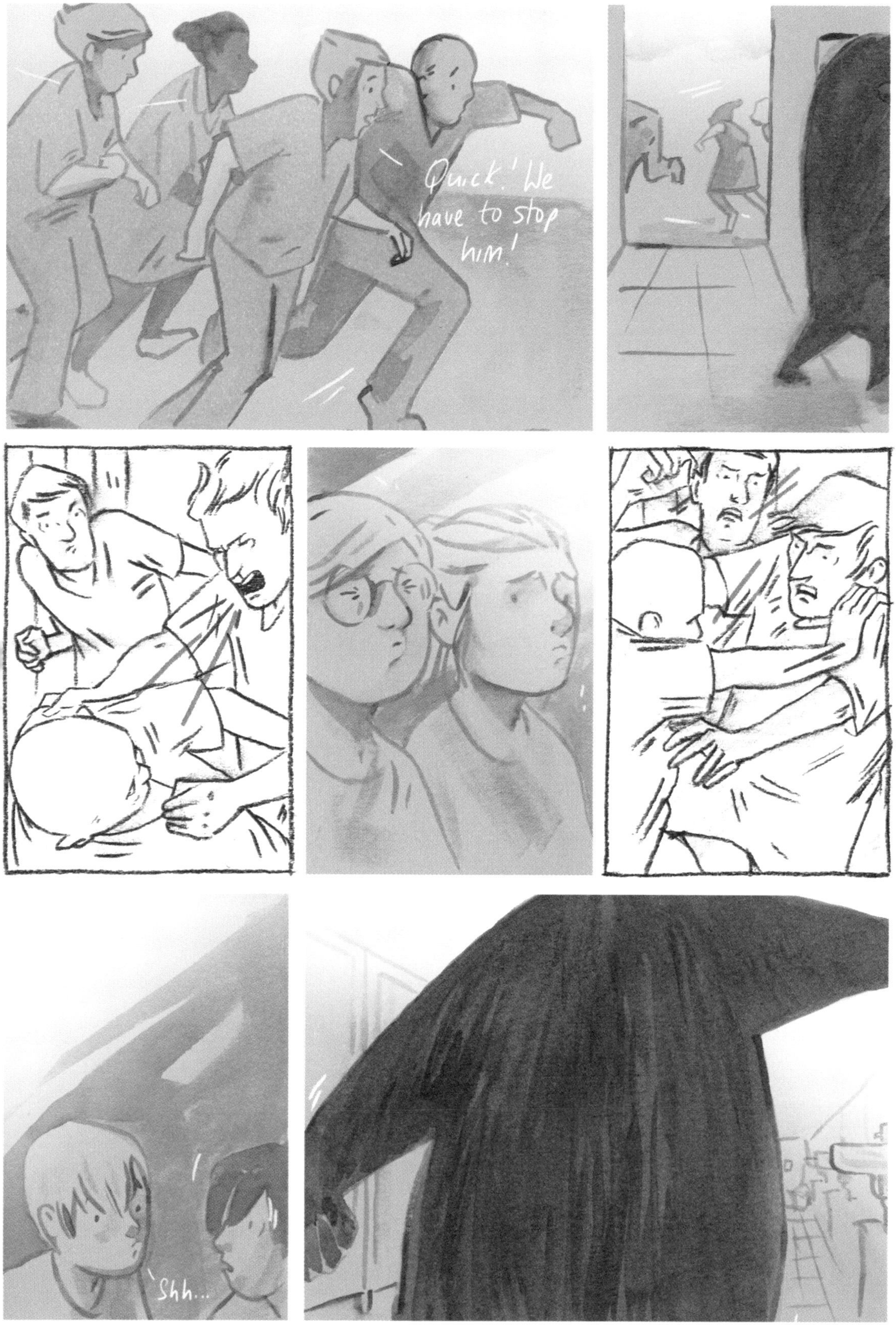
Quick! We have to stop him!
Shh...

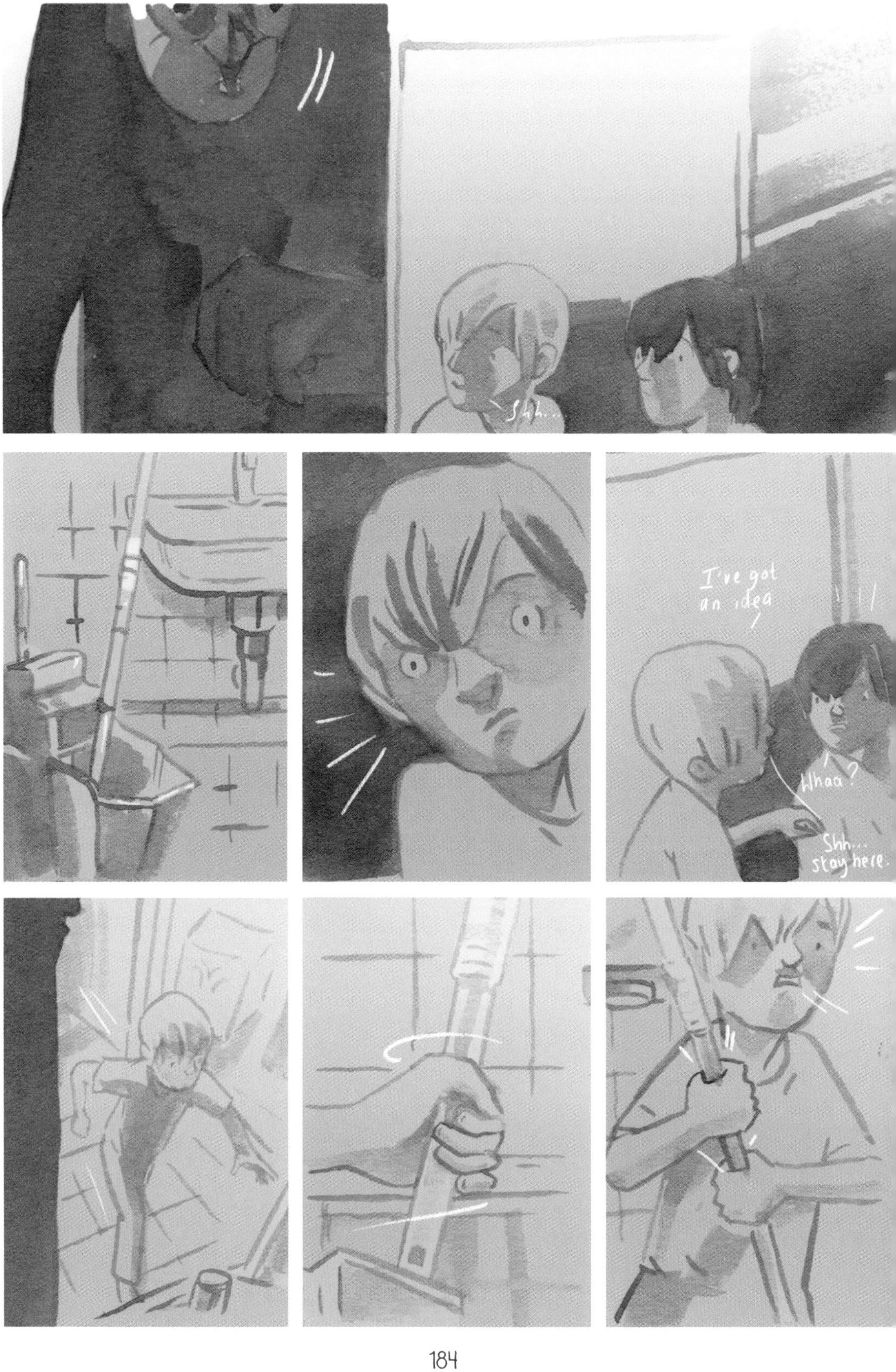
Shh...
I've got an idea
Whaa?
Shh... stay here.

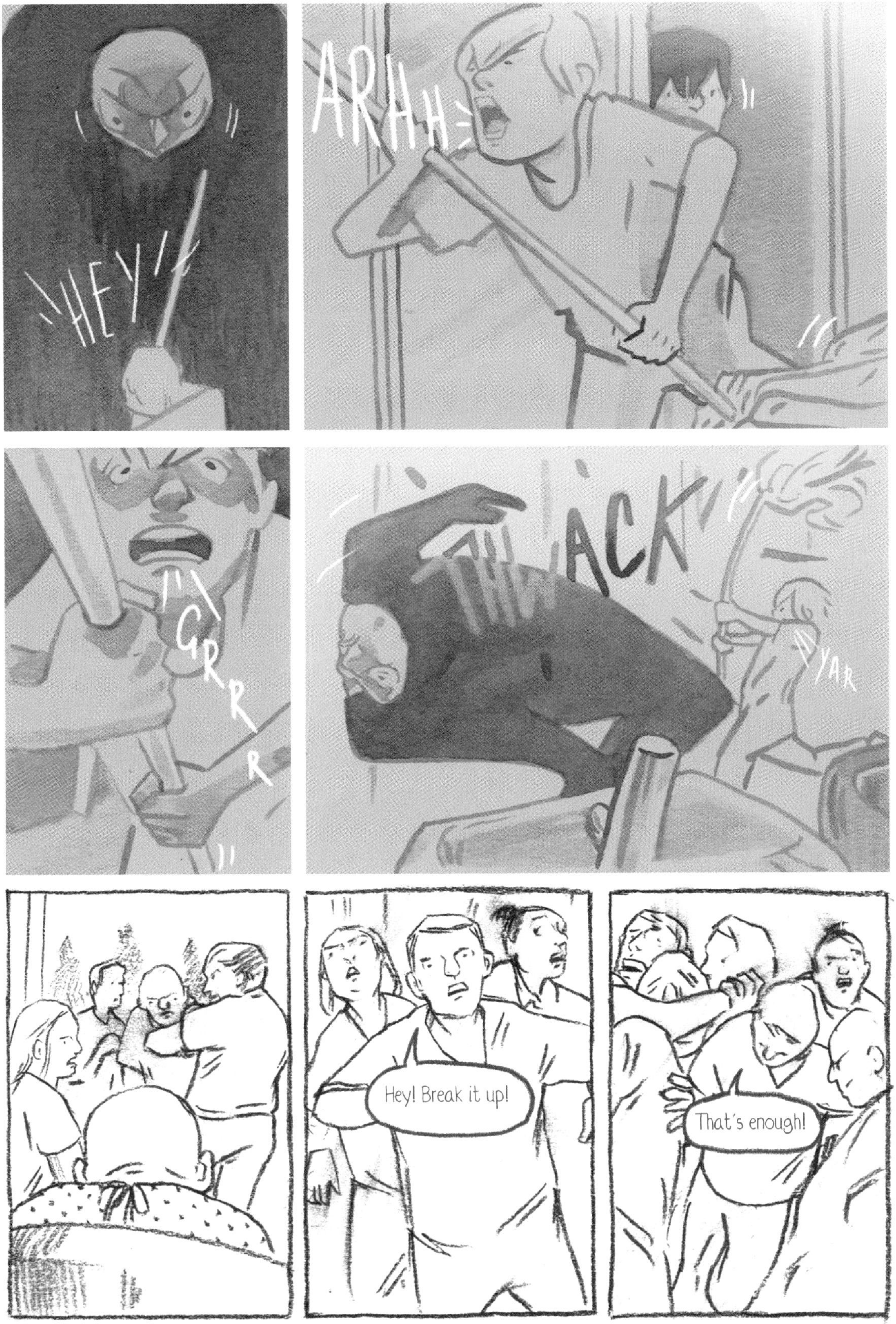
HEY
ARHH
GRRRR
THWACK
YAR
Hey! Break it up!
That's enough!

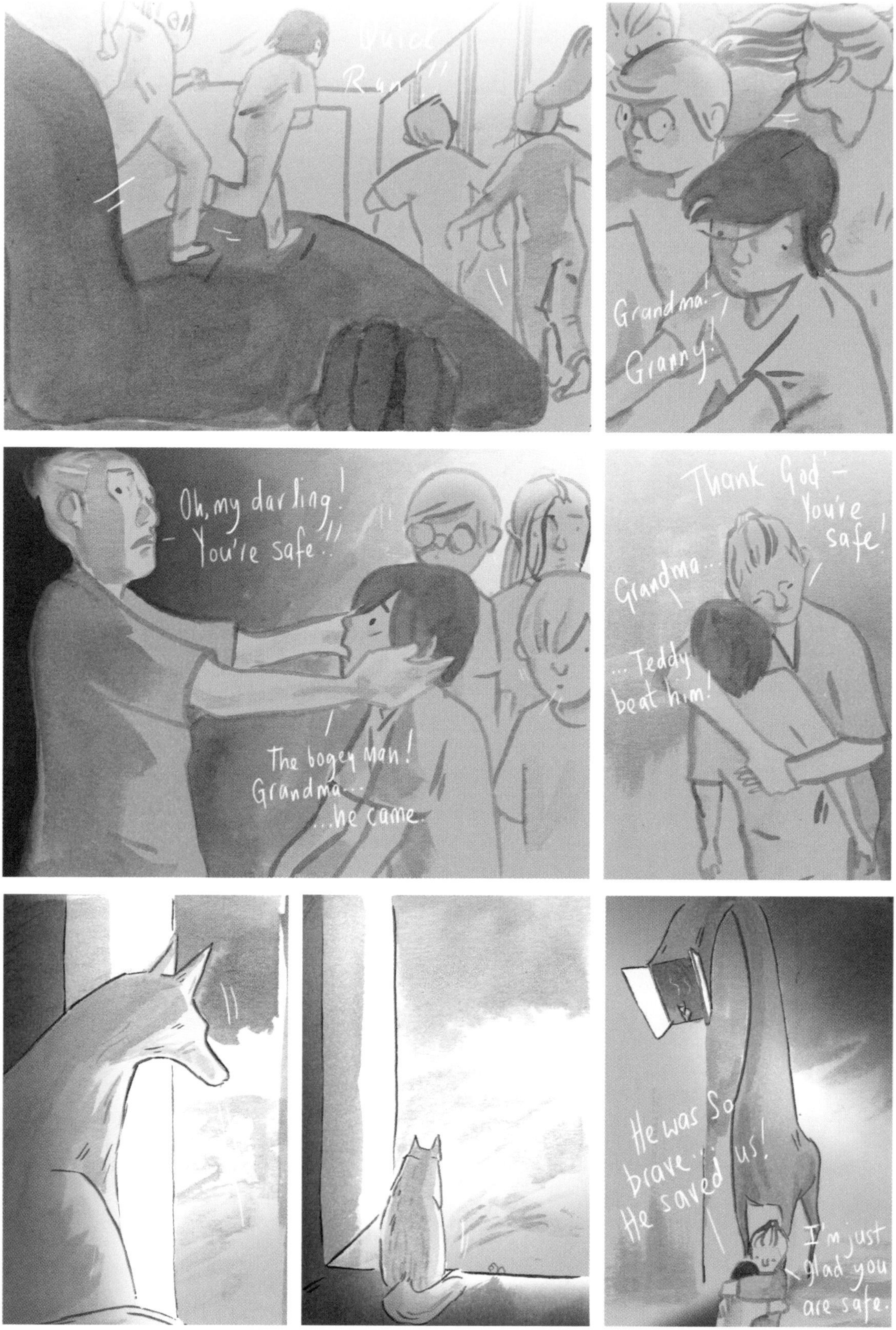

Quick
Run!!!
Grandma!
Granny!
Oh, my darling! You're safe!
The bogey man! Grandma... ...he came.
Thank God – You're safe!
Grandma...
...Teddy beat him!
He was so brave... He saved us!
I'm just glad you are safe.

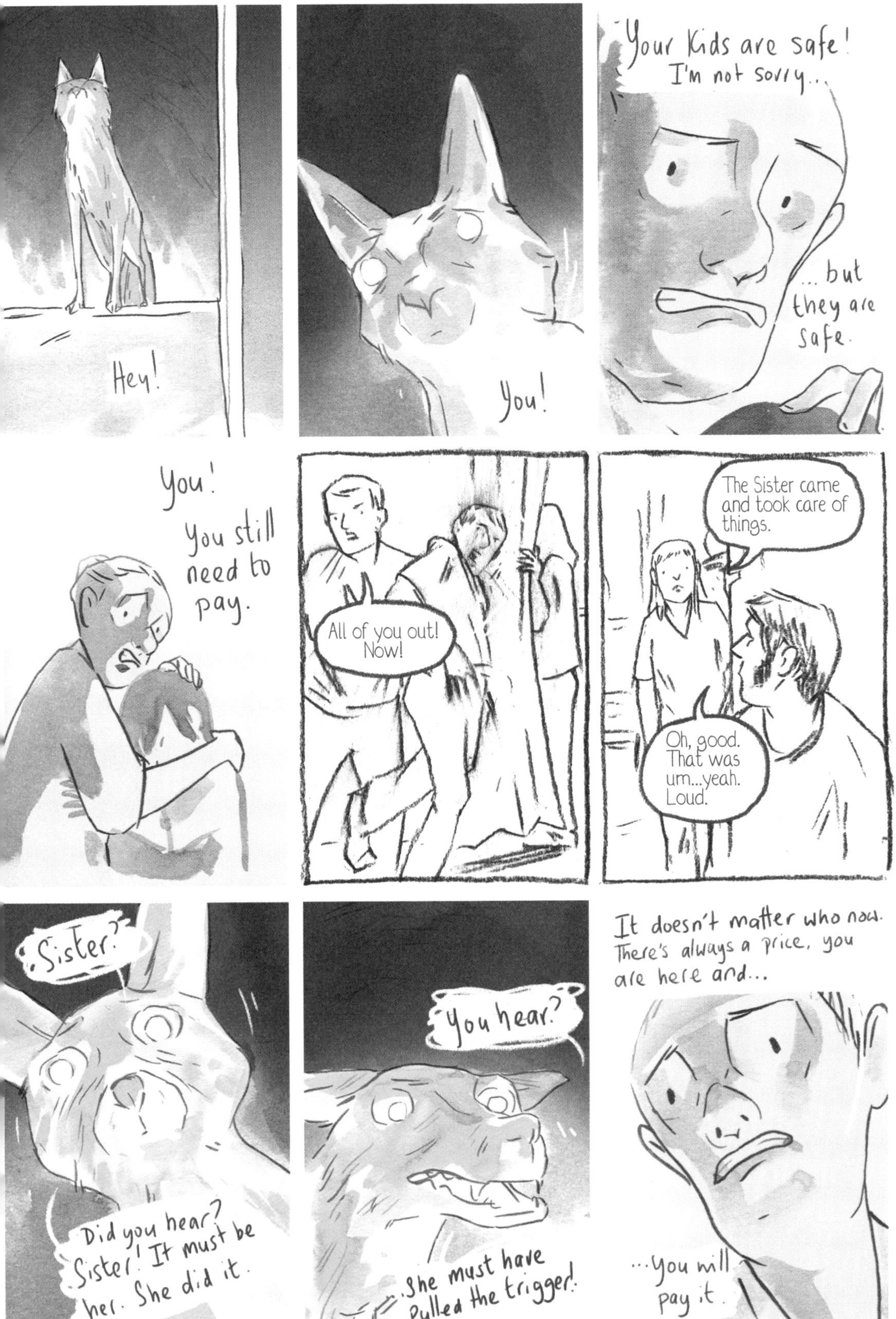

Hey!
You!
Your kids are safe! I'm not sorry...
...but they are safe.
You! You still need to pay.
All of you out! Now!
The Sister came and took care of things.
Oh, good. That was um...yeah. Loud.
Sister?
Did you hear? Sister! It must be her. She did it.
You hear?
She must have pulled the trigger!
It doesn't matter who now. There's always a price, you are here and...
...You will pay it.

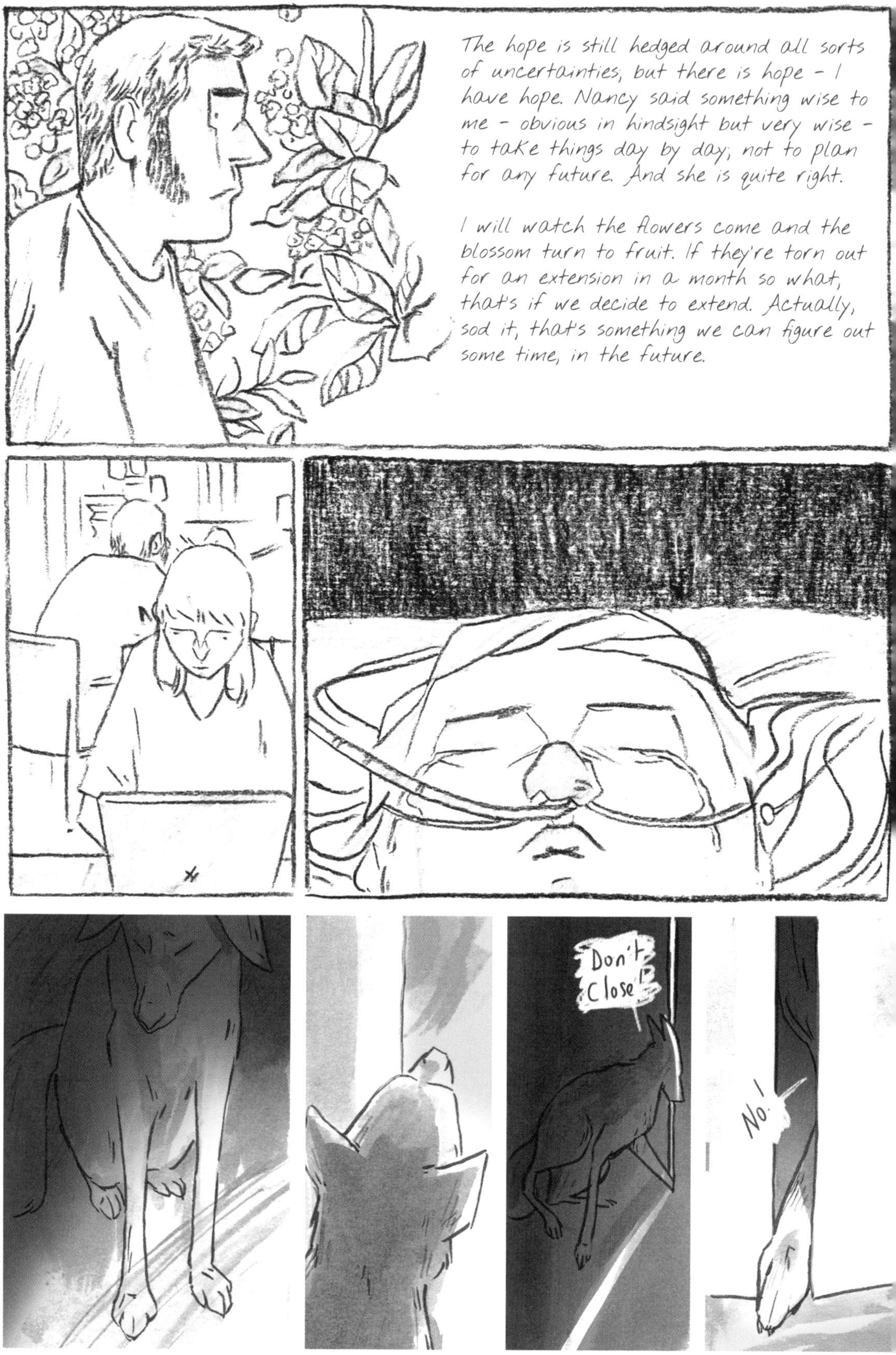
The hope is still hedged around all sorts of uncertainties; but there is hope - I have hope. Nancy said something wise to me - obvious in hindsight but very wise - to take things day by day; not to plan for any future. And she is quite right.
I will watch the flowers come and the blossom turn to fruit. If they're torn out for an extension in a month so what, that's if we decide to extend. Actually, sod it, that's something we can figure out some time, in the future.
Don't Close!
No!

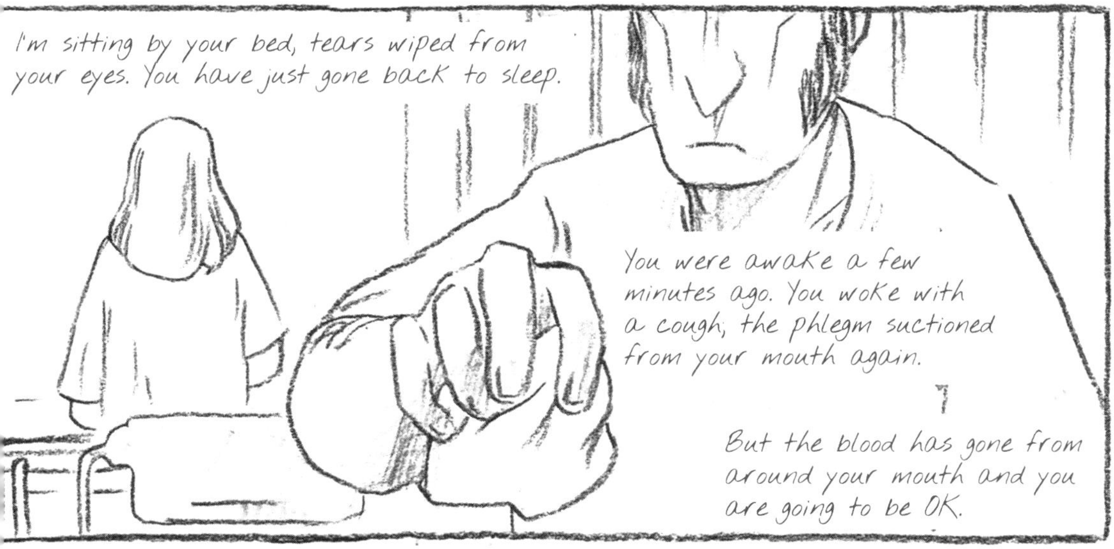
I'm sitting by your bed, tears wiped from your eyes. You have just gone back to sleep.
You were awake a few minutes ago. You woke with a cough; the phlegm suctioned from your mouth again.
But the blood has gone from around your mouth and you are going to be OK.

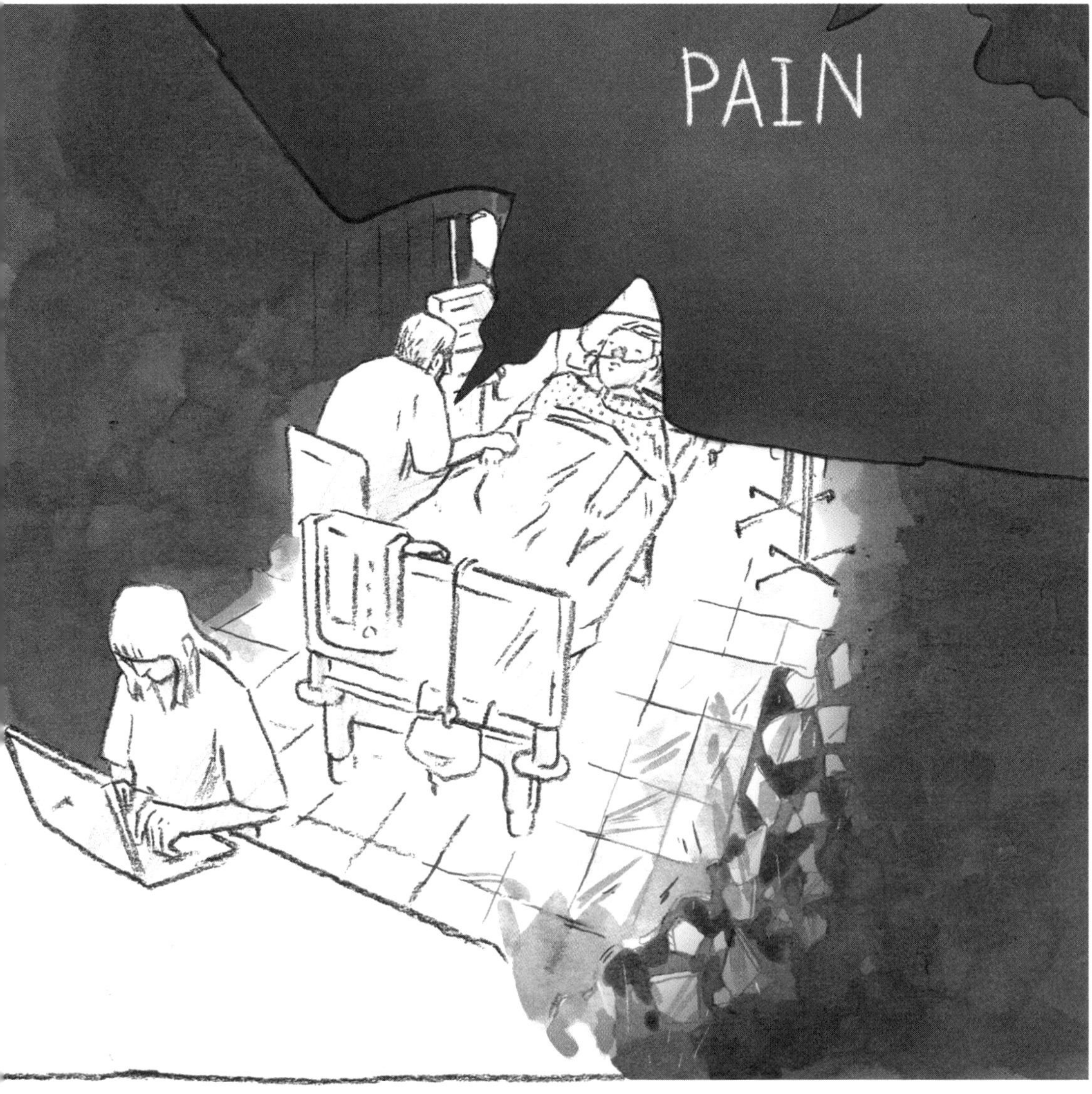
PAIN

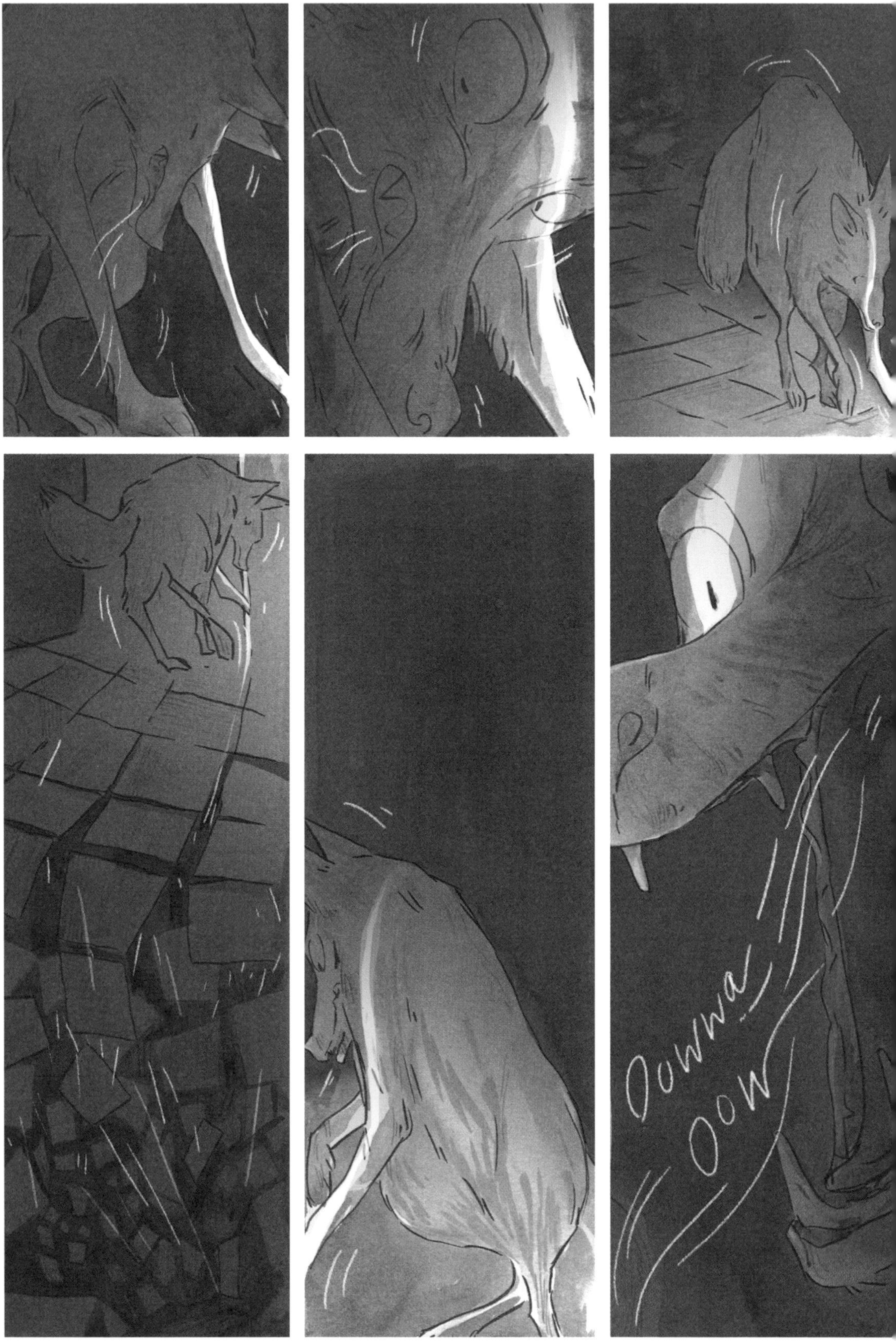
Oowwa
oow

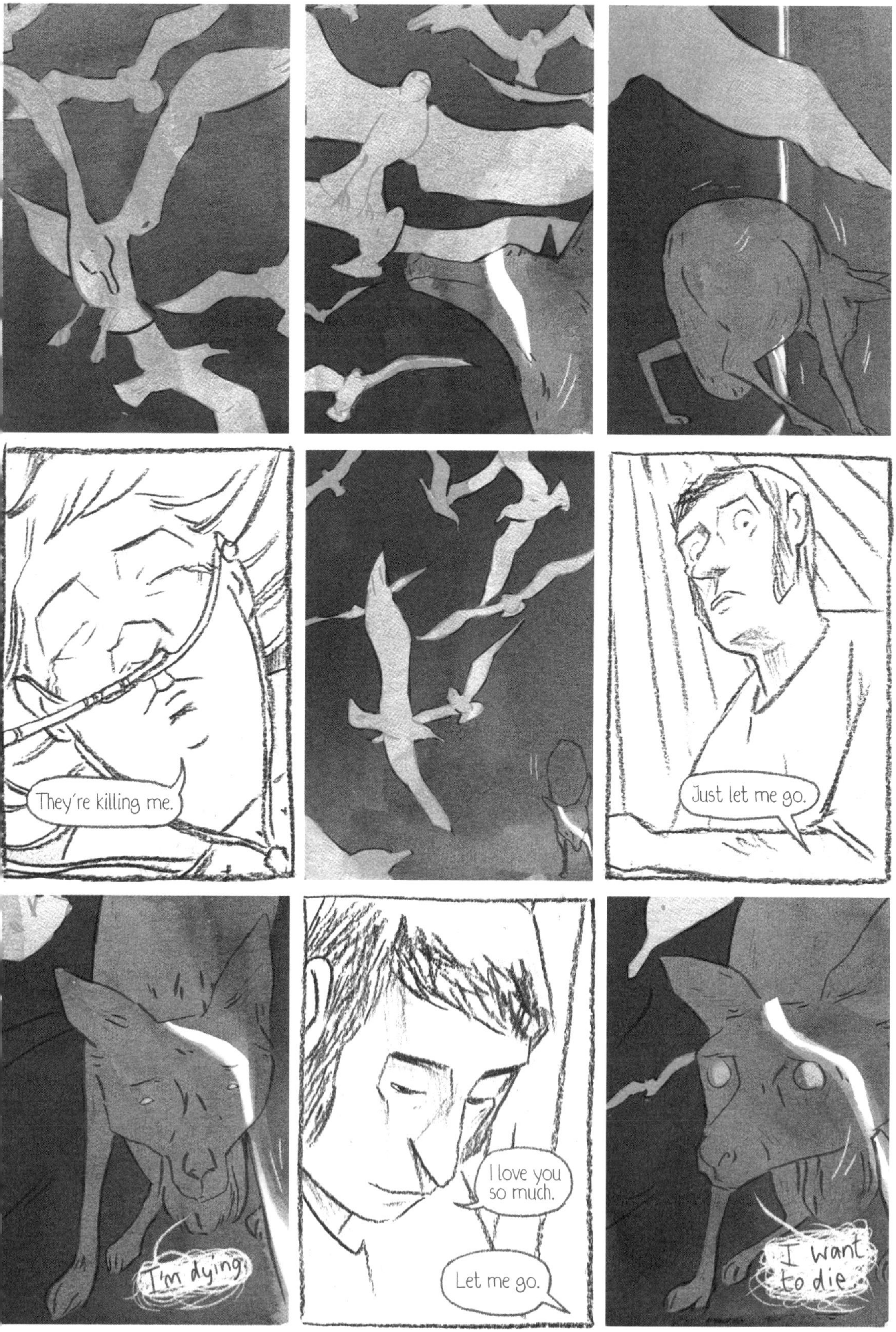
They're killing me.
Just let me go.
I'm dying.
I love you so much.
Let me go.
I want to die.

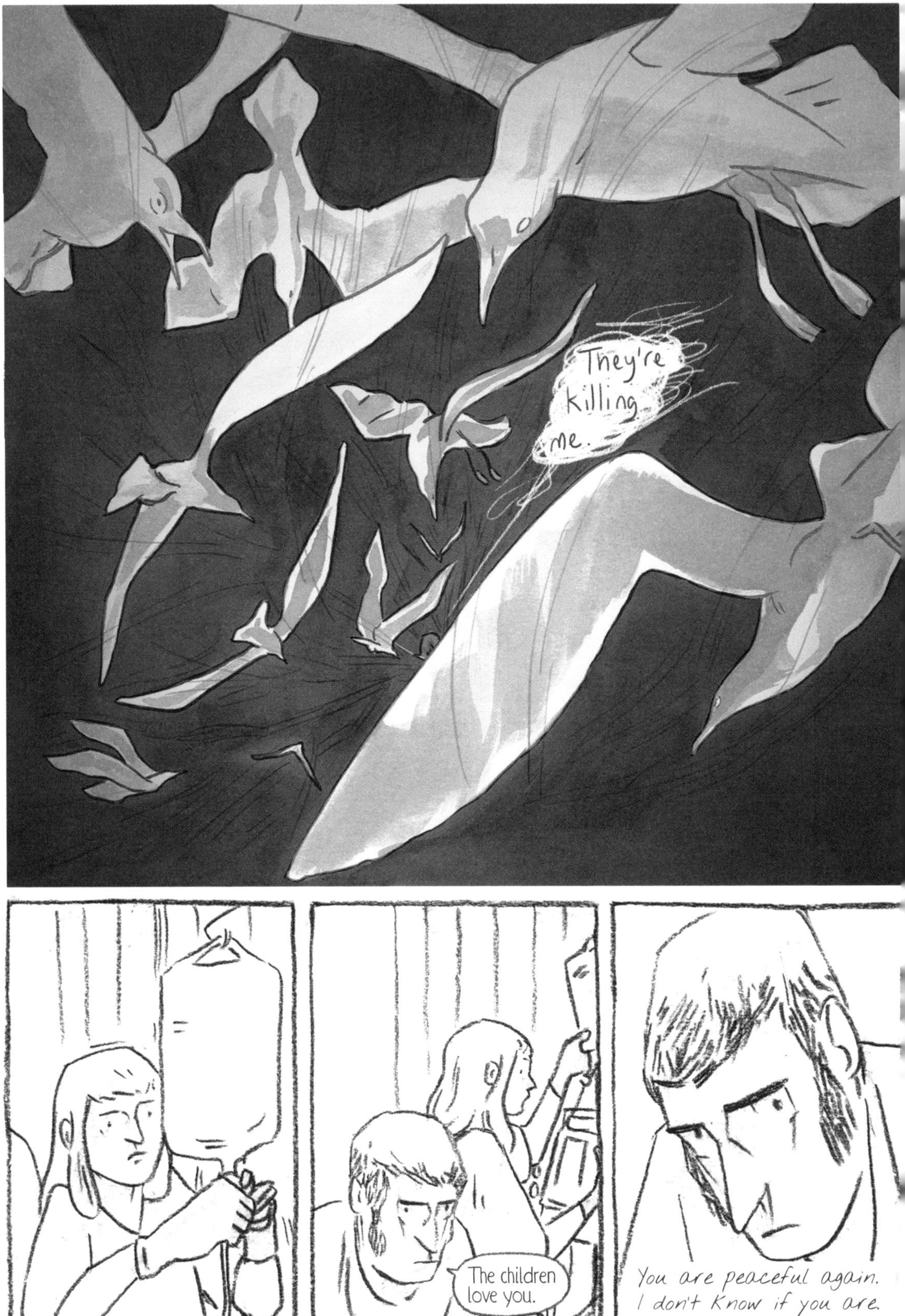
They're killing me.
The children love you.
You are peaceful again.
I don't know if you are.

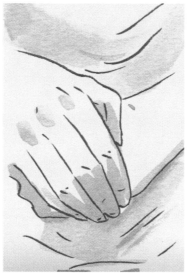

No.

No....
Don't
trust
them!

The wires!
Don't let
them!
Don't
listen to
them!

The wires...

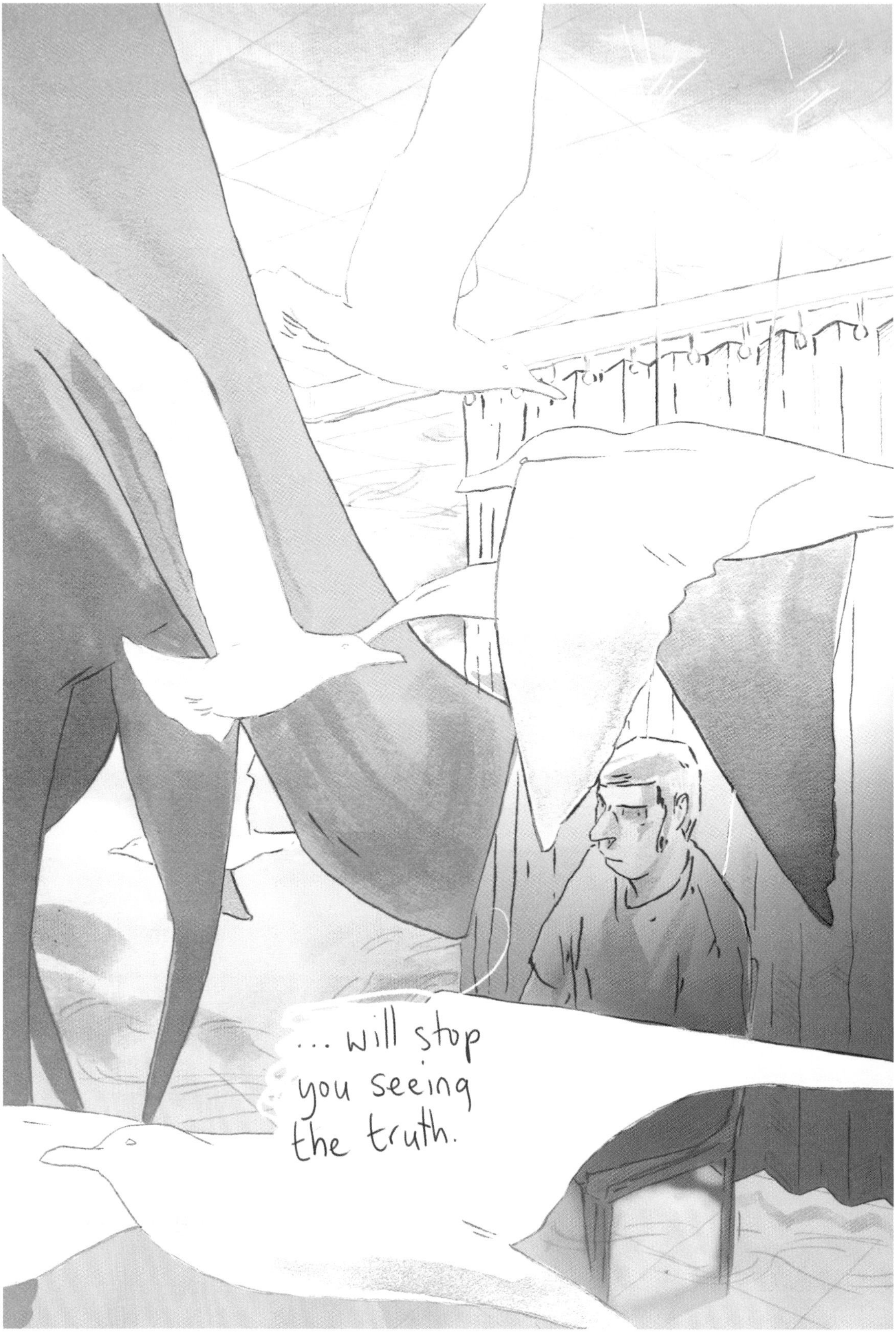
... will stop you seeing the truth.

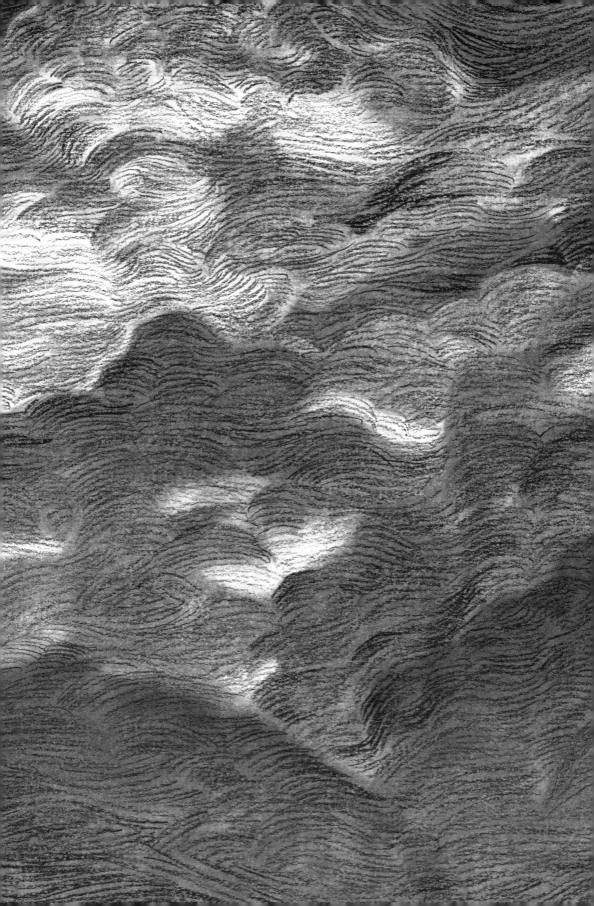

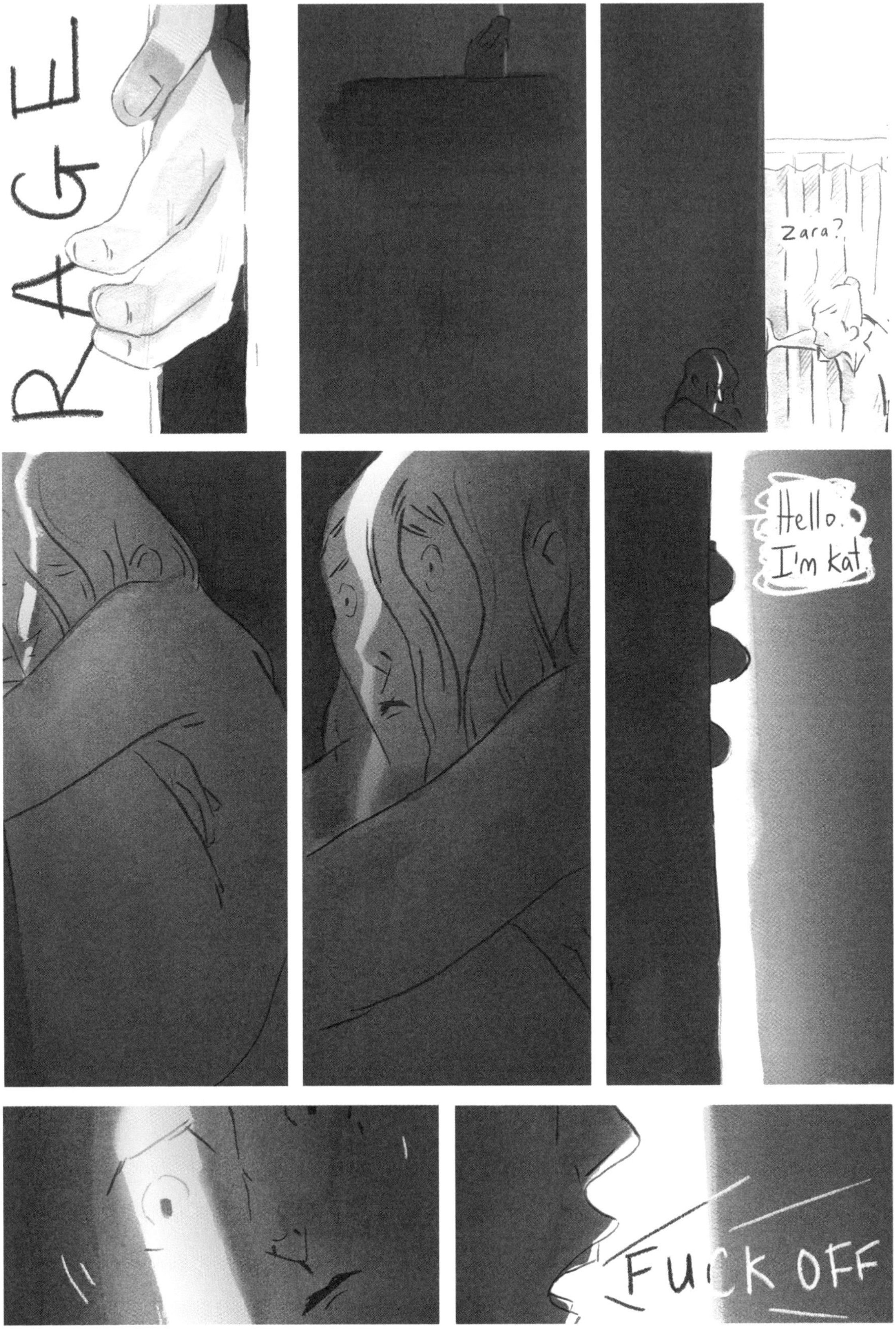
RAGE
Zara?
Hello. I'm kat.
FUCK OFF

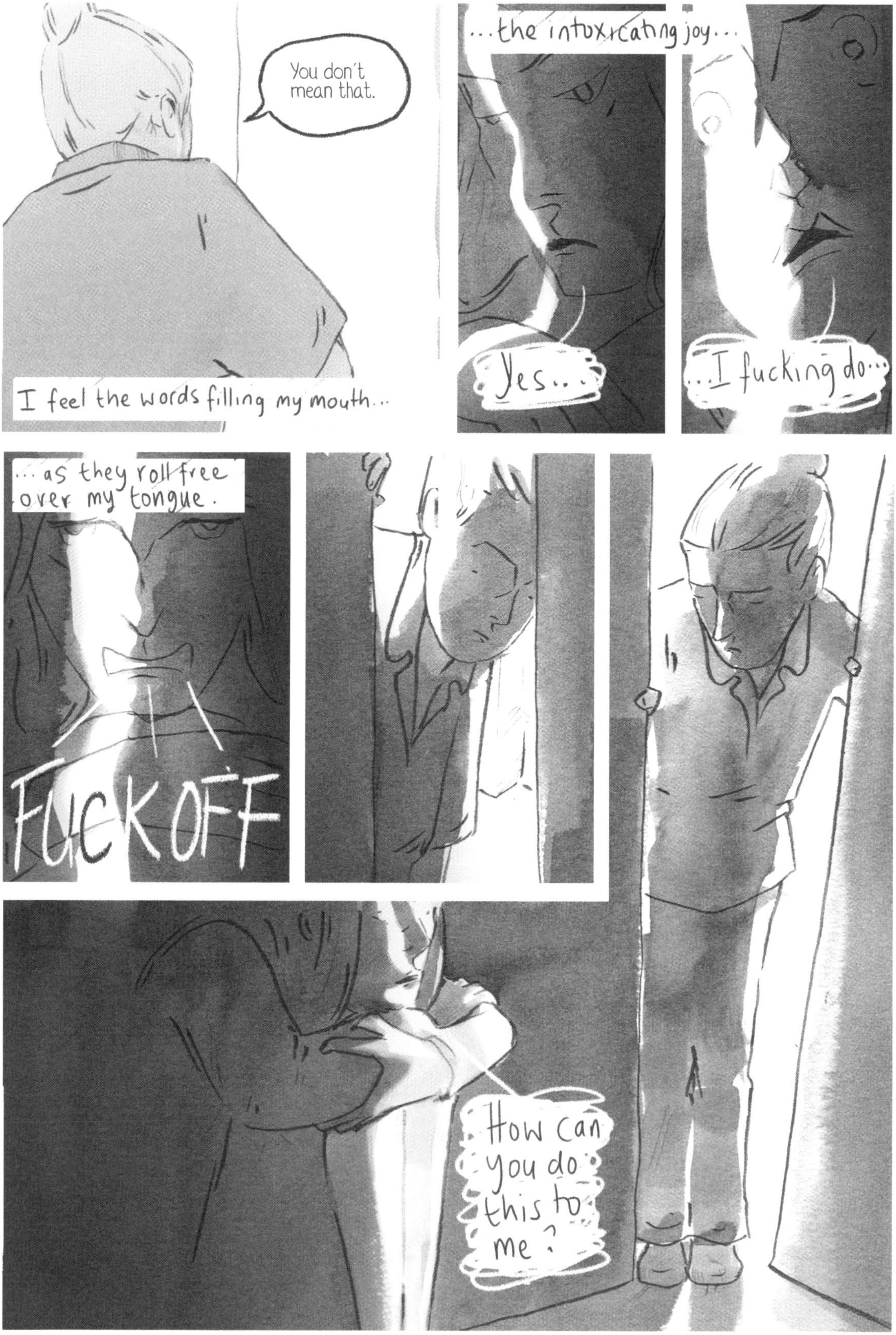
You don't mean that.
I feel the words filling my mouth...
...the intoxicating joy...
Yes...
...I fucking do...
...as they roll free over my tongue.
FUCK OFF
How can you do this to me?

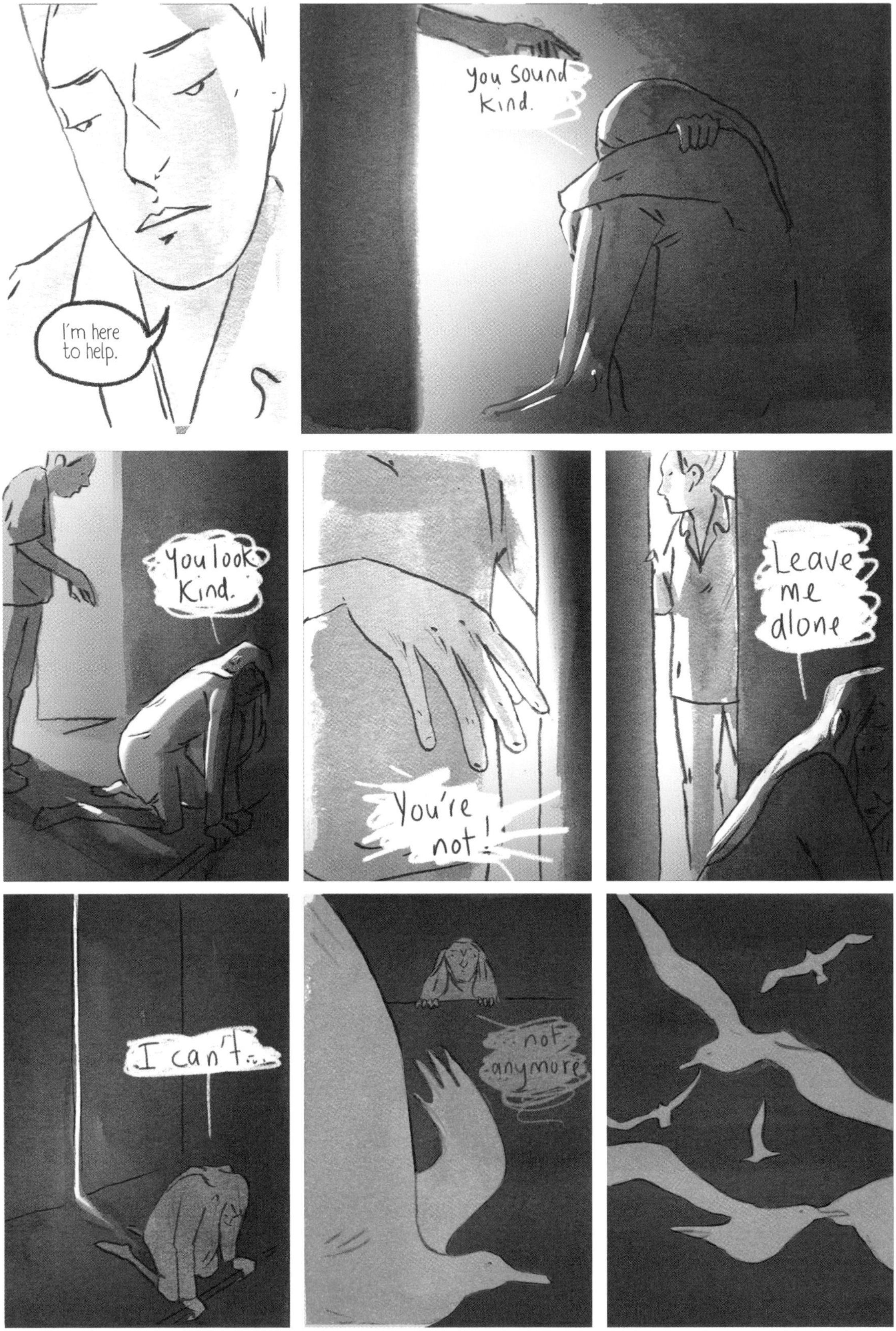
I'm here to help.
you sound kind.
You look kind.
You're not!
Leave me alone
I can't...
not anymore

SUNDAY 2nd JUNE

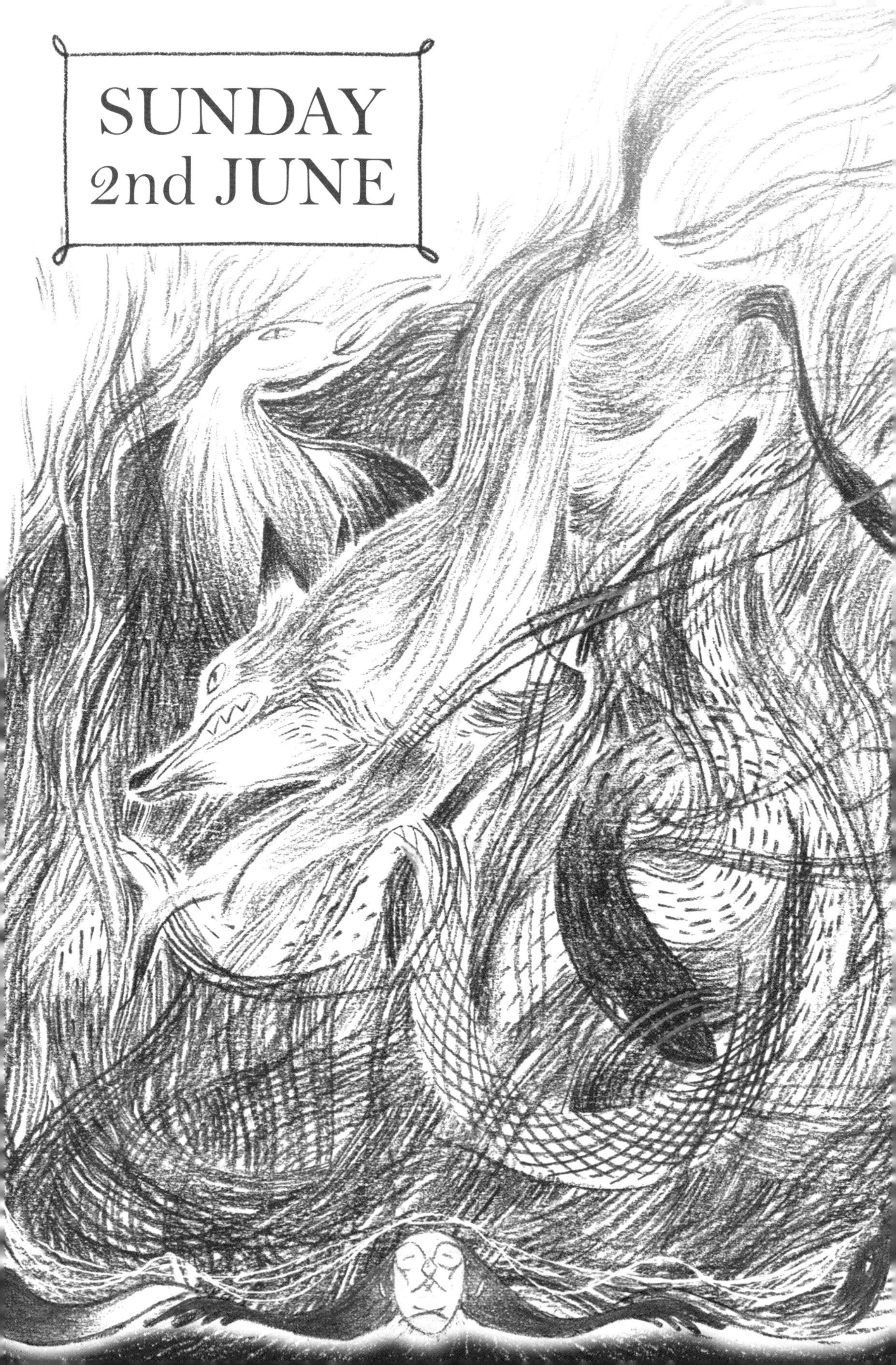

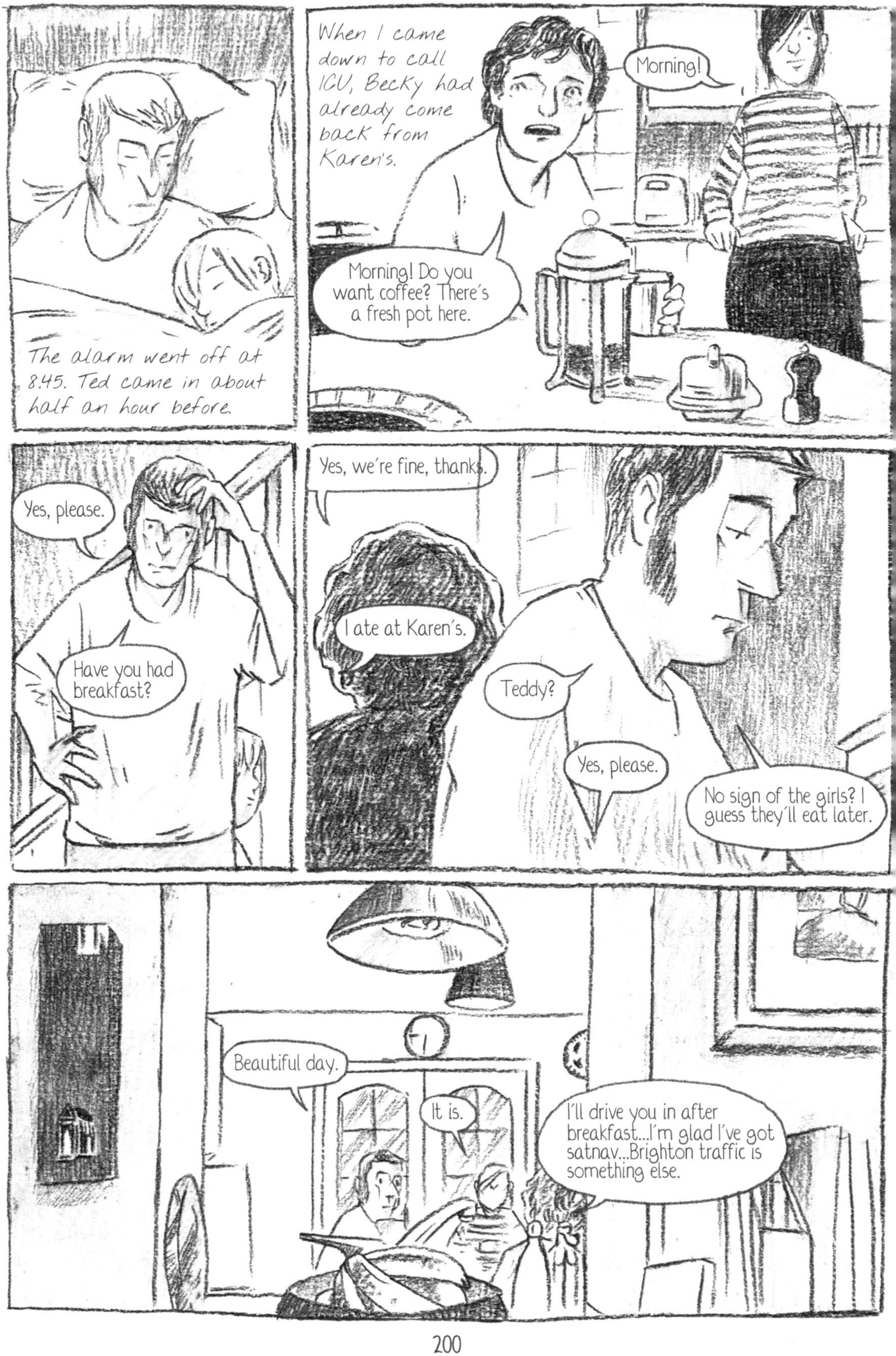
The alarm went off at 8.45. Ted came in about half an hour before.
When I came down to call ICU, Becky had already come back from Karen's.
Morning!
Morning! Do you want coffee? There's a fresh pot here.
Yes, please.
Have you had breakfast?
Yes, we're fine, thanks.
I ate at Karen's.
Teddy?
Yes, please.
No sign of the girls? I guess they'll eat later.
Beautiful day.
It is.
I'll drive you in after breakfast...I'm glad I've got satnav...Brighton traffic is something else.

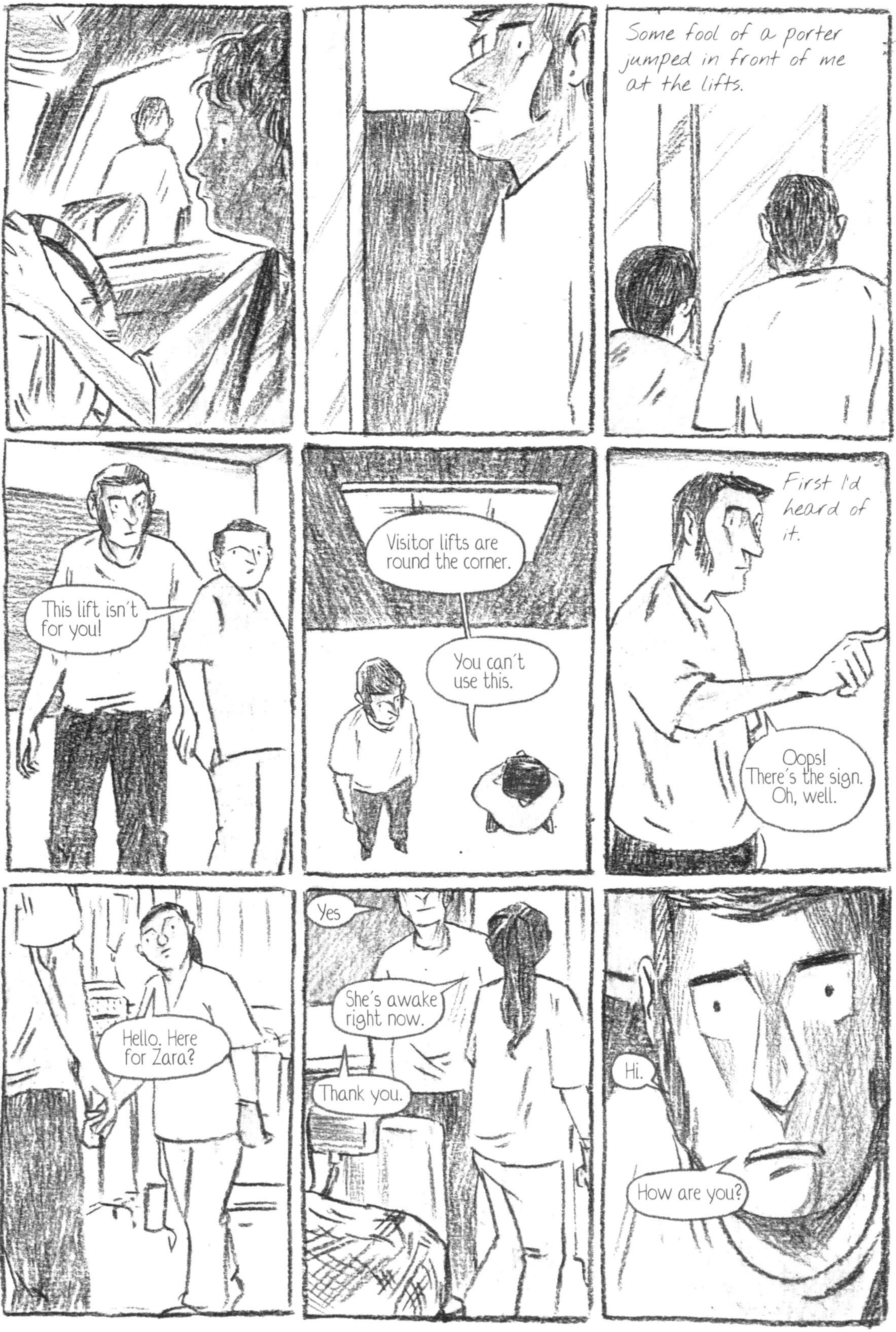
Some fool of a porter jumped in front of me at the lifts.
This lift isn't for you!
Visitor lifts are round the corner.
You can't use this.
First I'd heard of it.
Oops! There's the sign. Oh, well.
Hello. Here for Zara?
Yes
She's awake right now.
Thank you.
Hi.
How are you?

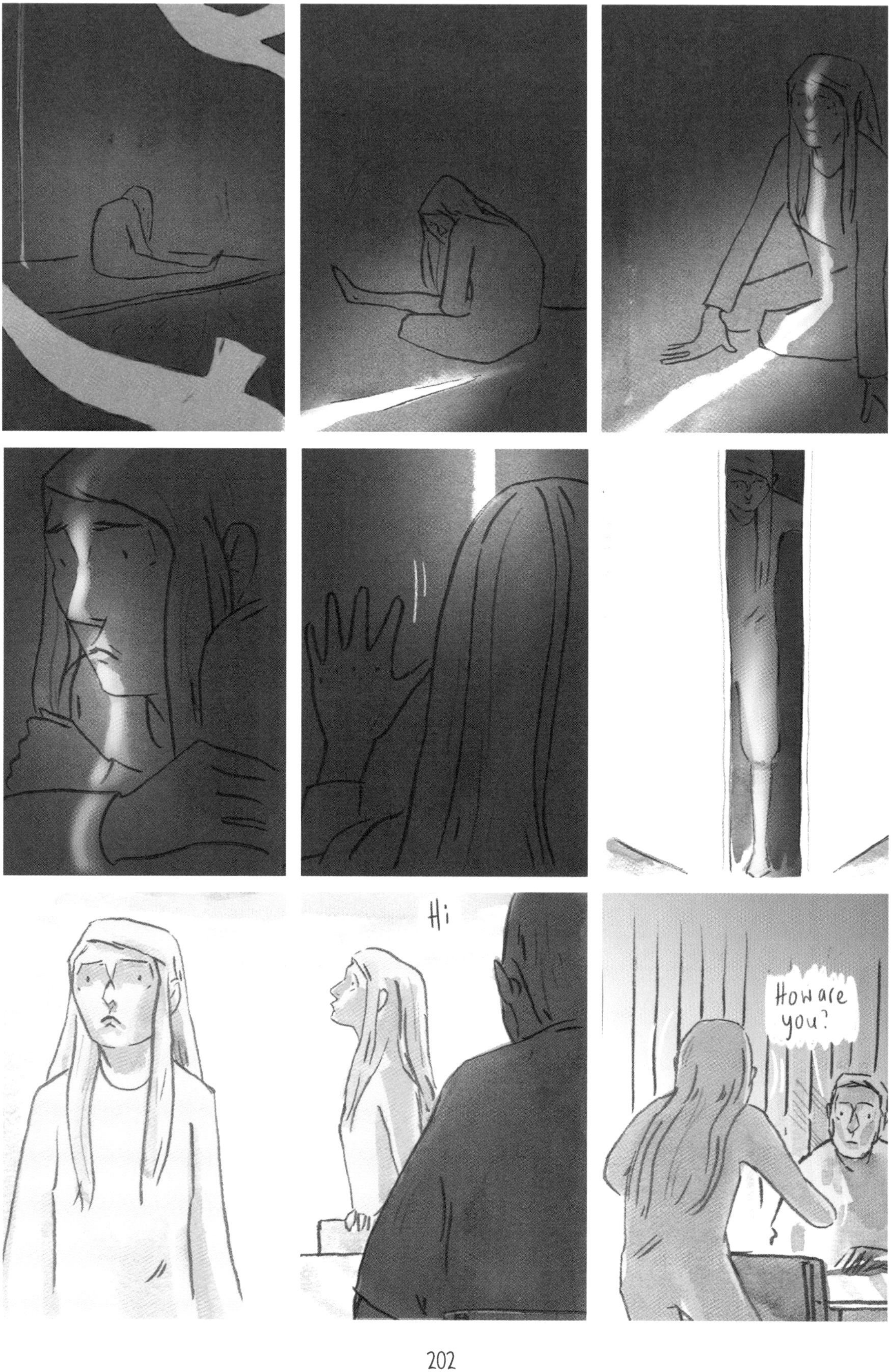
Hi
How are you?

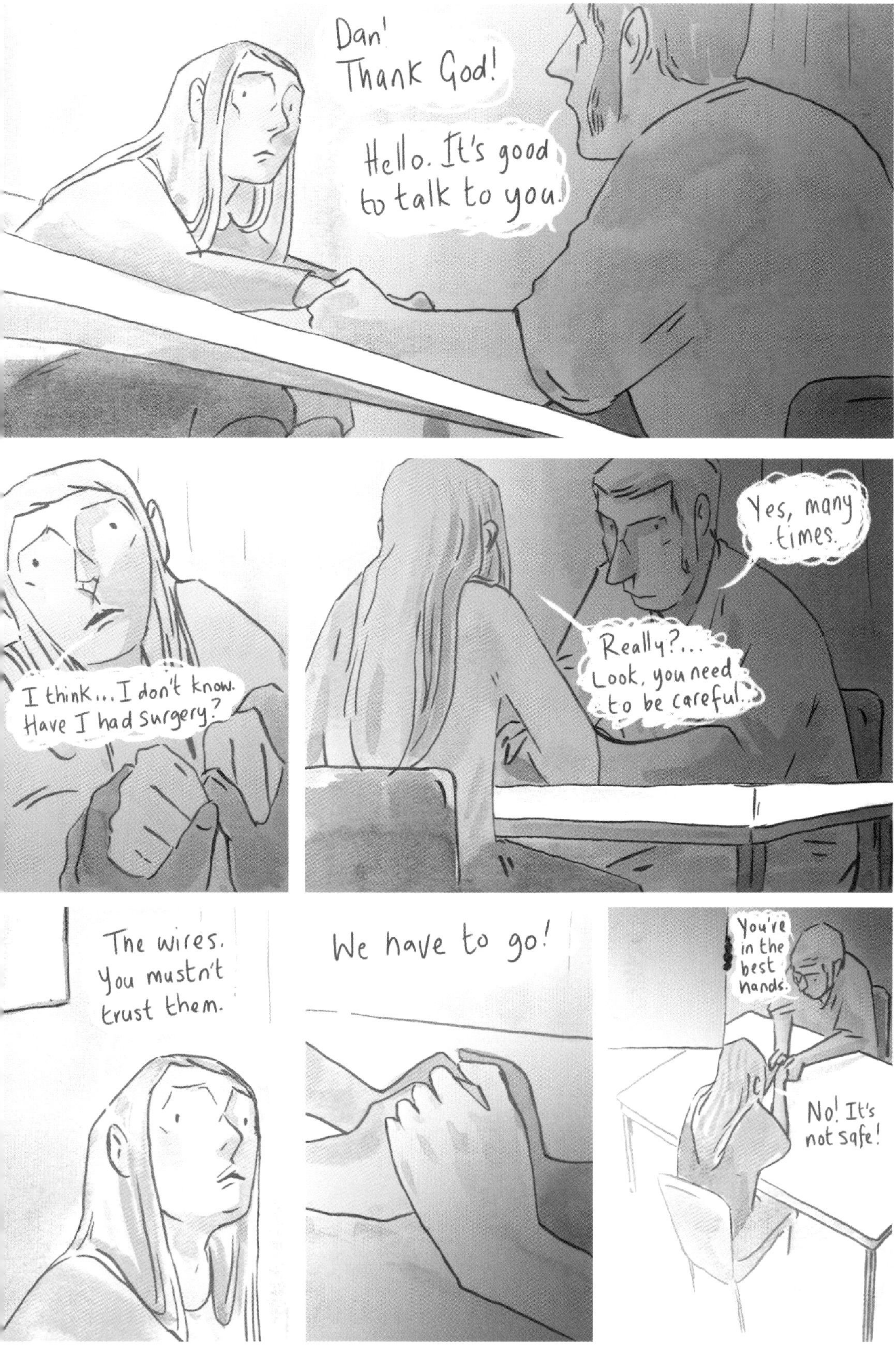
Dan! Thank God!
Hello. It's good to talk to you.
I think... I don't know. Have I had surgery?
Yes, many times.
Really?... Look, you need to be careful.
The wires. You mustn't trust them.
We have to go!
You're in the best hands.
No! It's not safe!

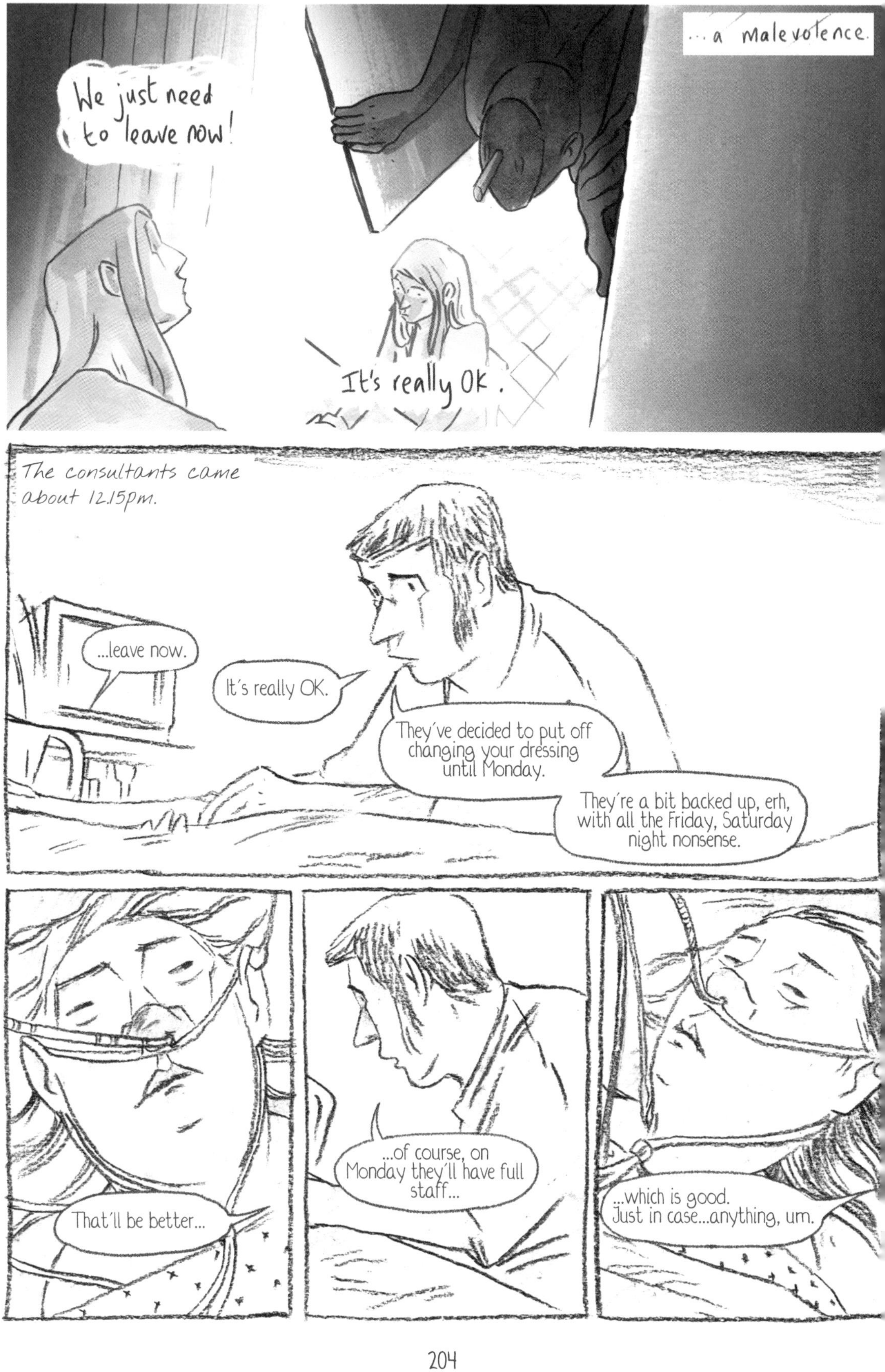
We just need to leave now!
...a malevolence.
It's really OK.
The consultants came about 12.15pm.
...leave now.
It's really OK.
They've decided to put off changing your dressing until Monday.
They're a bit backed up, erh, with all the Friday, Saturday night nonsense.
That'll be better...
...of course, on Monday they'll have full staff...
...which is good. Just in case...anything, um.

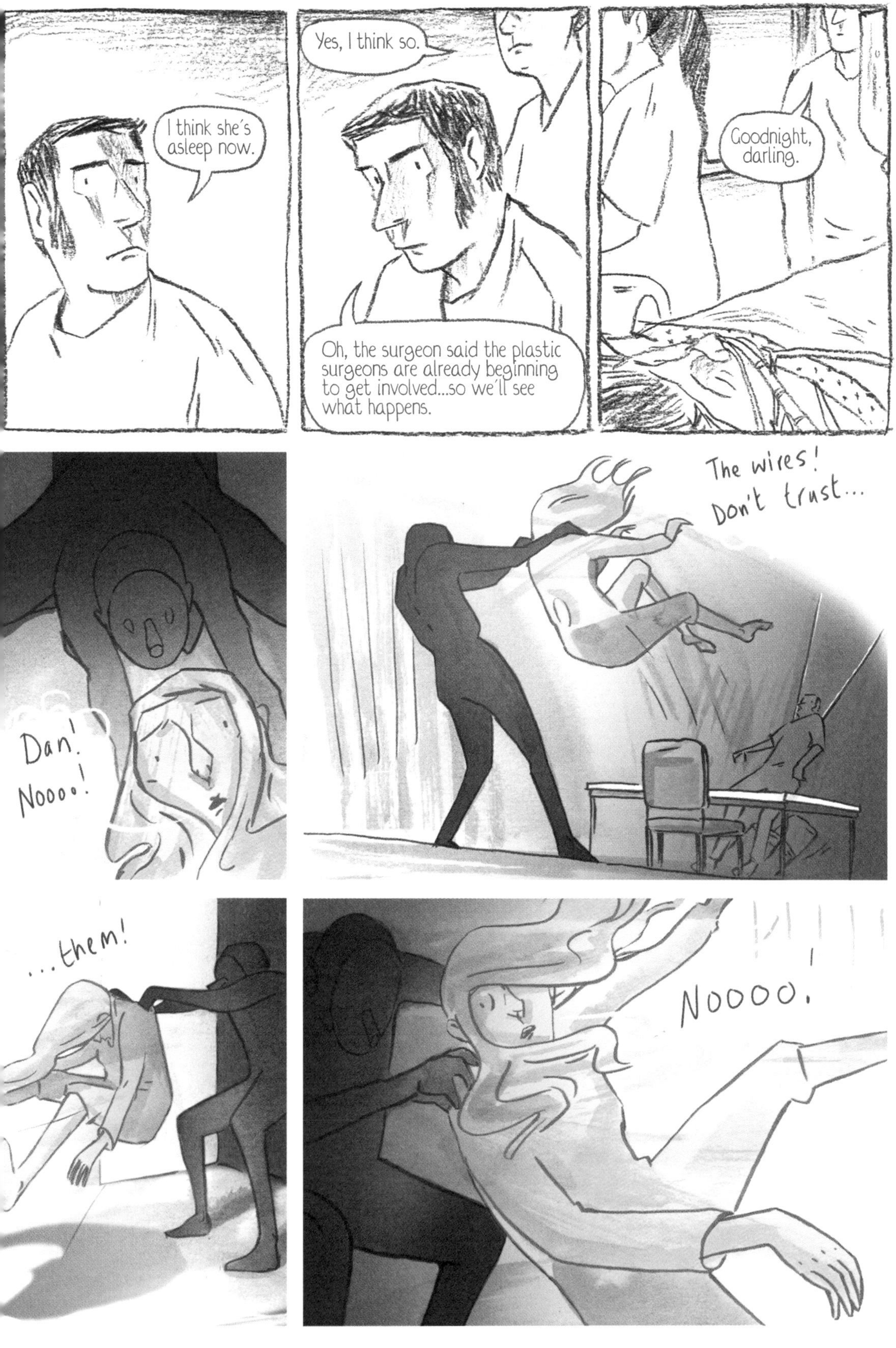

I think she's asleep now.
Yes, I think so.
Oh, the surgeon said the plastic surgeons are already beginning to get involved...so we'll see what happens.
Goodnight, darling.
Dan! Noooo!
The wires! Don't trust...
...them!
Noooo!

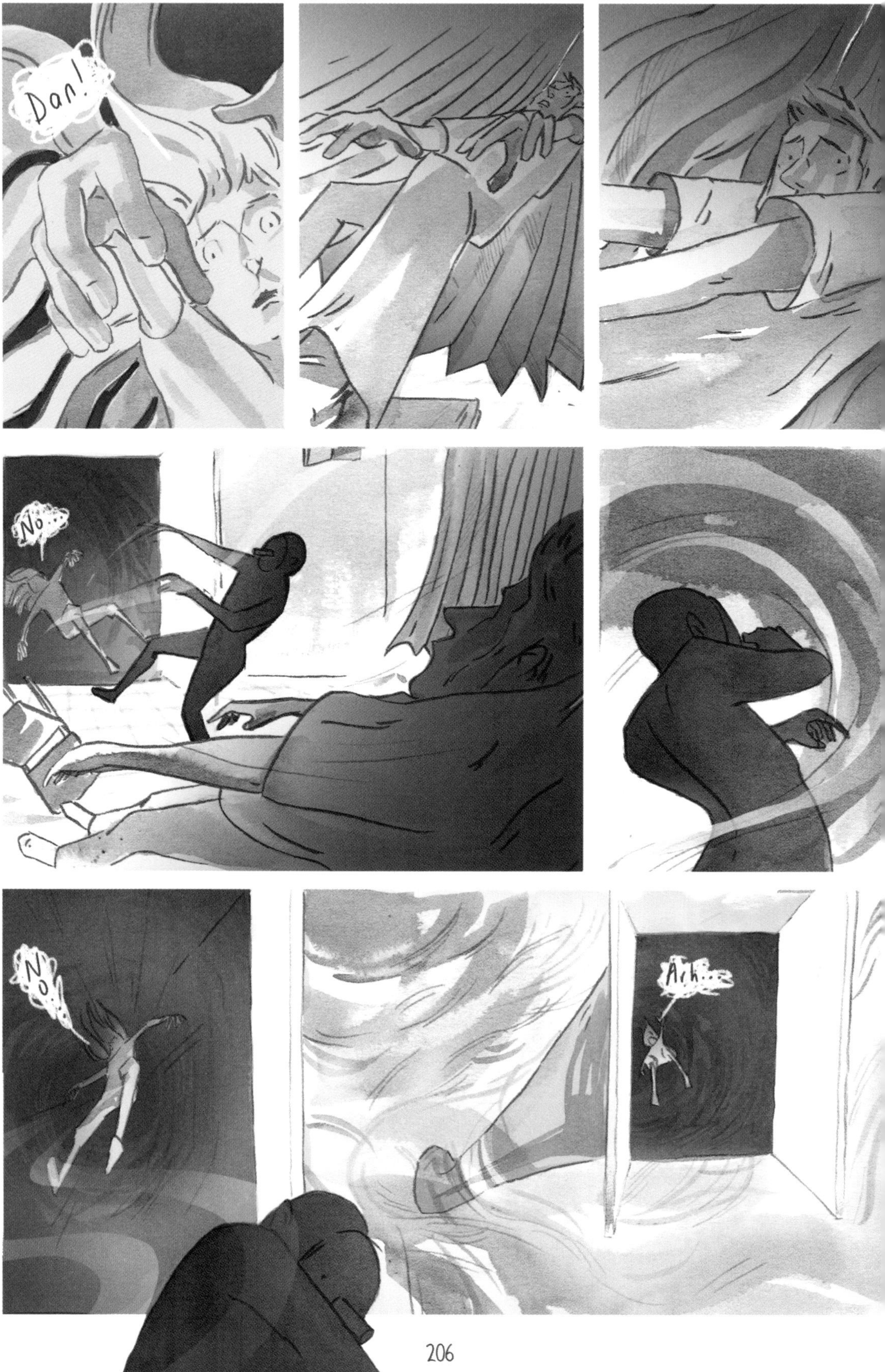
Dan!
No...
No
Ah...

MONDAY 3rd JUNE

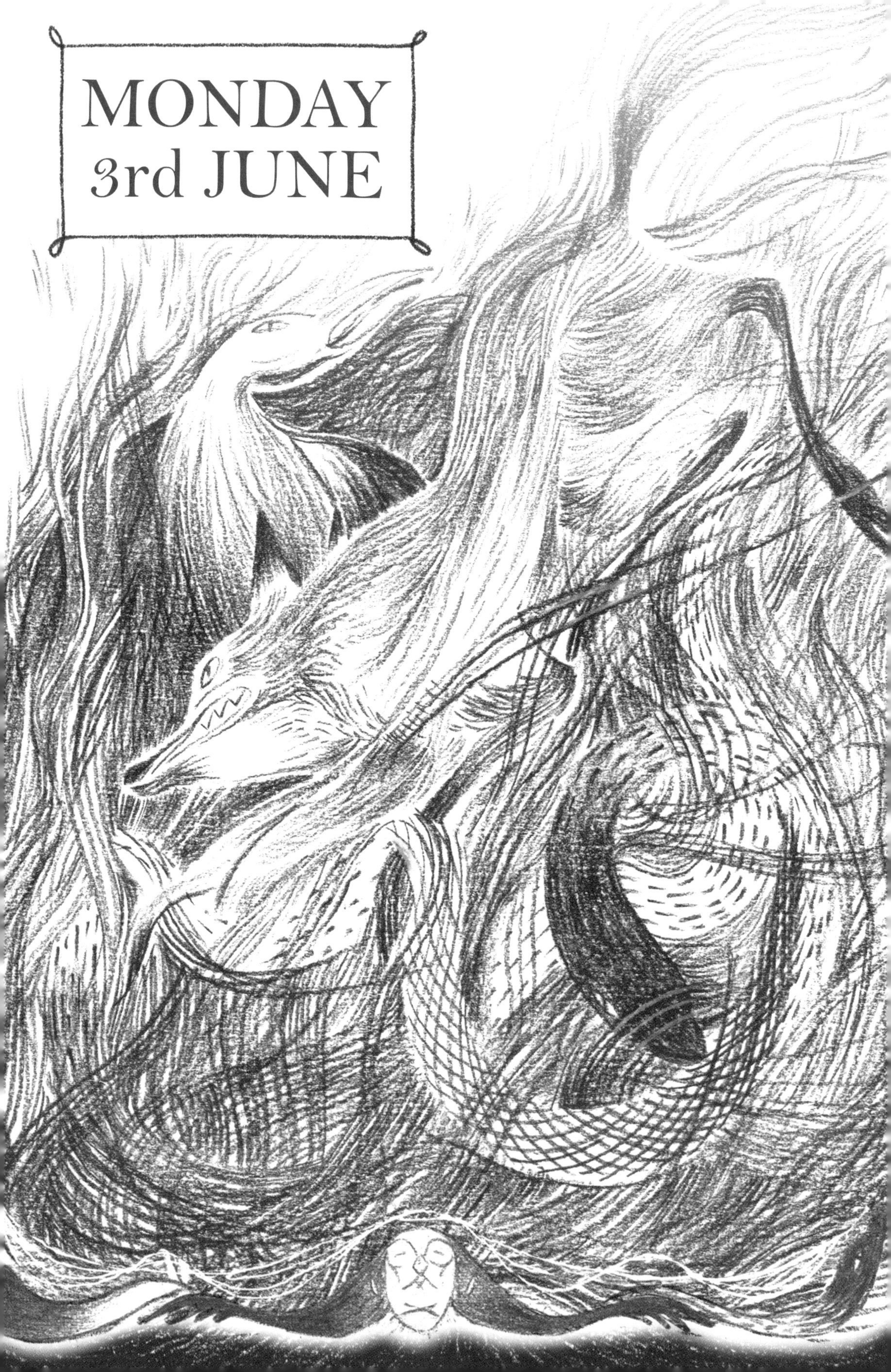

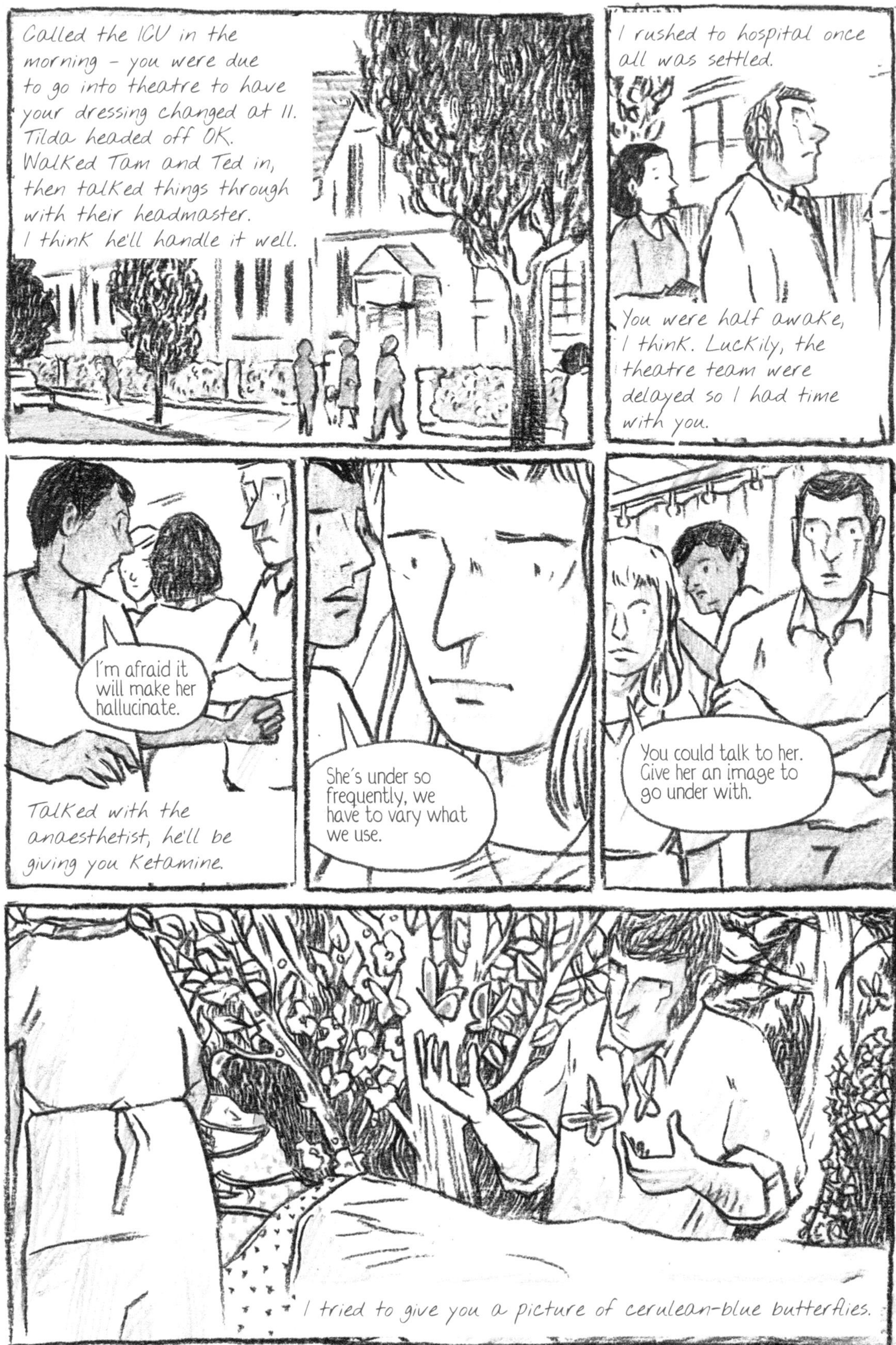
Called the ICU in the morning – you were due to go into theatre to have your dressing changed at 11. Tilda headed off OK. Walked Tam and Ted in, then talked things through with their headmaster. I think he'll handle it well.
I rushed to hospital once all was settled.
You were half awake, I think. Luckily, the theatre team were delayed so I had time with you.
I'm afraid it will make her hallucinate.
Talked with the anaesthetist, he'll be giving you Ketamine.
She's under so frequently, we have to vary what we use.
You could talk to her. Give her an image to go under with.
I tried to give you a picture of cerulean-blue butterflies.

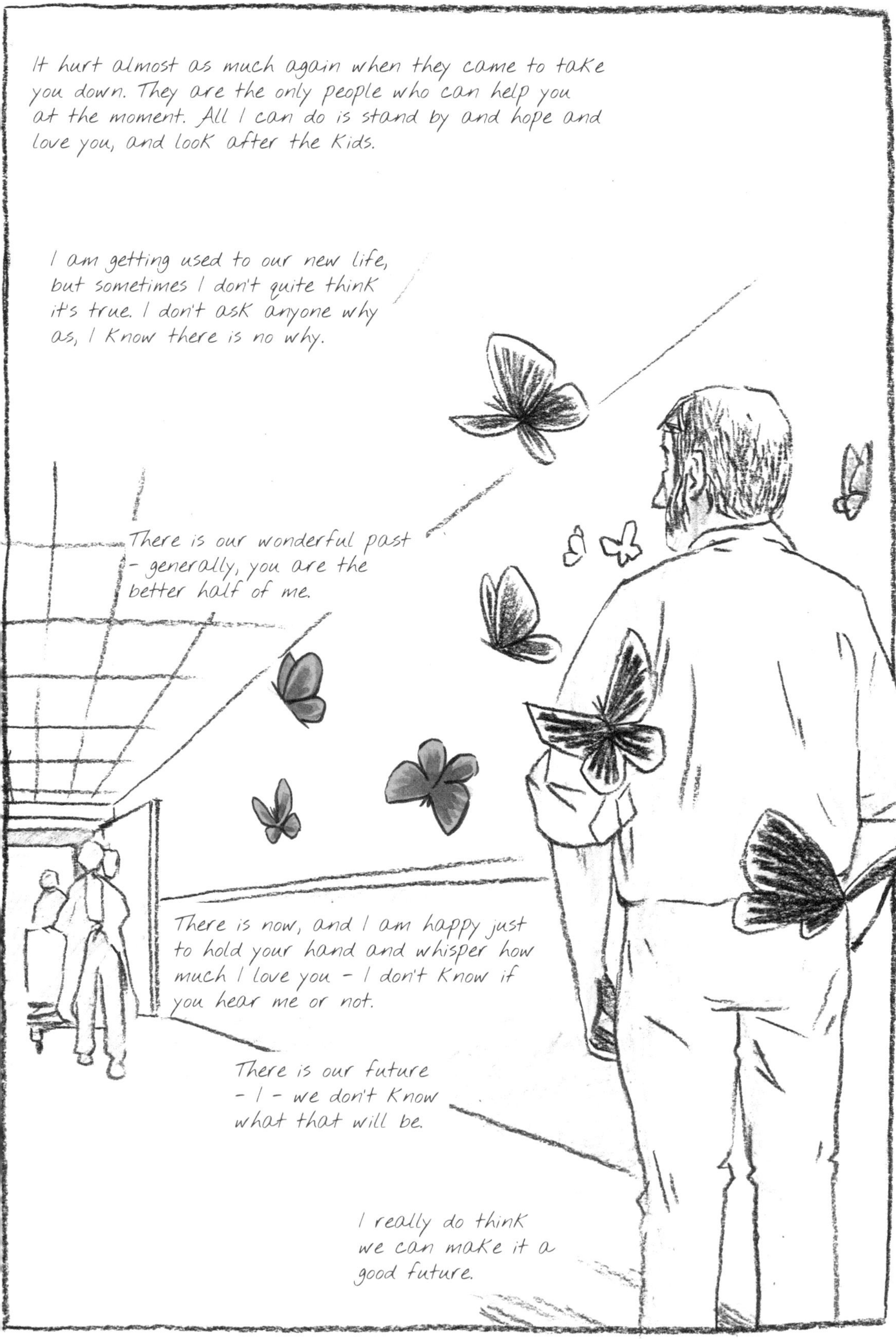
It hurt almost as much again when they came to take you down. They are the only people who can help you at the moment. All I can do is stand by and hope and love you, and look after the kids.
I am getting used to our new life, but sometimes I don't quite think it's true. I don't ask anyone why as, I know there is no why.
There is our wonderful past - generally, you are the better half of me.
There is now, and I am happy just to hold your hand and whisper how much I love you - I don't know if you hear me or not.
There is our future - I - we don't know what that will be.
I really do think we can make it a good future.

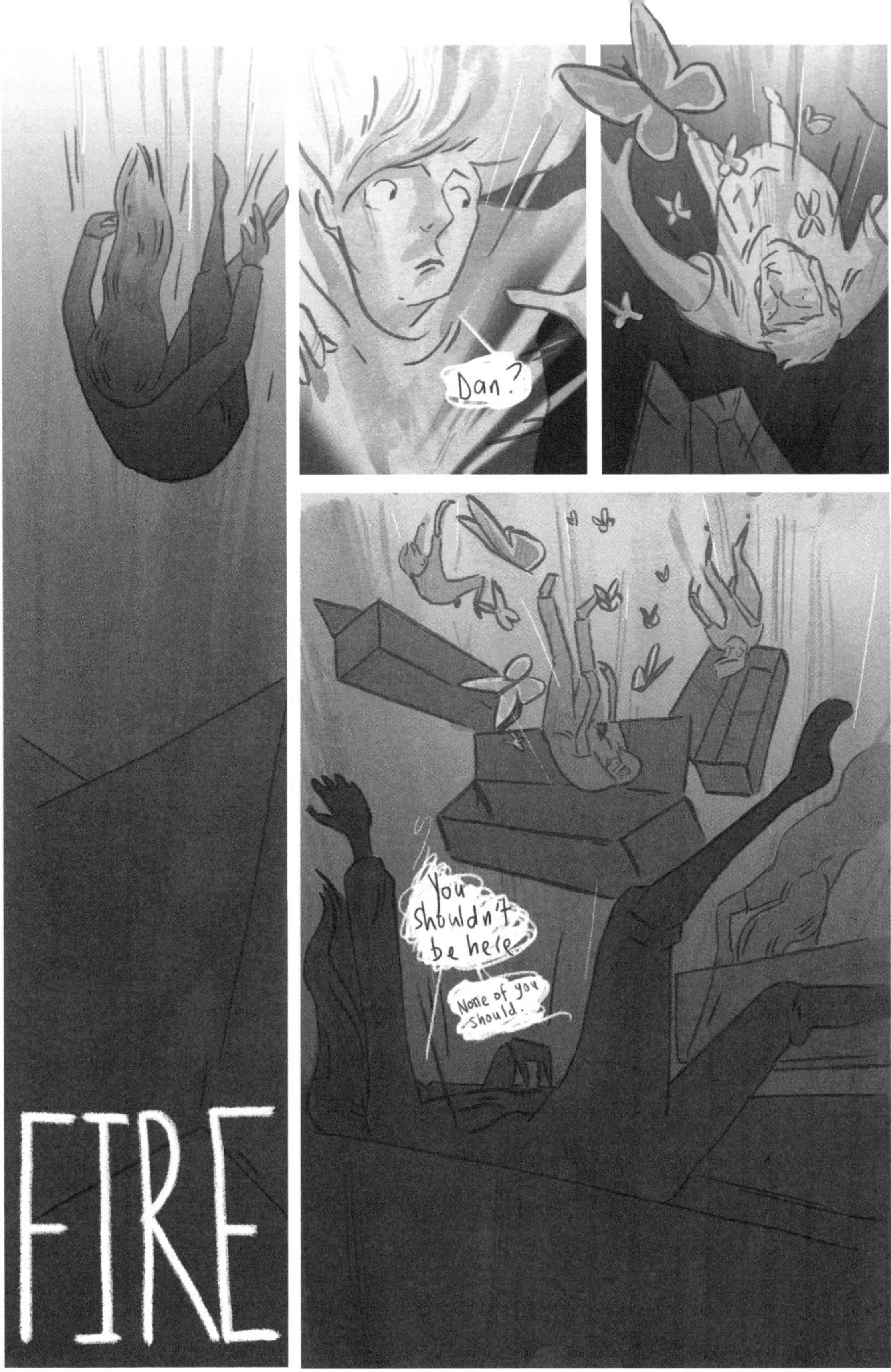
Dan?
You shouldn't be here
None of you should.
FIRE

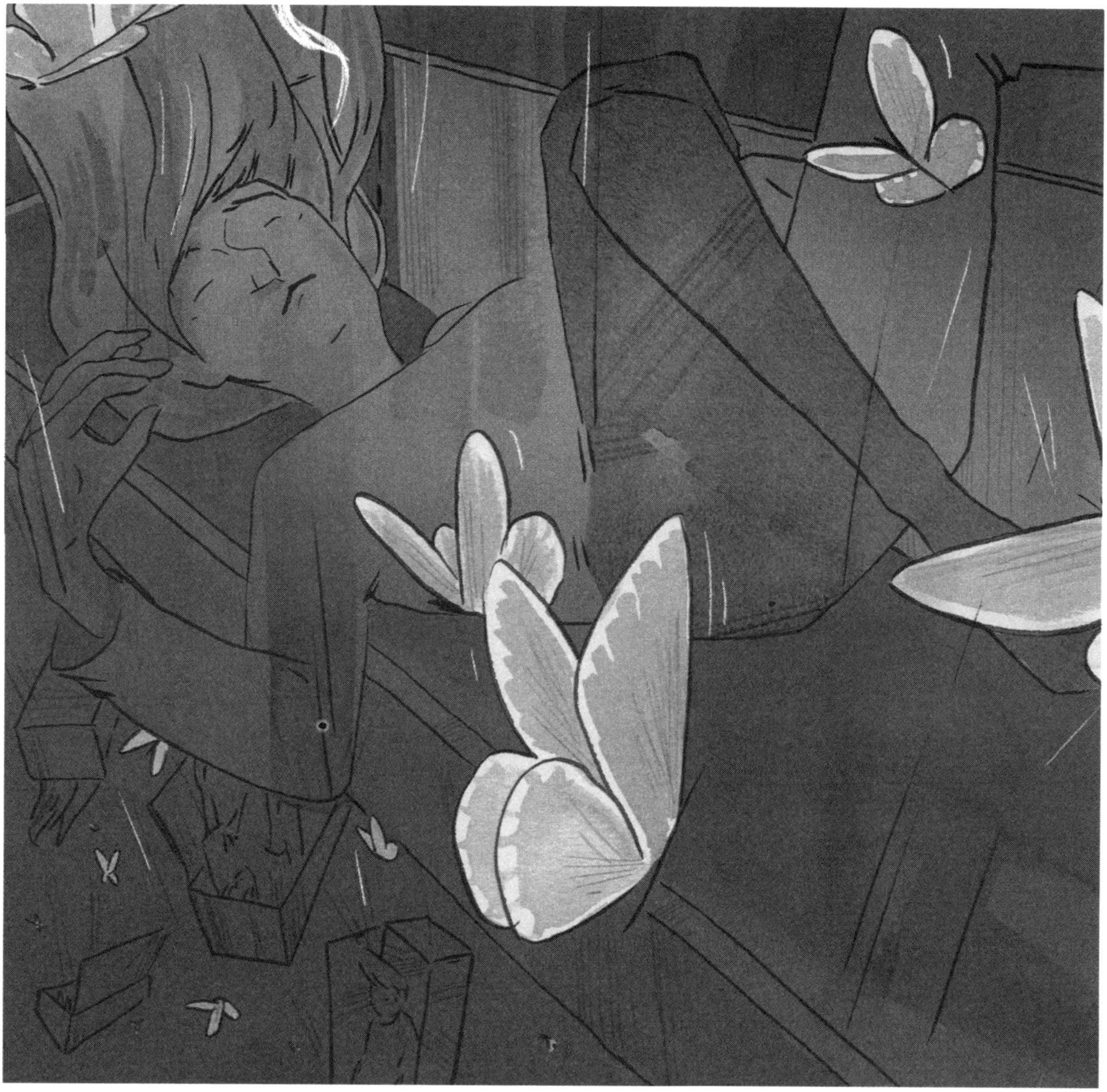

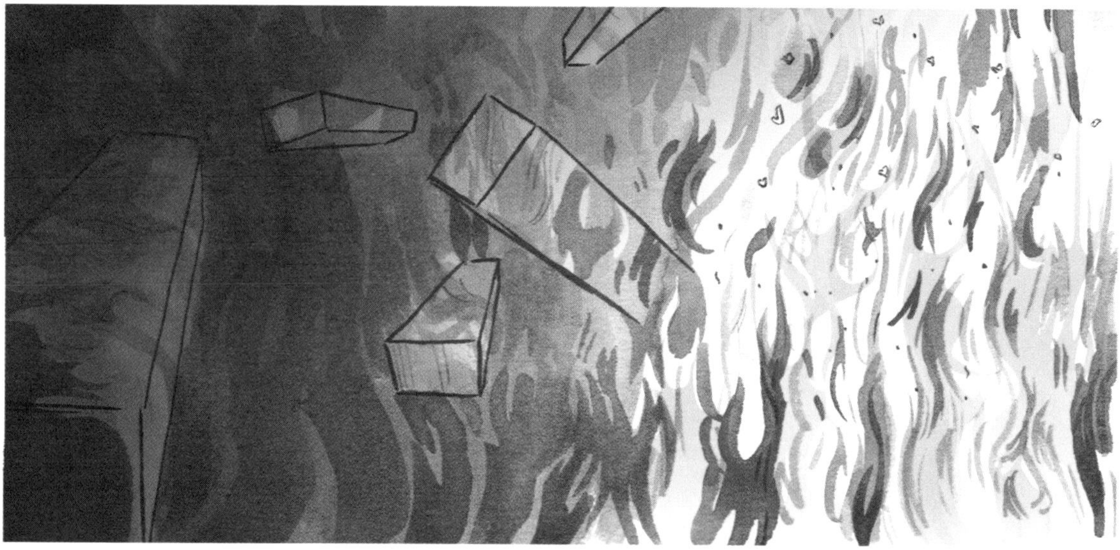

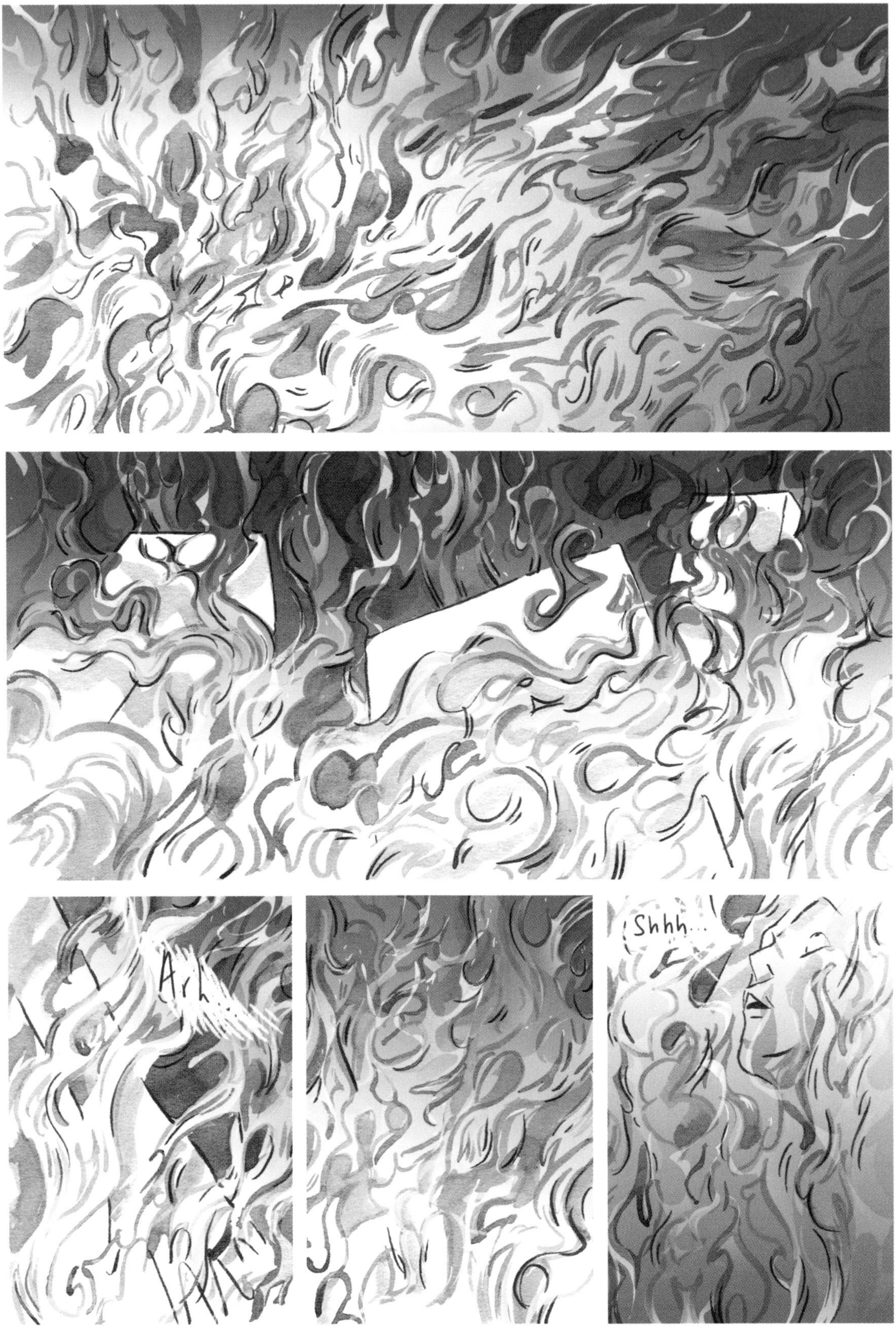
Arh
Shhh...

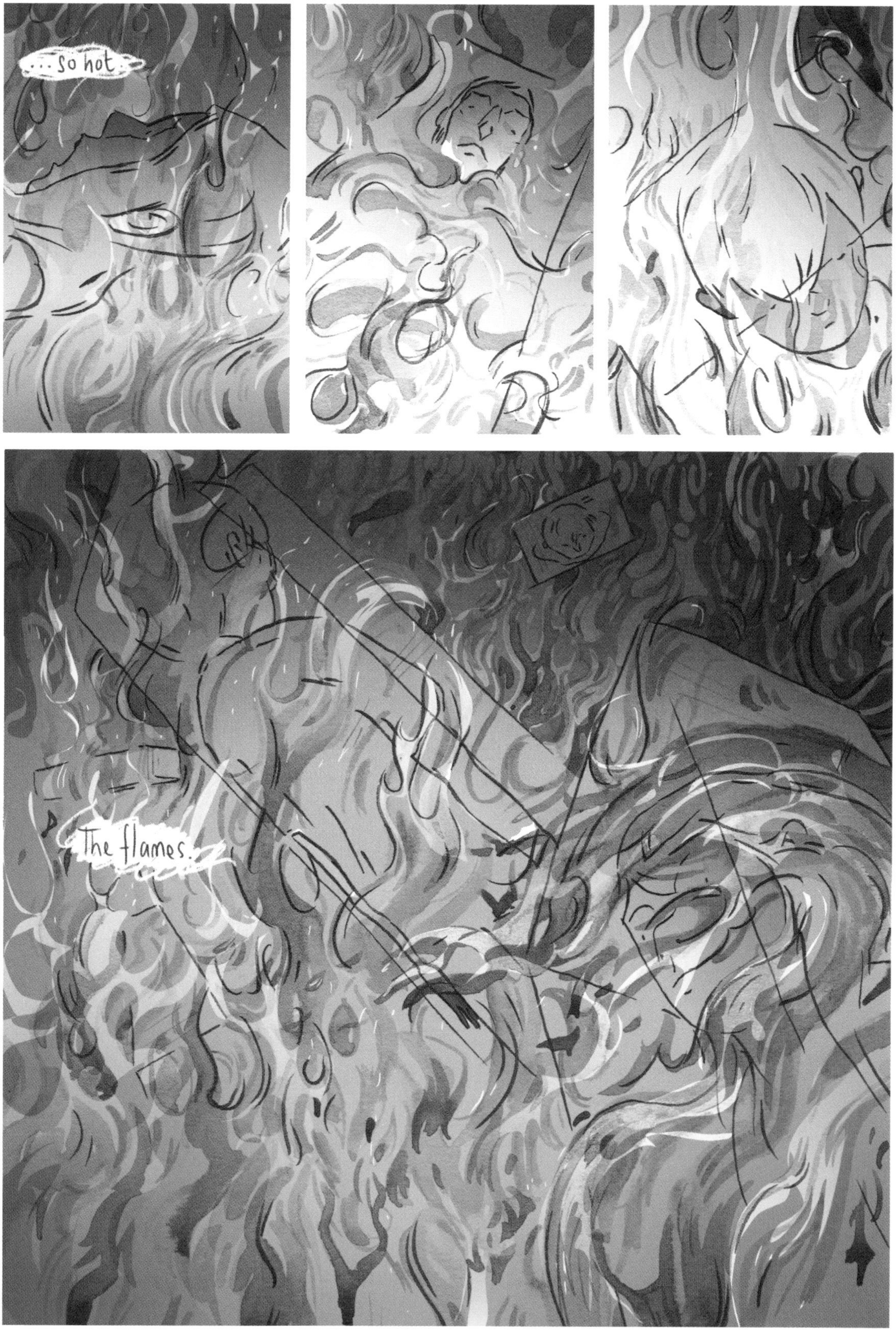
...so hot.
The flames.

...they aren't burning...
...them...
...me.

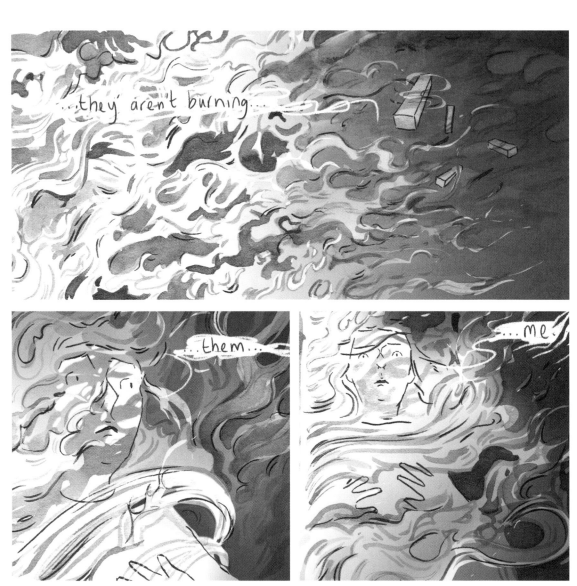

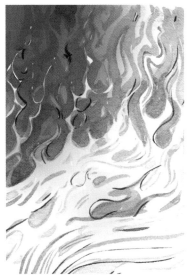

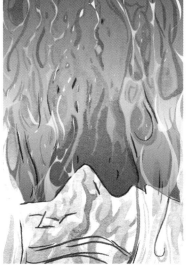

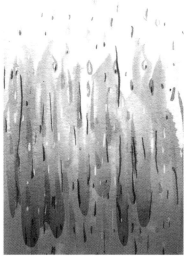

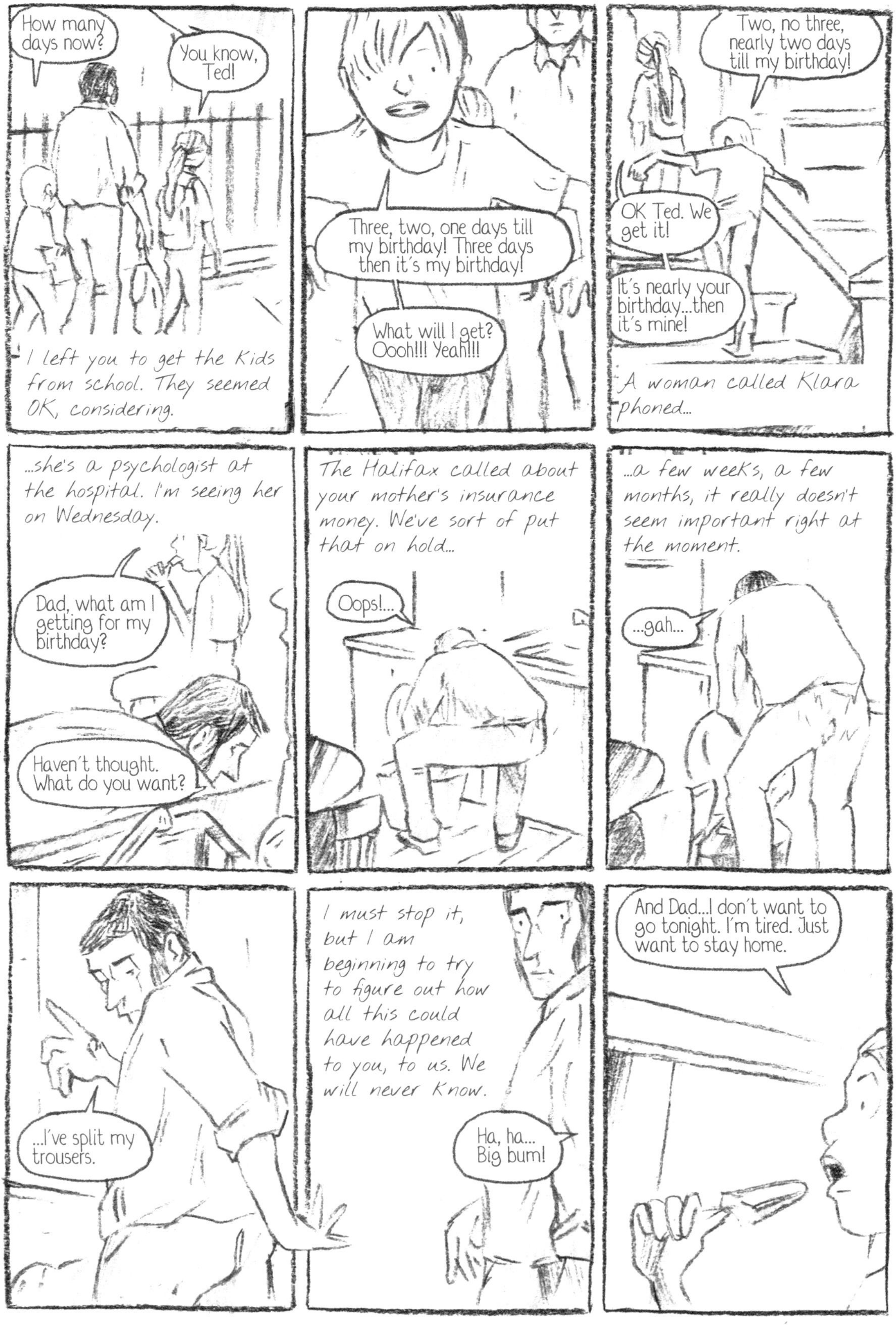
How many days now?
You know, Ted!
I left you to get the kids from school. They seemed OK, considering.
Three, two, one days till my birthday! Three days then it's my birthday!
What will I get? Oooh!!! Yeah!!!
Two, no three, nearly two days till my birthday!
OK Ted. We get it!
It's nearly your birthday...then it's mine!
A woman called Klara phoned...
...she's a psychologist at the hospital. I'm seeing her on Wednesday.
Dad, what am I getting for my birthday?
Haven't thought. What do you want?
The Halifax called about your mother's insurance money. We've sort of put that on hold...
Oops!...
...a few weeks, a few months, it really doesn't seem important right at the moment.
...gah...
...I've split my trousers.
I must stop it, but I am beginning to try to figure out how all this could have happened to you, to us. We will never know.
Ha, ha... Big bum!
And Dad...I don't want to go tonight. I'm tired. Just want to stay home.

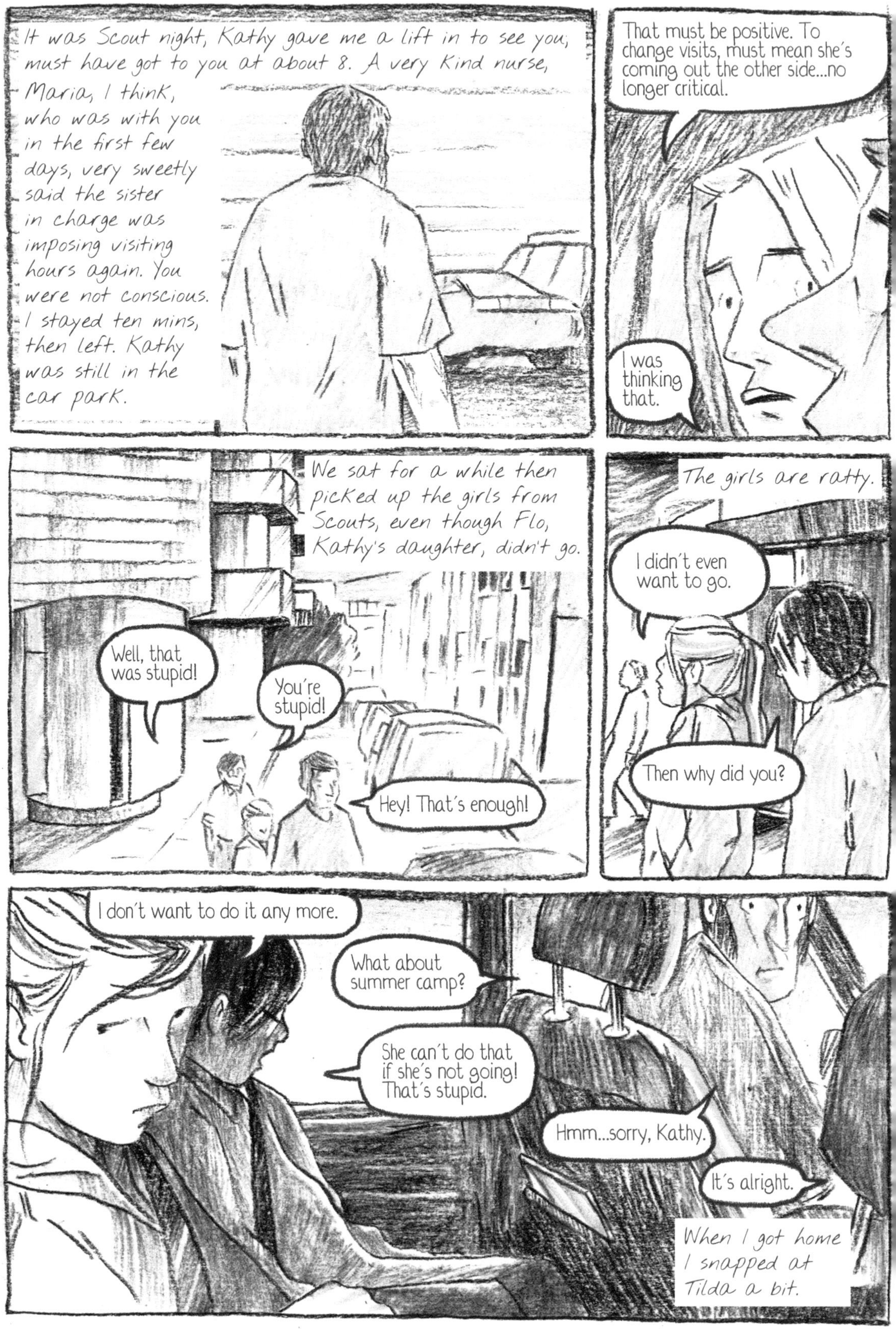
It was Scout night, Kathy gave me a lift in to see you; must have got to you at about 8. A very kind nurse, Maria, I think, who was with you in the first few days, very sweetly said the sister in charge was imposing visiting hours again. You were not conscious. I stayed ten mins, then left. Kathy was still in the car park.
That must be positive. To change visits, must mean she's coming out the other side...no longer critical.
I was thinking that.
We sat for a while then picked up the girls from Scouts, even though Flo, Kathy's daughter, didn't go.
Well, that was stupid!
You're stupid!
Hey! That's enough!
The girls are ratty.
I didn't even want to go.
Then why did you?
I don't want to do it any more.
What about summer camp?
She can't do that if she's not going! That's stupid.
Hmm...sorry, Kathy.
It's alright.
When I got home I snapped at Tilda a bit.

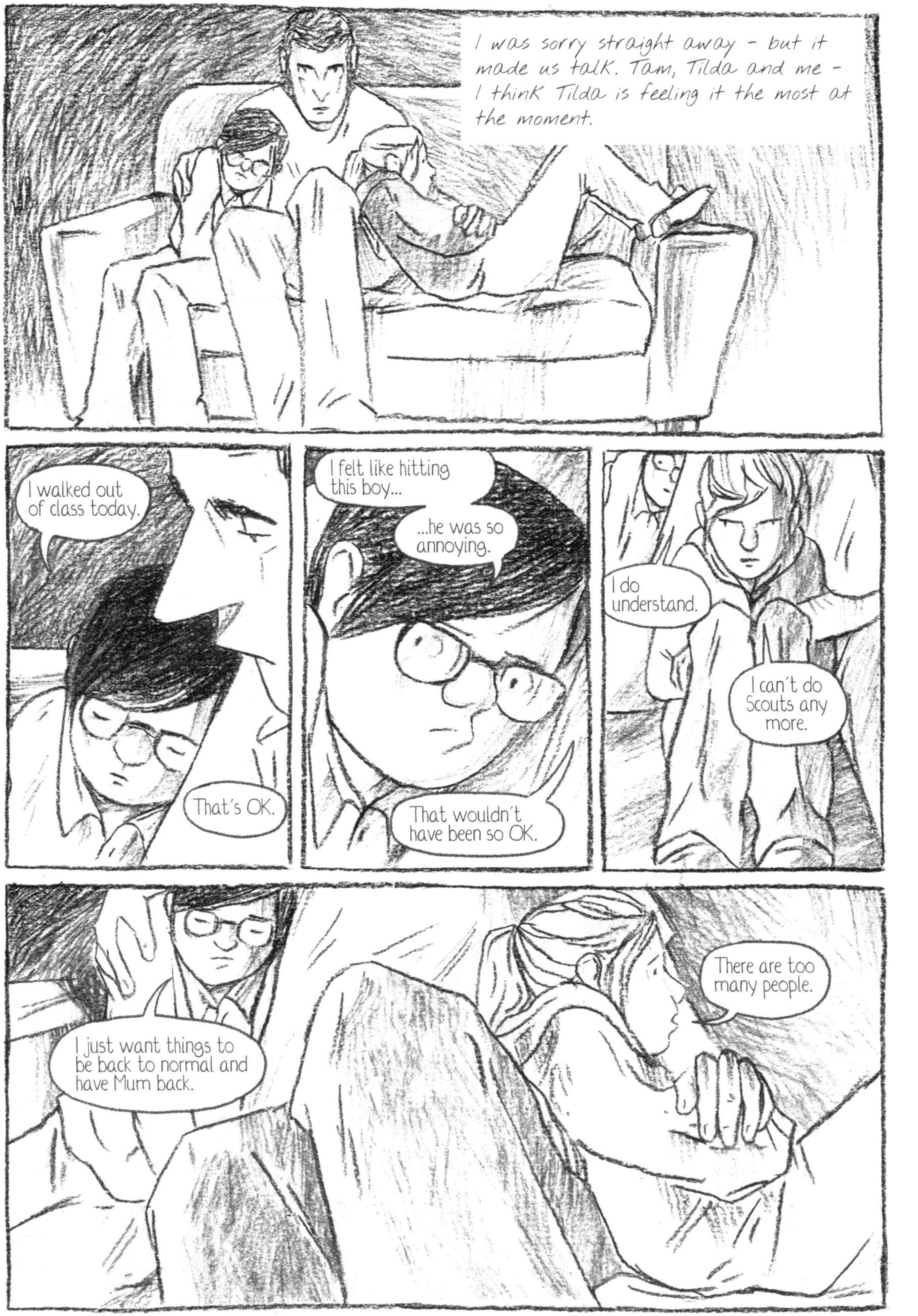
I was sorry straight away - but it made us talk. Tam, Tilda and me - I think Tilda is feeling it the most at the moment.
I walked out of class today.
That's OK.
I felt like hitting this boy...
...he was so annoying.
That wouldn't have been so OK.
I do understand.
I can't do Scouts any more.
I just want things to be back to normal and have Mum back.
There are too many people.

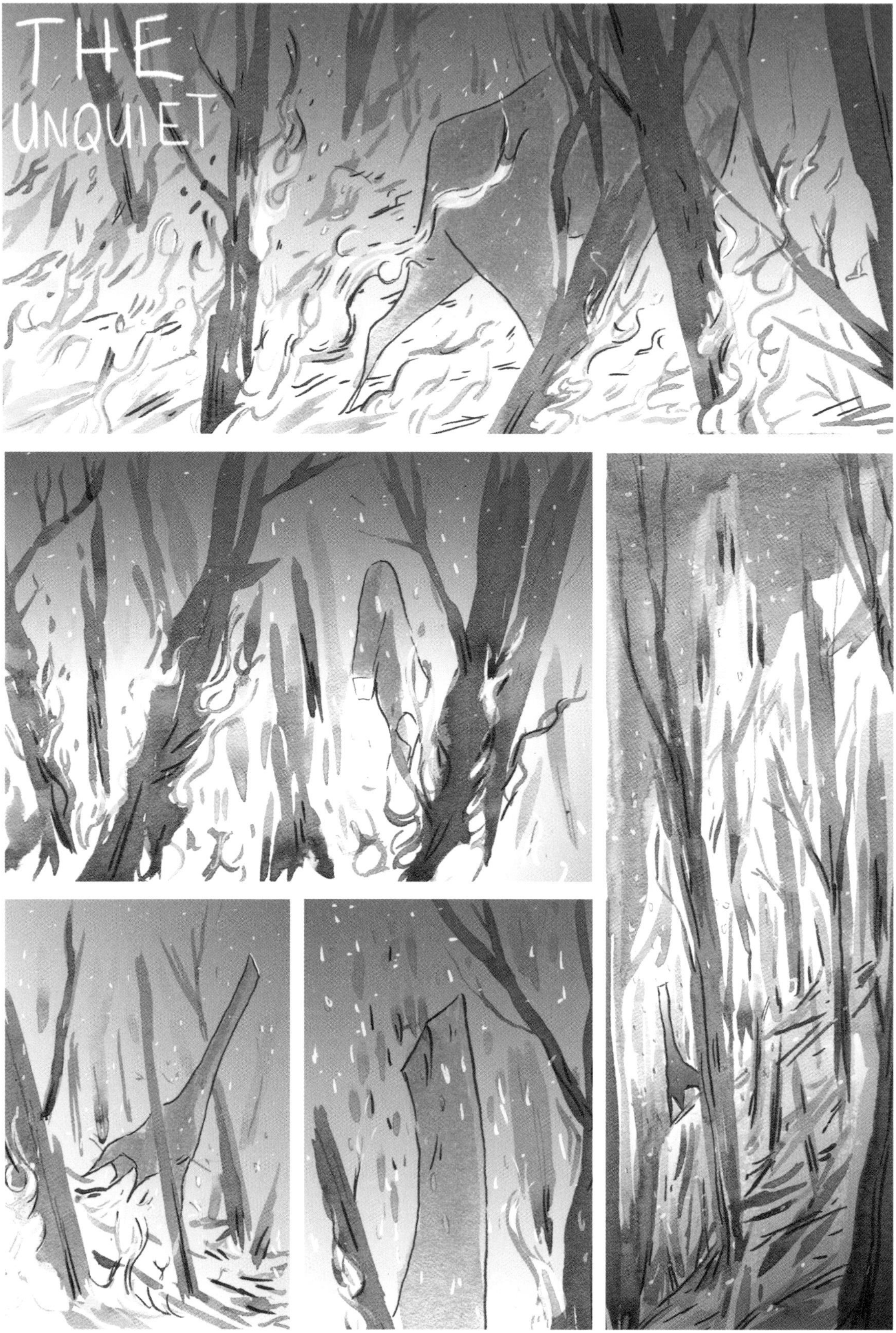
THE
UNQUIET

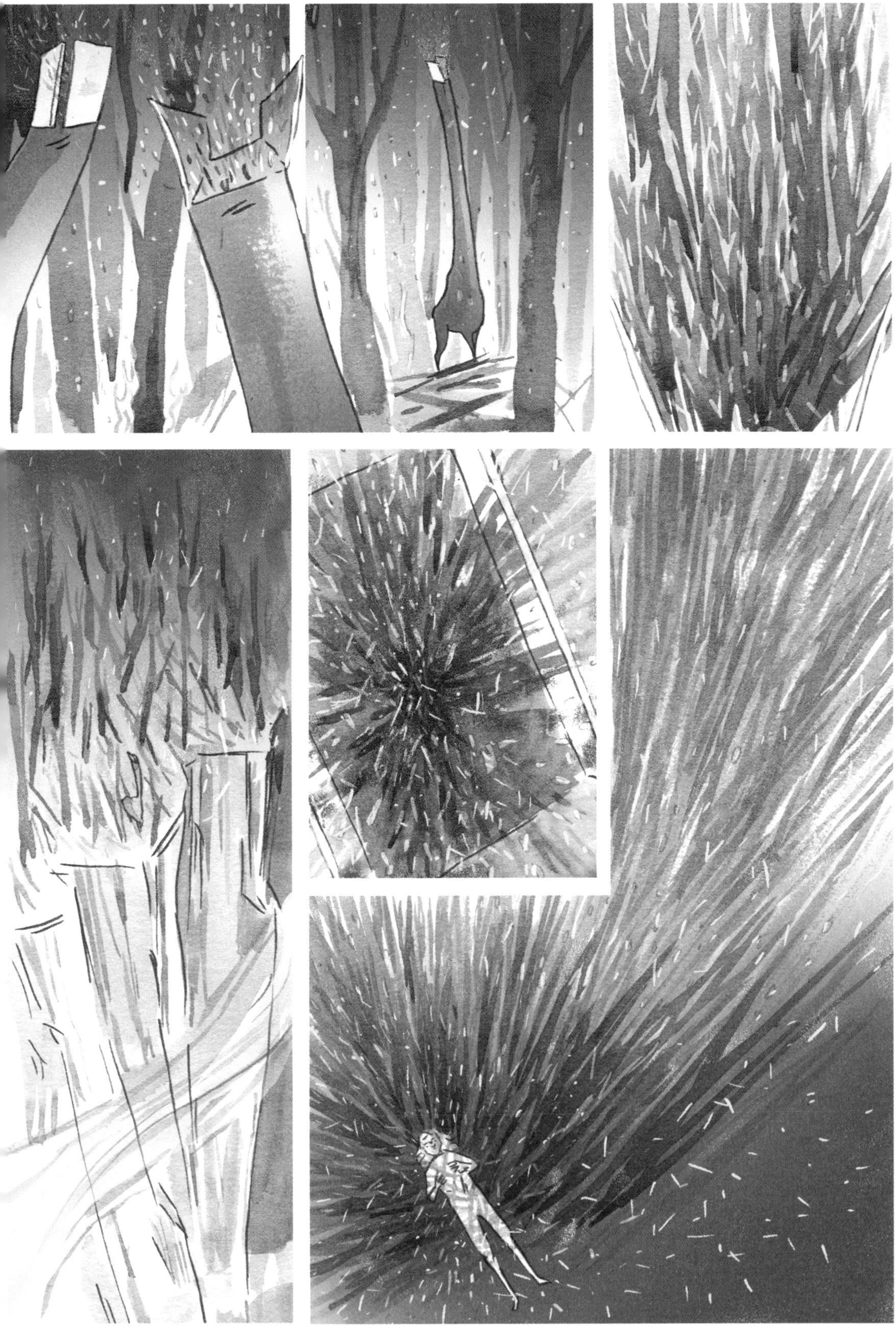

Please, go away.

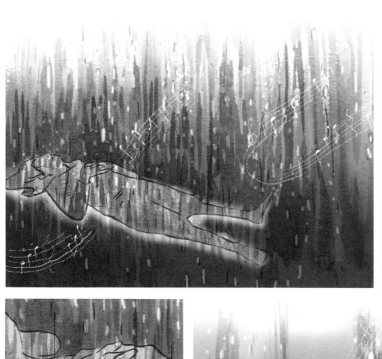

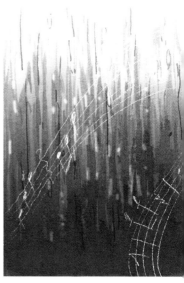

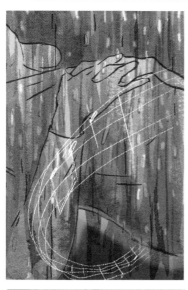

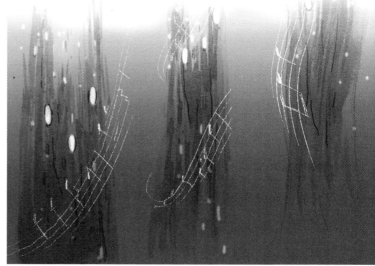

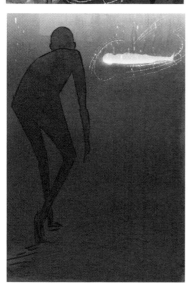

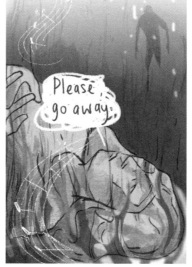

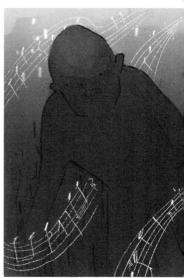

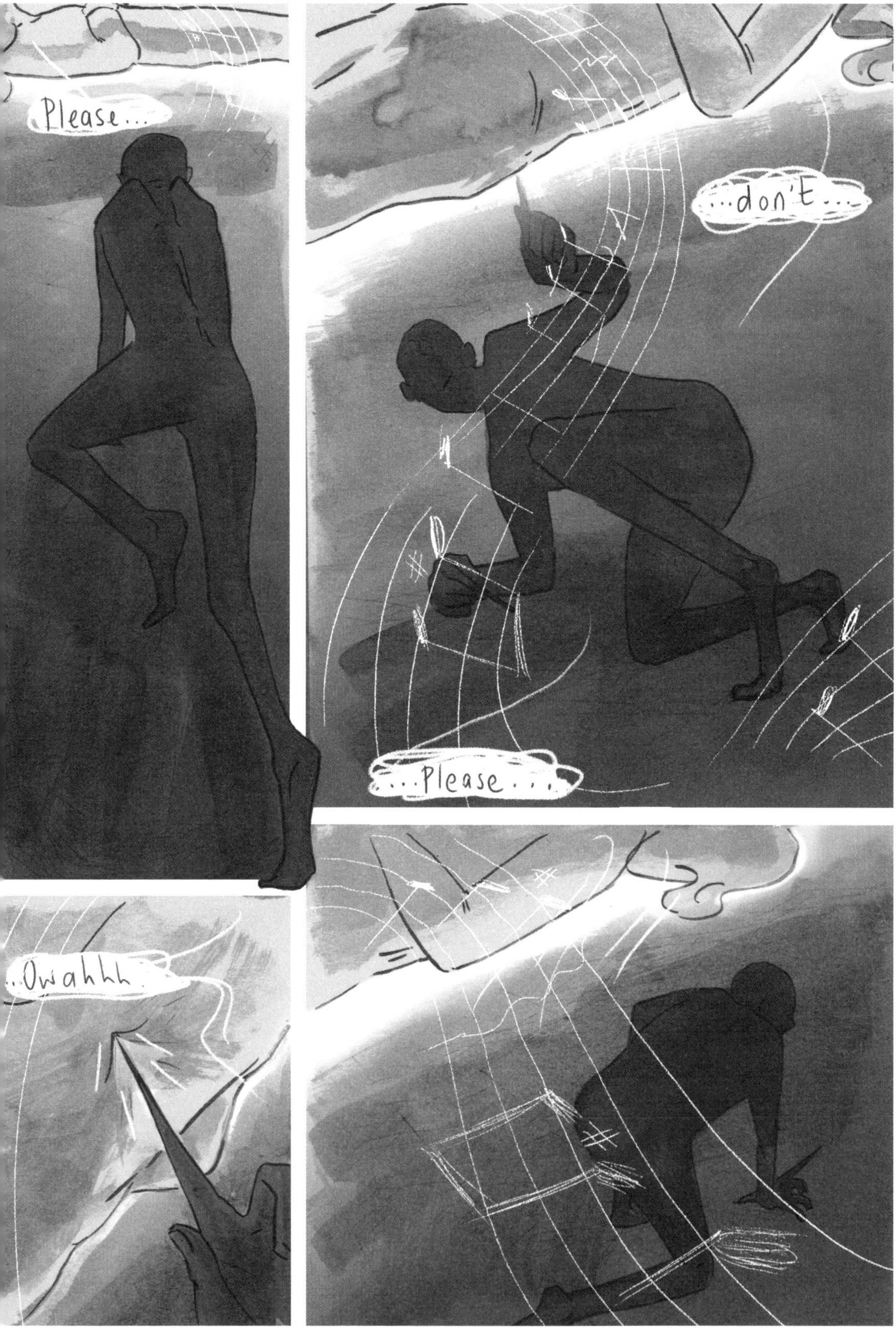
Please...
...don't...
...Please...
..Owahhh.

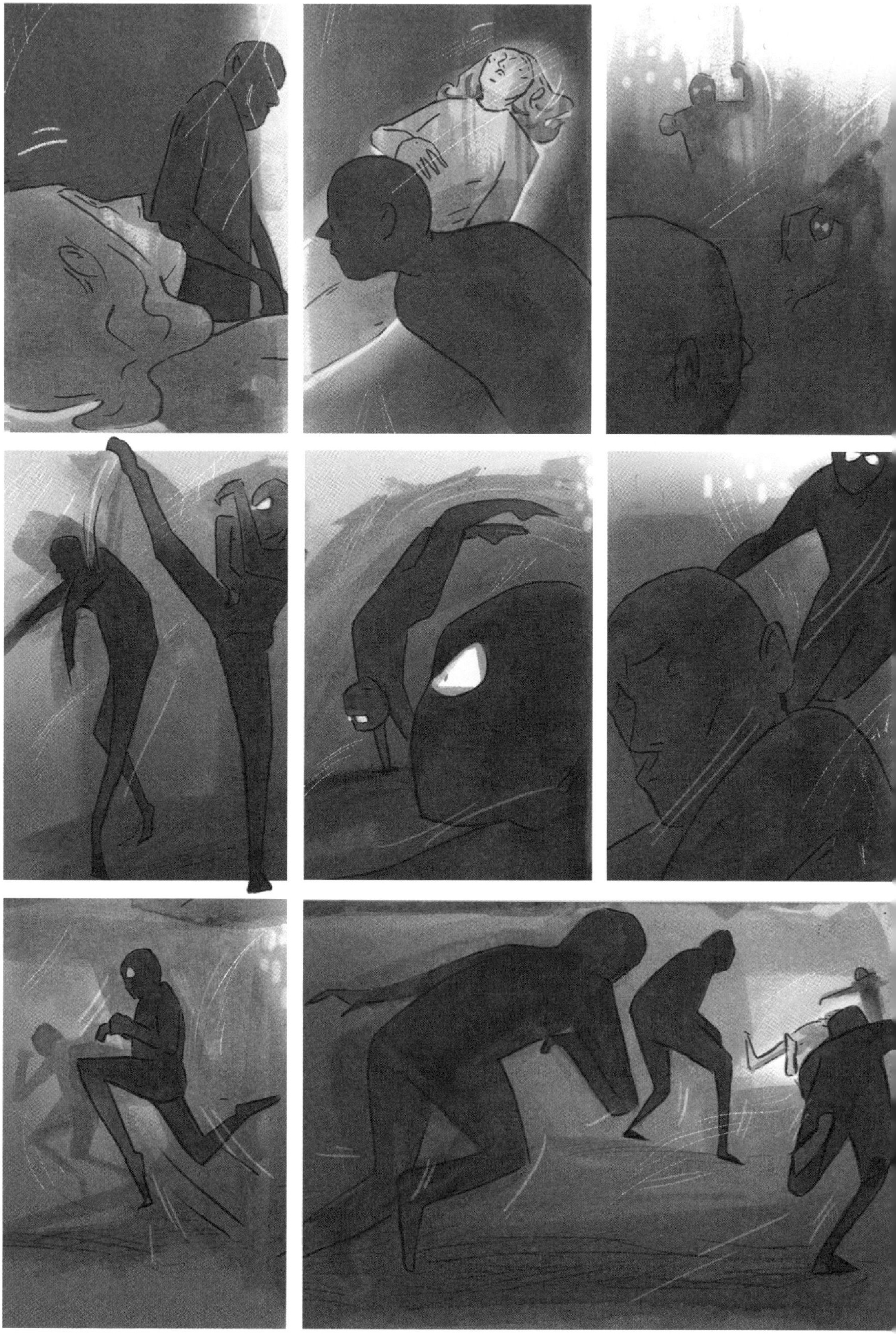

Circus Ninjas!

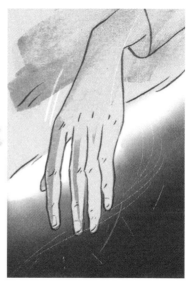

They're rescuing me?

Sob!

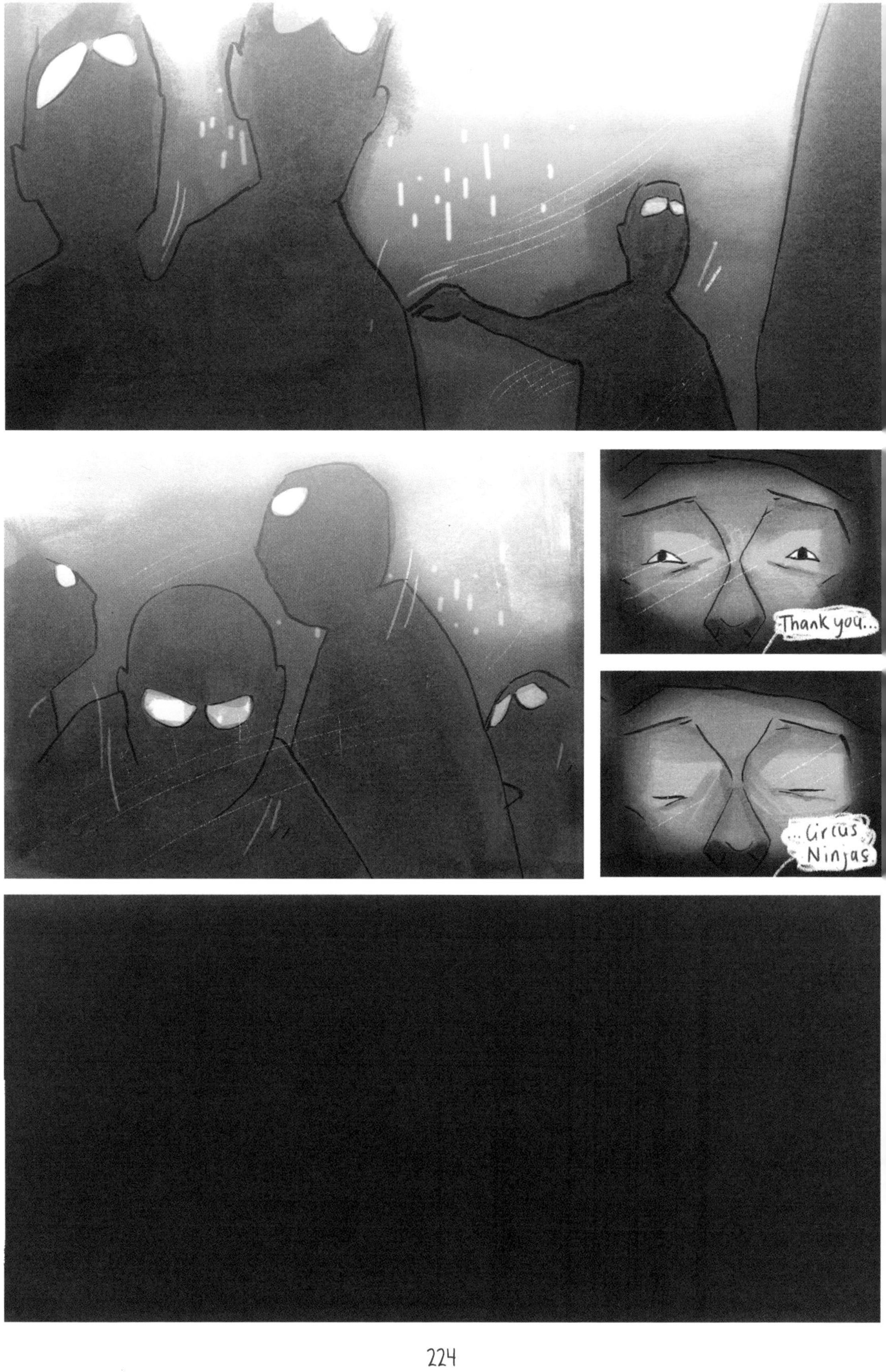
Thank you...
...Circus Ninjas.

TUESDAY 4th JUNE

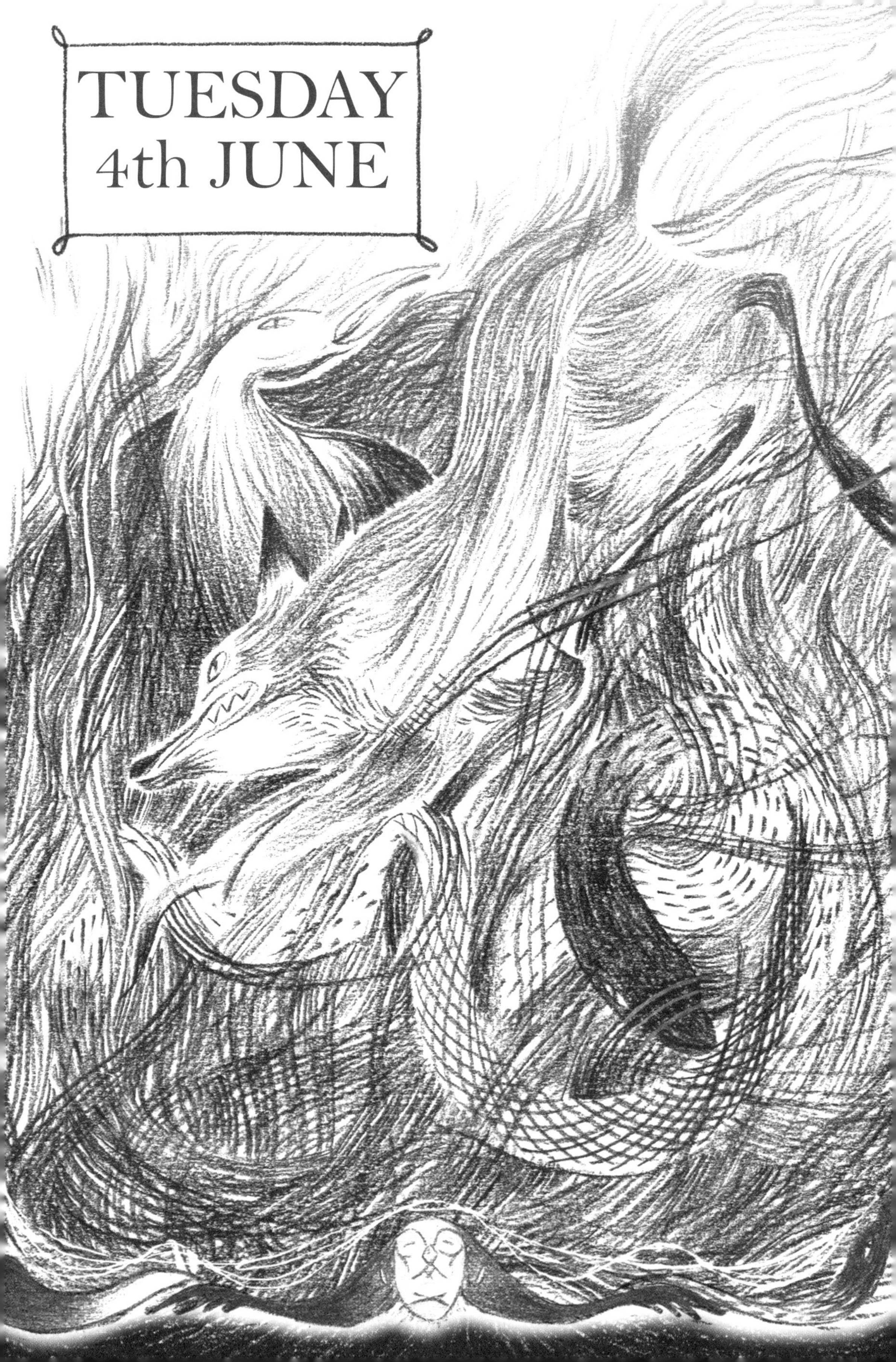

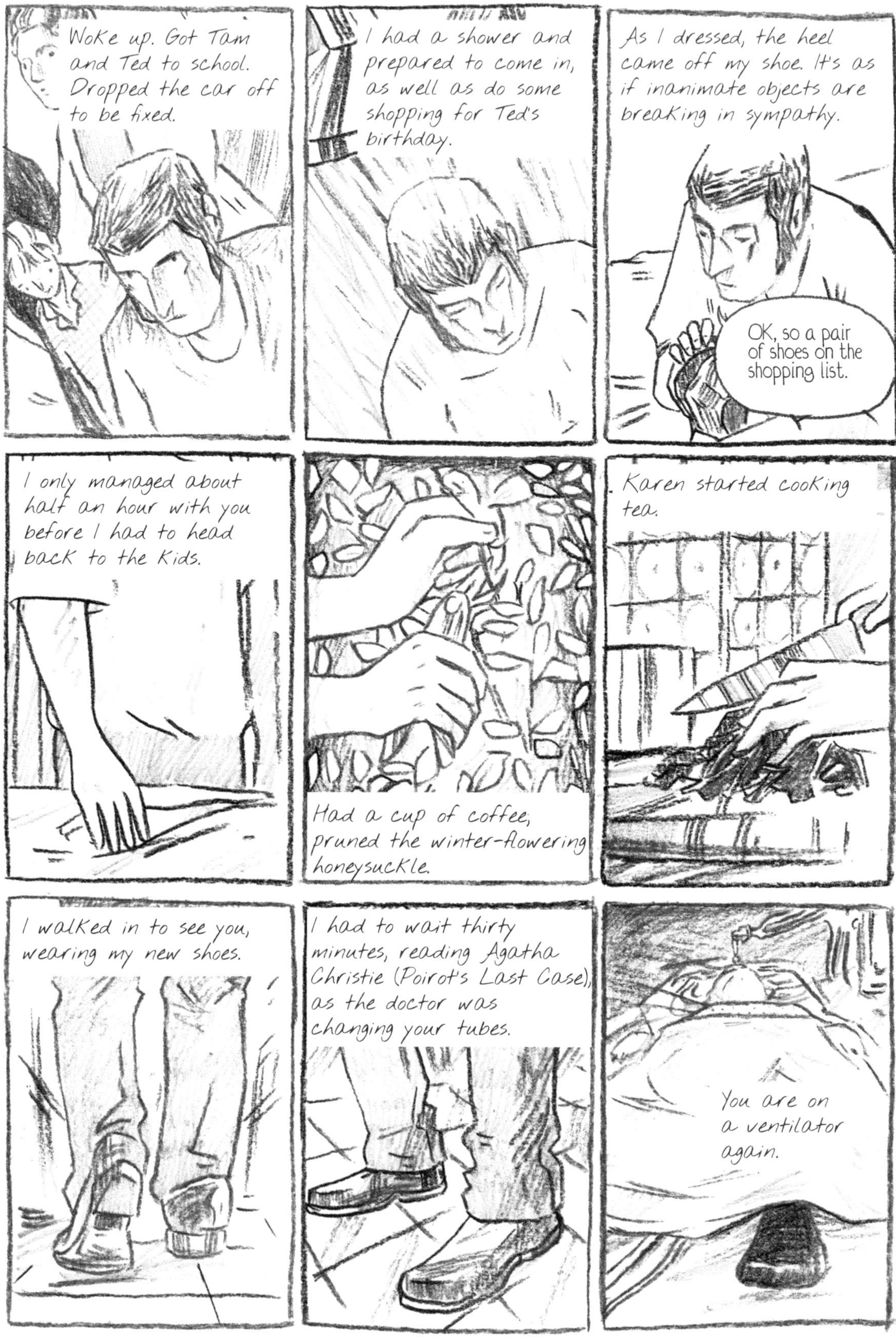
Woke up. Got Tam and Ted to school. Dropped the car off to be fixed.
I had a shower and prepared to come in, as well as do some shopping for Ted's birthday.
As I dressed, the heel came off my shoe. It's as if inanimate objects are breaking in sympathy.
OK, so a pair of shoes on the shopping list.
I only managed about half an hour with you before I had to head back to the kids.
Had a cup of coffee, pruned the winter-flowering honeysuckle.
Karen started cooking tea.
I walked in to see you, wearing my new shoes.
I had to wait thirty minutes, reading Agatha Christie (Poirot's Last Case), as the doctor was changing your tubes.
You are on a ventilator again.

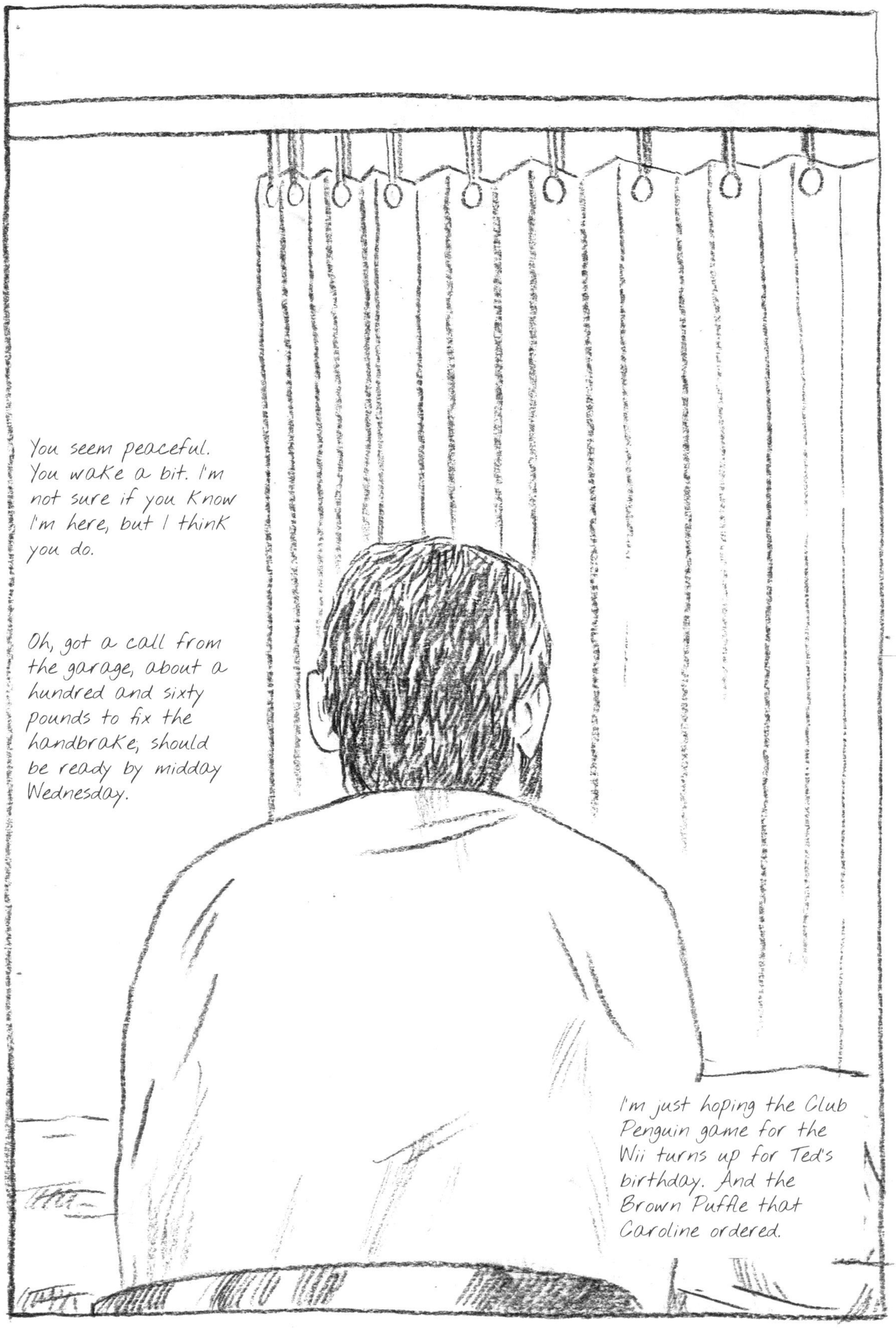
You seem peaceful. You wake a bit. I'm not sure if you know I'm here, but I think you do.
Oh, got a call from the garage, about a hundred and sixty pounds to fix the handbrake, should be ready by midday Wednesday.
I'm just hoping the Club Penguin game for the Wii turns up for Ted's birthday. And the Brown Puffle that Caroline ordered.

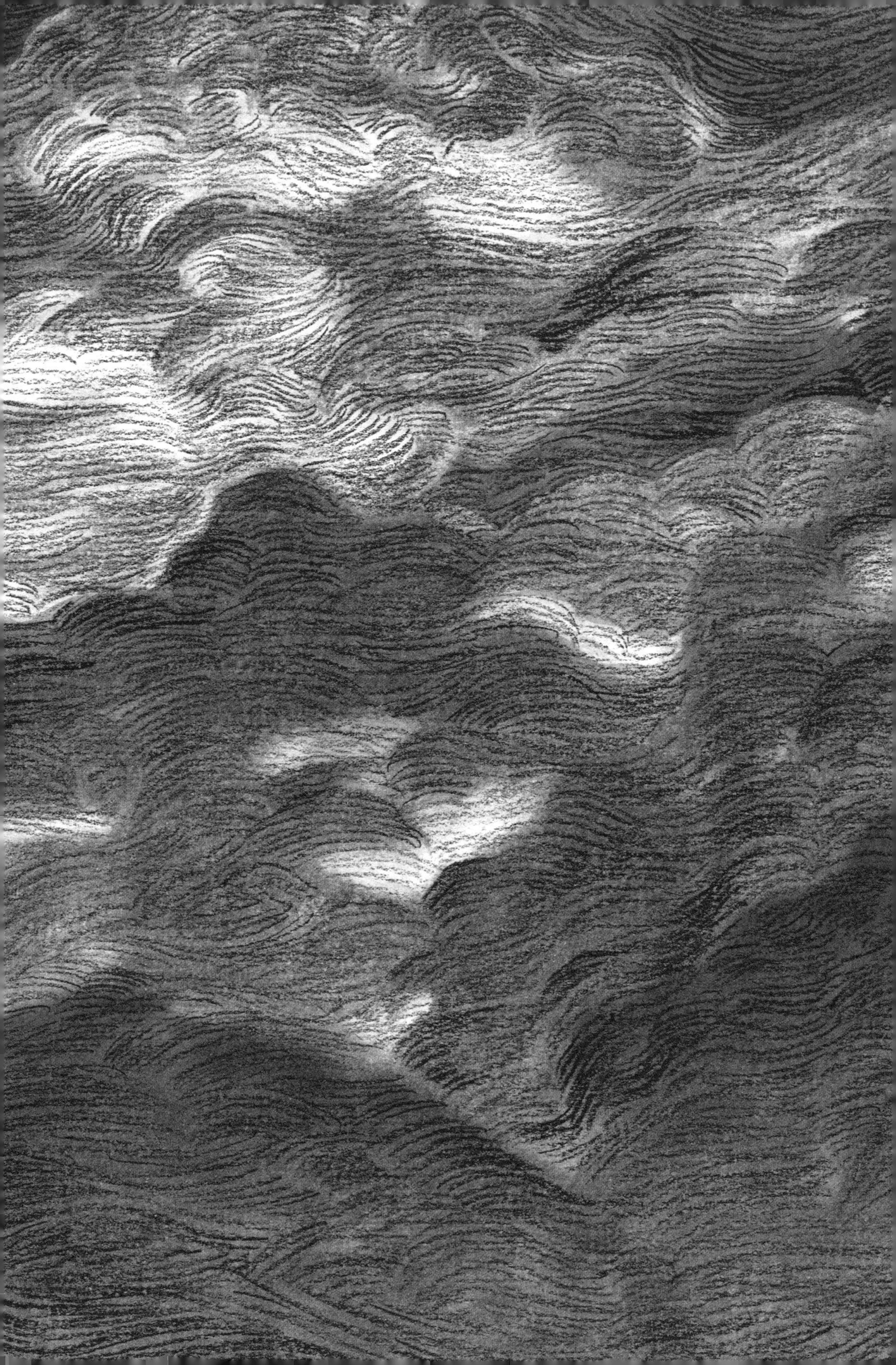

WEDNESDAY 5th JUNE

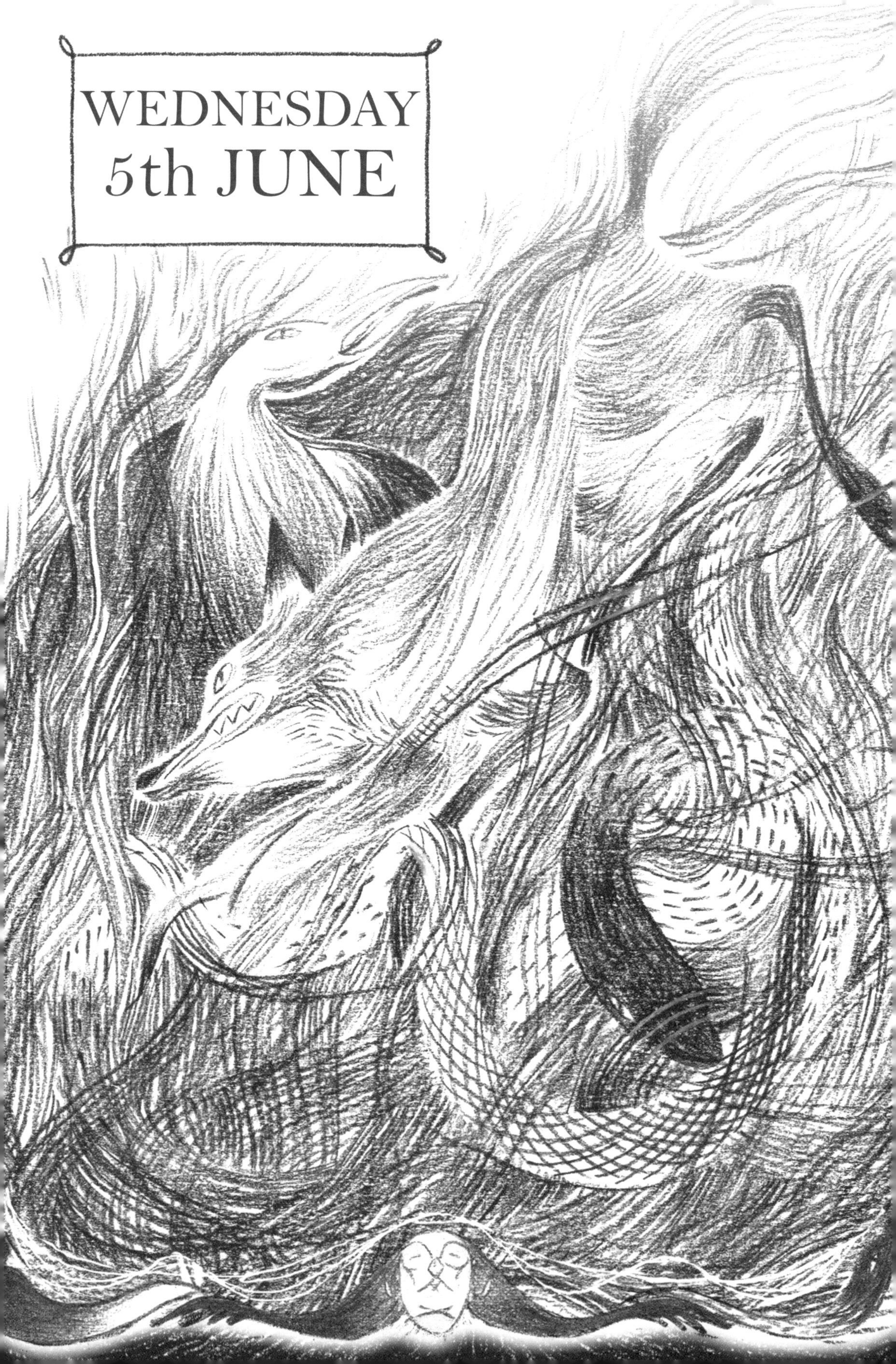

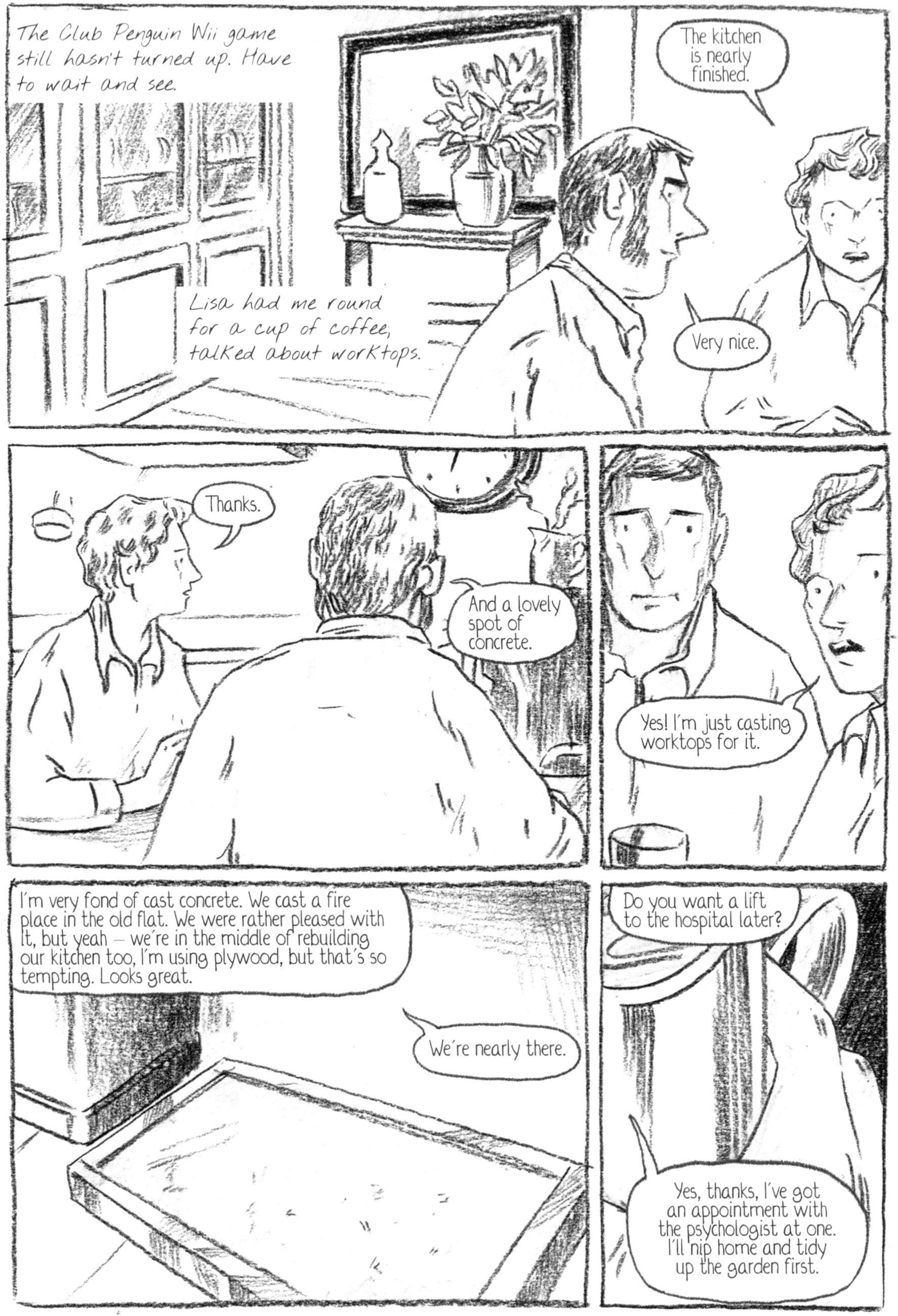

The Club Penguin Wii game still hasn't turned up. Have to wait and see.
The kitchen is nearly finished.
Lisa had me round for a cup of coffee, talked about worktops.
Very nice.
Thanks.
And a lovely spot of concrete.
Yes! I'm just casting worktops for it.
I'm very fond of cast concrete. We cast a fire place in the old flat. We were rather pleased with it, but yeah – we're in the middle of rebuilding our kitchen too, I'm using plywood, but that's so tempting. Looks great.
We're nearly there.
Do you want a lift to the hospital later?
Yes, thanks, I've got an appointment with the psychologist at one. I'll nip home and tidy up the garden first.

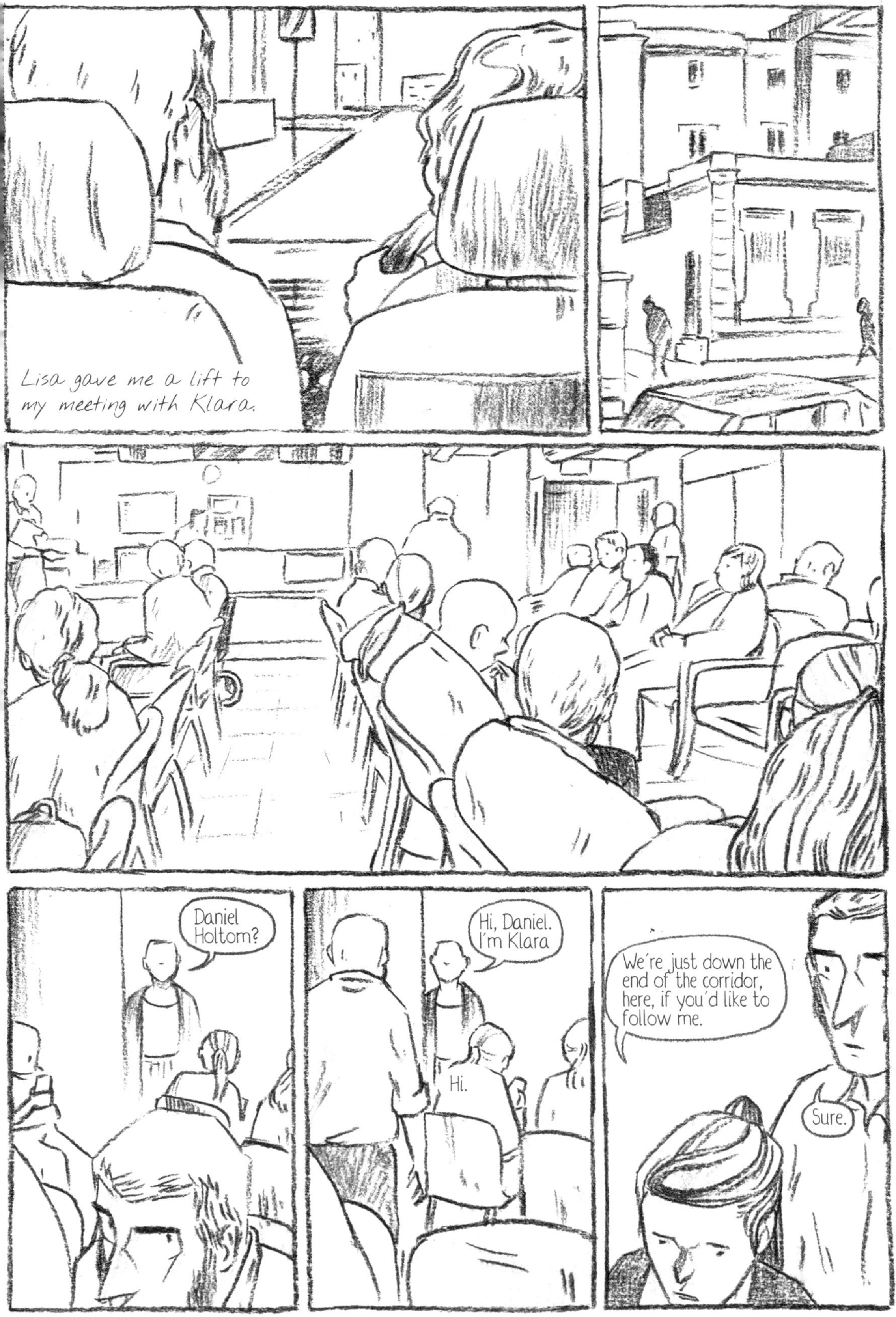
Lisa gave me a lift to my meeting with Klara.
Daniel Holtom?
Hi, Daniel. I'm Klara
Hi.
We're just down the end of the corridor, here, if you'd like to follow me.
Sure.

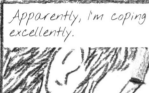
Apparently, I'm coping excellently.

Anyway, I'm in the waiting room, waiting to see you.

The doctor is putting something in your wrist at the moment.

You are still sedated and had a echo scan earlier today.

I believe they were checking for infection around your heart.

As nobody has taken me aside to a small quiet room, I'm assuming they didn't find any infection.

God – we have so much to go through. You, most of all.

One plus point.

Stumbled across a reduced copy of the Club Penguin game in Asda when buying party food junk for Ted's party.

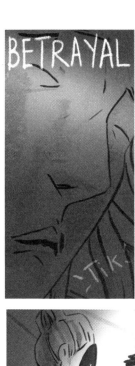

BETRAYAL

sister!

You? All this time! You dragged me back!

Tick, Tock, Tick

Tock,

what?

Hey? You're not nurses! This is a beautician's?

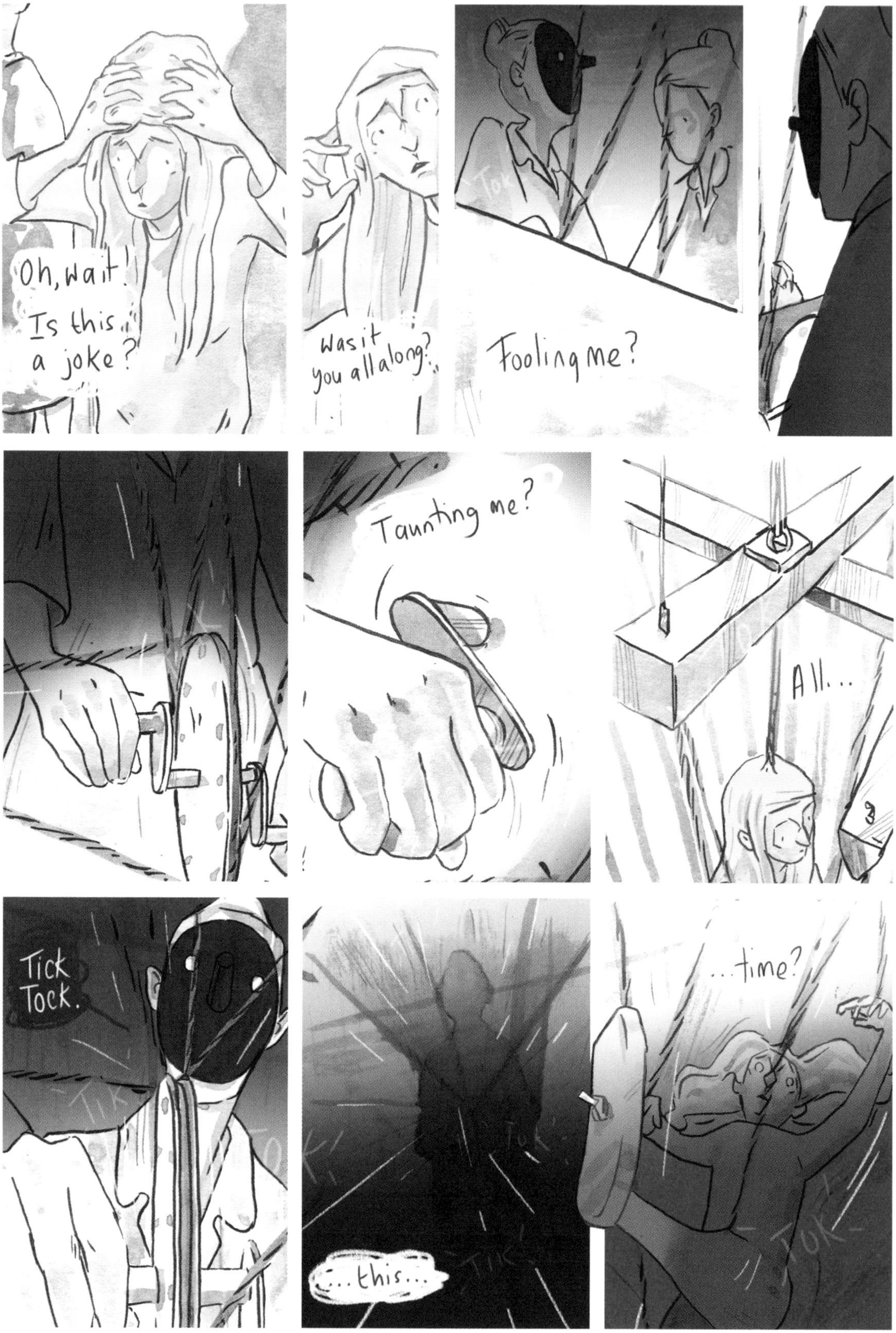
Oh, wait!
Is this a joke?
Was it you all along?
Fooling me?
TOK
Taunting me?
All...
Tick Tock.
TIK
TOK
...this...
TOK
TIK
...time?
TOK

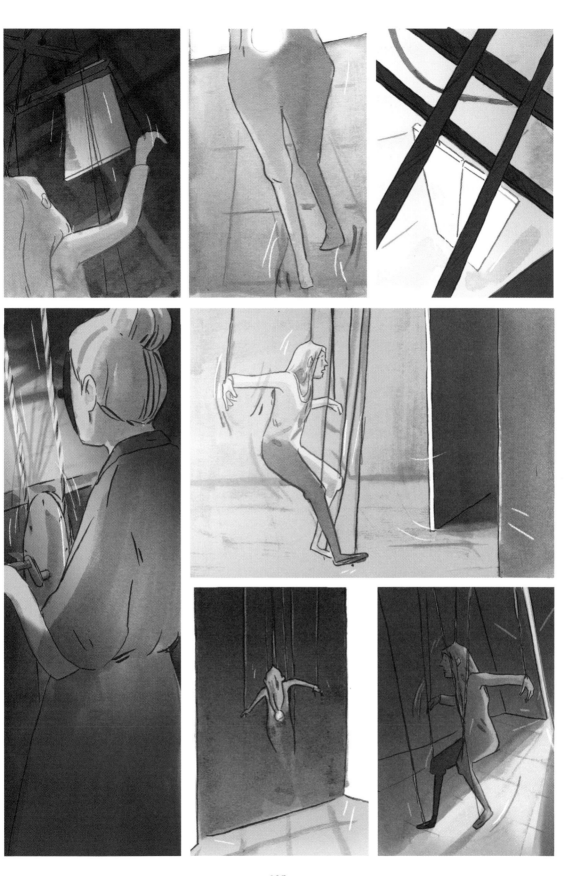

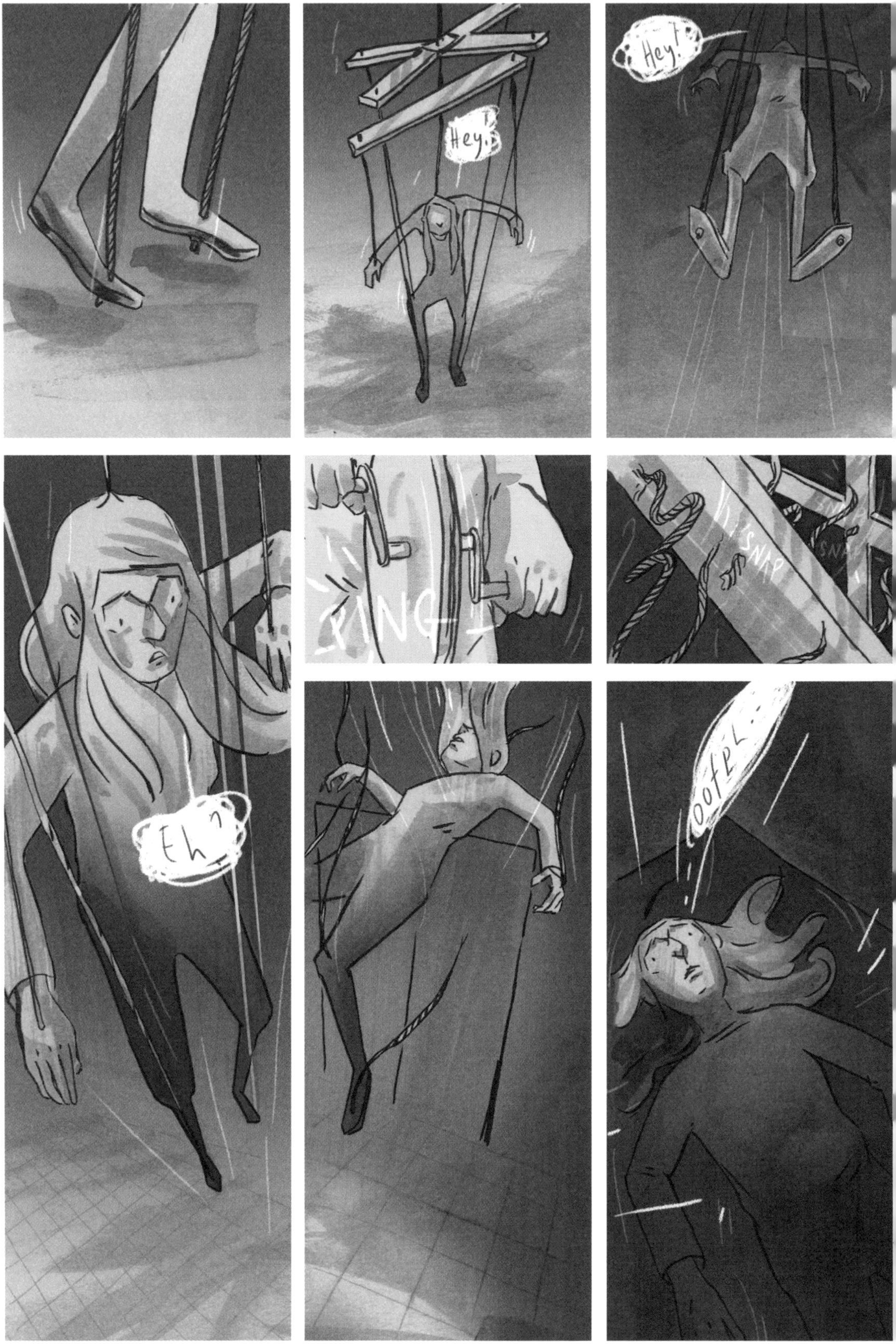

Hey!
Hey!
Eh?
PING
SNAP
Oofl..

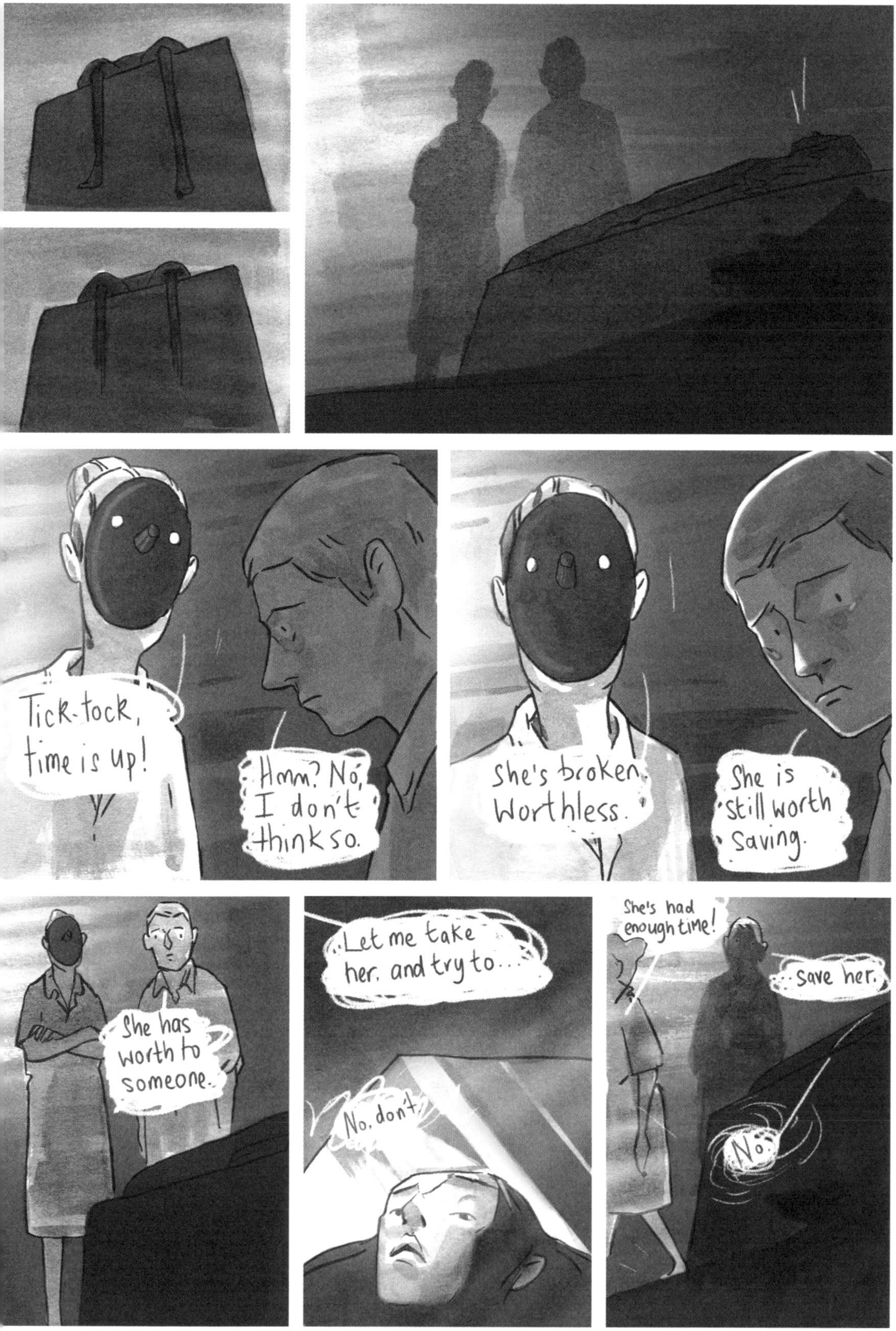
Tick-tock, time is up!
Hmm? No, I don't think so.
She's broken. Worthless.
She is still worth saving.
She has worth to someone.
Let me take her. and try to...
No, don't
She's had enough time!
...save her.
No.

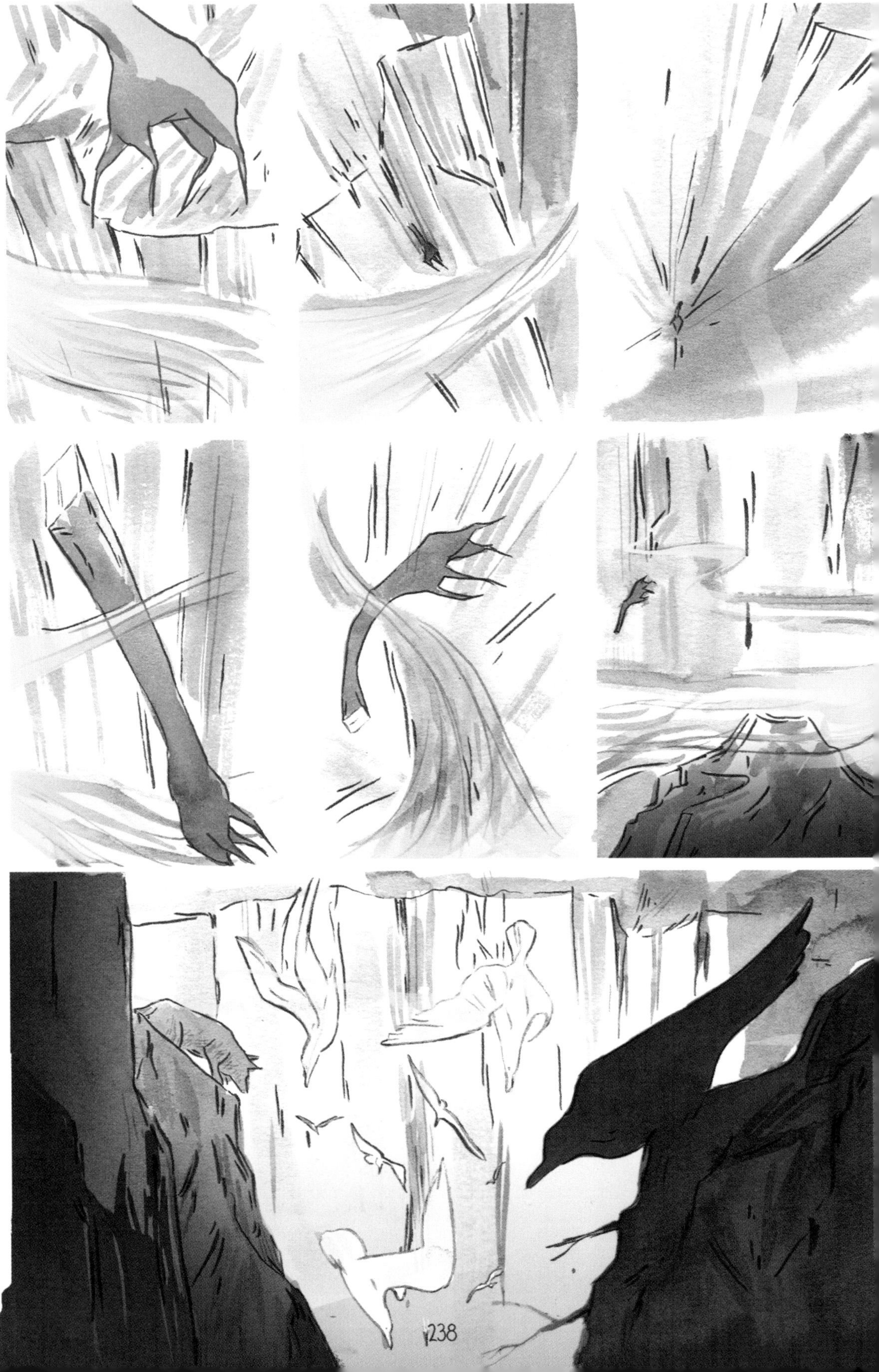

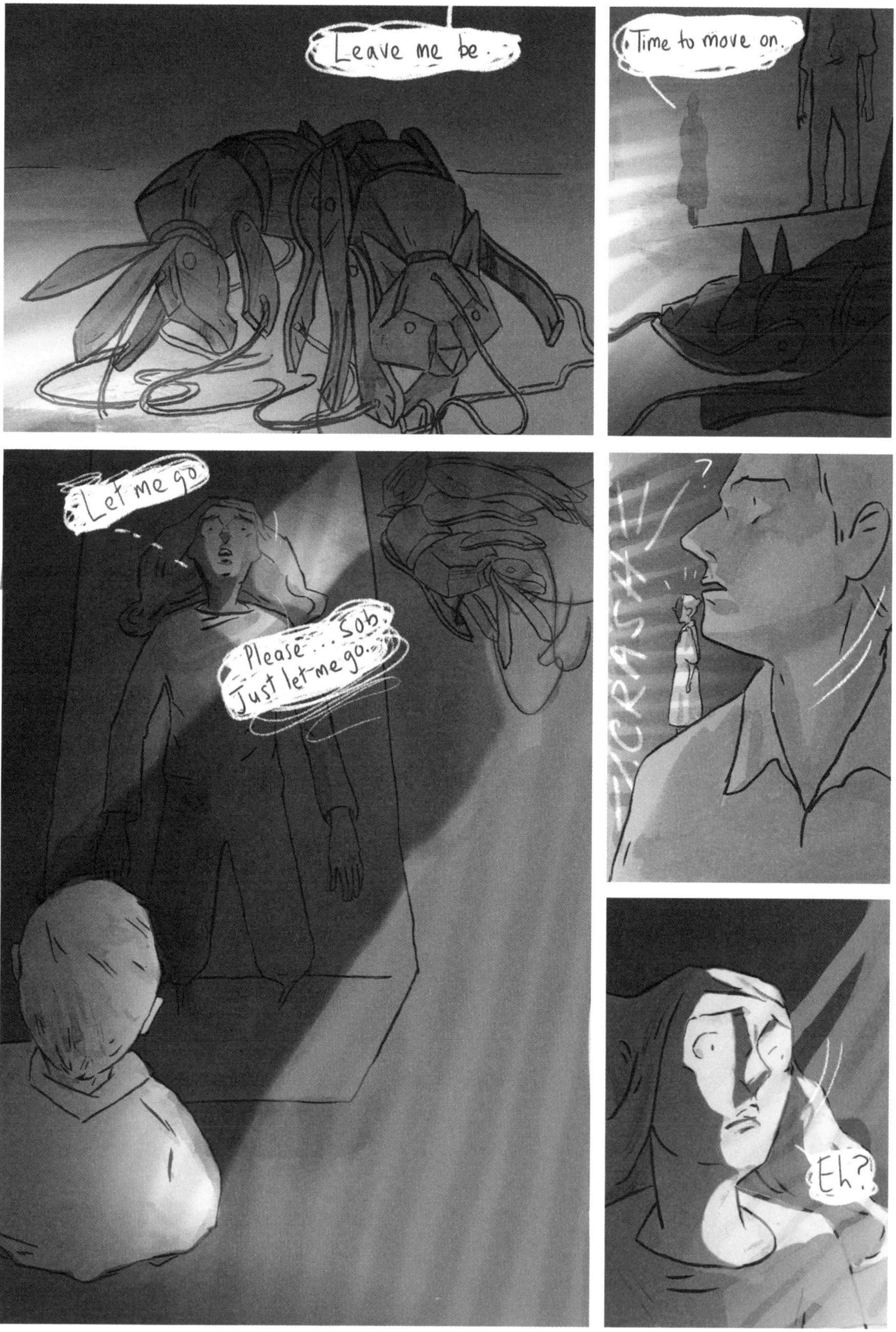
Leave me be..
Time to move on.
Let me go
Please...Sob.
Just let me go..
CRASH
Eh?

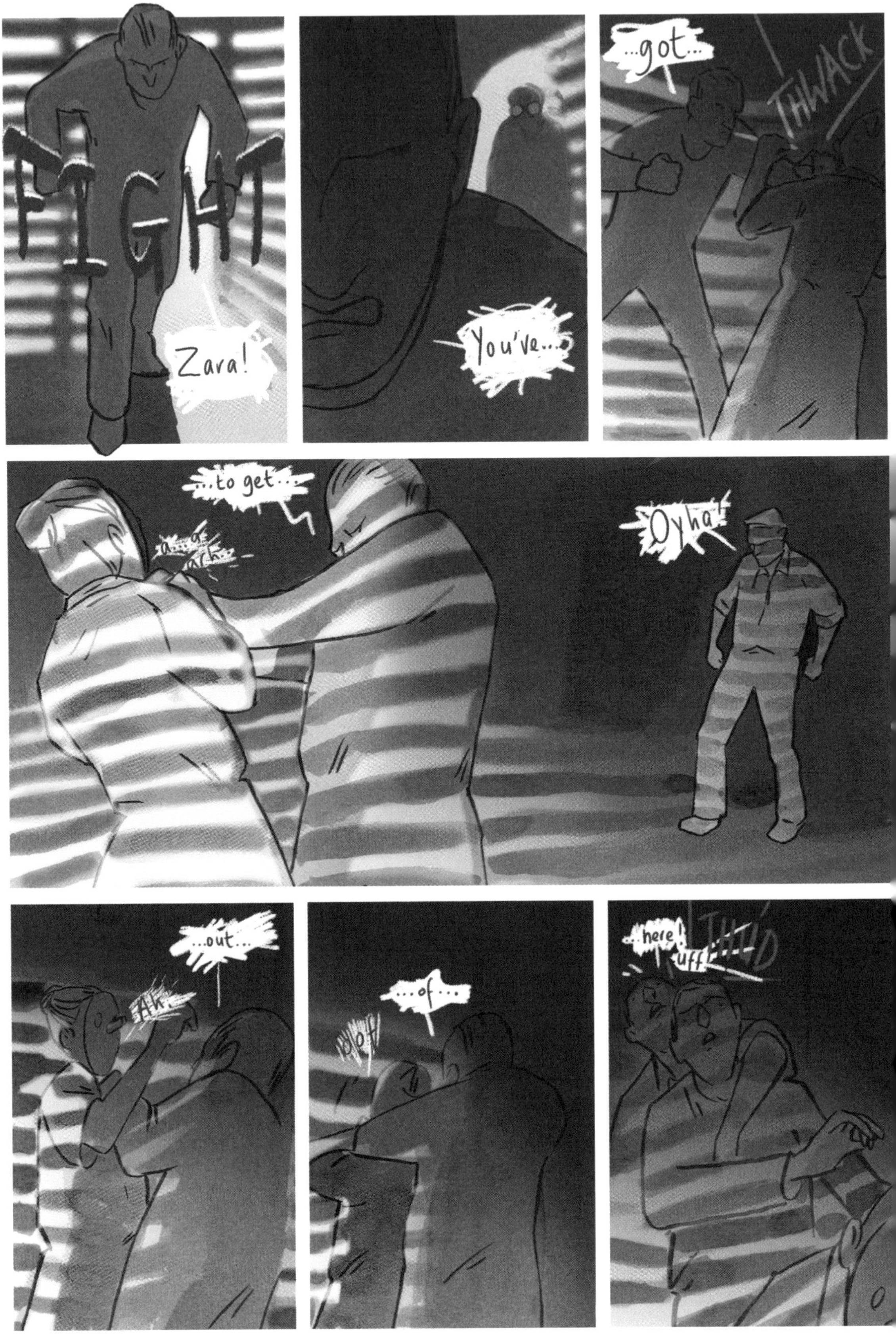
FIGHT
Zara!
You've...
...got...
THWACK
...to get...
Oyha!
...out...
Ah
...of...
oof
...here!
uff
THUD

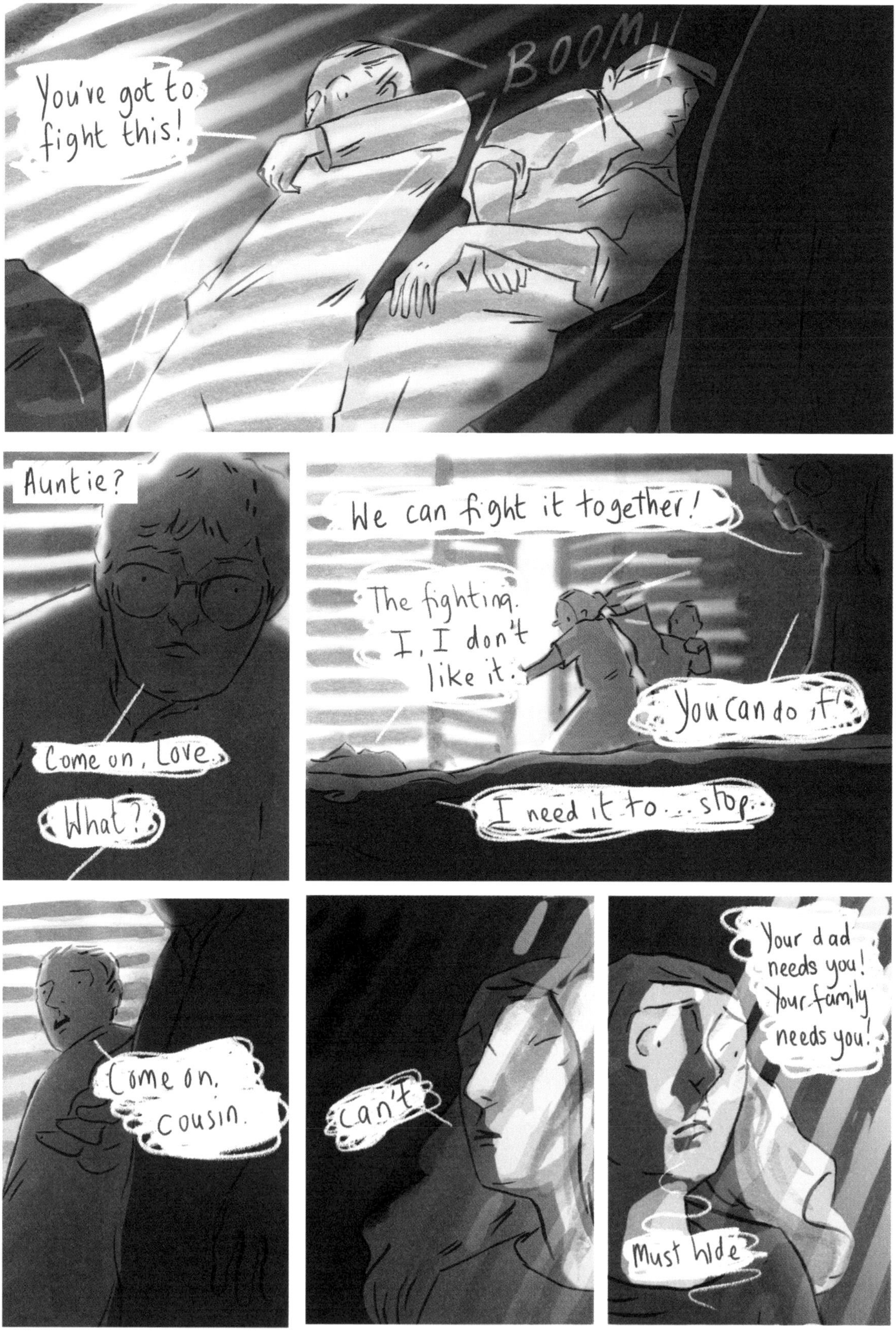
You've got to fight this!
BOOM!
Auntie?
Come on, Love.
What?
We can fight it together!
The fighting. I, I don't like it.
You can do it!
I need it to... stop.
Come on, cousin.
can't
Your dad needs you! Your family needs you!
Must hide

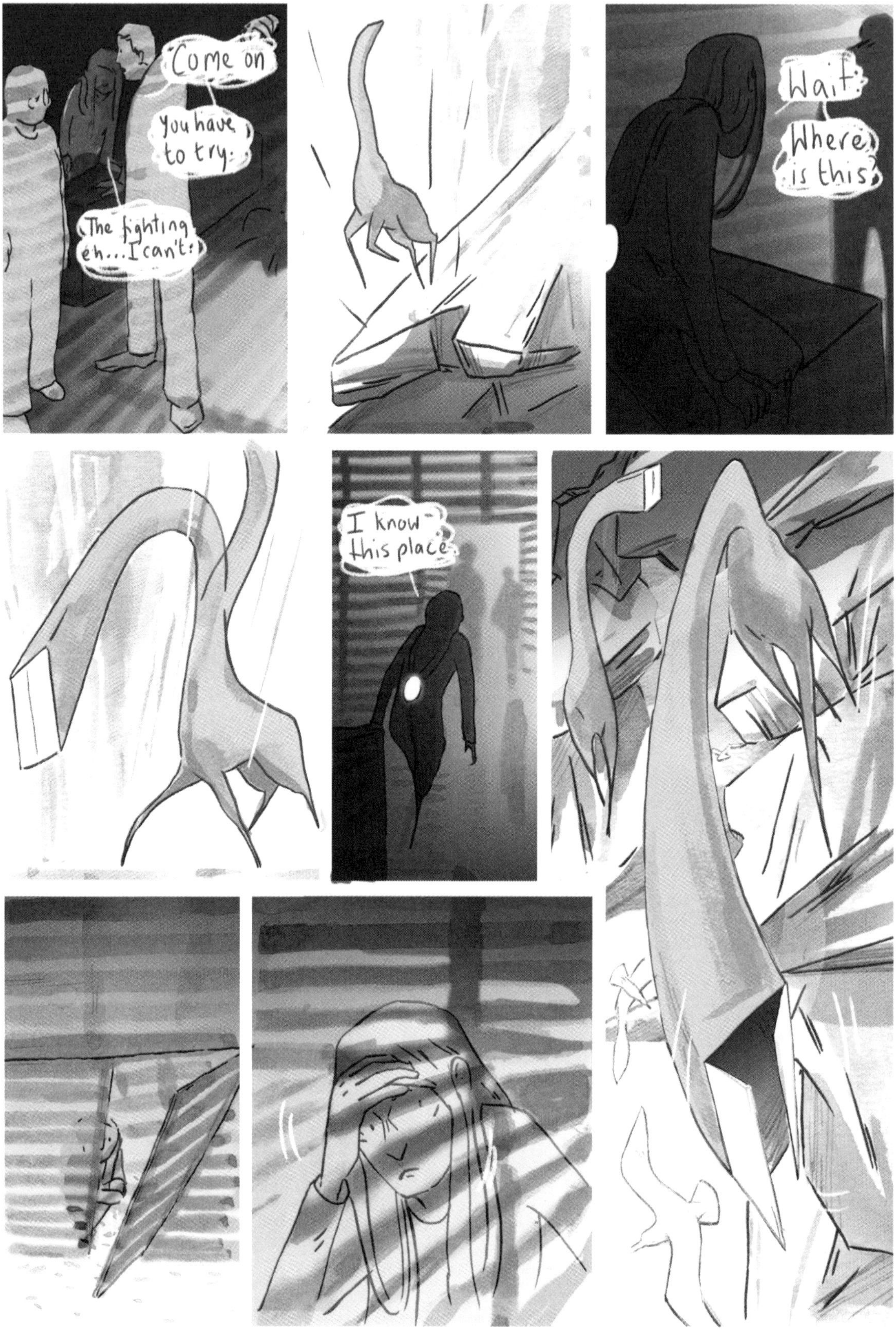

Come on
You have to try.
The fighting eh... I can't.
Wait
Where is this
I know this place

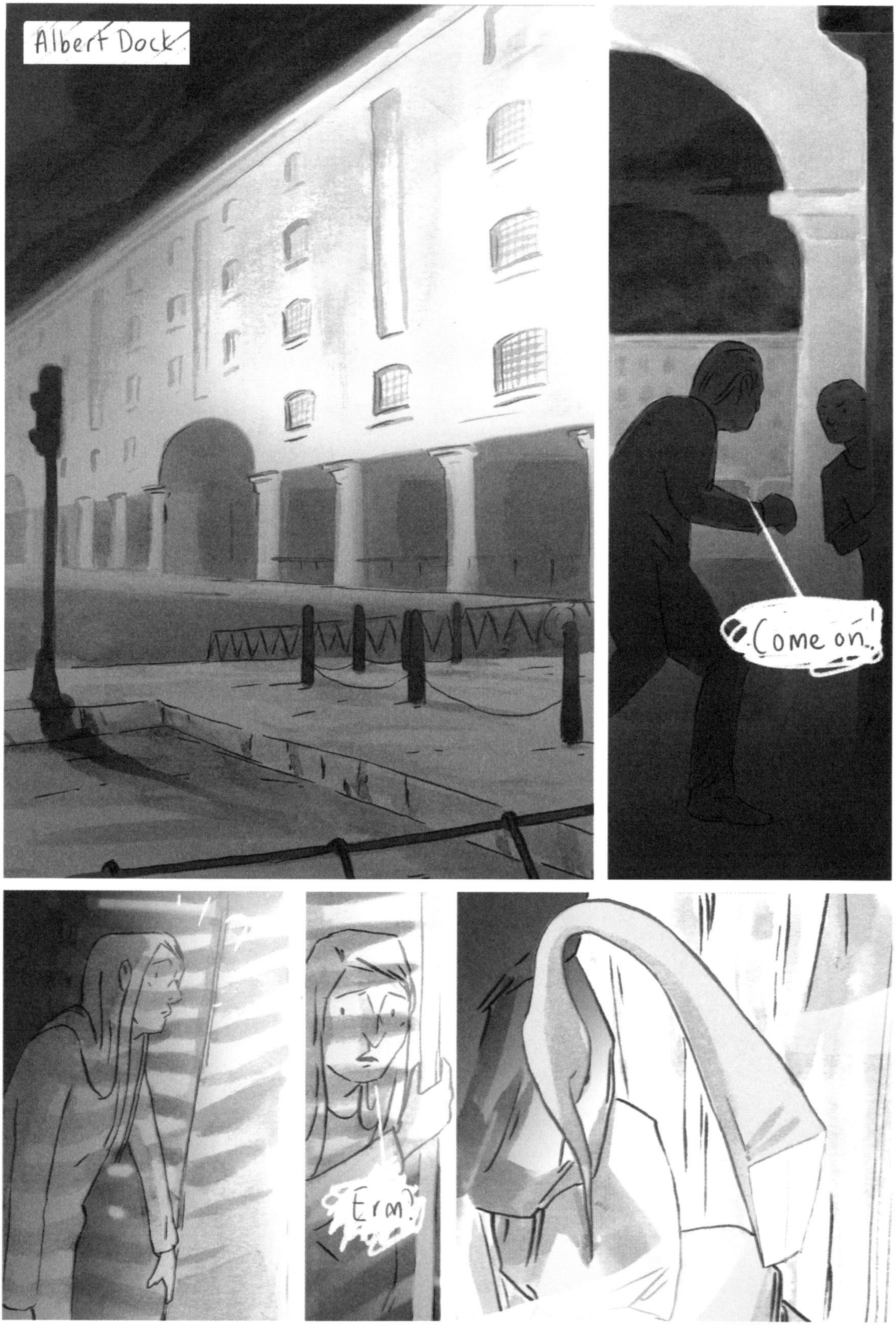
Albert Dock
Come on!
Erm?

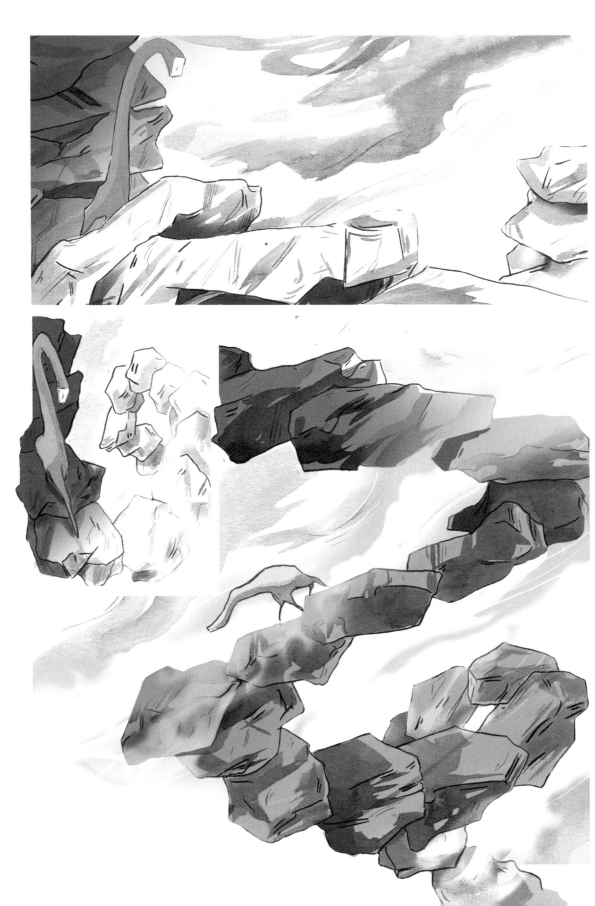

THURSDAY 6th JUNE

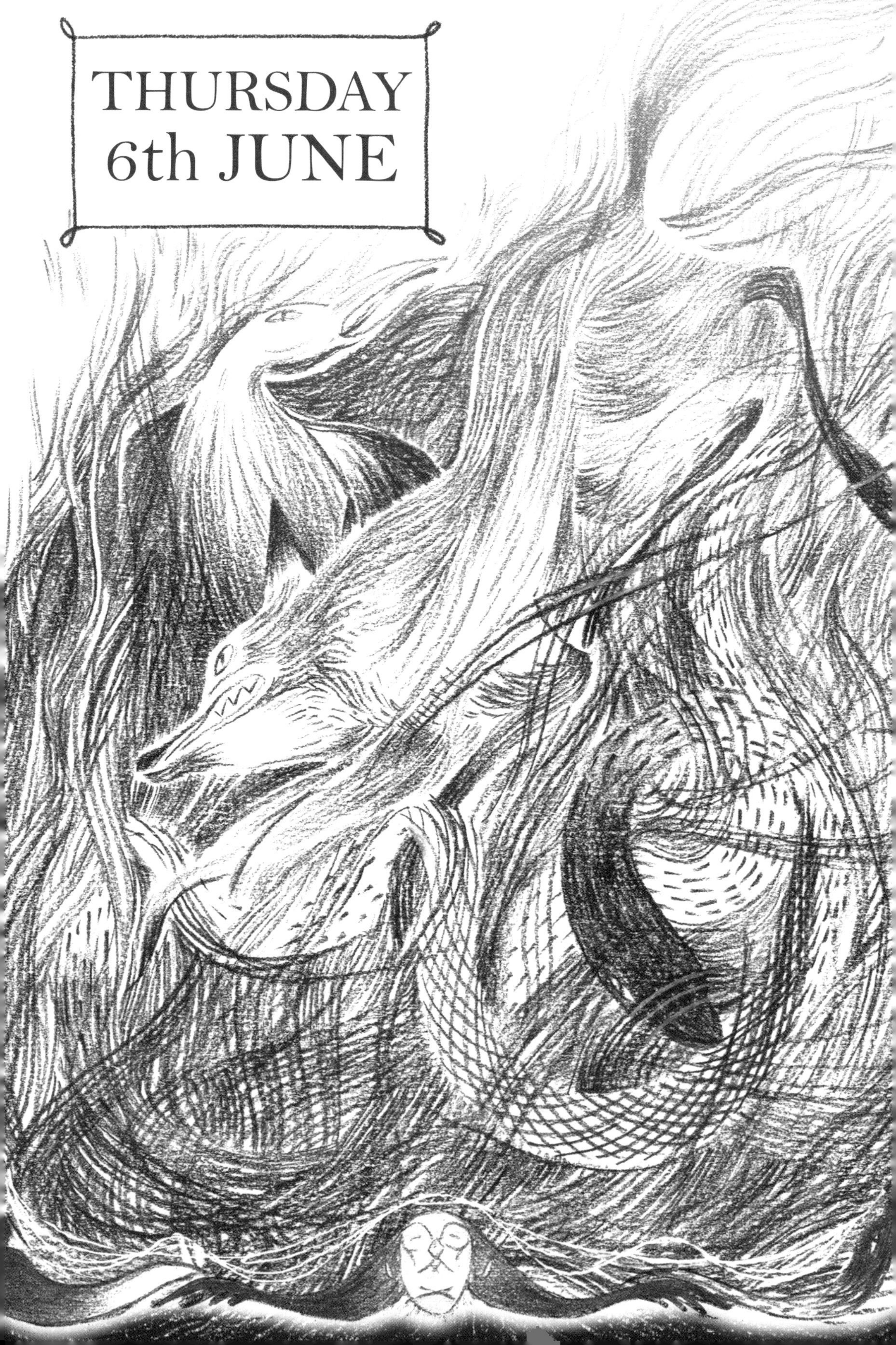

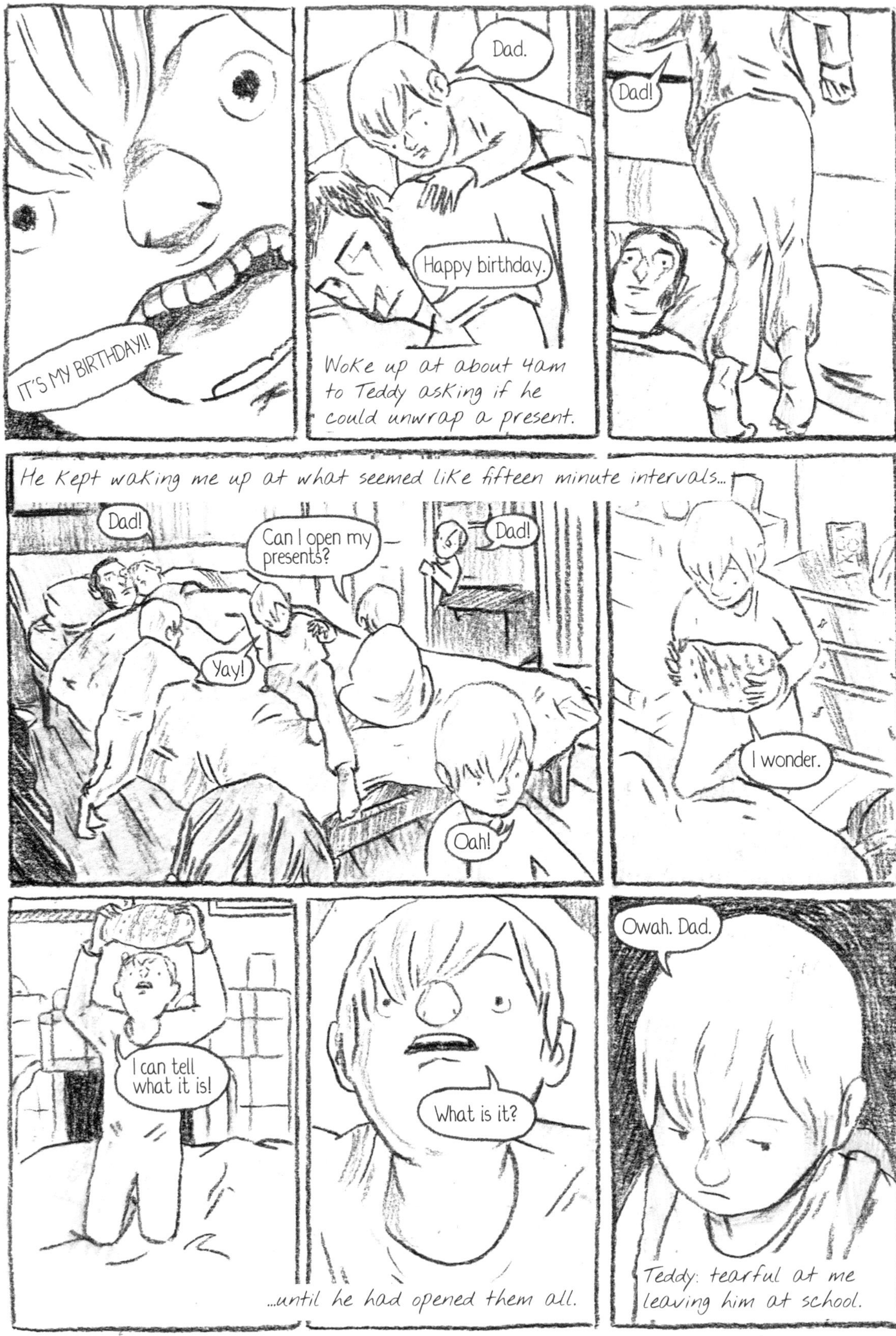
IT'S MY BIRTHDAY!!
Dad.
Happy birthday.
Woke up at about 4am to Teddy asking if he could unwrap a present.
Dad!
He kept waking me up at what seemed like fifteen minute intervals...
Dad!
Can I open my presents?
Dad!
Yay!
Oah!
I wonder.
I can tell what it is!
What is it?
...until he had opened them all.
Owah. Dad.
Teddy: tearful at me leaving him at school.

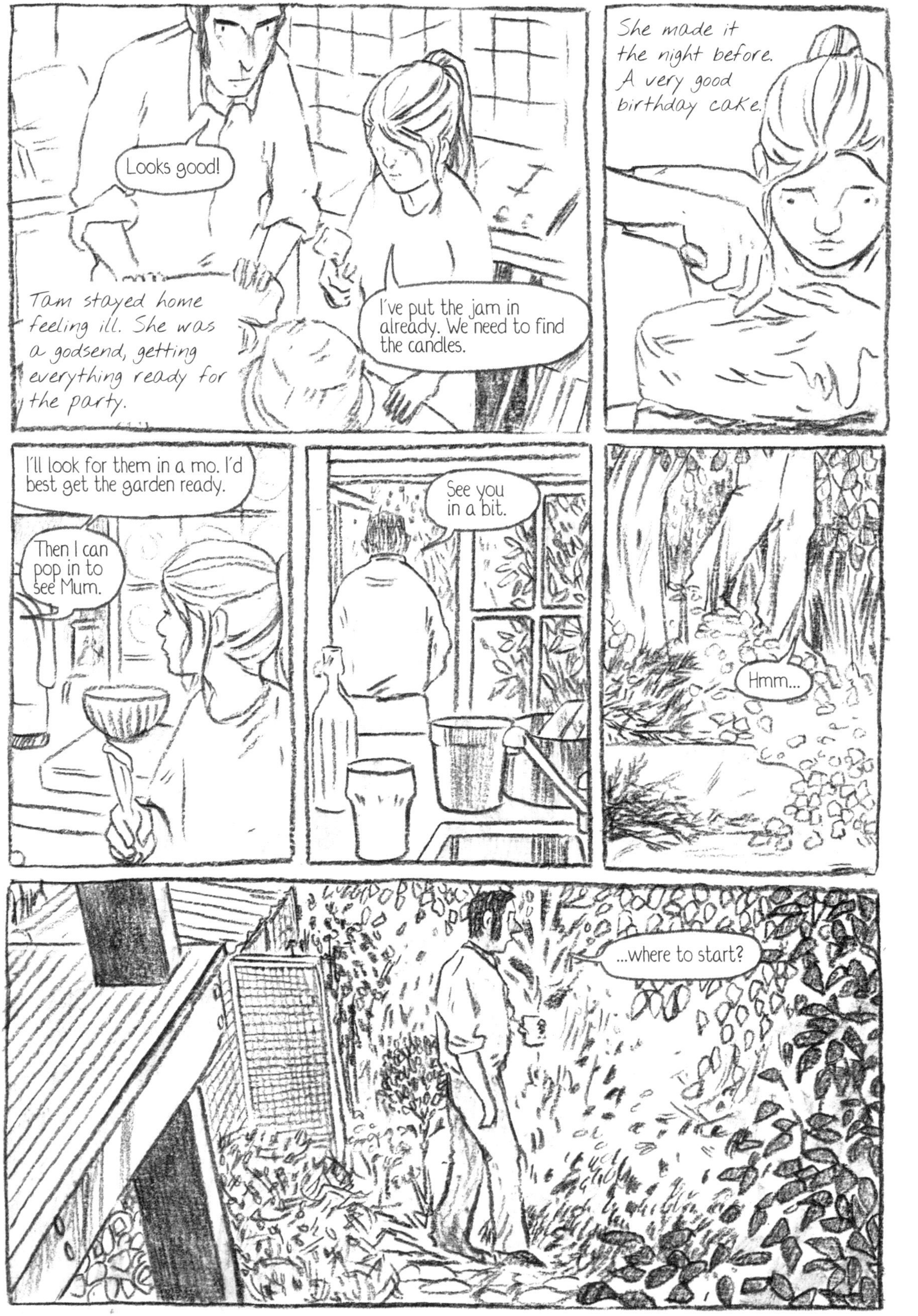
Looks good!
Tam stayed home feeling ill. She was a godsend, getting everything ready for the party.
I've put the jam in already. We need to find the candles.
She made it the night before. A very good birthday cake.
I'll look for them in a mo. I'd best get the garden ready.
Then I can pop in to see Mum.
See you in a bit.
Hmm...
...where to start?

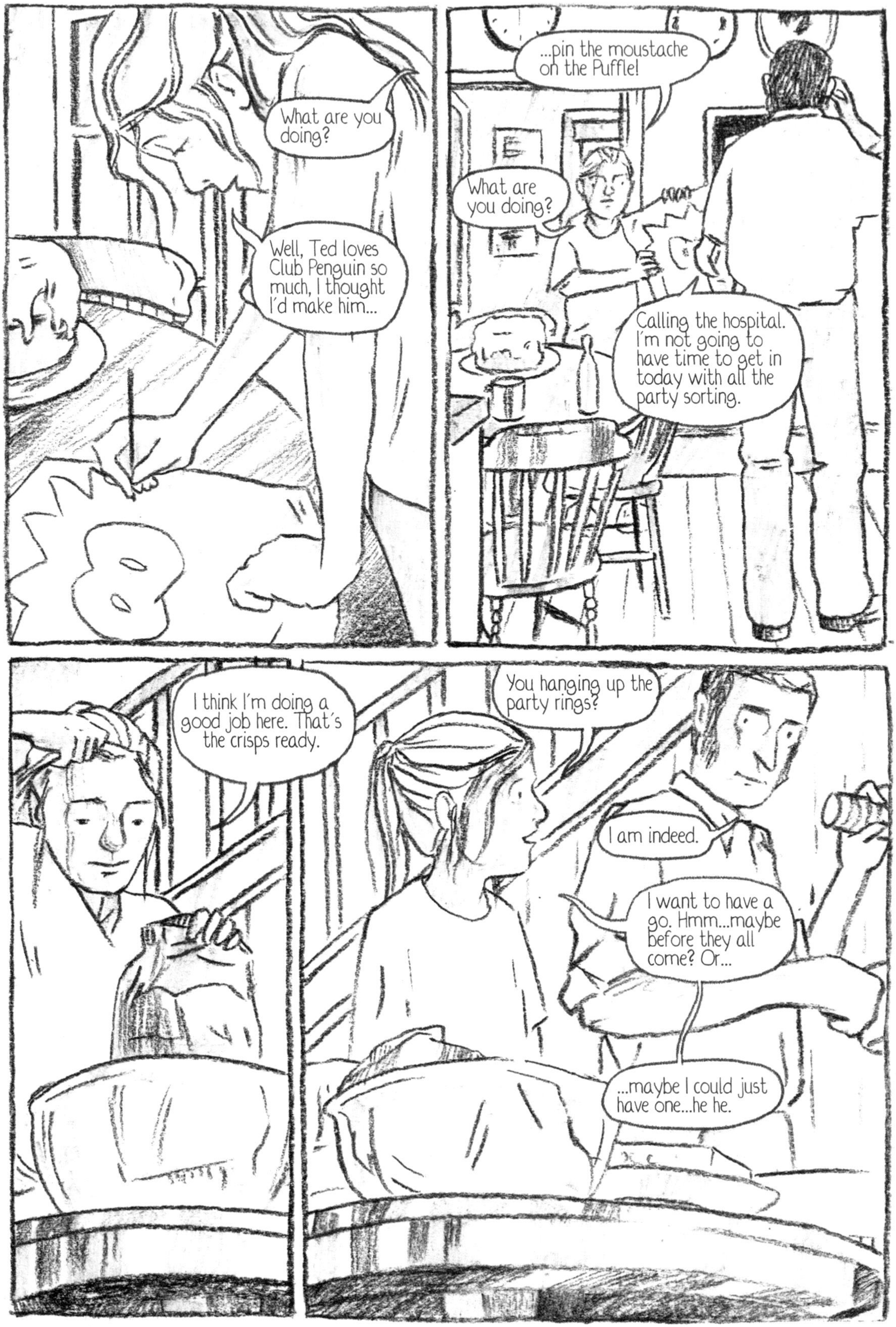
What are you doing?
Well, Ted loves Club Penguin so much, I thought I'd make him...
...pin the moustache on the Puffle!
What are you doing?
Calling the hospital. I'm not going to have time to get in today with all the party sorting.
I think I'm doing a good job here. That's the crisps ready.
You hanging up the party rings?
I am indeed.
I want to have a go. Hmm...maybe before they all come? Or...
...maybe I could just have one...he he.

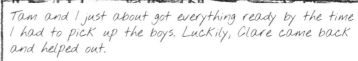
Tam and I just about got everything ready by the time I had to pick up the boys. Luckily, Clare came back and helped out.

The party started off fine, they're a nice bunch.

Wow, Tam, it looks amazing! Well done!

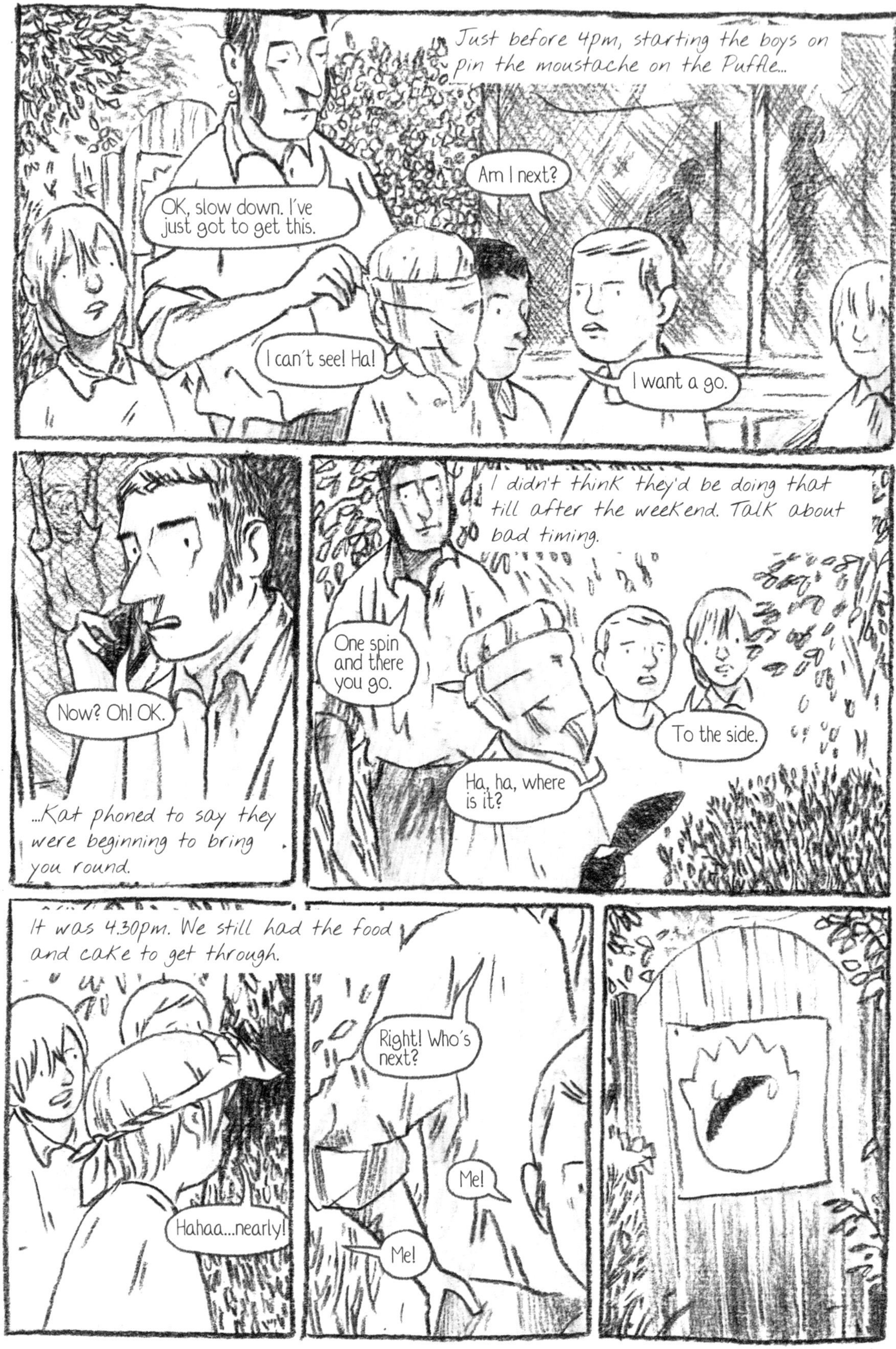

Just before 4pm, starting the boys on pin the moustache on the Puffle...
OK, slow down. I've just got to get this.
Am I next?
I can't see! Ha!
I want a go.
Now? Oh! OK.
...Kat phoned to say they were beginning to bring you round.
I didn't think they'd be doing that till after the weekend. Talk about bad timing.
One spin and there you go.
To the side.
Ha, ha, where is it?
It was 4.30pm. We still had the food and cake to get through.
Hahaa...nearly!
Right! Who's next?
Me!
Me!

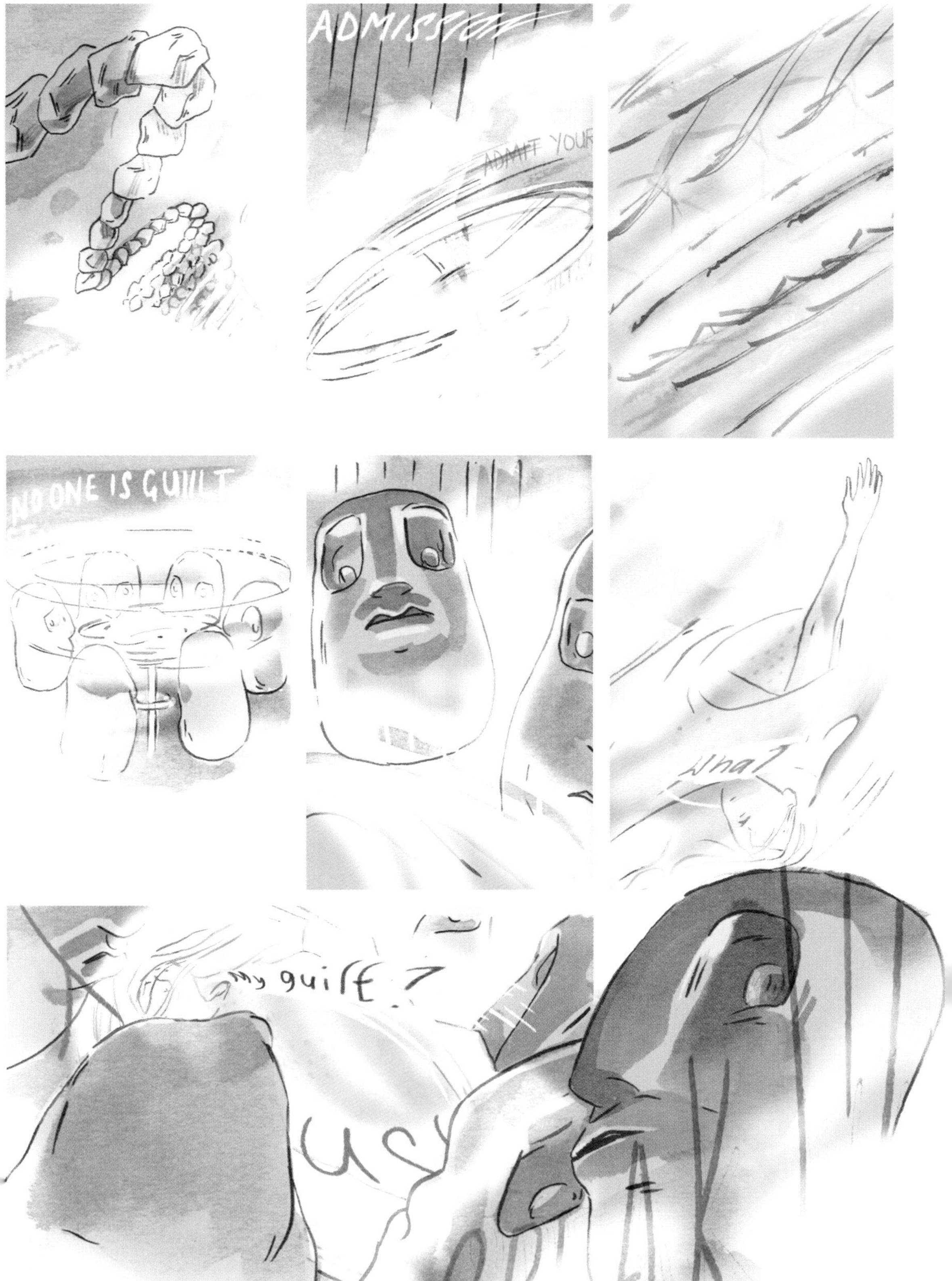

ADMISSION
ADMIT YOUR
NO ONE IS GUILT
Wha?
my guilt?

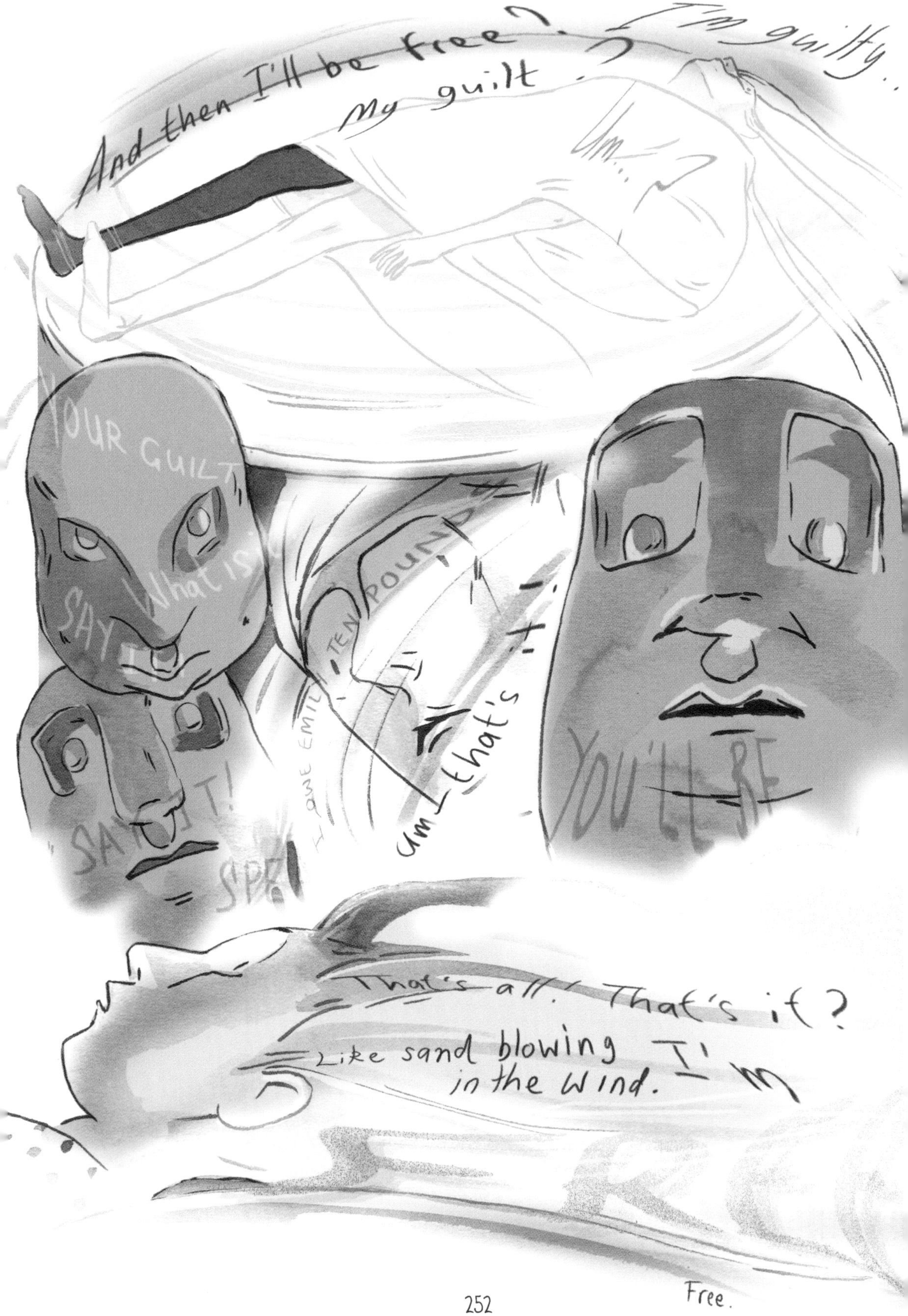
And then I'll be free?
I'm guilty..
My guilt.
YOUR GUILT
What is it
SAY IT!
I OWE EMILY TEN POUNDS
Um... that's
YOU'LL BE
That's all. That's it?
Like sand blowing in the wind.
I'm
Free.

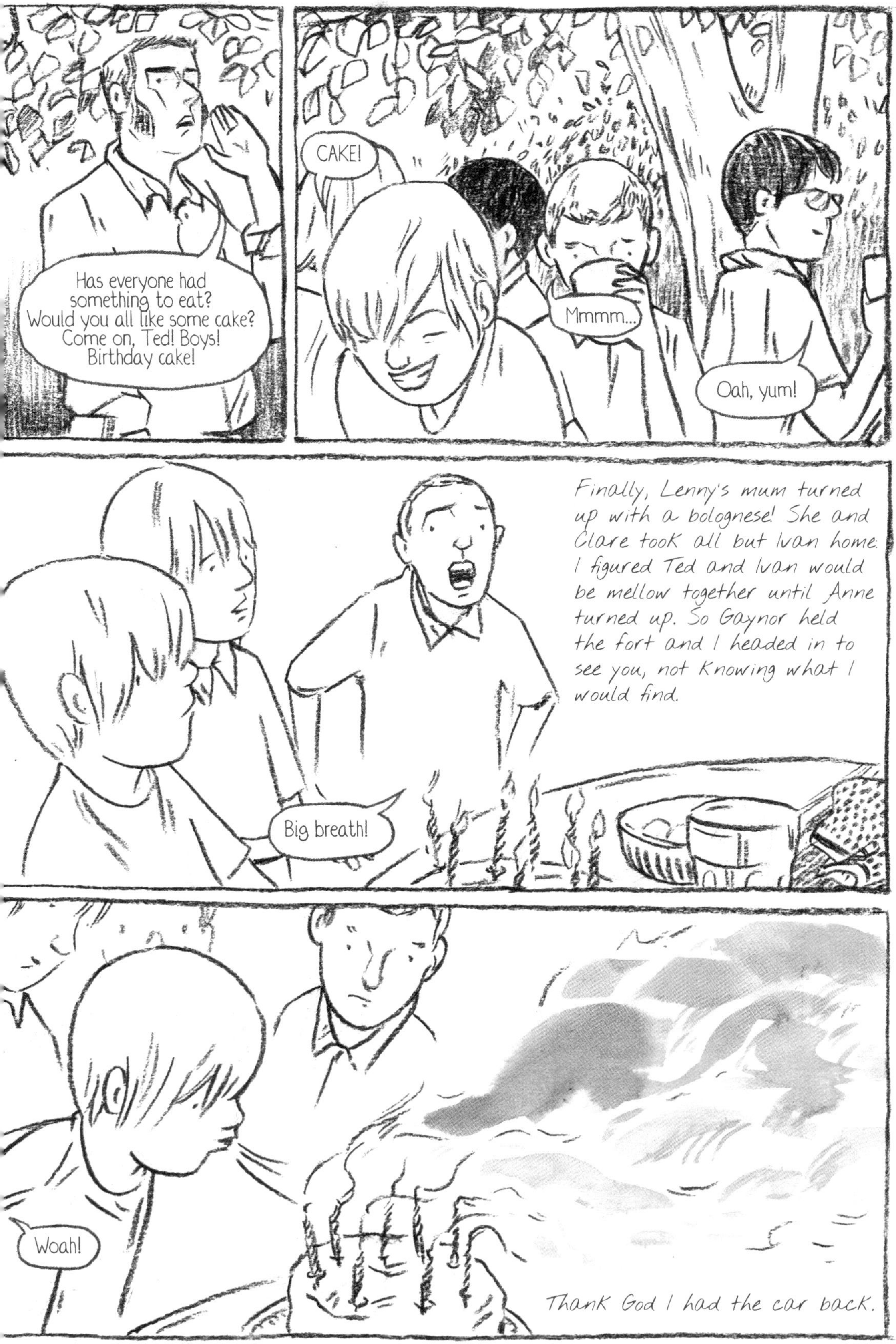
Has everyone had something to eat? Would you all like some cake? Come on, Ted! Boys! Birthday cake!
CAKE!
Mmmm...
Oah, yum!
Finally, Lenny's mum turned up with a bolognese! She and Clare took all but Ivan home. I figured Ted and Ivan would be mellow together until Anne turned up. So Gaynor held the fort and I headed in to see you, not knowing what I would find.
Big breath!
Woah!
Thank God I had the car back.

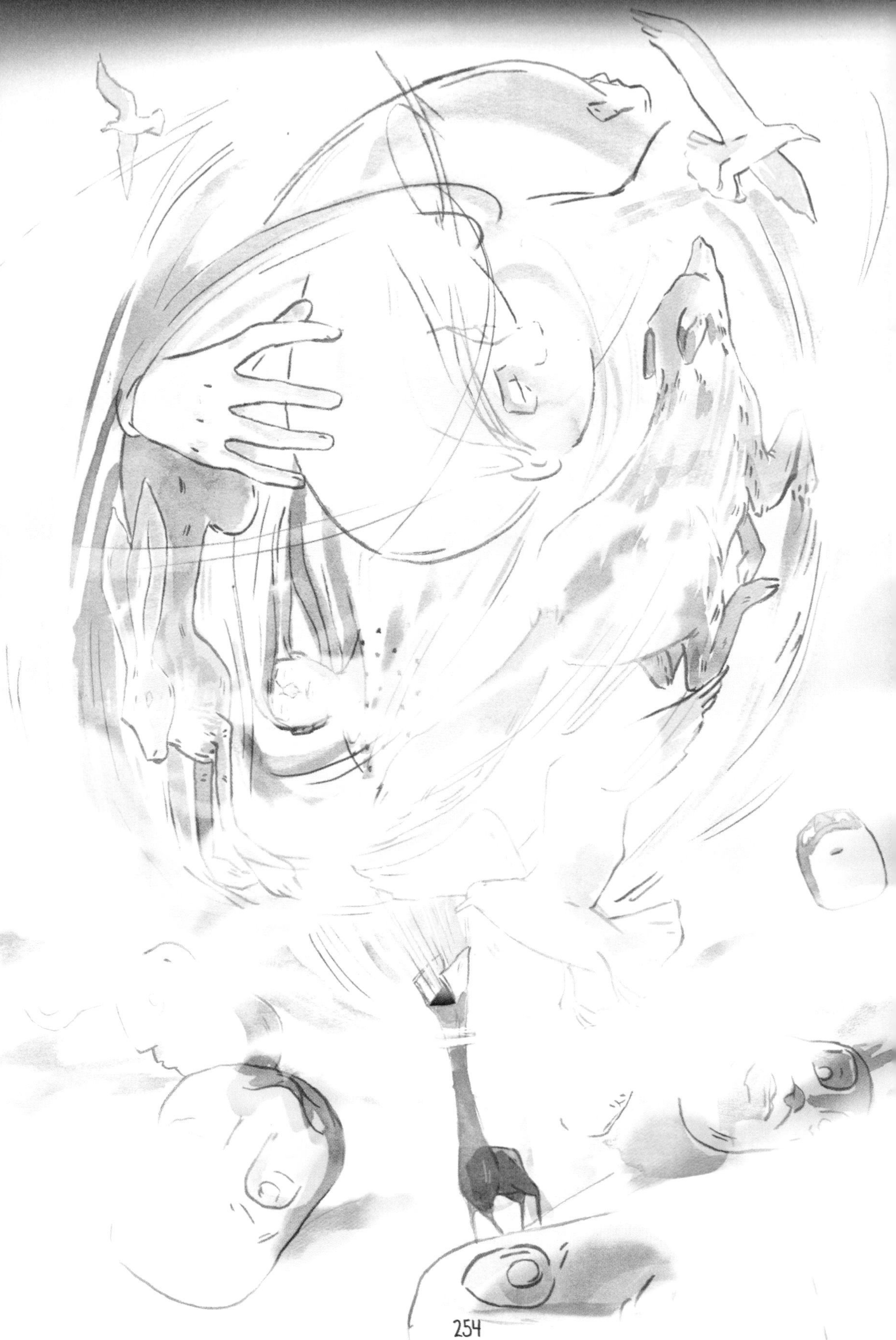

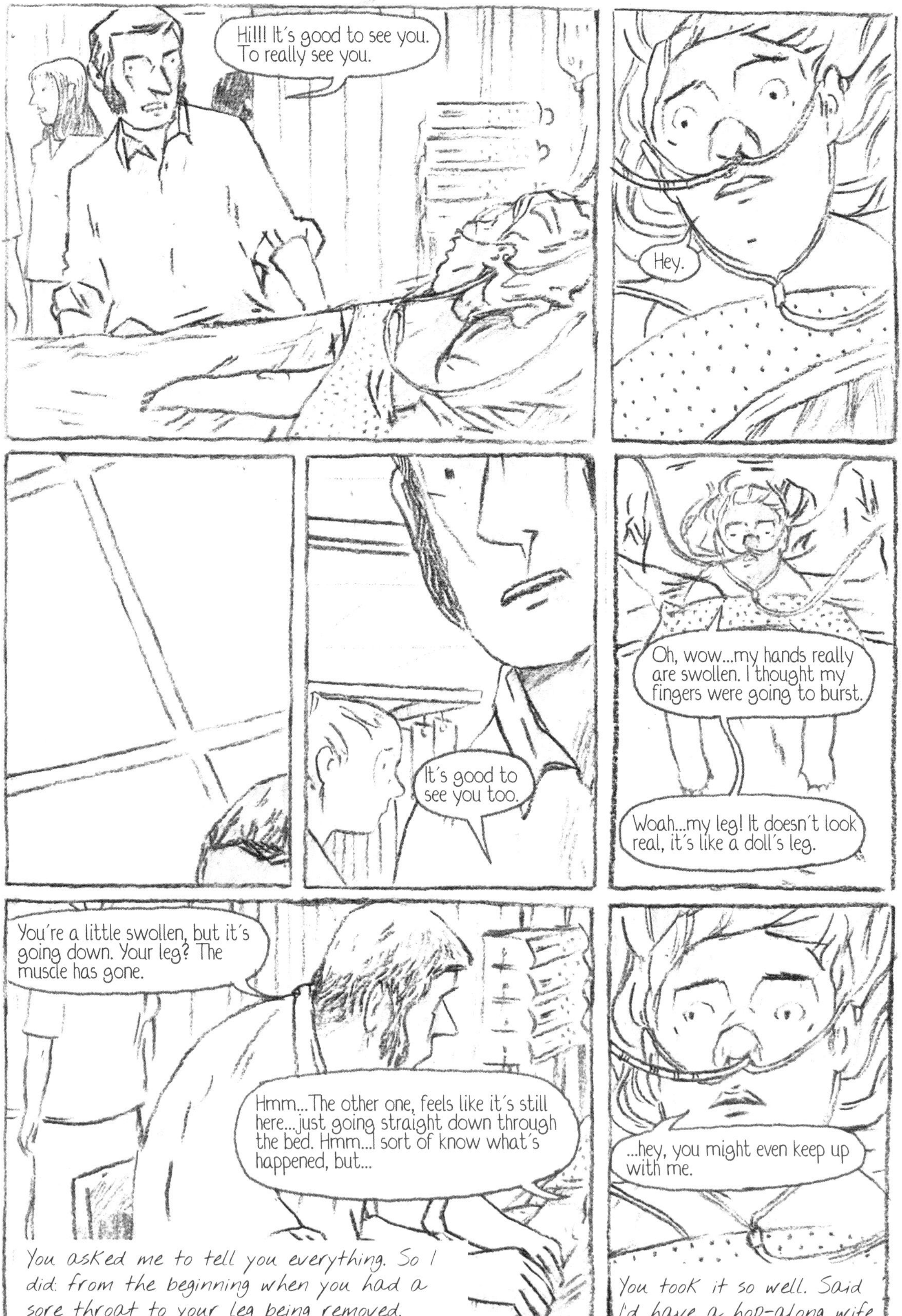
Hi!!! It´s good to see you. To really see you.
Hey.
It´s good to see you too.
Oh, wow...my hands really are swollen. I thought my fingers were going to burst.
Woah...my leg! It doesn´t look real, it´s like a doll´s leg.
You´re a little swollen, but it´s going down. Your leg? The muscle has gone.
Hmm...The other one, feels like it´s still here...just going straight down through the bed. Hmm...I sort of know what´s happened, but...
You asked me to tell you everything. So I did: from the beginning when you had a sore throat to your leg being removed.
...hey, you might even keep up with me.
You took it so well. Said I'd have a hop-along wife.

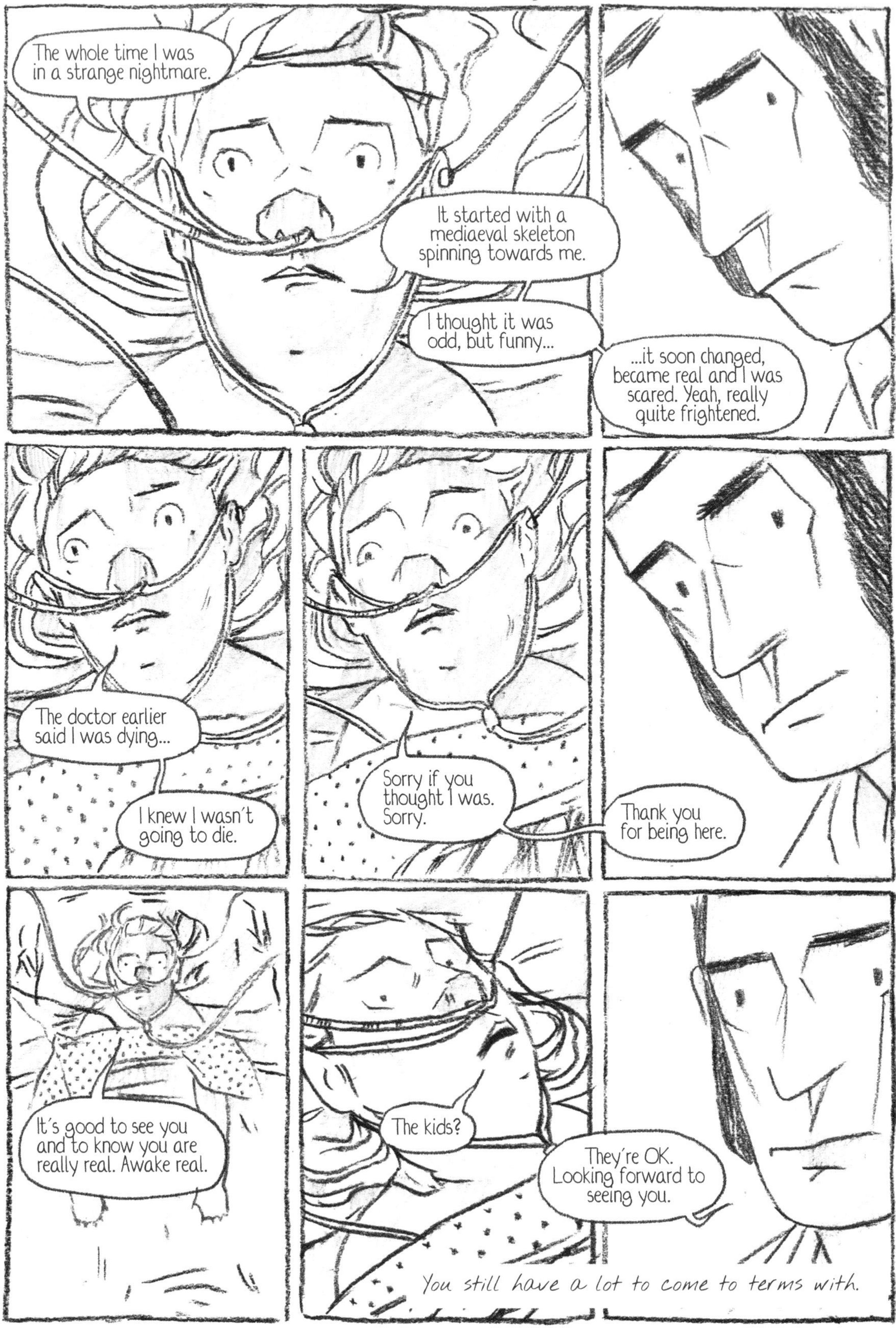
The whole time I was in a strange nightmare.
It started with a mediaeval skeleton spinning towards me.
I thought it was odd, but funny...
...it soon changed, became real and I was scared. Yeah, really quite frightened.
The doctor earlier said I was dying...
I knew I wasn't going to die.
Sorry if you thought I was. Sorry.
Thank you for being here.
It's good to see you and to know you are really real. Awake real.
The kids?
They're OK. Looking forward to seeing you.
You still have a lot to come to terms with.

SATURDAY 8th JUNE

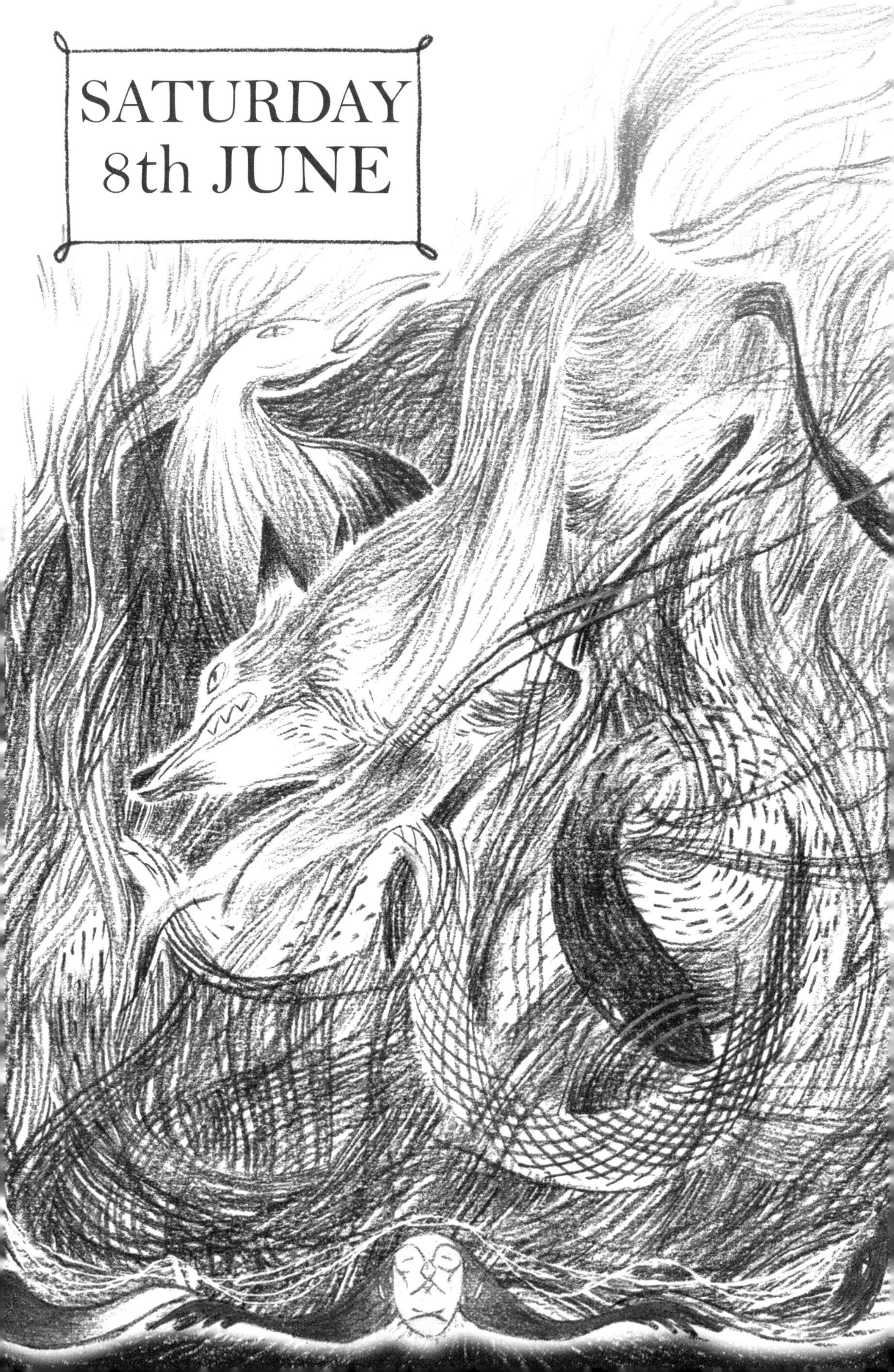

Darling, we are losing days, I am writing this on Saturday. Friday - I am not sure I remember much about it now, just one day later. I really can't remember.

I must have visited you in the morning. I brought the kids in after tea.

I have a few images in my head and that's all.

Tam holding your hand and crying, that was good.

Ted patting your arm.

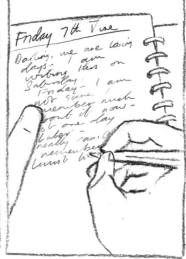

Friday 7th June

Darling, we are losing days, I am writing this on Saturday - I am not sure I remember much about it now - to one day later - I really can't remember this h...

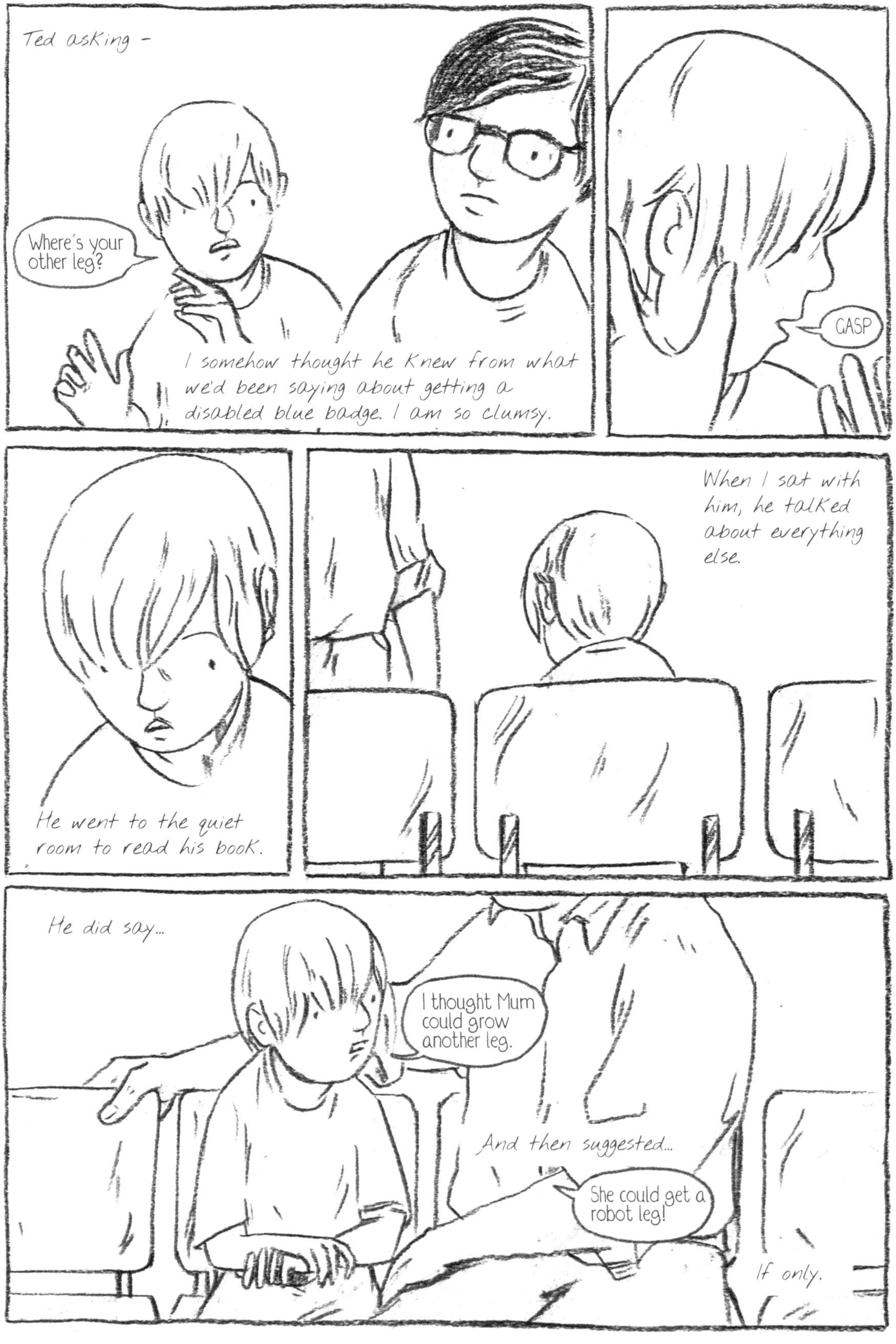
Ted asking -
Where's your other leg?
I somehow thought he knew from what we'd been saying about getting a disabled blue badge. I am so clumsy.
GASP
He went to the quiet room to read his book.
When I sat with him, he talked about everything else.
He did say...
I thought Mum could grow another leg.
And then suggested...
She could get a robot leg!
If only.

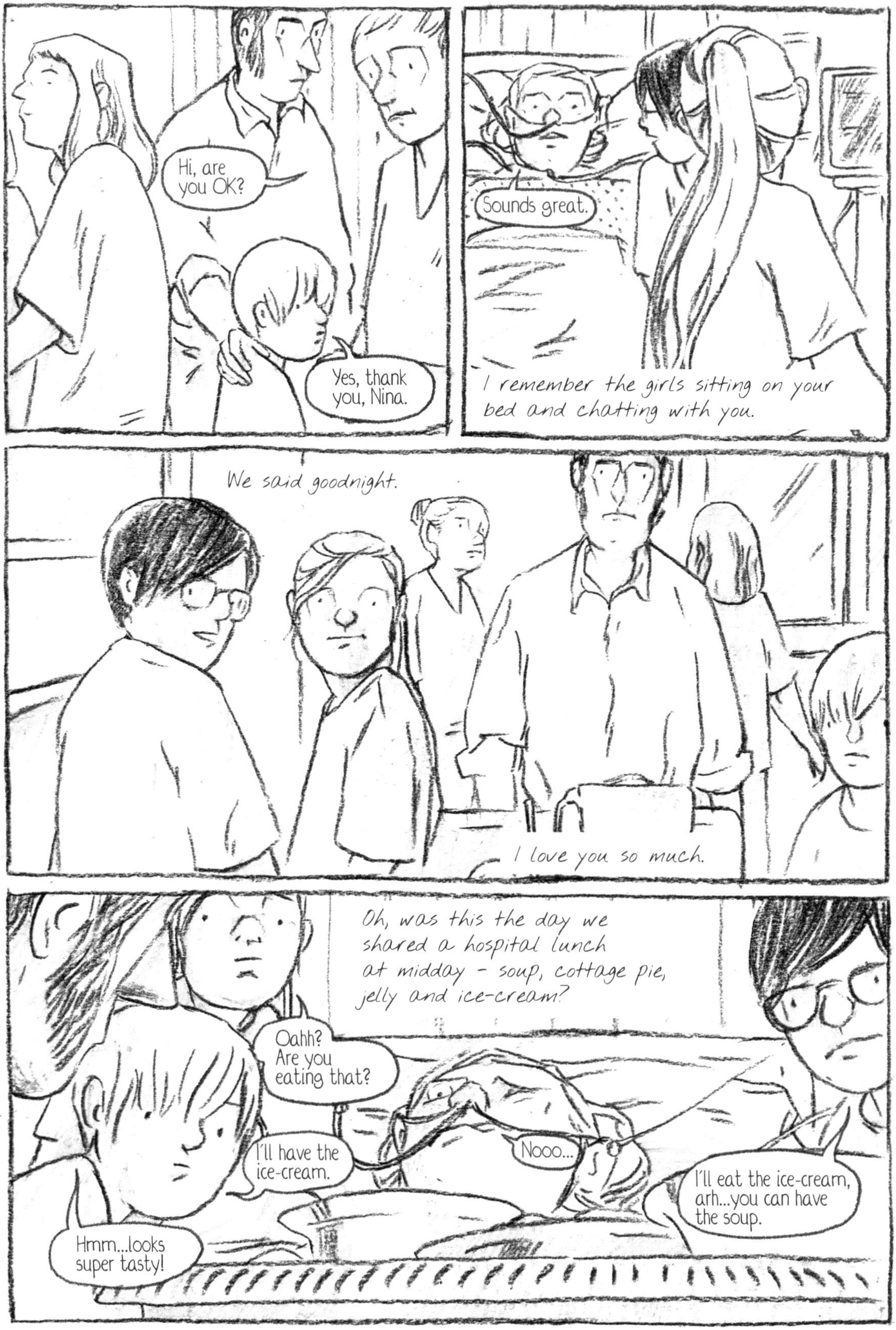
Hi, are you OK?
Yes, thank you, Nina.
Sounds great.
I remember the girls sitting on your bed and chatting with you.
We said goodnight.
I love you so much.
Oh, was this the day we shared a hospital lunch at midday - soup, cottage pie, jelly and ice-cream?
Oahh? Are you eating that?
I'll have the ice-cream.
Nooo...
I'll eat the ice-cream, arh...you can have the soup.
Hmm...looks super tasty!

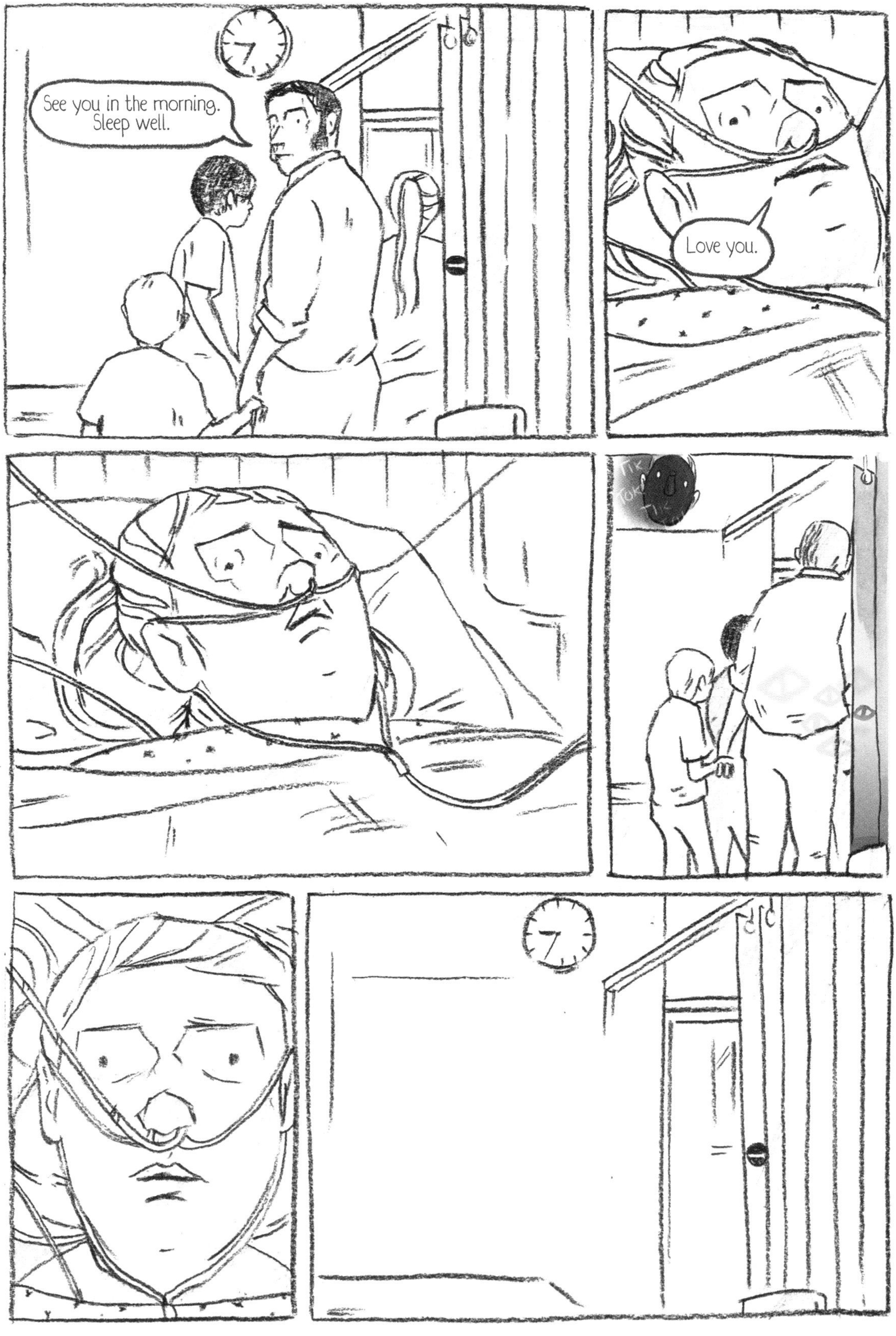

See you in the morning. Sleep well.
Love you.

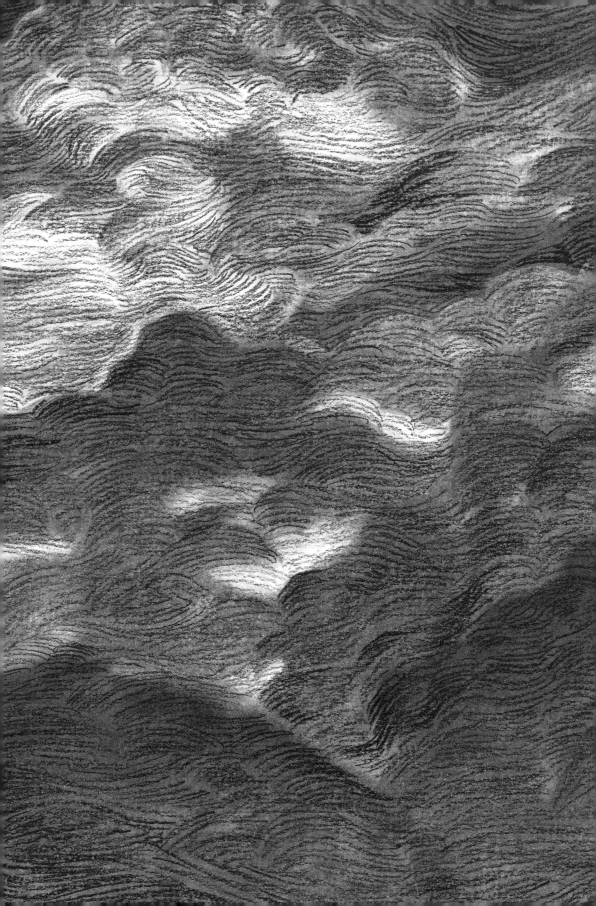

Dear Zara

9th June 2013

My name is Lucy. I am a nurse on the intensive care unit in Brighton. This diary is being written to help you understand what has been happening to you.

You came to the Royal Sussex County hospital on the 22nd May by ambulance. You had been suffering with severe back pain. You were admitted to the Clinical decisions unit for pain relief over night.

You were in a lot of pain in your back and leg and were given morphine to help relieve the pain. This did not help and you remained in lots of pain.

You became more unwell and the pain was impossible to manage. The doctors decided to send you for a scan, an MRI which did not show any obvious abnormalities. As the day progressed you were in more pain and again this was

not resolving with pain relief.
At around 11am you went
for a CT scan. Following
the scan you returned to the
ward very unwell. you had
a low blood pressure and
were grey & mottled. The
CT scan showed you had
  Gluteal myositis, similar to
necrotising fasciitis - This is
a rare infection of the deeper
layers of skin/muscle and
very fast spreading.
     you went to theatre
for lower limb surgery; but
by this time you were extremely
unwell. Initially the surgeons
tried to save your leg; carrying
out extensive debridement.
  Following theatre you were
transferred to the intensive care
unit.
    Your circulation was struggling
and needed support with a
drug called noradrenaline.
a tube was passed through your

mouth into your airway and was
attached to a ventilator to take
over the work of breathing.
Unfortunately your leg was bleeding
profusely. you needed lots of
blood & blood products. your kidneys
had stopped working and you
were extremely unwell.
Microbiology results indicated a group A
Streptoccal infection, with a
severe sepsis. and signs of
as On may the 24th it was
decided by all the various doctors,
that the only way to save your
life was a hind quarter amputation.
at the same time a colostomy was
formed; this is where a piece of
your large bowel comes to the surface
of your abdomen. In order to keep
the wound around the hind quarter
clean.
you continued to struggle with multi-
organ failure and the doctors talked
to your husband and told him you
may not survive.
over the next few days you

went to theatre a few more
times to have more tissue
removed.
Your kidneys were not working
and you were on a filter -
this was doing the work of your
kidneys, you remained unconscious
on a ventilator and you had
drugs to support your blood pressure.
You have a special dressing
that covers the area where
your buttock & leg were removed
- called a vac dressing.
You need to go back to theatre
quite regularly to have this
changed.
- So today, you have been
here for 18 days, you are
awake and breathing on your
own. Your blood pressure is
better and you are off of
the support for that. Your kidneys
are working again reasonably
well and are producing urine.
You remain very weak but
are much better. However;

We continue to keep a closely monitoring you as you are still at risk of infections.

But you are very determined and despite all the information you have been given are very optimistic.

Your husband and children have visited regularly.

This diary has been started to help you & your family under-stand what is happening to you. Your primary nurses are Marta & Dina & they will look after you when they are working.
— We hope that your family & friends will also contribute to this.

Lucy

hello its tilda.

its 8:40pm and im with dad. hes trying to wipe your nose... but its not working. hes not manly enough. its quite funny though because your like shouting at him.

we brought you some pinapple things and some more lemonade. oh and some haribos, for gathior but I was eating them, hehehe.

your looking better now you can move your head and fingers, so thats good.

~~we brought you an iPad yesterday~~
~~you look like your enjoying it but~~

We bought you an iPad yesterday
you look like your enjoying it
but you cant use it properly yet
because your hands are swollen
and you cant move your arms
that much.
But your looking well.
I love you.
and I think the nurses are doing
a brilliant job.

Tilda, over and out.

wednesday 19th June

Hi mum it's ted here Oh heres a ioke to cheer you ~~you~~ up: what is the sewers faviourete song?

hallopooya!

hahaha ha ha! sorry laughed to my own ioke orkward. Anyway I miss you and I take back all the times I shouted and screamed.

see ya!

Wednesday 19th June.

Hi mum it's tam.

I dont really know what to write ....

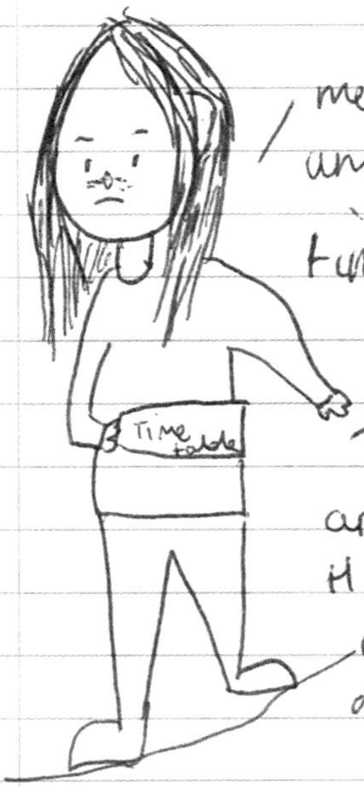
Time table

me when I couldn't understand ~~my tabtable~~ timetable.

Ted is reallllllllllly annoying at the moment. He keeps coming into my room when I dont want him to...

It's harder ~~or~~ in the mornings because dad is really bad at making packted lunches. (~~he tries~~ ~~tries~~
(he tries though)

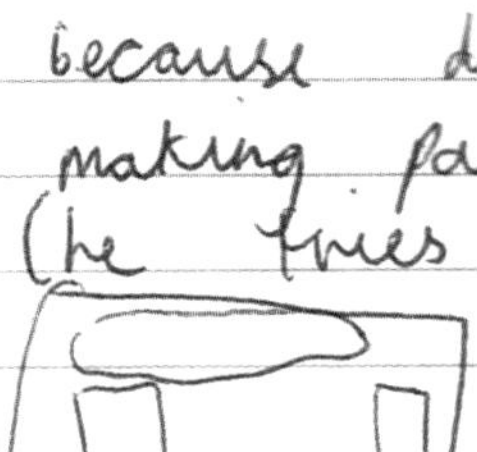

this is my new room layout

AFTERWORD

Fifteen days in an induced coma. Six weeks in intensive care. Three-and-a-half months in hospital. These are easily quantifiable. What's not easy to measure are the emotions that followed and the trauma to be worked through.

Elation was the first feeling that burst forth on being 'woken up'. After many dark nights, the veil of distrust and fear fell away. My heart beat with a renewed sense of self. I was me, positive and self-assured, minus a leg. Dan and the children had been spared their grief and we would soon resume our lives, albeit differently. What could be more simple?

Shock and bewilderment soon followed, and a mask of positivity concealed the trauma that was unfolding within. In constant pain, I'd lost a quarter of my body weight in flesh, bone and muscle, and my remaining muscles had atrophied.

I couldn't retain the information I'd been given and had no answers for the questions asked of me. I was wholly dependent on those that cared for me, for every aspect of my being.

Asking why this had happened to me was reasoned with, 'Why not?' I was unlucky. I balanced my luck, visualising the unlucky weight of infection with the lucky weight of survival; the unlucky weight of losing my leg with the lucky one of only having lost my leg. I was neither unlucky nor lucky. 'Why not' cancelled out 'why'.

Over time, I'd return to those first elated feelings. I'd ponder them, ridicule them, long for them, and then, eventually try to live by them — but not before coming to terms with a broken body and the ravages of an aggressive infection.

Rehabilitation was difficult and frequently lonely. Physical trauma exposed my pain; I was a wounded animal, instinctively compelled to hide. I visualised my route to health — an inescapably dark, pot-holed road — and determined to travel it. As I hopped cautiously along, I would once again find myself weighing up the odds, reasoning what it was to be 'othered': to be both seen and unseen by society.

Eventually, I grew a protective coat, one that shielded me from the harsh realities of life. Within it I garnered my strength and became more resilient. With the love of my family and Dan's gentle patience, I slowly healed, out-grew my protective layers and shed my skin.

Some of the names in this book have been changed.

Zara Slattery 2021

ACKNOWLEDGEMENTS

Thank you to Dan for writing the most beautiful diary; for bringing light to dark days and for letting me loose with your precious words.

To Tilda, Tamblyn and Ted, for your gorgeous diary entries. Thank you for letting me share your story and being the beautiful people you are.

Thank you to all at Myriad. Corinne Pearlman, my editor, for believing in my story and helping me to bring it out of the shadows. Vicki Health Silk. Dawn Sackett. And my agent, Becky Thomas.

To my comic compadres, Myfanwy Tristram, Michi Mathias and Hannah Eaton, for your friendship, eagle eyes and wonderful feedback. Simon Russell for all your technical support at the drop of a hat. And Mike Unwin, for answering my questions about snakes.

Thanks to Karrie Fransman and Alex Fitch for believing in me. Hannah Berry, Woodrow Phoenix and John Allison. To Shelley Warren — The Arts Foundation Futures Award.

To Bobbie Farsides and Barbara Philips from the Brighton and Sussex Medical School, thank you for your time and input. Dr Ian Williams and the the Graphic Medicine community and all at LDC for welcoming and encouraging my work-in-progress.

To the intensive care team at the Royal Sussex County Hospital, Brighton, without whom I wouldn't be here. Thank you for your professionalism, care and for being safety in the storm. The plastic surgeons and rehab team at the Queen Victoria Hospital, East Grinstead for putting me back together.

To Dee Cartedge, founder of the Lee Spark NF Foundation — for the work you do in supporting survivors and families of those effected by Necrotising Fasciitis. And the crucial role you play in raising awareness and educating about the symptoms of NF. Thank you for supporting research into the causes of NF.

A huge thank you to our family and friends, those mentioned in this book, and those not, for being wonderful friends. For being there in the worst and the best of times.

A special thank you to Dobbin. *From one side of the universe to the other*, thank you for sharing your love of comics with me and setting me along this crazy path. *Love, peace and flowers — Be really happy and be nice to everyone, until next time.* You set the standard X.